Contents

Preface

There has been a great change in the philosophy of craft teaching during the past few years. Craft education, from being a purely 'do-as-you-are-told' subject, taught mainly by instructional methods which scarcely involved the student intellectually, now requires the pupil to be responsible for the complete design of his or her own work. This means that the course has great intellectual content and that the student must think about the work in hand and must now make decisions regarding the choice of materials, method of construction, shape, fitness for purpose and finish. Previously all or almost all of these had been decided upon by the teacher, leaving the pupils with little opportunity to display any of their own personality in the work.

Because of this shift of emphasis, it is very important that students should be able to express their ideas clearly in a visual form. This enables proposals to be discussed with the teacher and possibly other students in order to clarify ideas, work out proportions and all the other details leading to a satisfactory design. Drawing is the normal way in which suggestions for practical work are expressed and this may be in the form of freehand sketching and/or mechanical drawing. The degree of ability with which students can do this is therefore a dominant factor in this approach to craft education.

All children can produce design ideas within the limits of their own natural ability and experience of making things; this design approach to craft education should be introduced at the very beginning of the course in the first form. Children soon adapt to the idea of designing their own work and this approach should begin with the first exercise and be pursued throughout the craft course. It will be found that the first possibly rather crude attempts to draw ideas for designs will soon improve with practice and this improvement will be noticeable over the whole ability range.

Previous experience in junior school craft work including making three dimensional models of various descriptions in paper, card, wood, etc. will have provided a useful background.

How might the design problem be presented? In the first instance it could be suggested to the class as a whole and either solved by group effort or individually. Then, possibly, problems can be given to small groups and soon to individuals. The problem may be stated in words or by an illustration of a particular situation which may be in the form of a well prepared sketch or a photograph. Towards the end of the course the student will suggest his own design problems in producing work which is uniquely his own, although not necessarily for the student's own personal use. It is the author's experience that students really give of their very best if the work is directed towards other people such as the sick and infirm, the elderly or for the benefit of the community at large.

Following the Preface are examples of a number of design sheets produced by boys of different age groups; the book is intended to develop further the visual literacy of woodwork and metalwork students through the media of graphics and the various types of projection used in technical drawing. The concept of sketching and technical drawing as a means of communication and expression of ideas has been further illustrated after the Introduction by including a wide selection of completed design sheets coupled with photographs of many pieces of work produced from them. In some cases these also include mock-ups and scale models. The design sheets have been carefully chosen to show work of different grades of difficulty in both wood and metal for the various age ranges. After studying these and examples of the various types of projections in common use the student is given the opportunity of solving a series of carefully graded problems and a selection of those set recently by various examining boards.

By involving the student in this way workshop drawing is shown to be a logical thinking process rather than being purely mechanical.

The book is a source of ideas to further encourage a creative approach to craft and design and its presentation.

TP

Examples of students' design sheets

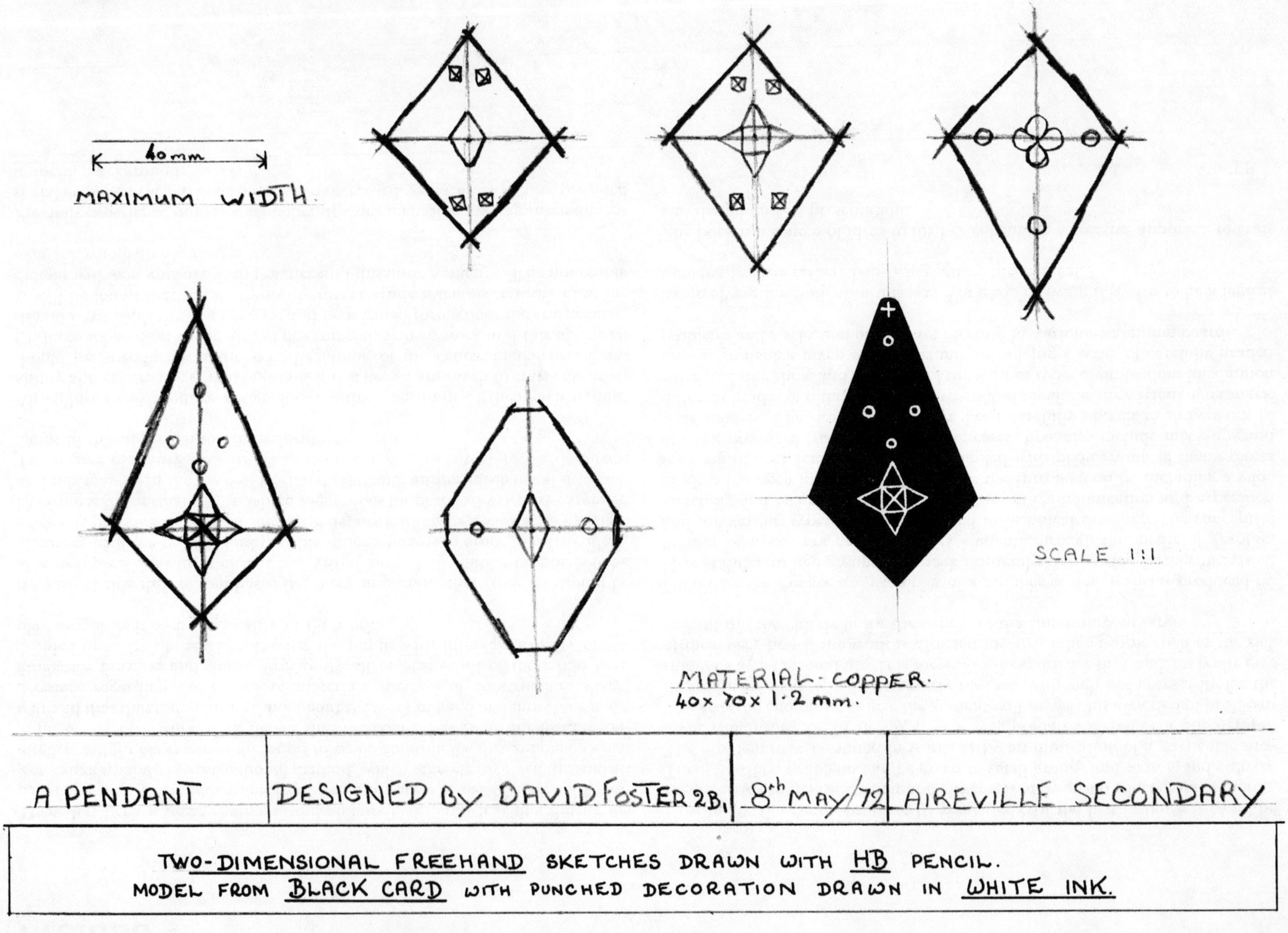
40mm
MAXIMUM WIDTH
SCALE 1:1
MATERIAL - COPPER.
40 x 70 x 1·2 mm.
A PENDANT
DESIGNED BY DAVID FOSTER 2B,
8th MAY/72
AIREVILLE SECONDARY
TWO-DIMENSIONAL FREEHAND SKETCHES DRAWN WITH HB PENCIL.
MODEL FROM BLACK CARD WITH PUNCHED DECORATION DRAWN IN WHITE INK.

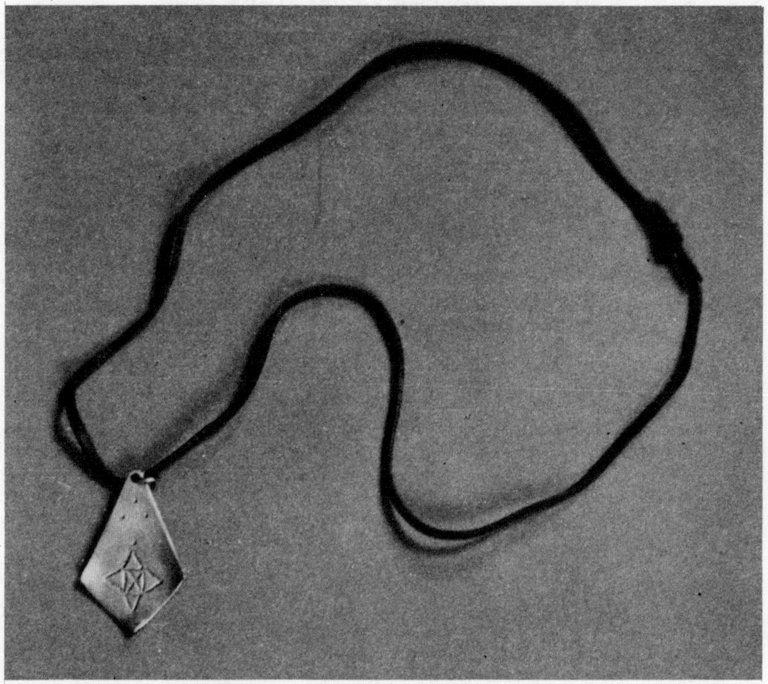

The completed pendant attached to a leather thong by a copper ring. The copper has been lacquered to prevent tarnishing.

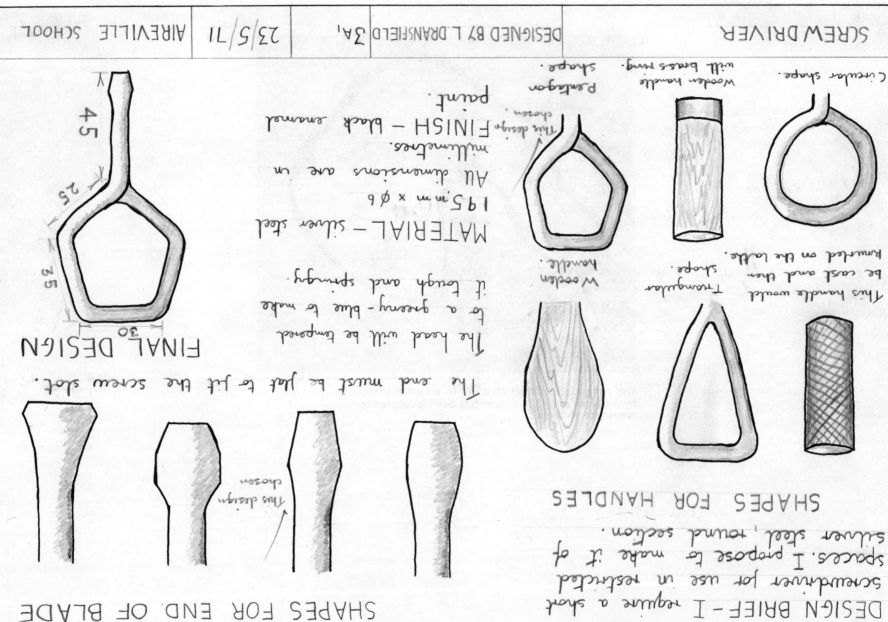

DESIGN BRIEF – I require a short screwdriver for use in restricted spaces. I propose to make it of silver steel, round section.

SHAPES FOR HANDLES

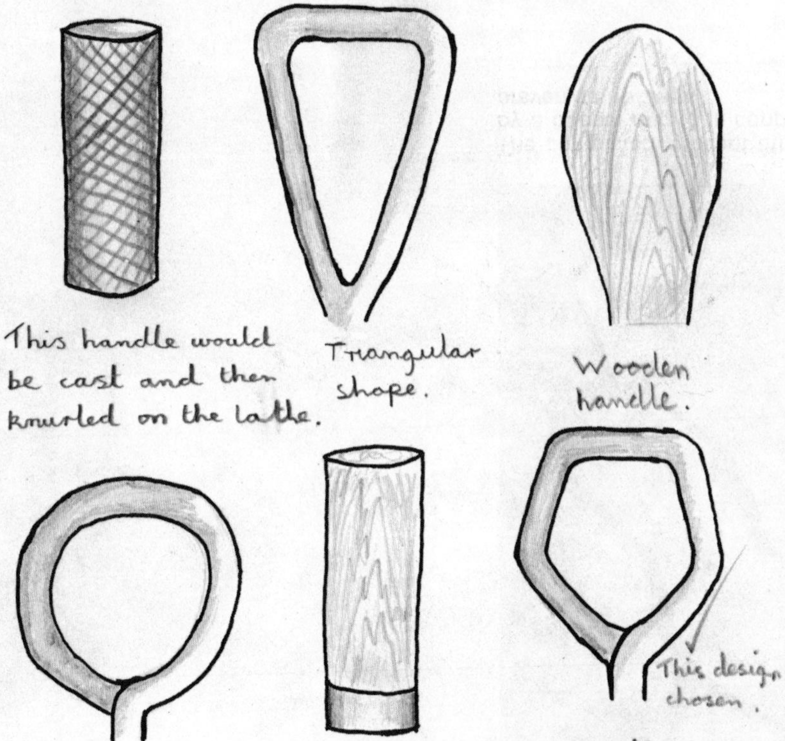

This handle would be cast and then knurled on the lathe.

Triangular shape.

Wooden handle.

Circular shape.

Wooden handle with brass ring.

Pentagon shape. This design chosen.

SHAPES FOR END OF BLADE

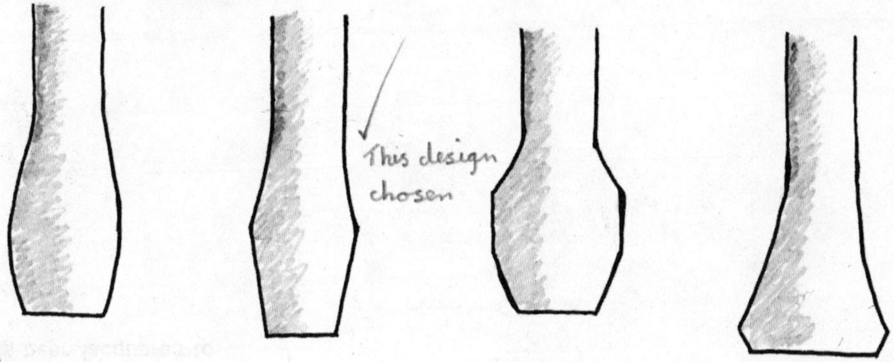
This design chosen

The end must be flat to fit the screw slot.

The head will be tempered to a greeny-blue to make it tough and springy.

MATERIAL – silver steel
195 mm × ⌀ 6
All dimensions are in millimetres.
FINISH – black enamel paint.

FINAL DESIGN

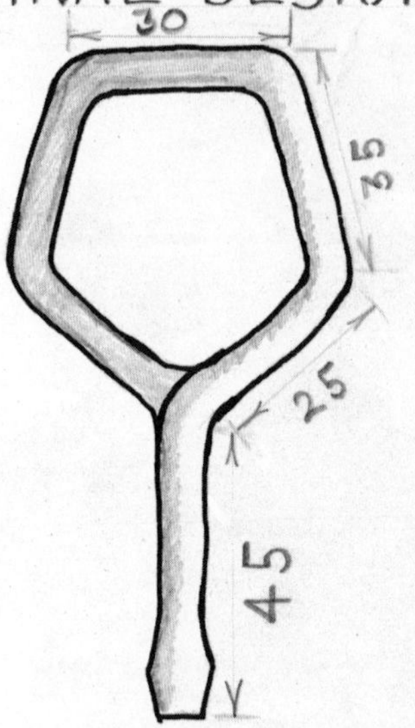
30
35
25
45

SCREWDRIVER	DESIGNED BY L. DRANSFIELD	3A₁	23/5/71	AIREVILLE SCHOOL

MAINLY TWO-DIMENSIONAL FREEHAND SKETCHES WITH HB PENCIL EDGED WITH BLACK FIBRE TIPPED PEN.

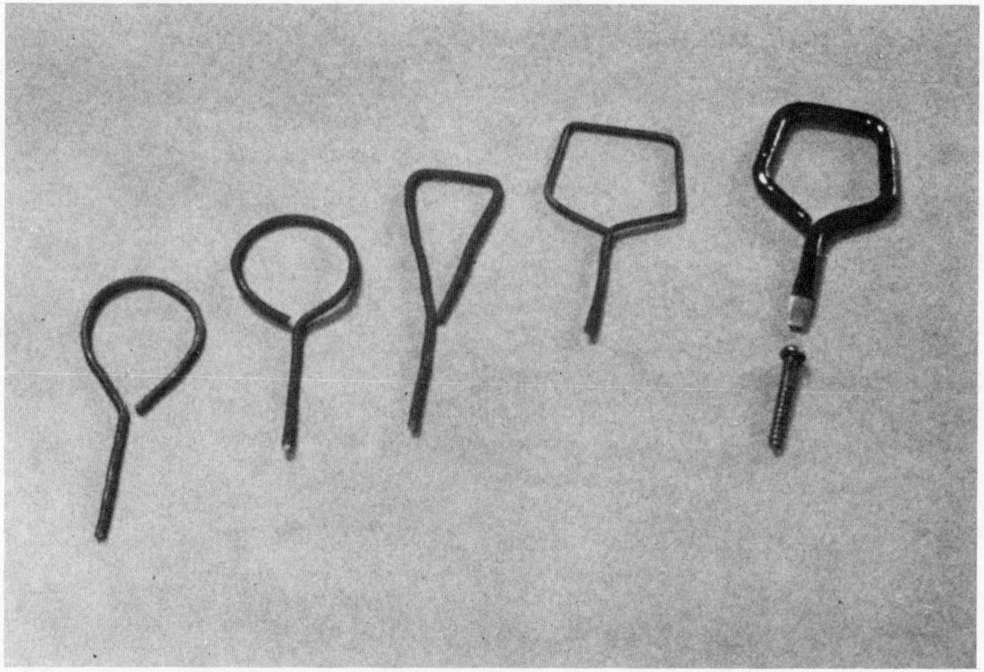

The illustration shows the completed screwdriver, hardened and tempered and finished with black enamel. You can see clearly that the wide handle will give good leverage when turning a screw. Note the range of wire mock-ups made to test leverage and comfortable holding in the palm of the hand.

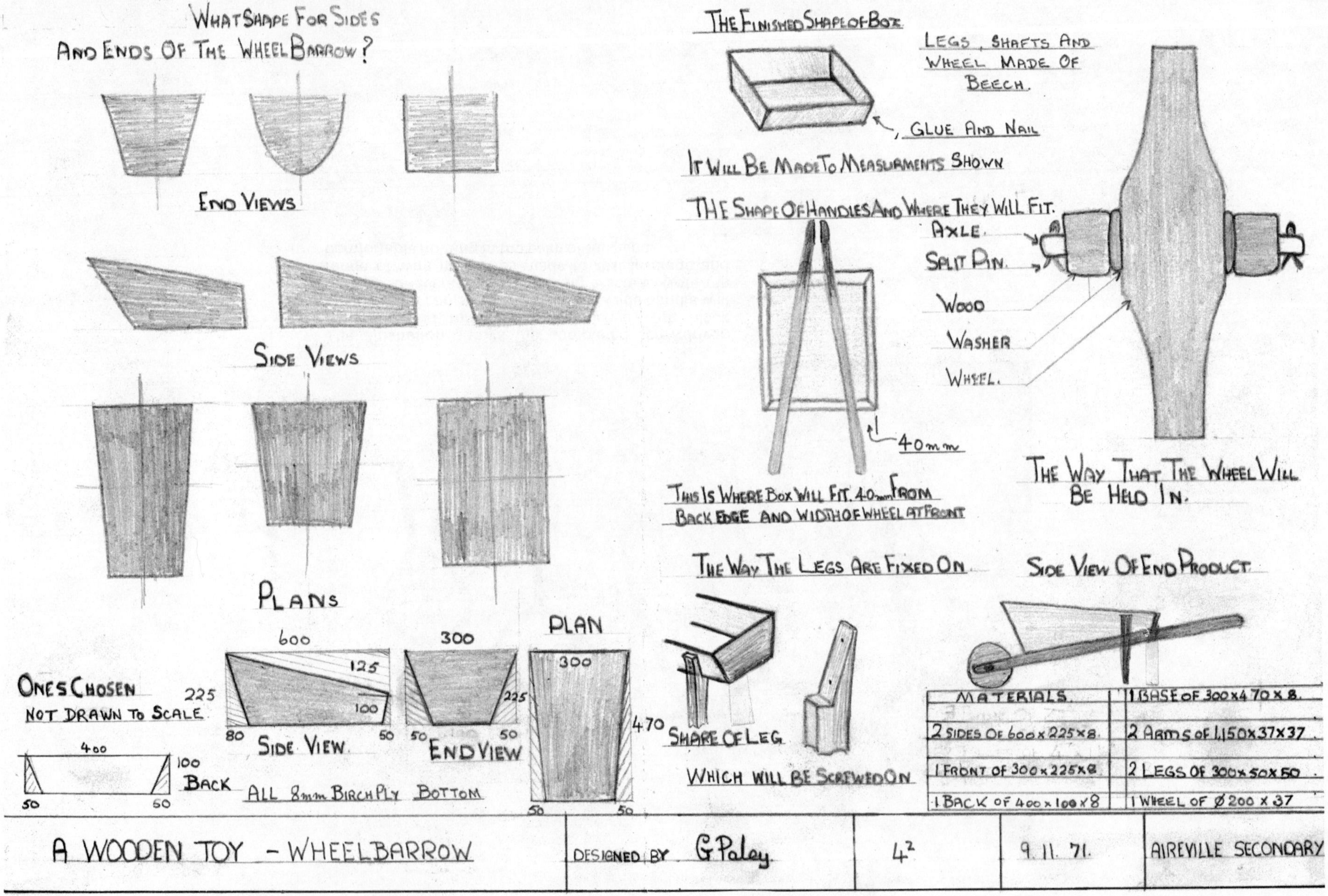
WHAT SHAPE FOR SIDES
AND ENDS OF THE WHEEL BARROW?
END VIEWS
SIDE VIEWS
PLANS
ONES CHOSEN
NOT DRAWN TO SCALE
600
125
225
100
80
50
SIDE VIEW
300
225
50
50
END VIEW
PLAN
300
470
50
50
400
100
BACK
50
50
ALL 8mm BIRCH PLY BOTTOM
THE FINISHED SHAPE OF BOX
GLUE AND NAIL
IT WILL BE MADE TO MEASURMENTS SHOWN
THE SHAPE OF HANDLES AND WHERE THEY WILL FIT.
40mm
THIS IS WHERE BOX WILL FIT. 40mm FROM
BACK EDGE AND WIDTH OF WHEEL AT FRONT
LEGS, SHAFTS AND
WHEEL MADE OF
BEECH.
AXLE.
SPLIT PIN.
WOOD
WASHER
WHEEL.
THE WAY THAT THE WHEEL WILL
BE HELD IN.
THE WAY THE LEGS ARE FIXED ON.
SHAPE OF LEG
WHICH WILL BE SCREWED ON
SIDE VIEW OF END PRODUCT
MATERIALS.
1 BASE OF 300×470×8.
2 SIDES OF 600×225×8.
2 ARMS OF 1,150×37×37.
1 FRONT OF 300×225×8
2 LEGS OF 300×50×50.
1 BACK OF 400×100×8
1 WHEEL OF Ø200×37
A WOODEN TOY - WHEELBARROW
DESIGNED BY G Paley.
4²
9. 11. 71.
AIREVILLE SECONDARY

FREEHAND TWO-DIMENSIONAL AND THREE-DIMENSIONAL SKETCHING WITH HB PENCIL.
SIMPLE SHADING WITH THE PENCIL TO GIVE SOME SOLIDITY TO THE SHAPES.

A scale model of the proposed wheelbarrow constructed from balsawood. The axle for the wheel is an ordinary pin and the whole model was assembled using balsa cement.

To give a true representation of the completed work the model was painted with blue and red water colours; the body blue and the wheel and frame red. Bright colours are ideal for childrens' toys.

BS 3443, The British Standard Code of Safety for Children's Toys and Playthings requires that wooden toys should be of good quality timber, well constructed and smoothly finished. Also, dyes, paint or other coatings should be free from lead and other toxic substances.

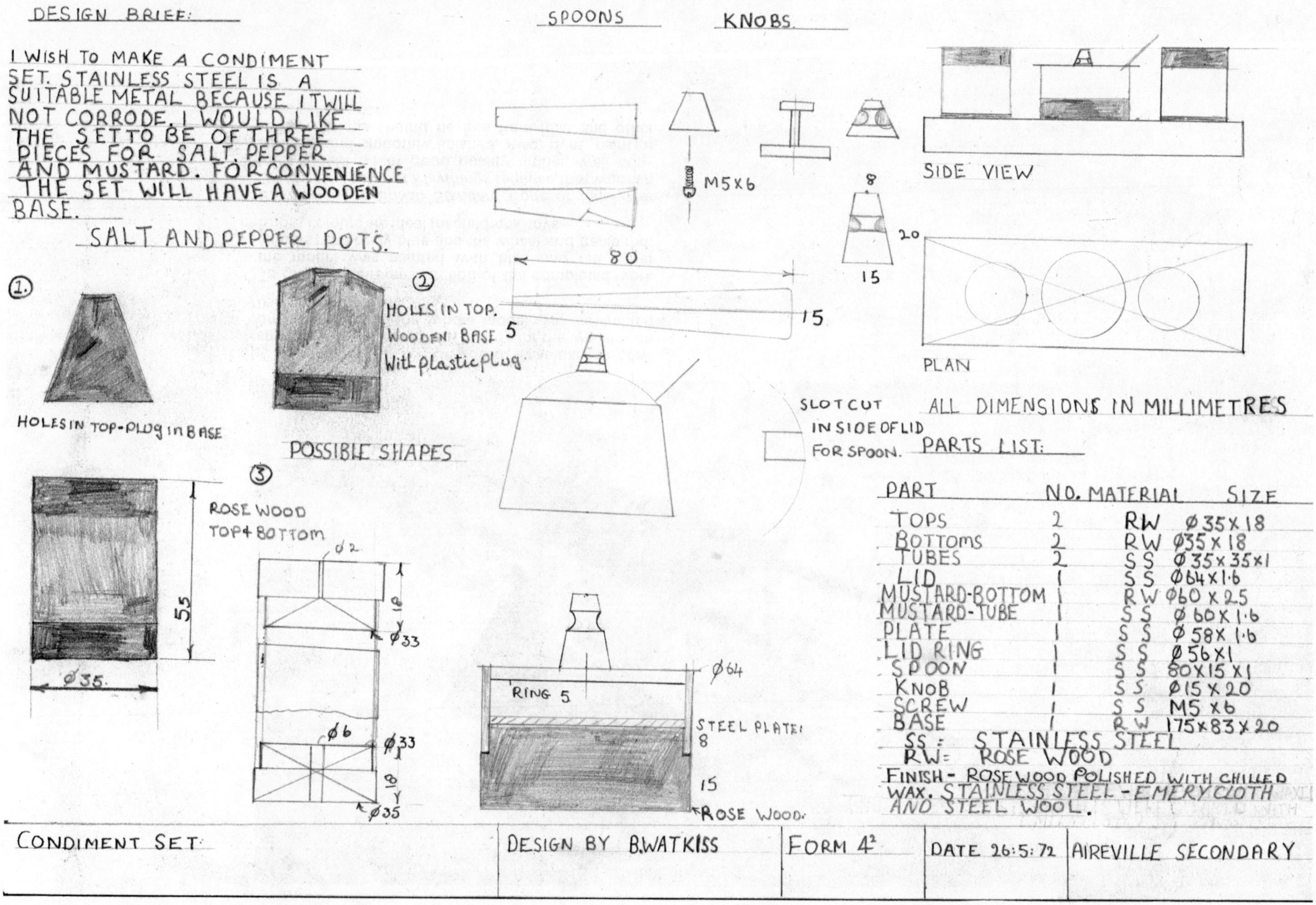
DESIGN BRIEF:
I WISH TO MAKE A CONDIMENT SET. STAINLESS STEEL IS A SUITABLE METAL BECAUSE IT WILL NOT CORRODE. I WOULD LIKE THE SET TO BE OF THREE PIECES FOR SALT, PEPPER AND MUSTARD. FOR CONVENIENCE THE SET WILL HAVE A WOODEN BASE.
SALT AND PEPPER POTS.
1.
HOLES IN TOP-PLUG IN BASE
2
HOLES IN TOP.
WOODEN BASE
With plastic plug
POSSIBLE SHAPES
3
ROSE WOOD
TOP + BOTTOM
55
Ø35
Ø2
18
Ø33
Ø6
Ø33
18
Ø35
SPOONS
KNOBS
M5x6
80
5
15
8
20
15
SLOT CUT
IN SIDE OF LID
FOR SPOON.
Ø64
RING 5
STEEL PLATE
8
15
ROSE WOOD.
SIDE VIEW
PLAN
ALL DIMENSIONS IN MILLIMETRES
PARTS LIST:
PART NO. MATERIAL SIZE
TOPS 2 RW Ø35x18
BOTTOMS 2 RW Ø35x18
TUBES 2 SS Ø35x35x1
LID 1 SS Ø64x1·6
MUSTARD-BOTTOM 1 RW Ø60x25
MUSTARD-TUBE 1 SS Ø60x1·6
PLATE 1 SS Ø58x1·6
LID RING 1 SS Ø56x1
SPOON 1 SS 80x15x1
KNOB 1 SS Ø15x20
SCREW 1 SS M5x6
BASE 1 RW 175x83x20
SS = STAINLESS STEEL
RW = ROSE WOOD
FINISH - ROSEWOOD POLISHED WITH CHILLED WAX. STAINLESS STEEL - EMERY CLOTH AND STEEL WOOL.
CONDIMENT SET
DESIGN BY B.WATKISS
FORM 4²
DATE 26:5:72
AIREVILLE SECONDARY

TWO-DIMENSIONAL SKETCHES DRAWN WITH HB PENCIL WITH SIDE ELEVATION AND PLAN IN ORTHOGRAPHIC PROJECTION.

You will see that by using different colours of card it was possible to represent both the wood and the stainless steel. Obtaining the correct proportions for height and diameter is important and so too is the relationship between the amount of wood used to the amount of steel. The model also gave a good indication as to how well the finished pieces could be held when in use.

Compare the card model with the completed work.

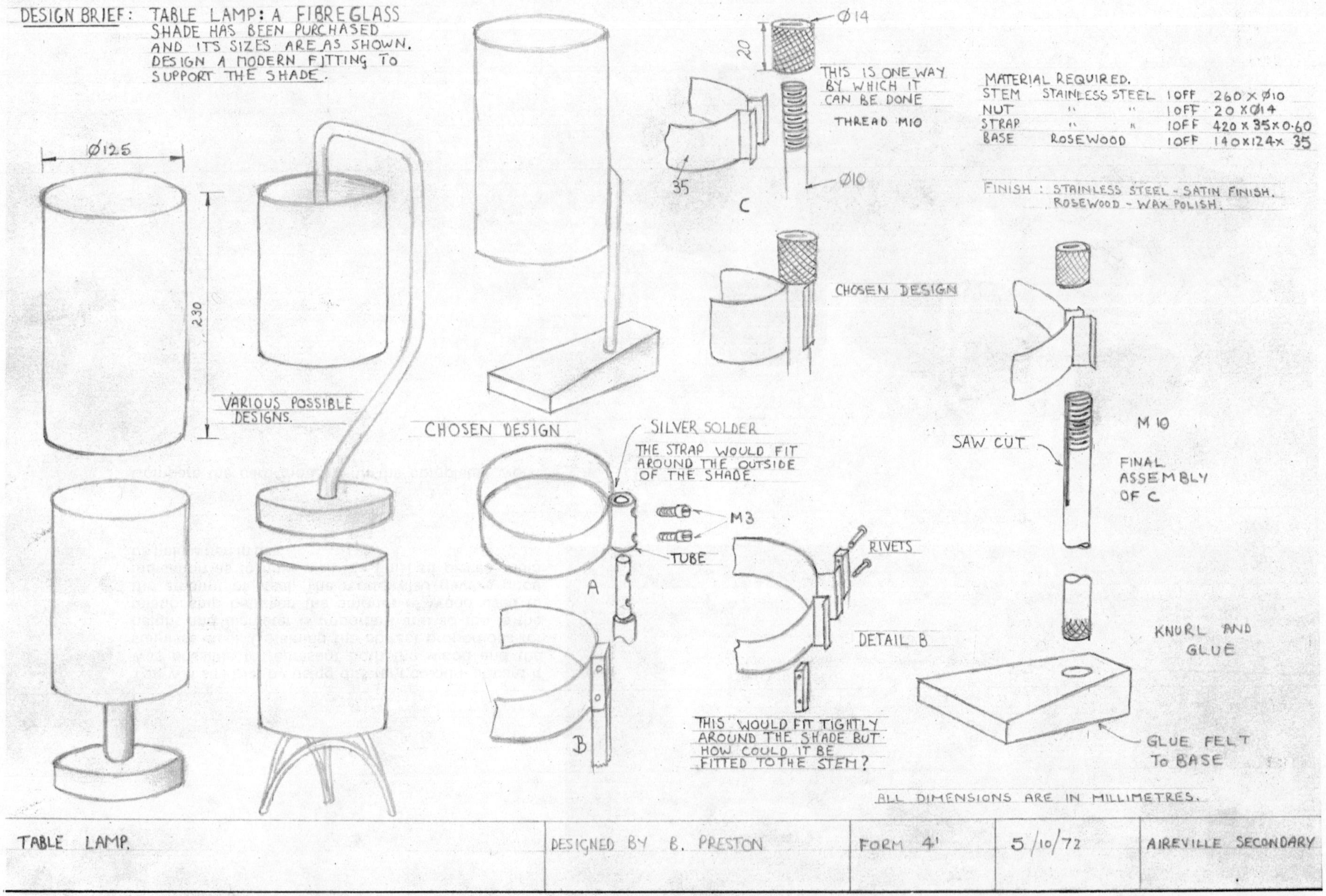
DESIGN BRIEF: TABLE LAMP: A FIBREGLASS SHADE HAS BEEN PURCHASED AND ITS SIZES ARE AS SHOWN. DESIGN A MODERN FITTING TO SUPPORT THE SHADE.
Ø125
230
VARIOUS POSSIBLE DESIGNS.
CHOSEN DESIGN
Ø14
20
THIS IS ONE WAY BY WHICH IT CAN BE DONE
THREAD M10
35
Ø10
C
MATERIAL REQUIRED.
STEM STAINLESS STEEL 1OFF 260 × Ø10
NUT " " 1OFF 20 × Ø14
STRAP " " 1OFF 420 × 35 × 0·60
BASE ROSEWOOD 1OFF 140 × 124 × 35
FINISH : STAINLESS STEEL - SATIN FINISH. ROSEWOOD - WAX POLISH.
CHOSEN DESIGN
SILVER SOLDER
THE STRAP WOULD FIT AROUND THE OUTSIDE OF THE SHADE.
M3
TUBE
A
RIVETS
DETAIL B
B
THIS WOULD FIT TIGHTLY AROUND THE SHADE BUT HOW COULD IT BE FITTED TO THE STEM?
M 10
SAW CUT
FINAL ASSEMBLY OF C
KNURL AND GLUE
GLUE FELT TO BASE
ALL DIMENSIONS ARE IN MILLIMETRES.
TABLE LAMP.
DESIGNED BY B. PRESTON
FORM 4'
5/10/72
AIREVILLE SECONDARY

FREEHAND ISOMETRIC AND PICTORIAL SKETCHES DRAWN WITH HB PENCIL.

The finished lamp. You should note the well balanced appearance, the beauty of the grain of the rosewood and how well it harmonises with the red shade and the stainless steel fittings.

Close-up of the assembly. A necessary part of the construction becomes an interesting decorative feature.

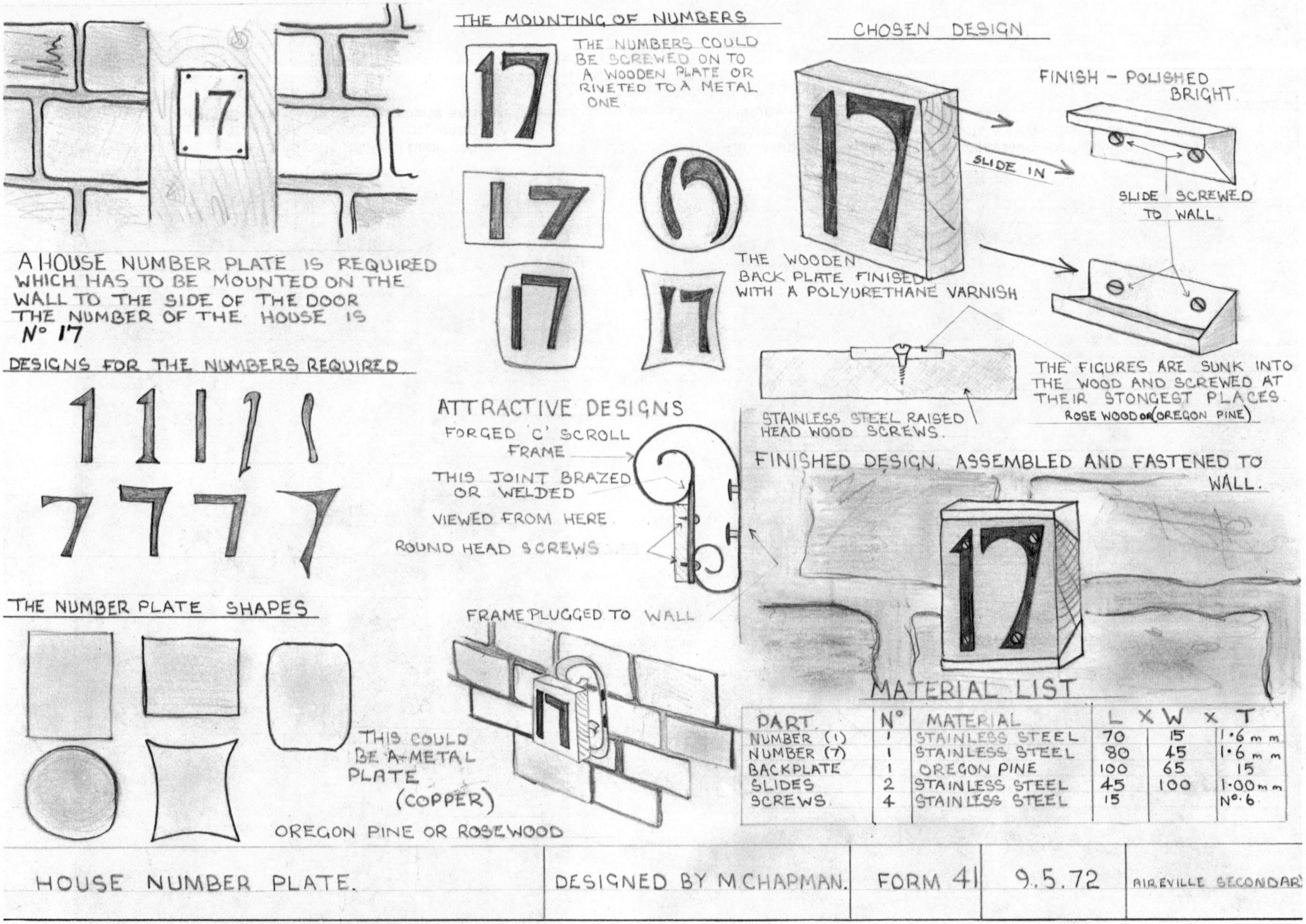
17
A HOUSE NUMBER PLATE IS REQUIRED WHICH HAS TO BE MOUNTED ON THE WALL TO THE SIDE OF THE DOOR THE NUMBER OF THE HOUSE IS N° 17
DESIGNS FOR THE NUMBERS REQUIRED
THE NUMBER PLATE SHAPES
THIS COULD BE A METAL PLATE (COPPER)
OREGON PINE OR ROSEWOOD
THE MOUNTING OF NUMBERS
THE NUMBERS COULD BE SCREWED ON TO A WOODEN PLATE OR RIVETED TO A METAL ONE
ATTRACTIVE DESIGNS
FORGED 'C' SCROLL FRAME
THIS JOINT BRAZED OR WELDED
VIEWED FROM HERE
ROUND HEAD SCREWS
FRAME PLUGGED TO WALL
CHOSEN DESIGN
FINISH - POLISHED BRIGHT.
SLIDE IN
SLIDE SCREWED TO WALL
THE WOODEN BACK PLATE FINISED WITH A POLYURETHANE VARNISH
THE FIGURES ARE SUNK INTO THE WOOD AND SCREWED AT THEIR STONGEST PLACES
ROSE WOOD OR (OREGON PINE)
STAINLESS STEEL RAISED HEAD WOOD SCREWS.
FINISHED DESIGN, ASSEMBLED AND FASTENED TO WALL.
MATERIAL LIST
PART | N° | MATERIAL | L × W × T
NUMBER (1) | 1 | STAINLESS STEEL | 70 | 15 | 1·6 mm
NUMBER (7) | 1 | STAINLESS STEEL | 80 | 45 | 1·6 mm
BACKPLATE | 1 | OREGON PINE | 100 | 65 | 15
SLIDES | 2 | STAINLESS STEEL | 45 | 100 | 1·00 mm
SCREWS | 4 | STAINLESS STEEL | 15 | | N° 6
HOUSE NUMBER PLATE.
DESIGNED BY M CHAPMAN.
FORM 41
9.5.72
AIREVILLE SECONDARY

TWO-DIMENSIONAL, ISOMETRIC AND OBLIQUE FREEHAND SKETCHING WITH HB PENCIL.
ALTERNATIVE DESIGNS HAVE BEEN CONSIDERED, THERE ARE MANY EXPLANATORY NOTES AND A COMPREHENSIVE MATERIAL LIST.

Card model and tinplate mock-up of one of the two slides. You should note the simple development involved in setting out the card. This was then cut out very quickly and easily and when folded was tested on the wood for correct fitting.

Mocking-up in tinplate gave practice in folding sheet metal before making both slides in stainless steel.

17

The completed number plate mounted on the brick-work near to the door at a height easily seen.

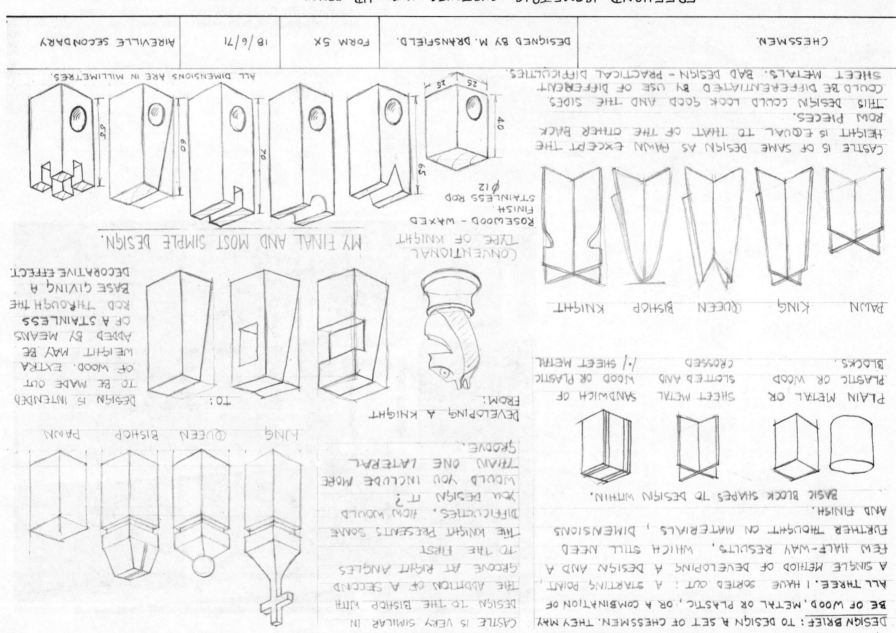

DESIGN BRIEF: TO DESIGN A SET OF CHESSMEN. THEY MAY BE OF WOOD, METAL OR PLASTIC, OR A COMBINATION OF ALL THREE. I HAVE SORTED OUT: A STARTING POINT, A SINGLE METHOD OF DEVELOPING A DESIGN AND A FEW HALF-WAY RESULTS, WHICH STILL NEED FURTHER THOUGHT ON MATERIALS, DIMENSIONS AND FINISH.

BASIC BLOCK SHAPES TO DESIGN WITHIN.

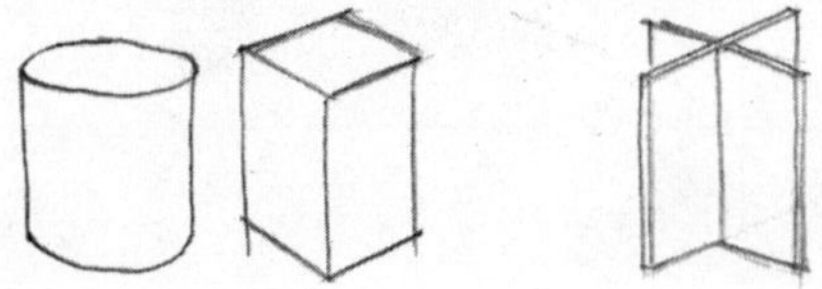

PLAIN METAL OR PLASTIC OR WOOD BLOCKS. | SHEET METAL SLOTTED AND CROSSED | SANDWICH OF WOOD OR PLASTIC /·/ SHEET METAL

PAWN KING QUEEN BISHOP KNIGHT

CASTLE IS OF SAME DESIGN AS PAWN EXCEPT THE HEIGHT IS EQUAL TO THAT OF THE OTHER BACK ROW PIECES.
THIS DESIGN COULD LOOK GOOD AND THE SIDES COULD BE DIFFERENTIATED BY USE OF DIFFERENT SHEET METALS. BAD DESIGN - PRACTICAL DIFFICULTIES.

CASTLE IS VERY SIMILAR IN DESIGN TO THE BISHOP WITH THE ADDITION OF A SECOND GROOVE AT RIGHT ANGLES TO THE FIRST
THE KNIGHT PRESENTS SOME DIFFICULTIES. HOW WOULD YOU DESIGN IT?
WOULD YOU INCLUDE MORE THAN ONE LATERAL GROOVE.

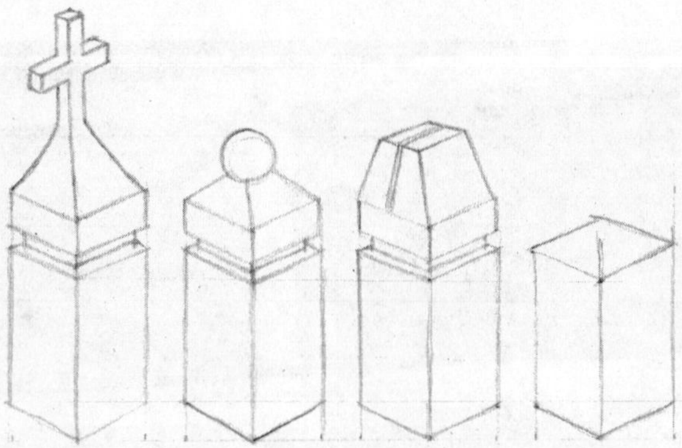

KING QUEEN BISHOP PAWN

DEVELOPING A KNIGHT FROM:

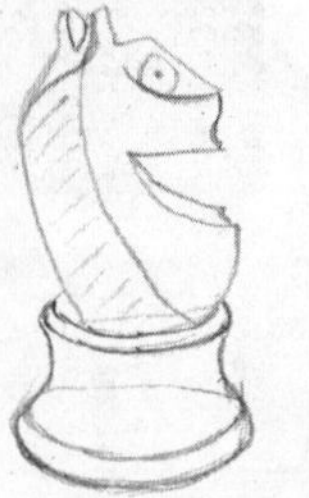

CONVENTIONAL TYPE OF KNIGHT

TO:

DESIGN IS INTENDED TO BE MADE OUT OF WOOD. EXTRA WEIGHT MAY BE ADDED BY MEANS OF A STAINLESS ROD THROUGH THE BASE GIVING A DECORATIVE EFFECT.

MY FINAL AND MOST SIMPLE DESIGN.

ROSEWOOD - WAXED FINISH.
STAINLESS ROD
$\phi 12$

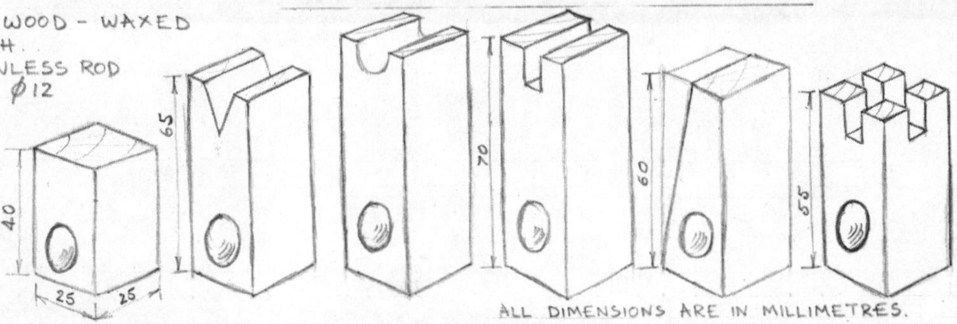
40
25
25
65
70
60
55

ALL DIMENSIONS ARE IN MILLIMETRES.

CHESSMEN.	DESIGNED BY M. DRANSFIELD.	FORM 5X	18/6/71	AIREVILLE SECONDARY

FREEHAND ISOMETRIC SKETCHES WITH HB PENCIL.
NOTE THE ABUNDANT PRINTED DESCRIPTIONS WHICH ACCOMPANY THE SKETCHES.

From left to right, a Castle, Knight, King, Queen, Bishop and Pawn. The clean-cut lines and simple shapes of the pieces together with the stainless steel insert, which contrasts with the rich colour of the rosewood, combine to give a very pleasing effect.

It is proposed to make the corresponding set from sycamore with a black plastic insert.

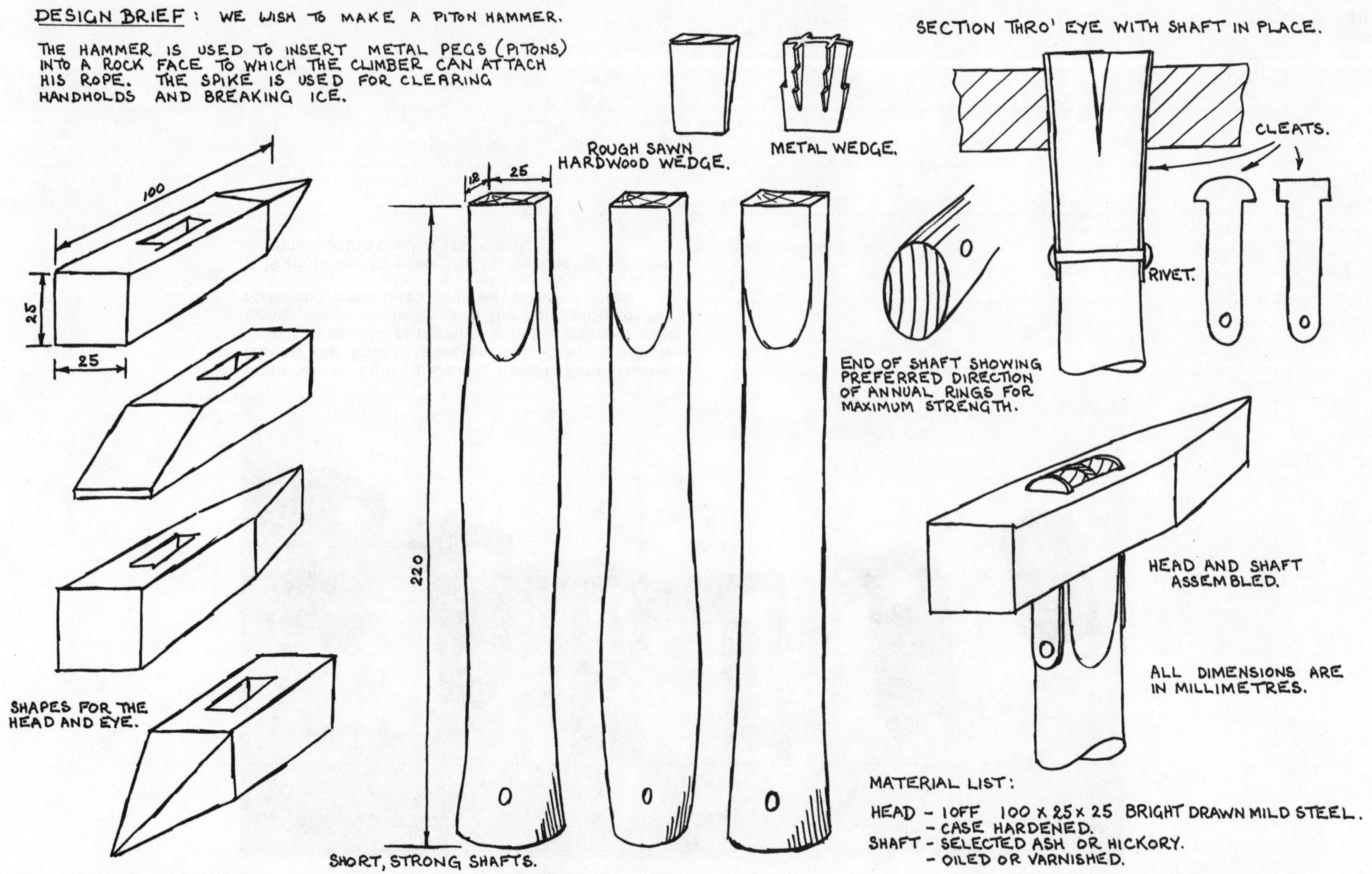
DESIGN BRIEF : WE WISH TO MAKE A PITON HAMMER.
THE HAMMER IS USED TO INSERT METAL PEGS (PITONS) INTO A ROCK FACE TO WHICH THE CLIMBER CAN ATTACH HIS ROPE. THE SPIKE IS USED FOR CLEARING HANDHOLDS AND BREAKING ICE.
100
25
25
SHAPES FOR THE HEAD AND EYE.
ROUGH SAWN HARDWOOD WEDGE.
METAL WEDGE.
12
25
220
SHORT, STRONG SHAFTS.
SECTION THRO' EYE WITH SHAFT IN PLACE.
CLEATS.
RIVET.
END OF SHAFT SHOWING PREFERRED DIRECTION OF ANNUAL RINGS FOR MAXIMUM STRENGTH.
HEAD AND SHAFT ASSEMBLED.
ALL DIMENSIONS ARE IN MILLIMETRES.
MATERIAL LIST :
HEAD - 1OFF 100 x 25 x 25 BRIGHT DRAWN MILD STEEL.
- CASE HARDENED.
SHAFT - SELECTED ASH OR HICKORY.
- OILED OR VARNISHED.

PITON HAMMERS.	DESIGNED BY C. BRIGHT AND D. WEAR.	FORM 5Y	3/9/67	AIREVILLE SECONDARY.

AN EDITED DRAWING TO SHOW METRIC MEASUREMENTS. DRAWING AND PRINTING MADE ENTIRELY BY THE USE OF A BLACK FIBRE TIPPED PEN. THE 'LAKELAND' MARKER 33 IS IDEAL FOR THIS PURPOSE AND IS AVAILABLE IN A VARIETY OF COLOURS. THE BOLD, FREELY MADE LINES ALLOW CLEAR AND RAPID SKETCHING OF IDEAS.

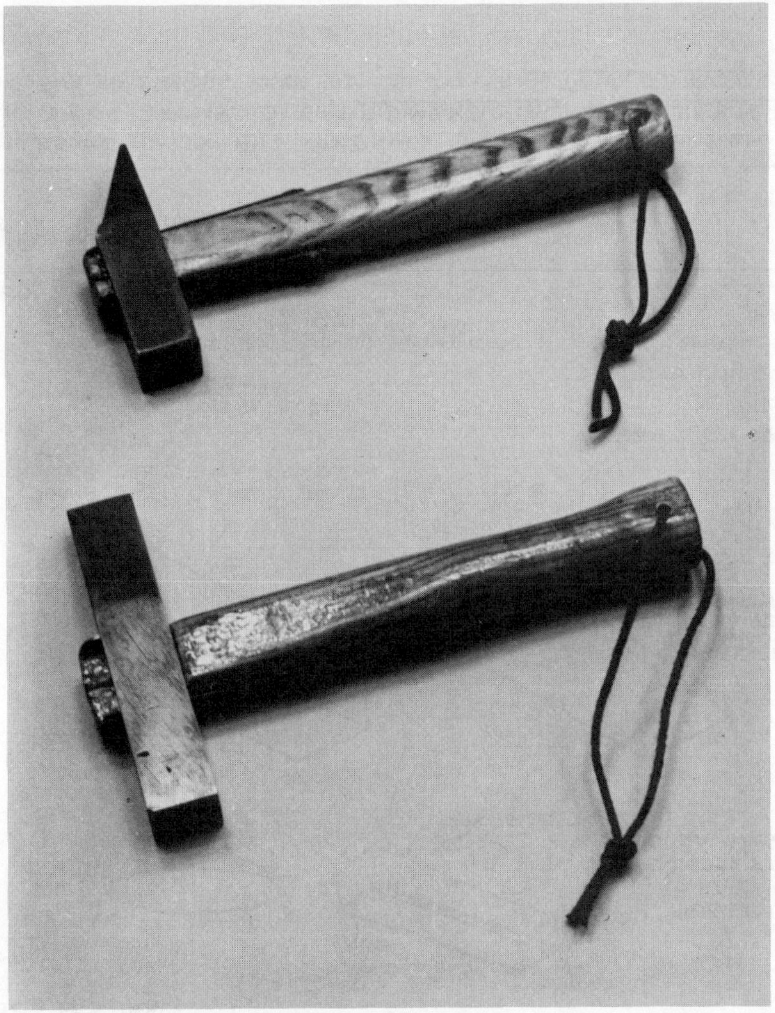

The two hammers when completed.

Note the different shapes of head, this being dependent on the designer's preference.

The cleats are riveted through the handle for maximum security of the head.

You should notice also the different shapes of the handle, both of which allow a secure grip. One is fitted with a leather thong and the other with a stout cord.

THE FOLLOWING DESIGN BRIEF WAS GIVEN TO A GROUP OF BOYS FOLLOWING A REQUEST FOR ASSISTANCE FROM THE LOCAL HOSPITAL. THE HOSPITAL STAFF WERE CONCERNED FOR THE SAFETY OF CERTAIN PATIENTS WHO WERE CONFINED TO THEIR BEDS AND WHO ENJOYED SMOKING. DUE TO THEIR CONDITION THEY HAD DIFFICULTY IN HANDLING CIGARETTES SO THAT THERE WAS A PERSONAL HAZARD IN THAT THEY MIGHT BURN THEIR HANDS OR, WORSE STILL, SET FIRE TO THE BED. THERE WAS A DISTINCT POSSIBILITY THAT THEY MAY HAVE HAD TO BE DENIED ONE OF THEIR FEW REMAINING PLEASURES.

CIGARETTE HOLDER : SPECIAL REQUIREMENTS.

1. OF SIMPLE CONSTRUCTION TO ENABLE SEVERAL TO BE MADE EASILY. CAPABLE OF 'MASS PRODUCTION' WITHIN THE FACILITIES OF THE SCHOOL.
2. IT MUST BE STRONG AND DURABLE.
3. EASILY AND SECURELY FITTED TO THE BED TABLE.
4. BE EASILY DETACHED FOR EMPTYING.
5. BE EASILY CLEANED AND WASHED – MUST BE NON-CORROSIVE.
6. HOLD THE CIGARETTE FIRMLY.
7. CATCH ALL THE ASH AND THE STUB IF IT FALLS.
8. THE PATIENT MUST NOT MAKE DIRECT CONTACT.

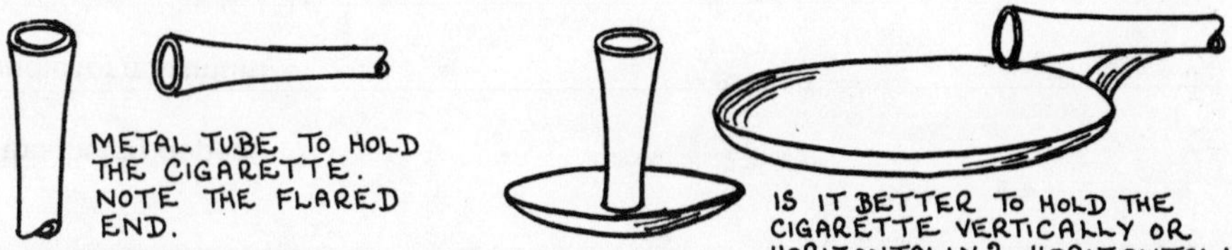
METAL TUBE TO HOLD THE CIGARETTE. NOTE THE FLARED END.
IS IT BETTER TO HOLD THE CIGARETTE VERTICALLY OR HORIZONTALLY? HORIZONTALLY ALLOWS THE ASH TO FALL CLEAR AND EASY CONNECTION OF THE TUBE.

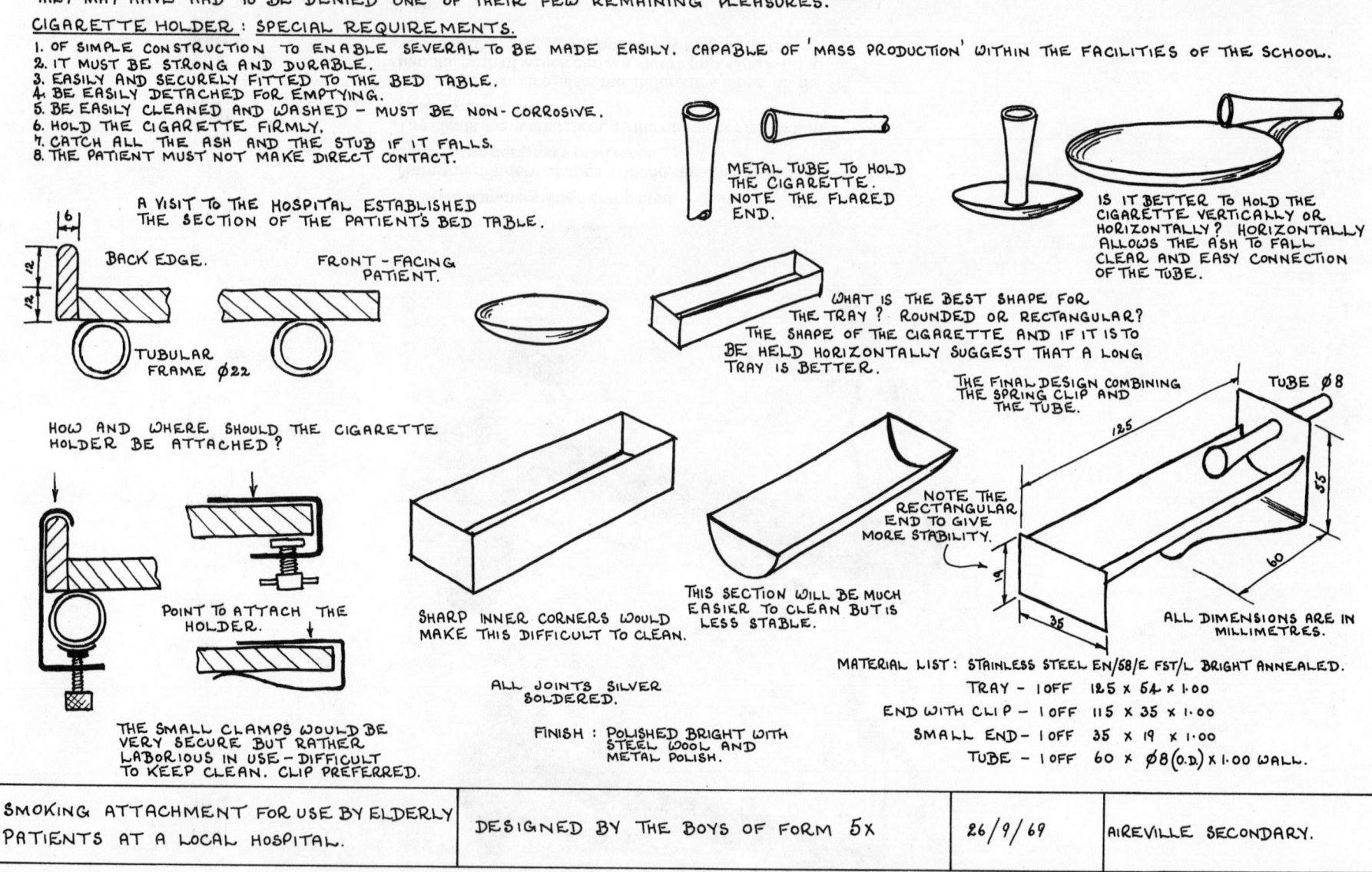

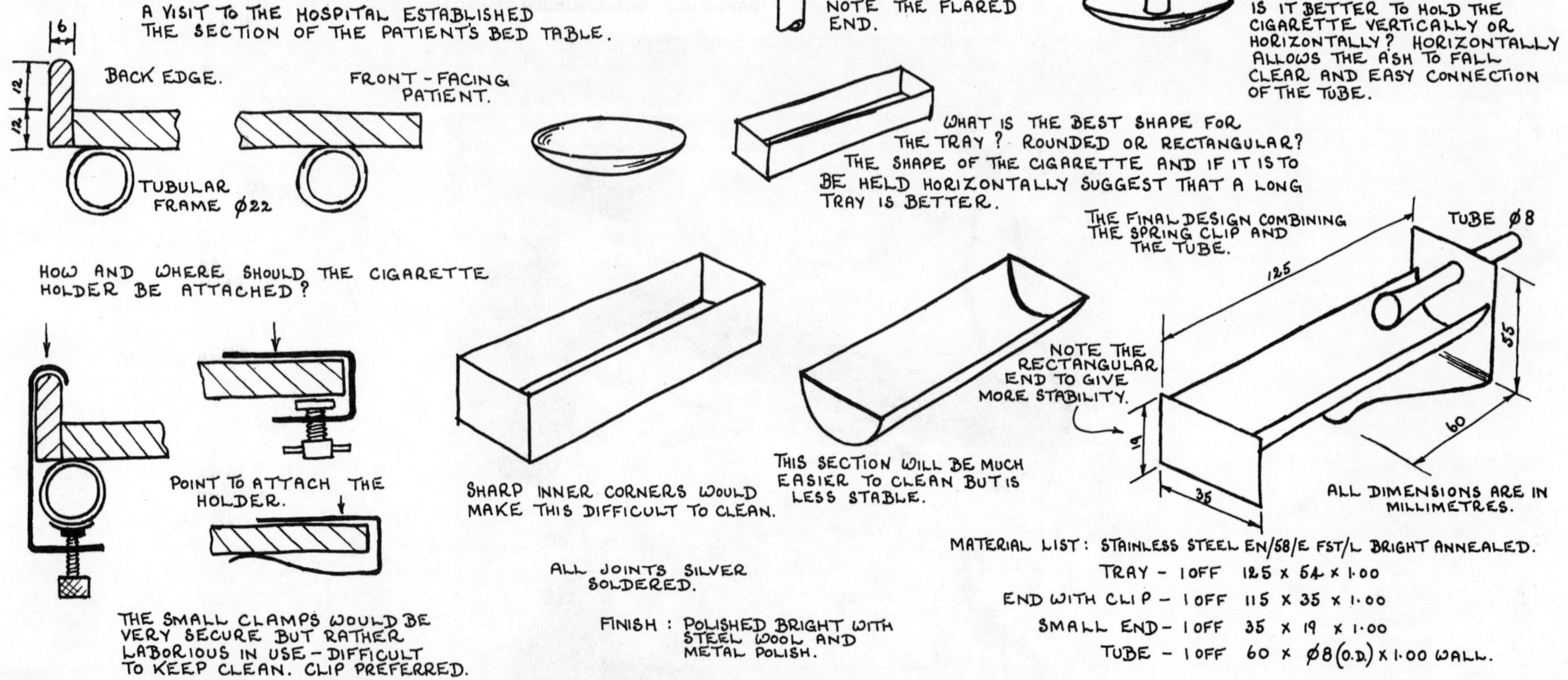
A VISIT TO THE HOSPITAL ESTABLISHED THE SECTION OF THE PATIENT'S BED TABLE.
6
12
12
BACK EDGE.
FRONT - FACING PATIENT.
TUBULAR FRAME Ø22
WHAT IS THE BEST SHAPE FOR THE TRAY? ROUNDED OR RECTANGULAR? THE SHAPE OF THE CIGARETTE AND IF IT IS TO BE HELD HORIZONTALLY SUGGEST THAT A LONG TRAY IS BETTER.
THE FINAL DESIGN COMBINING THE SPRING CLIP AND THE TUBE.
TUBE Ø8
125
55
60
19
35
HOW AND WHERE SHOULD THE CIGARETTE HOLDER BE ATTACHED?
NOTE THE RECTANGULAR END TO GIVE MORE STABILITY.
POINT TO ATTACH THE HOLDER.
SHARP INNER CORNERS WOULD MAKE THIS DIFFICULT TO CLEAN.
THIS SECTION WILL BE MUCH EASIER TO CLEAN BUT IS LESS STABLE.
ALL DIMENSIONS ARE IN MILLIMETRES.
MATERIAL LIST : STAINLESS STEEL EN/58/E FST/L BRIGHT ANNEALED.
TRAY - 1 OFF 125 x 54 x 1·00
END WITH CLIP - 1 OFF 115 x 35 x 1·00
SMALL END - 1 OFF 35 x 19 x 1·00
TUBE - 1 OFF 60 x Ø8 (O.D.) x 1·00 WALL.
ALL JOINTS SILVER SOLDERED.
FINISH : POLISHED BRIGHT WITH STEEL WOOL AND METAL POLISH.
THE SMALL CLAMPS WOULD BE VERY SECURE BUT RATHER LABORIOUS IN USE – DIFFICULT TO KEEP CLEAN. CLIP PREFERRED.

SMOKING ATTACHMENT FOR USE BY ELDERLY PATIENTS AT A LOCAL HOSPITAL.	DESIGNED BY THE BOYS OF FORM 5X	26/9/69	AIREVILLE SECONDARY.

AN EDITED DRAWING TO SHOW METRIC MEASUREMENTS AND COMBINING THE INDIVIDUAL DESIGN SUGGESTIONS OF THE GROUP WHICH LED TO THE FINAL PROPOSAL. THE DRAWING SHOWS EXAMPLES OF TWO-DIMENSIONAL AND ISOMETRIC SKETCHING AND WAS MADE WITH A BLACK FIBRE TIPPED PEN. THE LETTERING AND DIMENSIONS WERE ADDED WITH A ROTRING 0·5 MICRONORM TECHNICAL DRAWING PEN.

A card mock-up was made followed by a model in tinplate.

The six pieces required were then made in stainless steel. They were made quickly by group effort on a 'factory' day.

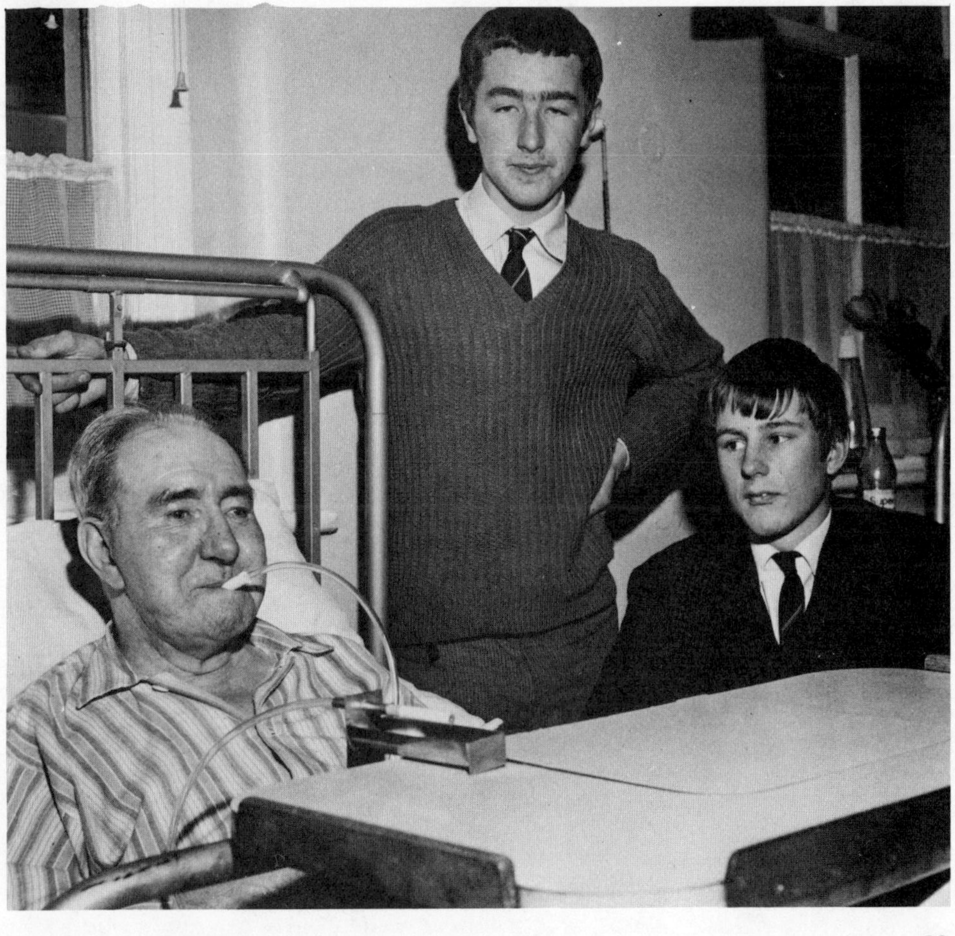

Two of the boys with a patient testing one of the attachments. The hospital supplied plastic tubes with mouth pieces which were fitted with filters. The test proved the holder to be satisfactory.

Introduction

From prehistoric days to the present time man has recorded his activities and ideas by means of drawings and paintings. Some of his earliest works have been preserved to the present day in the form of cave paintings depicting hunting scenes and animals of the period. The need to hunt in order to eat being predominant in man's fight for survival. Tools for hunting were developed and over the centuries as life for man became more positive he produced tools to help him in his work. With this change man's inventiveness became more and more evident leading to our very civilized society of today with its multiplicity of sophisticated products. Of comparatively modern times, Leonardo da Vinci (1452–1519), was a most prolific artist and designer. Evidence of the products of his fertile brain and infinite skill remain for us to see in his works of art and also in the form of freehand sketches of ideas for various machines, to be used in both war and peace. Many of these sketches are so detailed and refined that working models have been made from them quite recently, such as the boring machine illustrated (page 25).

The ability to express oneself visually in this way is important when designing craftwork so as to produce completely acceptable designs.
Preliminary ideas expressed as drawings enable the designer to correct and modify his work until he is satisfied that the design produced is a suitable solution to the design problem.

Ideas for designs may be expressed visually using a number of different media and different styles of drawing and projection. In this introductory chapter there are many examples of design sheets to enable students to apply an appropriate method to their own work. These illustrations range from junior to senior work in both wood and metal and from each example it can be seen how the design has led to the finished work often with the aid of mock-ups and scale models. The many variations help to demonstrate and encourage individuality in presentation of design.

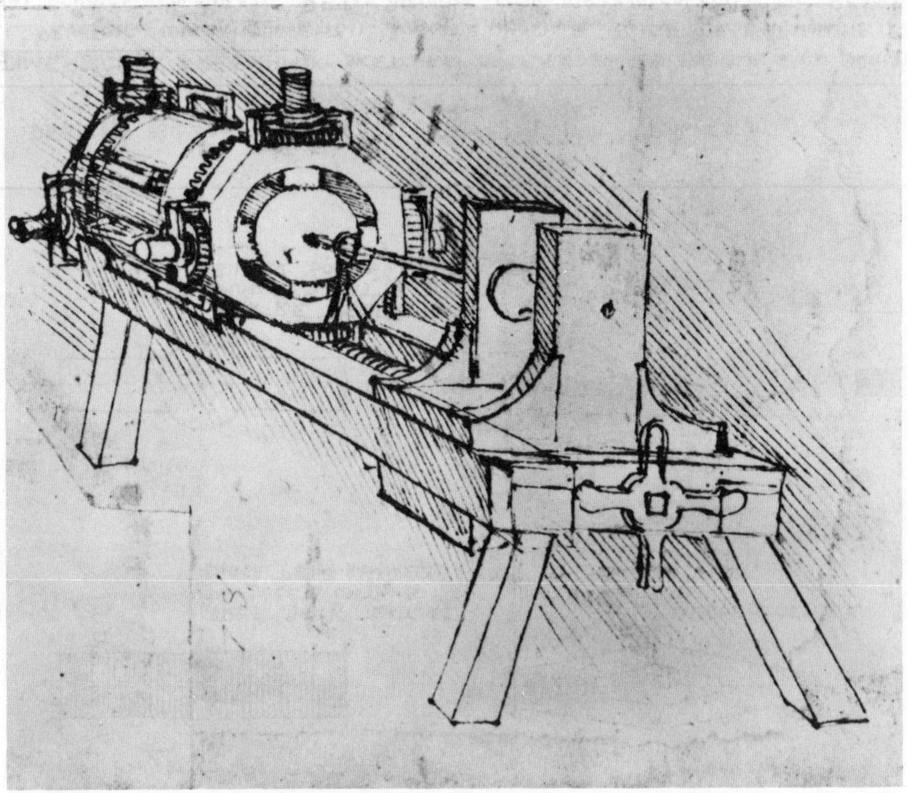

Sketch for a boring machine.
Leonardo da Vinci 1452-1519.

A model made from the design sketch.

Further specimen design sheets

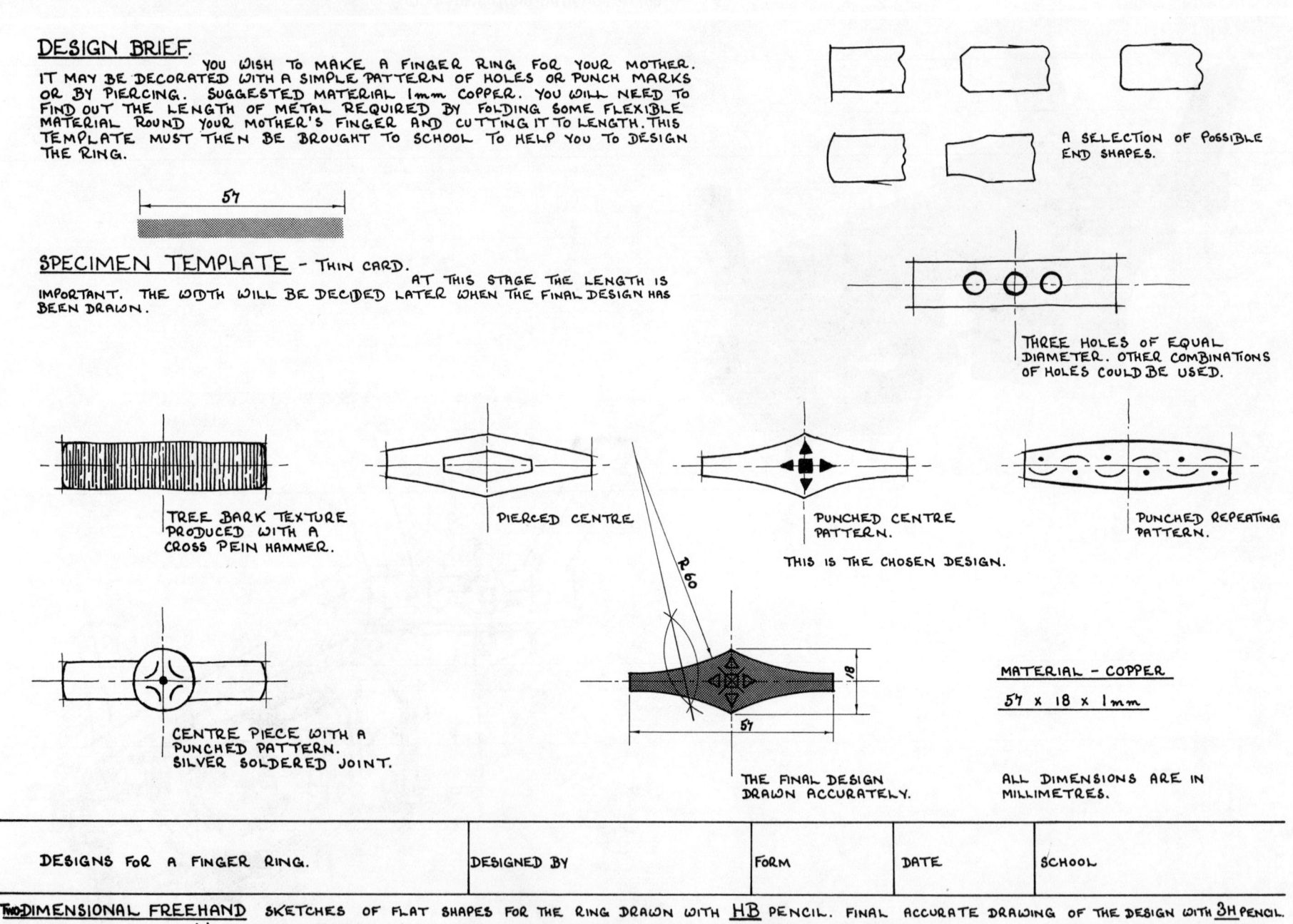

DESIGN BRIEF. YOU WISH TO MAKE A FINGER RING FOR YOUR MOTHER. IT MAY BE DECORATED WITH A SIMPLE PATTERN OF HOLES OR PUNCH MARKS OR BY PIERCING. SUGGESTED MATERIAL 1mm COPPER. YOU WILL NEED TO FIND OUT THE LENGTH OF METAL REQUIRED BY FOLDING SOME FLEXIBLE MATERIAL ROUND YOUR MOTHER'S FINGER AND CUTTING IT TO LENGTH. THIS TEMPLATE MUST THEN BE BROUGHT TO SCHOOL TO HELP YOU TO DESIGN THE RING.

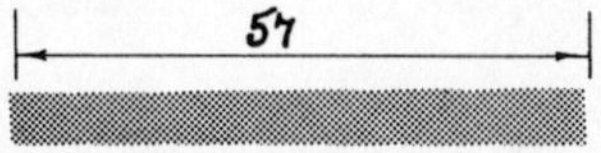
57

SPECIMEN TEMPLATE - THIN CARD. AT THIS STAGE THE LENGTH IS IMPORTANT. THE WIDTH WILL BE DECIDED LATER WHEN THE FINAL DESIGN HAS BEEN DRAWN.

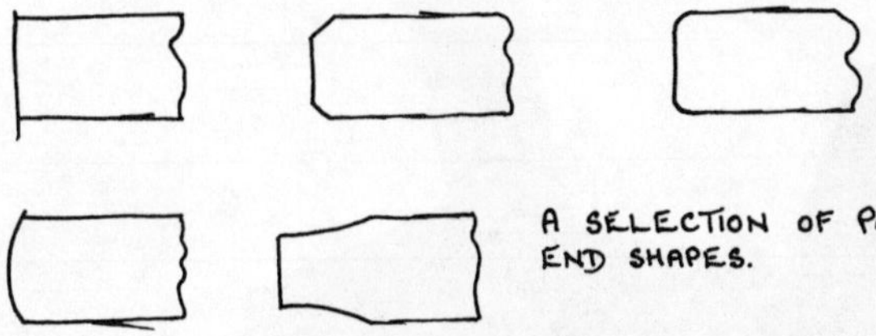

A SELECTION OF POSSIBLE END SHAPES.

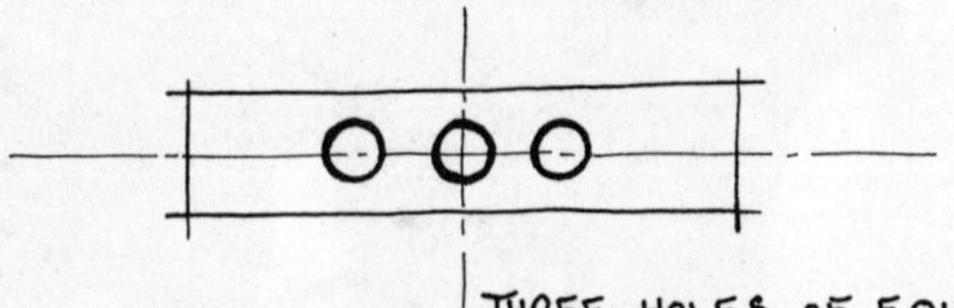

THREE HOLES OF EQUAL DIAMETER. OTHER COMBINATIONS OF HOLES COULD BE USED.

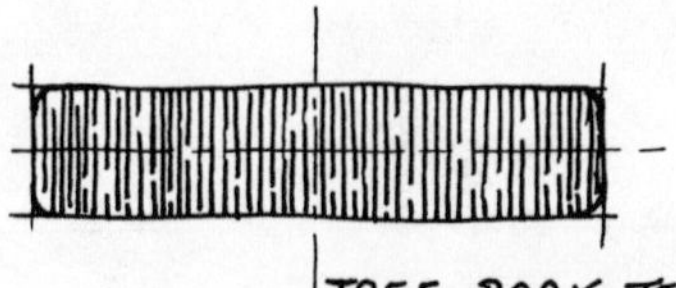

TREE BARK TEXTURE PRODUCED WITH A CROSS PEIN HAMMER.

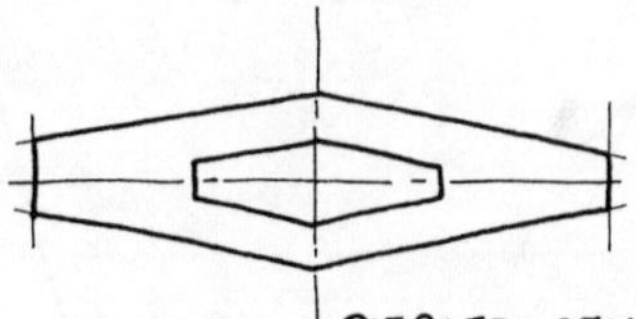

PIERCED CENTRE

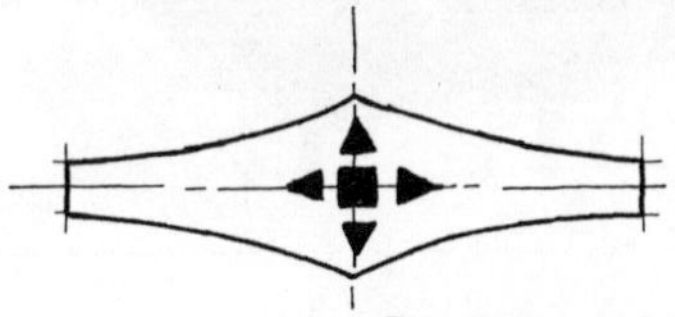

PUNCHED CENTRE PATTERN.

THIS IS THE CHOSEN DESIGN.

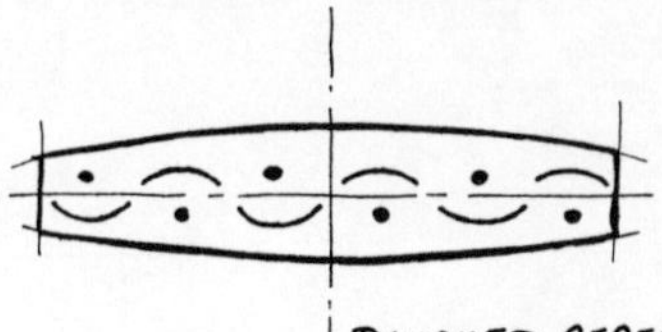

PUNCHED REPEATING PATTERN.

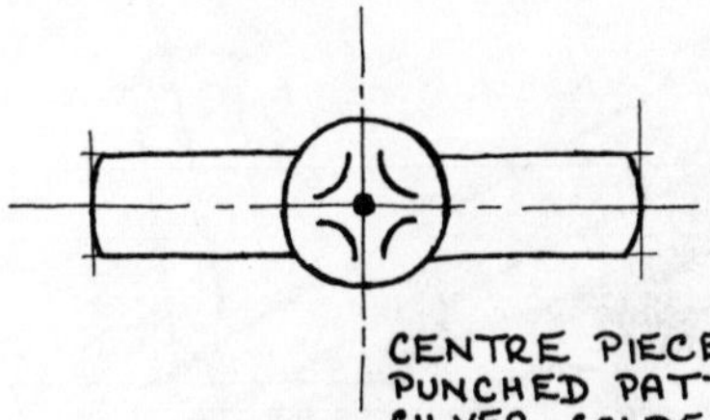

CENTRE PIECE WITH A PUNCHED PATTERN. SILVER SOLDERED JOINT.

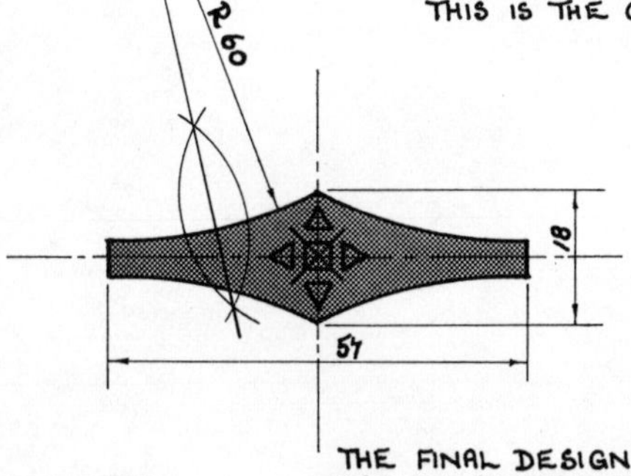
R60
18
57

THE FINAL DESIGN DRAWN ACCURATELY.

MATERIAL - COPPER

57 x 18 x 1mm

ALL DIMENSIONS ARE IN MILLIMETRES.

DESIGNS FOR A FINGER RING.	DESIGNED BY	FORM	DATE	SCHOOL

TWO-DIMENSIONAL FREEHAND SKETCHES OF FLAT SHAPES FOR THE RING DRAWN WITH HB PENCIL. FINAL ACCURATE DRAWING OF THE DESIGN WITH 3H PENCIL. ALL PRINTING WITH H PENCIL. NOTE HOW A BRIEF DESCRIPTION IS GIVEN OF EACH IDEA AND THE IMPORTANCE OF TRYING SEVERAL DESIGNS. FINAL CHOICE COLOURED RED-BROWN WITH WATER COLOURS TO REPRESENT COPPER.

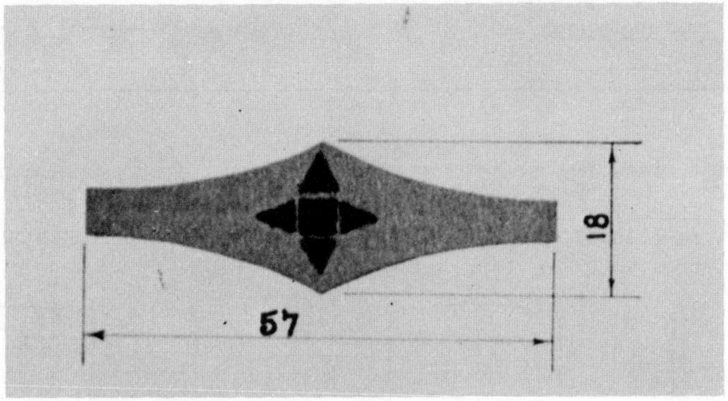
18
57

A card model, drawn and cut accurately to shape with the proposed punched pattern drawn in.

As a further check this may be taken home and tested for size. You will also be able to see if it is going to look well when it is worn on a finger. In this way the model enables you to see whether or not the chosen design is satisfactory in size, shape and appearance.

The completed ring. Note the pleasant overall shape, the punched pattern and the well finished surface.

DESIGN BRIEF. THE MANUFACTURERS OF MODERN NON-STICK SAUCE-PANS AND FRYING PANS OFTEN SUPPLY A PLASTIC SPATULA FOR USE WITH THEIR PRODUCTS. IT IS ESSENTIAL TO AVOID THE USE OF METAL UTENSILS WITH THESE PANS TO PREVENT DAMAGE TO THE NON-STICK PLASTIC COATING. UNFORTUNATELY, THESE PLASTIC SPATULAS CAN BE EASILY DAMAGED BY HEAT AND USUALLY HAVE ONLY A LIMITED LIFE.

BECAUSE OF THIS YOU ARE ASKED TO DESIGN A SPATULA TO BE MADE OF WOOD. IT SHOULD BE HARD WEARING AND EASY TO CLEAN. IT MUST BE EASY TO HOLD AND LONG ENOUGH TO AVOID BURNS TO THE HAND FROM SPLASHING FAT, ETC. THE END MUST BE SHAPED SO THAT IT WILL REACH INTO THE CORNERS OF PANS FOR SCRAPING AND HAVE A BIG ENOUGH AREA TO BE ABLE TO LIFT BACON, FRIED EGGS, ETC. OUT OF THE PAN WHEN THEY HAVE BEEN COOKED.

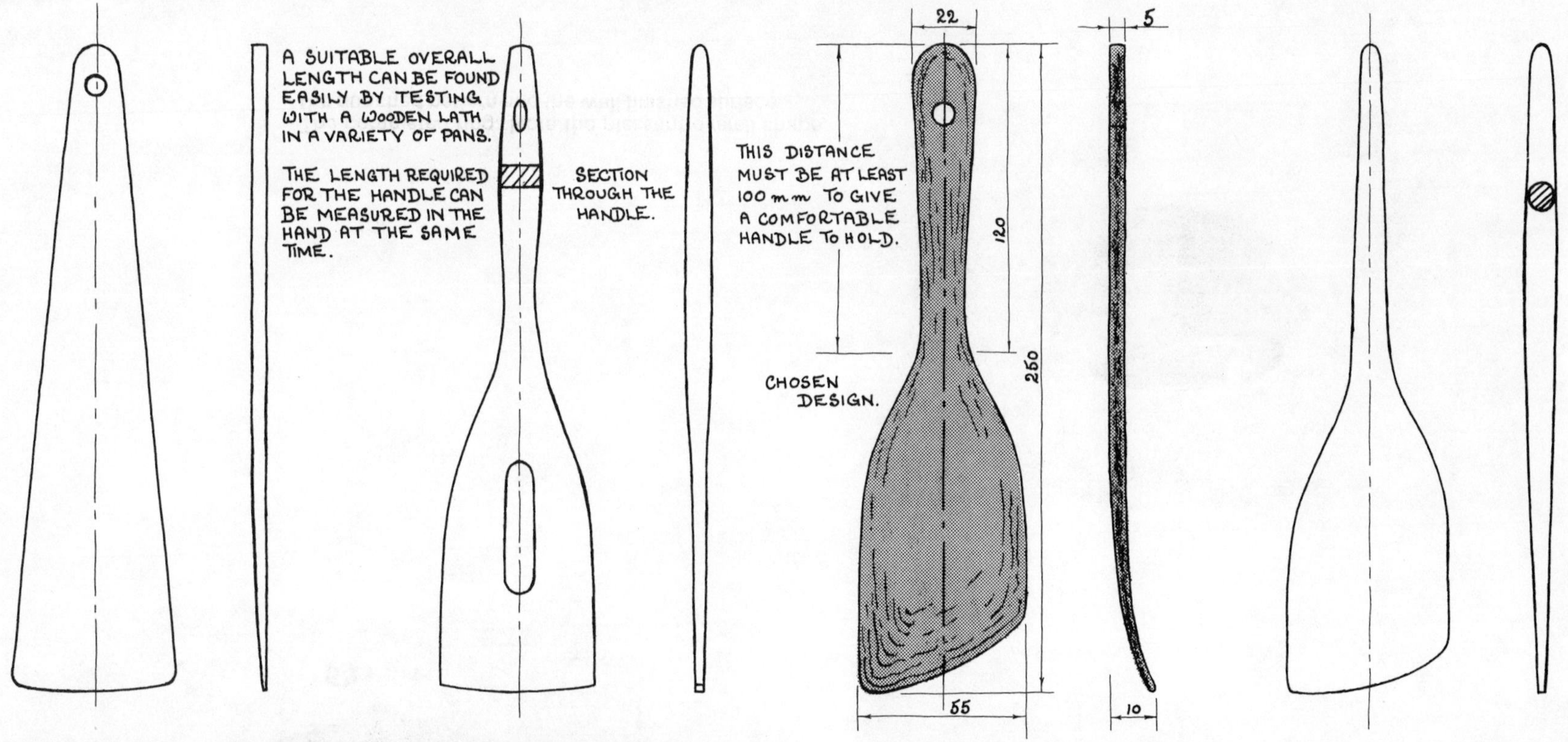
A SUITABLE OVERALL LENGTH CAN BE FOUND EASILY BY TESTING WITH A WOODEN LATH IN A VARIETY OF PANS.
THE LENGTH REQUIRED FOR THE HANDLE CAN BE MEASURED IN THE HAND AT THE SAME TIME.
SECTION THROUGH THE HANDLE.
THIS DISTANCE MUST BE AT LEAST 100 mm TO GIVE A COMFORTABLE HANDLE TO HOLD.
CHOSEN DESIGN.
22
5
120
250
55
10

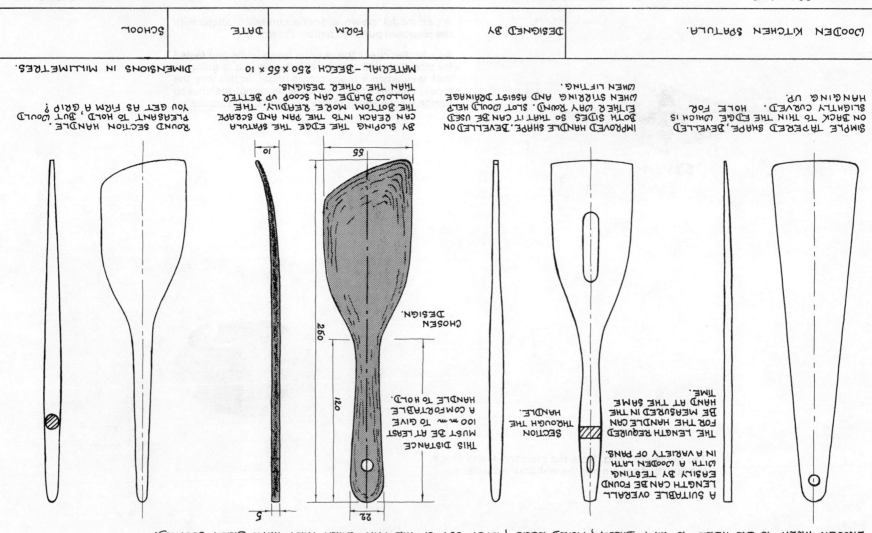

SIMPLE TAPERED SHAPE, BEVELLED ON BACK TO THIN THE EDGE WHICH IS SLIGHTLY CURVED. HOLE FOR HANGING UP.

IMPROVED HANDLE SHAPE. BEVELLED ON BOTH SIDES SO THAT IT CAN BE USED EITHER WAY ROUND. SLOT WOULD HELP WHEN STIRRING AND ASSIST DRAINAGE WHEN LIFTING.

BY SLOPING THE EDGE THE SPATULA CAN REACH INTO THE PAN AND SCRAPE THE BOTTOM MORE READILY. THE HOLLOW BLADE CAN SCOOP UP BETTER THAN THE OTHER DESIGNS.

ROUND SECTION HANDLE. PLEASANT TO HOLD, BUT WOULD YOU GET AS FIRM A GRIP?

MATERIAL – BEECH 250 x 55 x 10

DIMENSIONS IN MILLIMETRES.

WOODEN KITCHEN SPATULA.	DESIGNED BY	FORM	DATE	SCHOOL

IT IS GOOD PRACTICE TO DRAW SEVERAL IDEAS FROM WHICH THE DESIGN FOR THE ONE TO BE MADE CAN BE SELECTED. THE PROPOSED DIMENSIONS CAN THEN BE ADDED AND A SIMPLE MODEL MADE TO CHECK THEM. ANY FURTHER ALTERATIONS CAN THEN BE MADE BEFORE BEGINNING THE WORK. <u>TWO-DIMENSIONAL FREEHAND</u> SKETCHES WITH <u>HB</u> PENCIL AND <u>PRINTING, ETC.</u> WITH <u>H</u>. COLOUR <u>YELLOW-BROWN</u> WITH WAX CRAYONS.

Testing for length with a lath in four different pans. The length suitable for the largest pan was also suitable for the smaller ones.

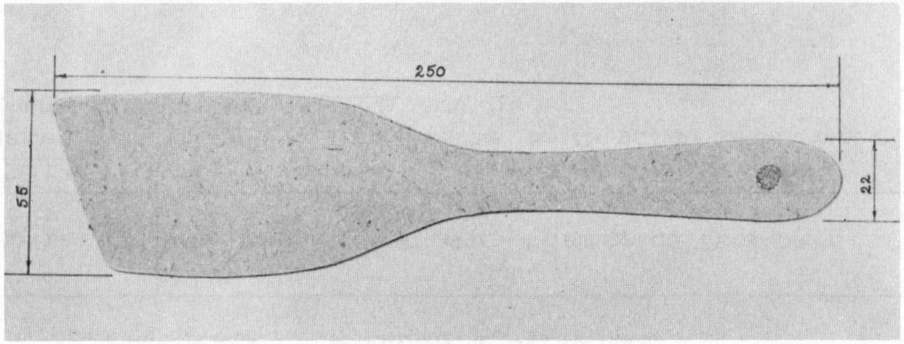
250
55
22

Mock-up in strawboard of the chosen design.

The final piece made in beech.

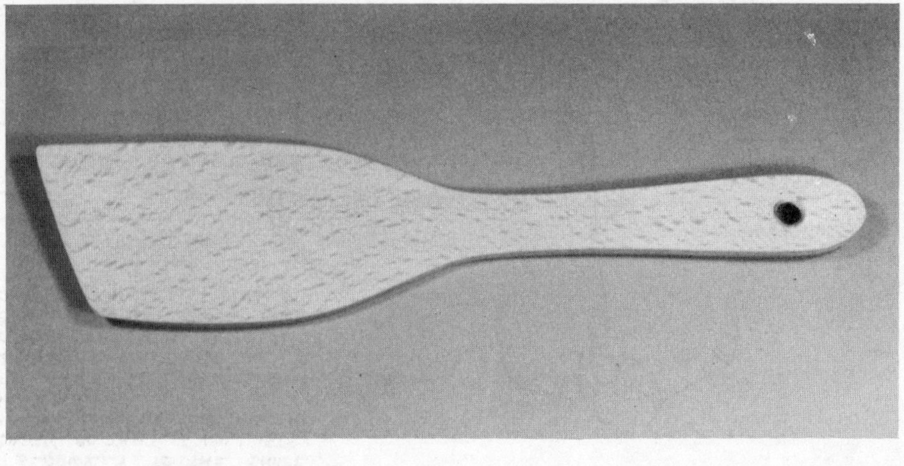

PROBLEM - TO DESIGN A TIE CLIP.

THE CLIP MUST HOLD THE TIE SECURELY TO THE SHIRT FRONT. IT SHOULD NOT BE TOO HEAVY BUT SHOULD BE STRONG AND SPRINGY SO THAT IT WILL STAY IN POSITION. THERE MUST NOT BE ANY SHARP EDGES OR POINTS WHICH MAY DAMAGE THE TIE OR THE SHIRT. THE CLIP MUST ALSO BE ATTRACTIVE TO LOOK AT - THIS IS MOST IMPORTANT.

BY HOLDING THE TIE BACK TO THE SHIRT THE CLIP WILL HELP TO PREVENT POSSIBLE WORKSHOP ACCIDENTS AND HELP TO KEEP A TIDY APPEARANCE AT ALL TIMES.

STAINLESS STEEL WILL BE A SUITABLE MATERIAL FROM WHICH TO MAKE IT AS IT WILL NOT CAUSE ANY METAL STAINS ON THE SHIRT OR TIE. IT IS A STRONG, TOUGH METAL AND THEREFORE A HEAVY GAUGE WILL NOT BE REQUIRED. ARE ANY OTHER METALS SUITABLE?

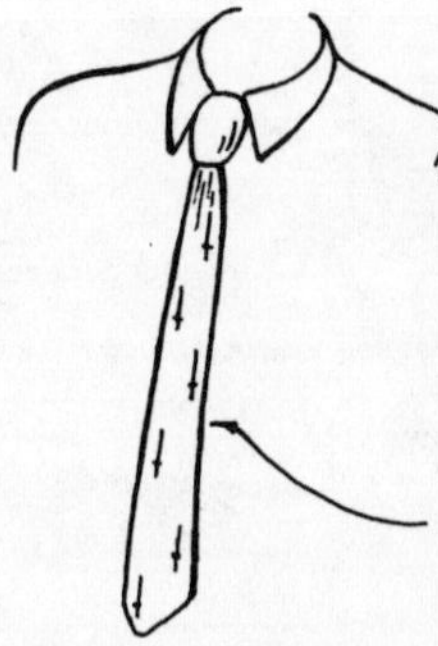

POSITION FOR THE CLIP.

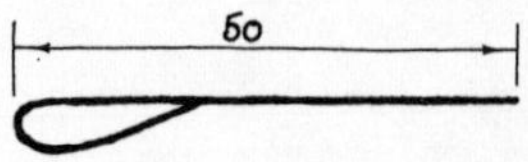

50

WRONG. SPRING CLIP TOO SHORT AND WOULD BE DIFFICULT TO OPEN AND PLACE IN POSITION. MAY DAMAGE THE SHIRT AND WRINKLE THE EDGE OF THE TIE.

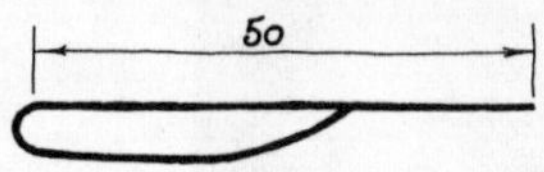

50

ALSO WRONG. ALTHOUGH LONGER, HAS SAME FAULTS AS PREVIOUS DESIGN AND MAY NOT HOLD WELL BECAUSE IT IS ONLY GRIPPING AT ONE POINT.

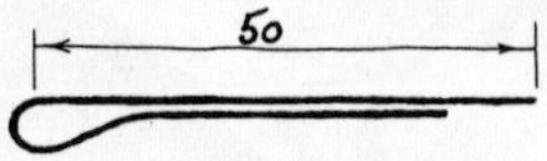

50

BETTER DESIGN. WILL GRIP THE TIE AND SHIRT OVER A GREATER AREA SO IT WILL STAY IN PLACE, BUT WOULD BE DIFFICULT TO OPEN AND TO SLIDE INTO POSITION.

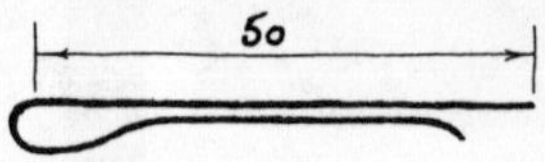

50

FURTHER IMPROVEMENT. BY TURNING THE END UP IT CAN BE OPENED EASILY AND WILL SLIDE INTO POSITION EASILY WITHOUT DAMAGE TO TIE OR SHIRT.

THE CLIP MUST HOLD THESE TOGETHER AND SHOULD SLIDE IN FROM THIS DIRECTION.

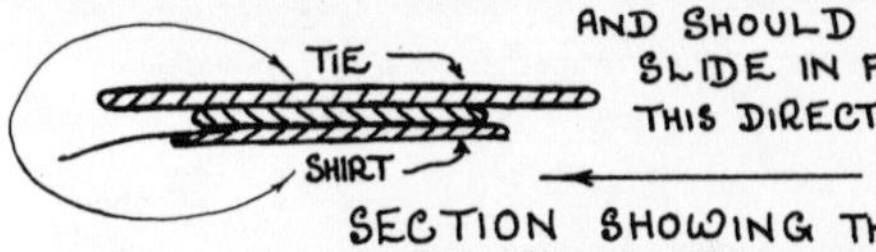

TIE
SHIRT

SECTION SHOWING THE SHIRT FRONT AND THE DOUBLE THICKNESS OF THE TIE.

TOTAL THICKNESS 3 mm

WIDTH OF THE TIE AT THIS POINT 50 mm

SUGGESTIONS FOR THE FRONT OF THE CLIP WITH SIMPLE DRILLED OR PUNCHED DESIGNS.

IDEAS FOR CLIPS WITH APPLIED FRONTS.

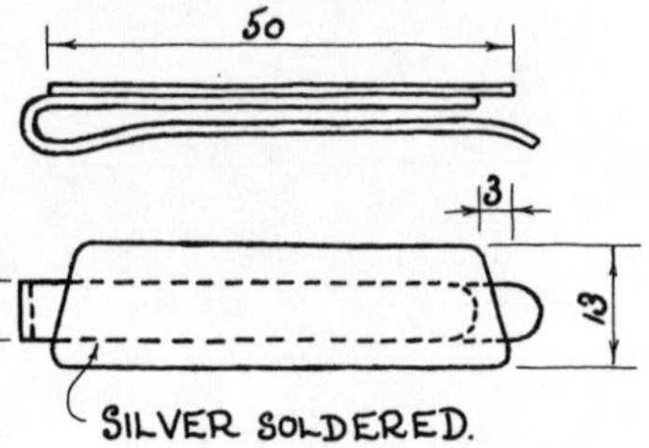

50
3
6
13
SILVER SOLDERED.

MATERIAL - STAINLESS STEEL.

CLIP - 100 x 6 x 0·80 mm
FRONT - 50 x 13 x 1·00 mm

FINAL DESIGN. DIMENSIONS IN MILLIMETRES.

COMPARE THESE DIMENSIONS WITH THOSE OF YOUR OWN TIE AND SHIRT.

TIE CLIP.	DESIGNED BY D. HOWES	FORM $3B_2$	SEPT. 1971.	AIREVILLE SECONDARY.

EXAMPLES OF TWO-DIMENSIONAL SKETCHING. NOTE THE USE OF SIMPLE GUIDE LINES AS AN AID TO SKETCHING THE FRONTS OF THE CLIPS. SEVERAL POSSIBILITIES HAVE BEEN DRAWN BEFORE MAKING THE FINAL CHOICE. FREEHAND ORTHOGRAPHIC SKETCH OF THE CHOSEN DESIGN SHOWING THE ARRANGEMENT FOR THE CLIP AND THE SHAPE OF THE FRONT. ALL SKETCHING WITH HB PENCIL AND PRINTING WITH H.

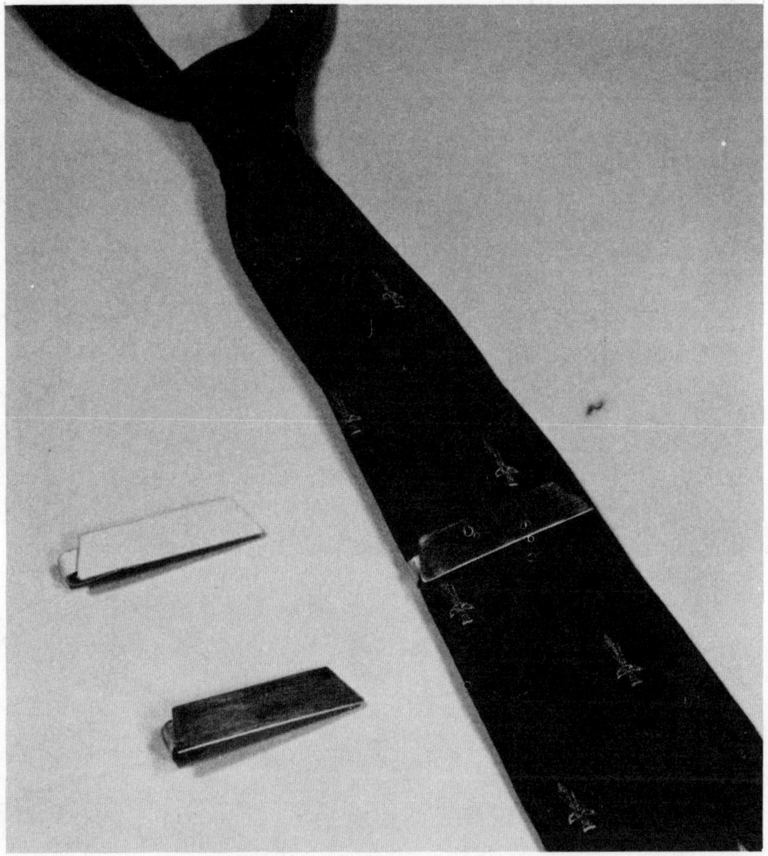

A card model, a tinplate model and the finished piece on the tie.

The card model was quickly and easily made to prove that the shape was acceptable. The tinplate model could be used to prove that in addition to the shape being satisfactory the clip was also efficient when in use. Following this test the final piece was made from stainless steel.

DESIGN PROBLEM.

THE THREE GRADES OF PENCILS MOST OFTEN USED FOR TECHNICAL DRAWING ARE AS FOLLOWS:–

1. 3H FOR MECHANICAL DRAWING USING DRAWING INSTRUMENTS.
2. H FOR ADDING DIMENSIONS AND PRINTING TO DRAWINGS.
3. HB FOR FREEHAND SKETCHING.

YOU ARE REQUIRED TO DESIGN A SIMPLE WOODEN BLOCK WHICH WOULD STAND NEAR TO YOUR DRAWING BOARD AND WHICH WOULD HOLD ONE PENCIL OF EACH GRADE. THE ADVANTAGE IN HAVING A PENCIL STAND IS THAT PENCILS ARE ALWAYS READILY TO HAND AND DO NOT BECOME DAMAGED.

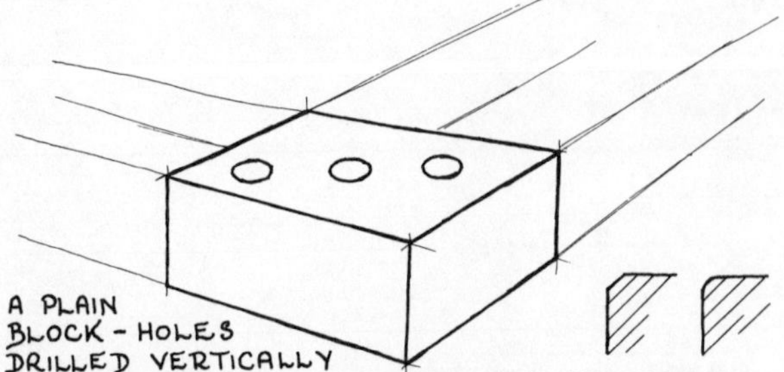

A PLAIN BLOCK – HOLES DRILLED VERTICALLY ON A DIAGONAL. THE CORNERS AND EDGES MAY BE CHAMFERED OR ROUNDED OFF.

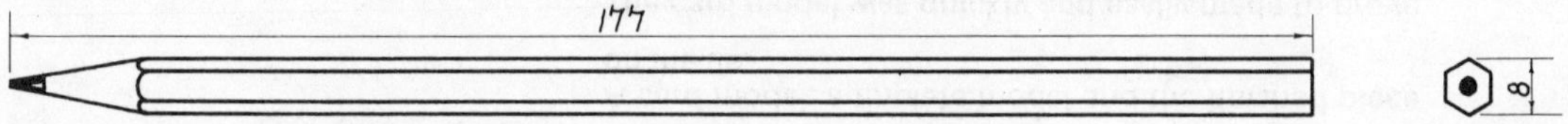
177
8

A STANDARD HEXAGONAL PENCIL. HOLE REQUIRED Ø8

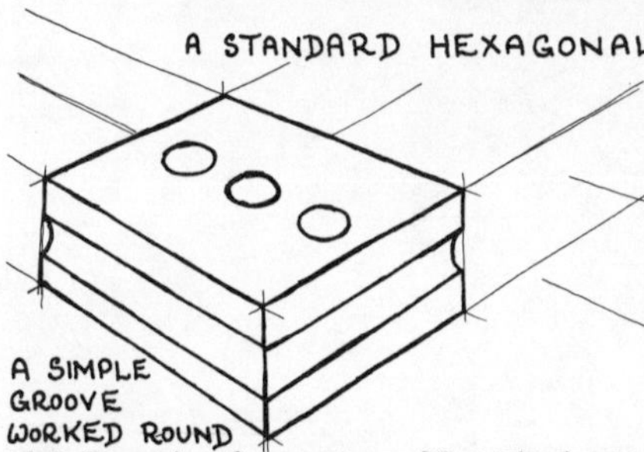

A SIMPLE GROOVE WORKED ROUND THE BLOCK OR ON TWO OPPOSITE SIDES WOULD MAKE THE SHAPE MORE INTERESTING AND EASIER TO PICK UP.

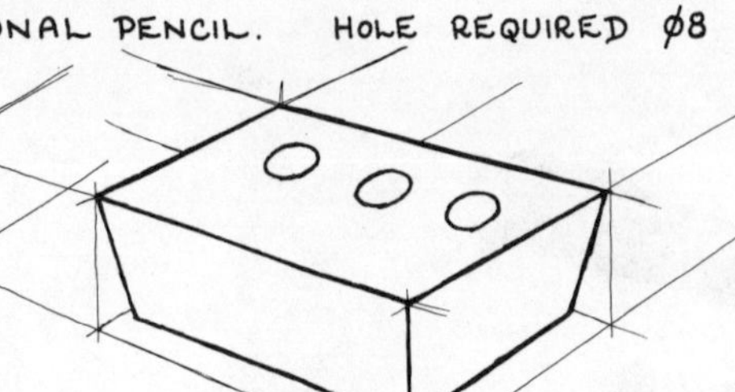

SIDES SLOPED OUTWARD FROM THE BOTTOM TO GIVE A BETTER GRIP.

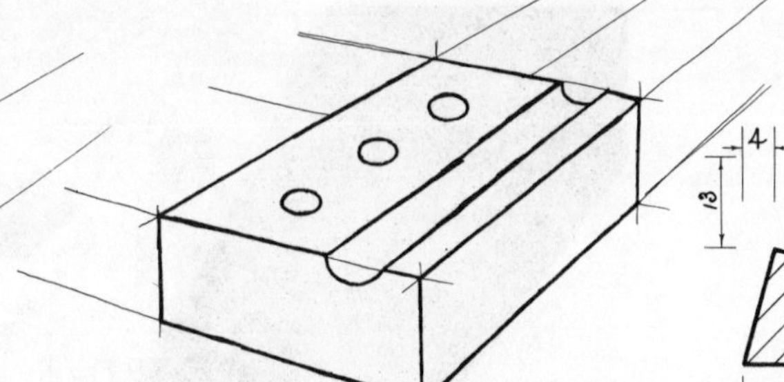

WITH THE HOLES OFFSET A PENCIL REST CAN BE WORKED ALONG THE TOP.

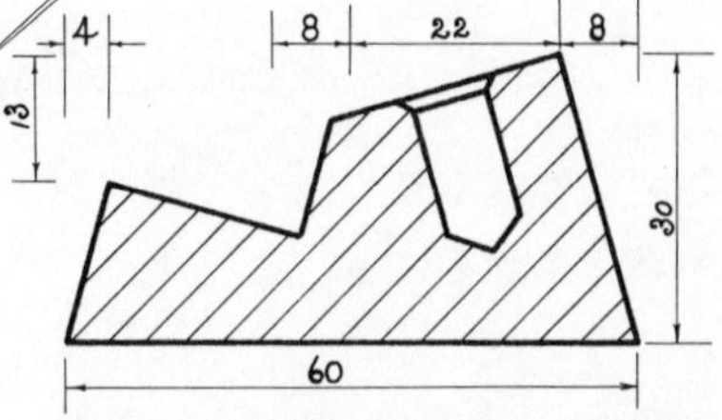
4
8
22
8
13
30
60

SECTIONAL SHAPE OF THE CHOSEN DESIGN THRO' ONE OF THE PENCIL HOLES.

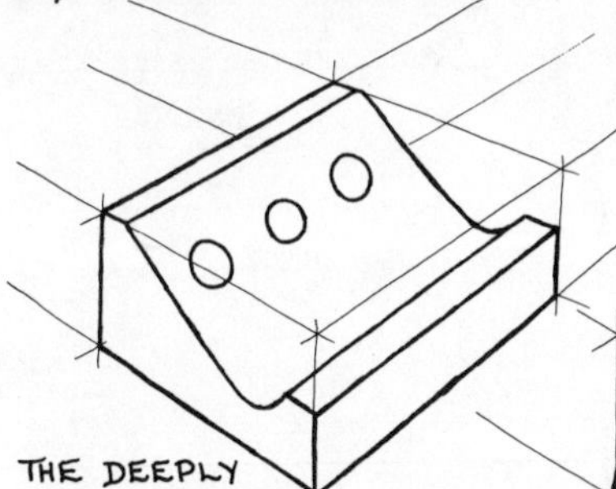

THE DEEPLY CUT GROOVE IS A NOTABLE FEATURE OF THIS DESIGN.

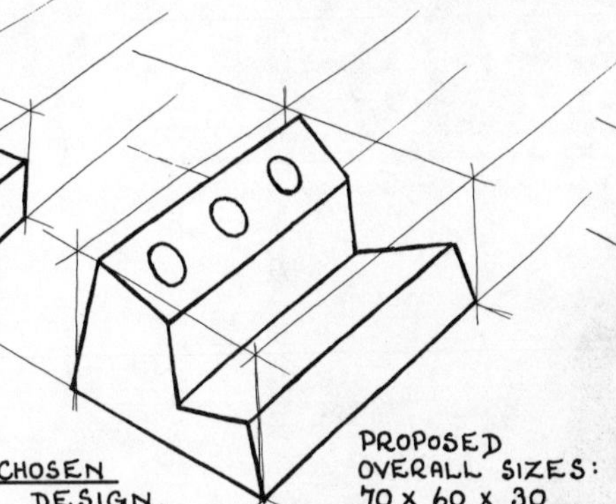

CHOSEN DESIGN.

PROPOSED OVERALL SIZES: 70 x 60 x 30

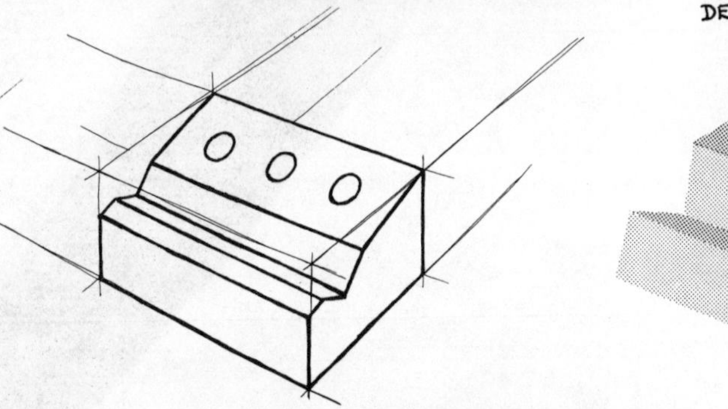

AN ALTERNATIVE DESIGN WITH A SIMILAR GROOVE.

MATERIAL: ROSEWOOD 70 x 60 x 30
FINISH: POLISHED WITH CHILLED WAX.

PENCIL BLOCK.	DESIGNED BY	FORM	DATE	SCHOOL

SKETCHES IN FREE PERSPECTIVE DRAWN WITH HB PENCIL. SECTIONAL SHAPE OF THE FINAL DESIGN DRAWN WITH 3H PENCIL. DIMENSIONS AND PRINTING ADDED WITH H PENCIL. FINAL SKETCH OF THE CHOSEN DESIGN COLOURED RED-BROWN WITH COTMAN WATER COLOURS TO REPRESENT THE ROSEWOOD.

An exact replica of the proposed piece made in red-wood. This gave practical experience of the necessary setting out, cutting and drilling.

It was also possible to test it in use during design lessons. Any necessary modifications to the design could then have been made before beginning the work proper.

Note the use of the 'slipper' to hold the work securely at the correct angle for drilling.

The completed work. A hardwood is more suitable on account of its durability and can be fashioned to shape more accurately. It is also heavier and therefore more stable in use.

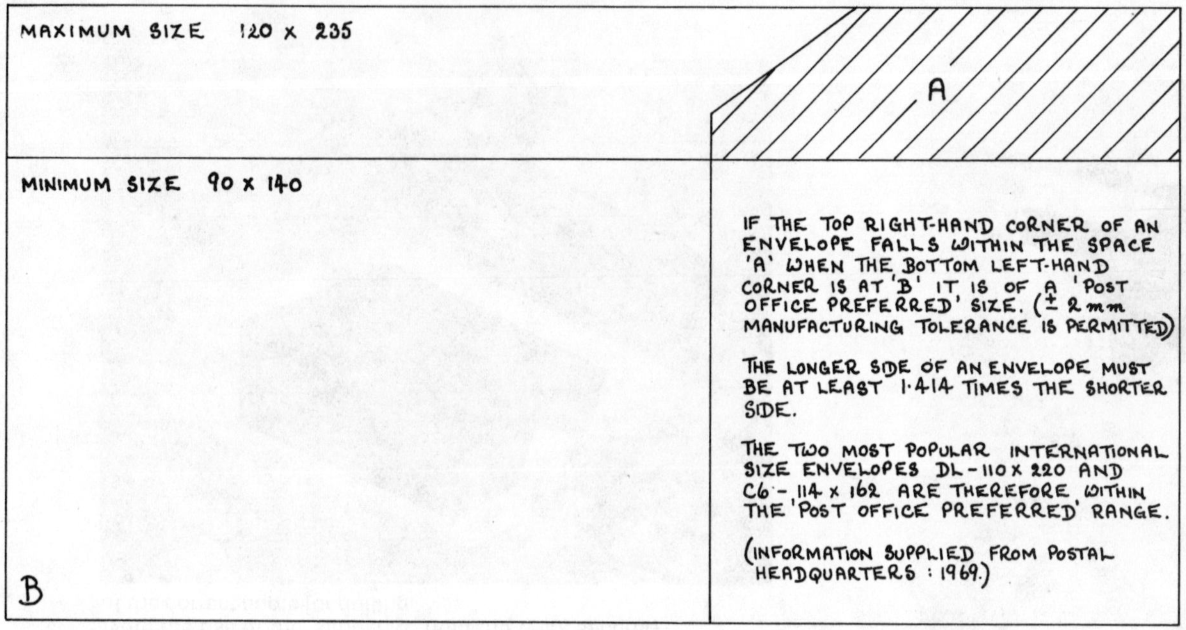
MAXIMUM SIZE 120 x 235
A
MINIMUM SIZE 90 x 140
B
IF THE TOP RIGHT-HAND CORNER OF AN ENVELOPE FALLS WITHIN THE SPACE 'A' WHEN THE BOTTOM LEFT-HAND CORNER IS AT 'B' IT IS OF A 'POST OFFICE PREFERRED' SIZE. (± 2 mm MANUFACTURING TOLERANCE IS PERMITTED)
THE LONGER SIDE OF AN ENVELOPE MUST BE AT LEAST 1·414 TIMES THE SHORTER SIDE.
THE TWO MOST POPULAR INTERNATIONAL SIZE ENVELOPES DL - 110 x 220 AND C6 - 114 x 162 ARE THEREFORE WITHIN THE 'POST OFFICE PREFERRED' RANGE.
(INFORMATION SUPPLIED FROM POSTAL HEADQUARTERS : 1969.)

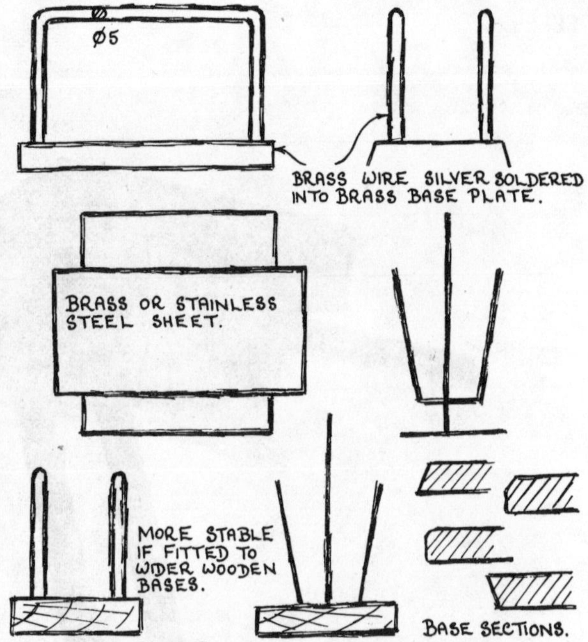
Ø5
BRASS WIRE SILVER SOLDERED INTO BRASS BASE PLATE.
BRASS OR STAINLESS STEEL SHEET.
MORE STABLE IF FITTED TO WIDER WOODEN BASES.
BASE SECTIONS.

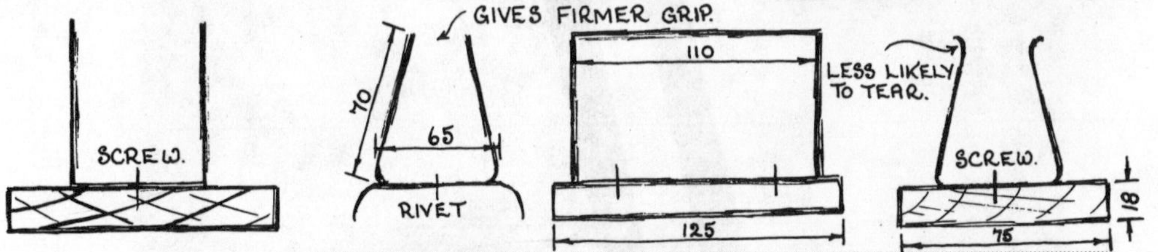
GIVES FIRMER GRIP.
SCREW.
70
65
RIVET
110
125
LESS LIKELY TO TEAR.
SCREW.
18
75

THE ABOVE DIAGRAM INDICATES THE MAXIMUM AND MINIMUM SIZES OF 'POST OFFICE PREFERRED' ENVELOPES.
LARGER ENVELOPES OUTSIDE THE 'PREFERRED' RANGE ARE STILL USED.
A SURVEY MADE AT SCHOOL INDICATED THAT THREE POPULAR SIZES ARE 90 x 150 ; 100 x 230 AND 178 x 238

PROBLEM.

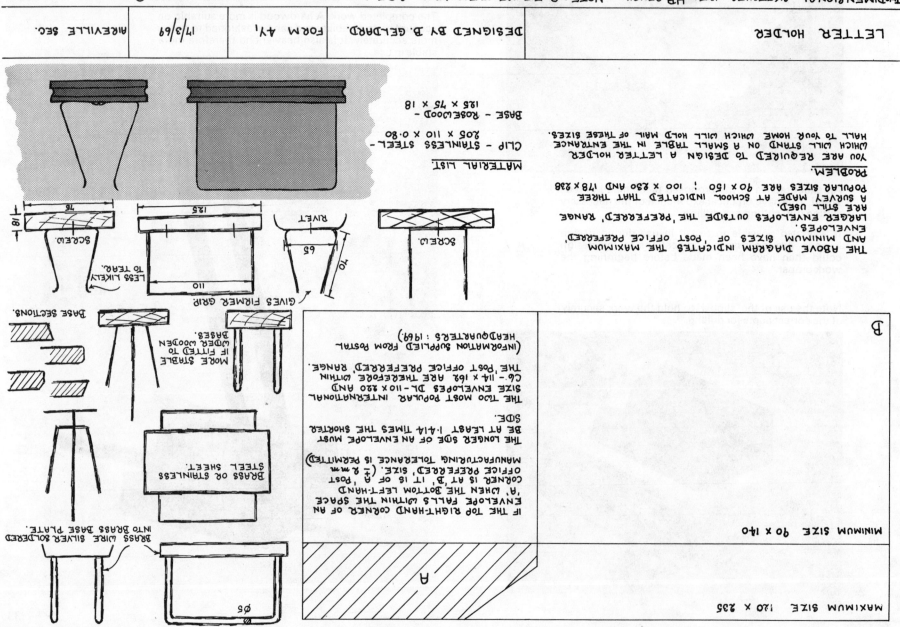

YOU ARE REQUIRED TO DESIGN A LETTER HOLDER WHICH WILL STAND ON A SMALL TABLE IN THE ENTRANCE HALL TO YOUR HOME WHICH WILL HOLD MAIL OF THESE SIZES.

MATERIAL LIST.

CLIP - STAINLESS STEEL - 205 x 110 x 0·80

BASE - ROSEWOOD - 125 x 75 x 18

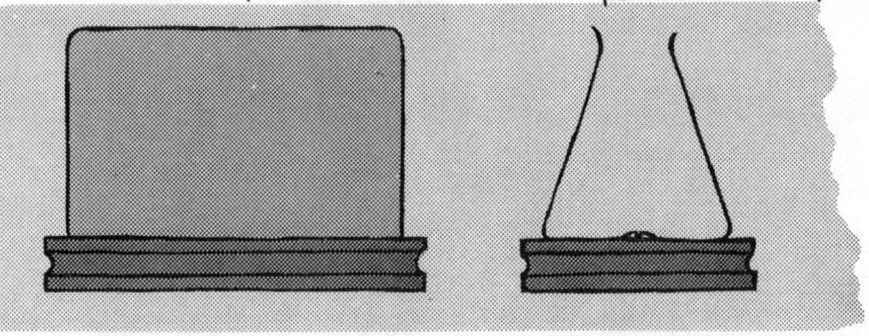

LETTER HOLDER	DESIGNED BY B. GELDARD.	FORM 4Y1	17/3/69	AIREVILLE SEC.

TWO-DIMENSIONAL SKETCHES WITH HB PENCIL. NOTE: ① THE USE OF TWO VIEWS - SIDE AND END - TO ILLUSTRATE THE IDEAS. ② THE COMBINATION OF WOOD AND METAL. ③ HOW THE DETAILS OF CONSTRUCTION HAVE BEEN INDICATED. ④ DIMENSIONS ADDED AS THE DESIGN IS NEARING COMPLETION AND THE SIZES ARE BEING WORKED OUT. COLOUR WASH ON FINAL DESIGN - STAINLESS STEEL - PALE BLUE ; ROSEWOOD - RED BROWN ; BACKGROUND - GREY.

Mock-up from tinplate and softwood nailed together with round wire nails. This model was used to find out if envelopes would stand securely.

The finished model in stainless steel and rosewood. Note the raised head screws used for fixing.

The letter clip in use.

BATH

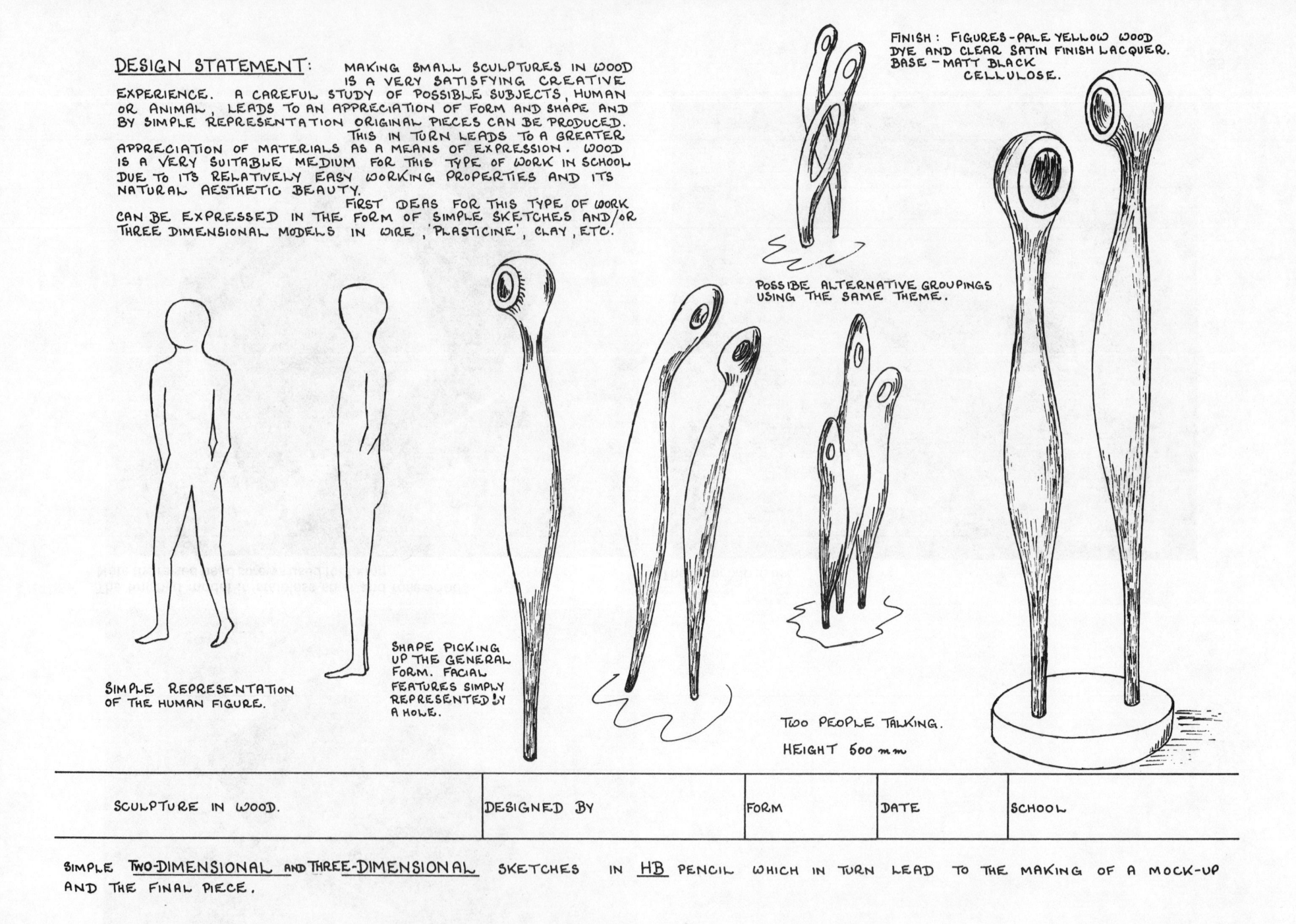

DESIGN STATEMENT: MAKING SMALL SCULPTURES IN WOOD IS A VERY SATISFYING CREATIVE EXPERIENCE. A CAREFUL STUDY OF POSSIBLE SUBJECTS, HUMAN OR ANIMAL, LEADS TO AN APPRECIATION OF FORM AND SHAPE AND BY SIMPLE REPRESENTATION ORIGINAL PIECES CAN BE PRODUCED.

THIS IN TURN LEADS TO A GREATER APPRECIATION OF MATERIALS AS A MEANS OF EXPRESSION. WOOD IS A VERY SUITABLE MEDIUM FOR THIS TYPE OF WORK IN SCHOOL DUE TO ITS RELATIVELY EASY WORKING PROPERTIES AND ITS NATURAL AESTHETIC BEAUTY.

FIRST IDEAS FOR THIS TYPE OF WORK CAN BE EXPRESSED IN THE FORM OF SIMPLE SKETCHES AND/OR THREE DIMENSIONAL MODELS IN WIRE, 'PLASTICINE', CLAY, ETC.

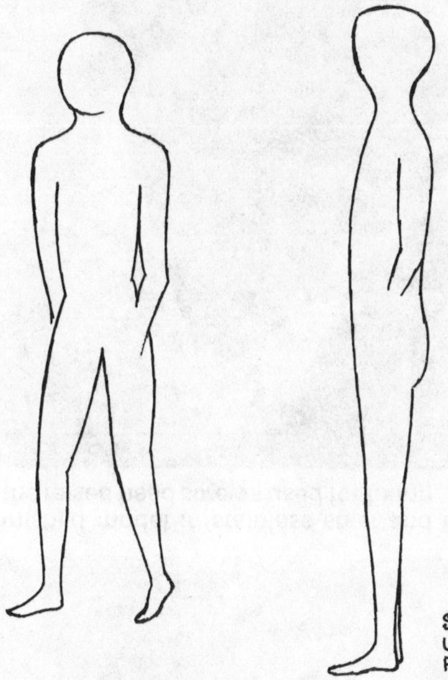

SIMPLE REPRESENTATION OF THE HUMAN FIGURE.

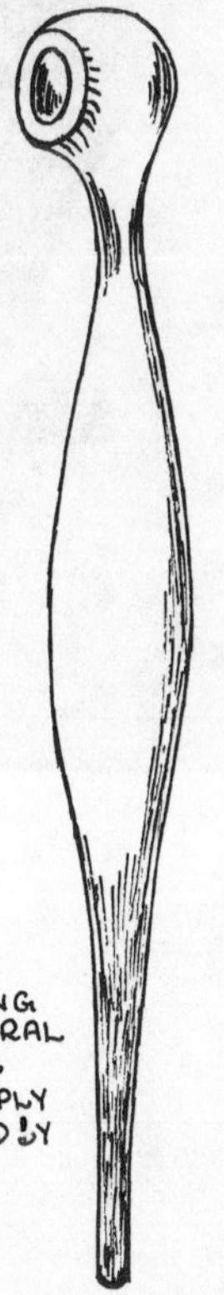

SHAPE PICKING UP THE GENERAL FORM. FACIAL FEATURES SIMPLY REPRESENTED BY A HOLE.

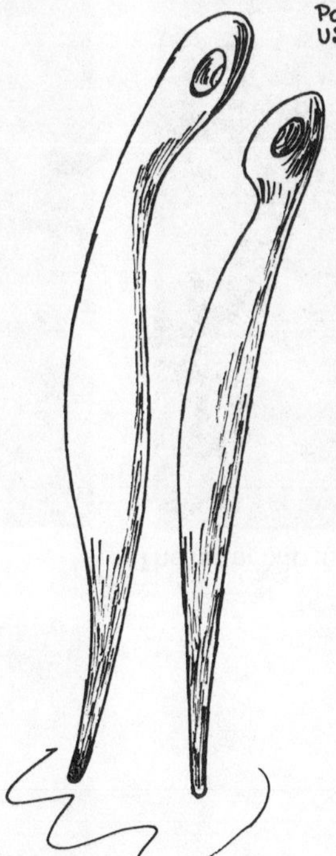

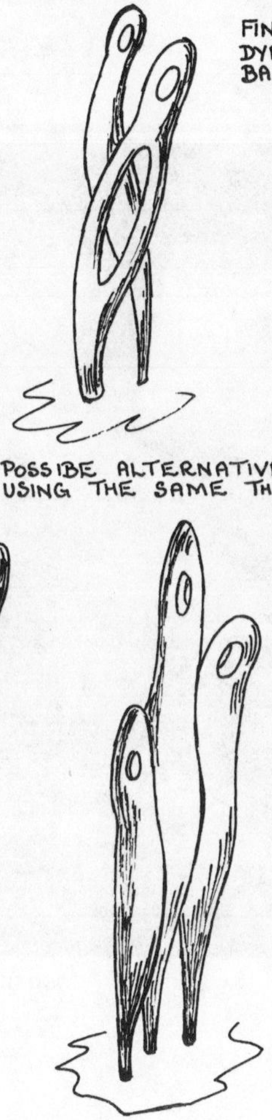

POSSIBE ALTERNATIVE GROUPINGS USING THE SAME THEME.

FINISH: FIGURES - PALE YELLOW WOOD DYE AND CLEAR SATIN FINISH LACQUER. BASE - MATT BLACK CELLULOSE.

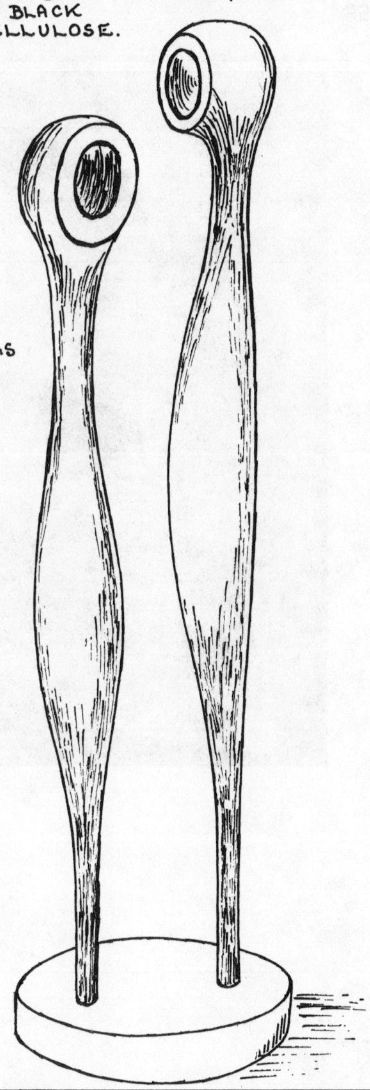

TWO PEOPLE TALKING.

HEIGHT 500 mm

SCULPTURE IN WOOD.	DESIGNED BY	FORM	DATE	SCHOOL

SIMPLE TWO-DIMENSIONAL AND THREE-DIMENSIONAL SKETCHES IN HB PENCIL WHICH IN TURN LEAD TO THE MAKING OF A MOCK-UP AND THE FINAL PIECE.

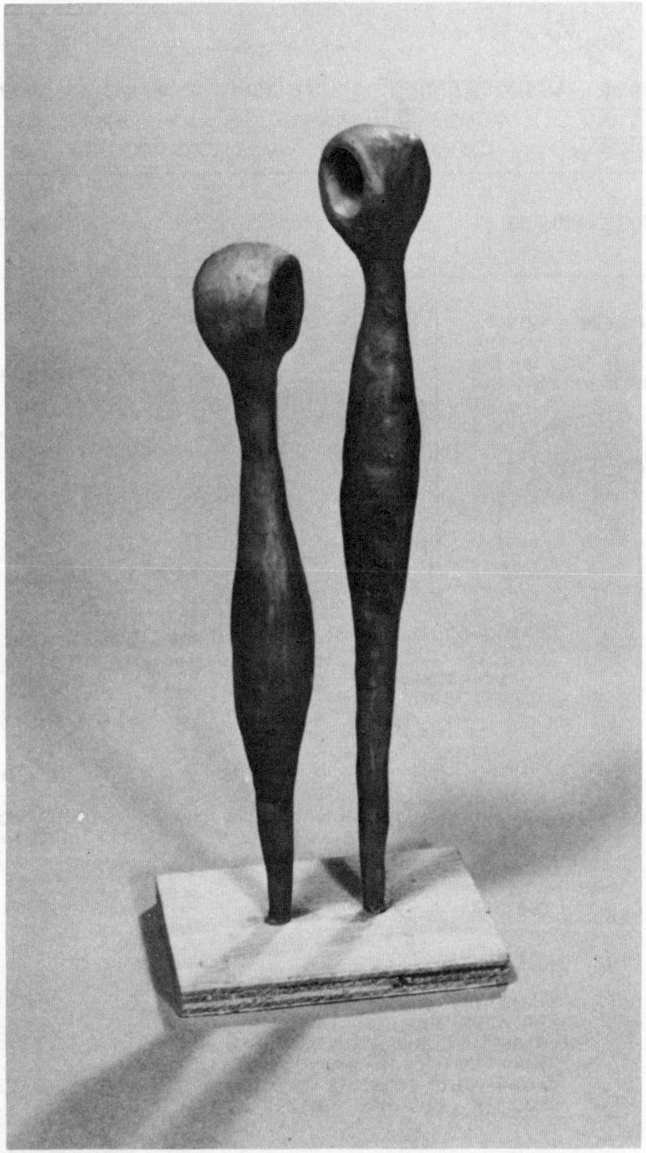

Mock-up in 'Plasticine' which has been modelled round a central wire to give it rigidity. A simple model such as this gives a good indication of what the finished piece will look like and what can be improved upon. For example the figures should be taller and more care needs to be taken with the shape of the space between them.

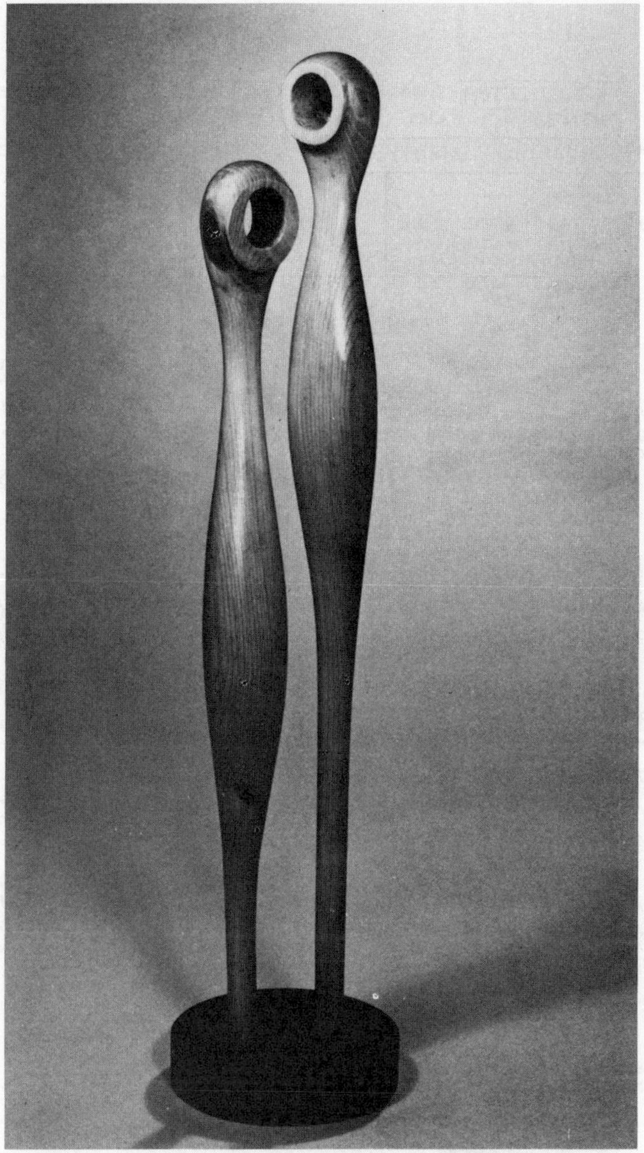

You should compare the finished piece with the model and note the improved shape. The grain of the wood adds to its aesthetic appearance which is also enhanced by the contrast between the yellow dye and the black base.

DESIGN BRIEF : A SHOE-HORN IS REQUIRED FOR FAMILY USE.

PURPOSE : TO EASE THE PUTTING ON OF SHOES WITHOUT DOUBLING DOWN AND DAMAGING THE BACK OF THE SHOES.

THE HEEL OF THE FOOT MUST BE ABLE TO SLIDE DOWN THE SHOE HORN EASILY AND INTO THE SHOE.

IT SHOULD BE OF A STRONG MATERIAL, EASY TO HOLD SECURELY AND OF PLEASING APPEARANCE.

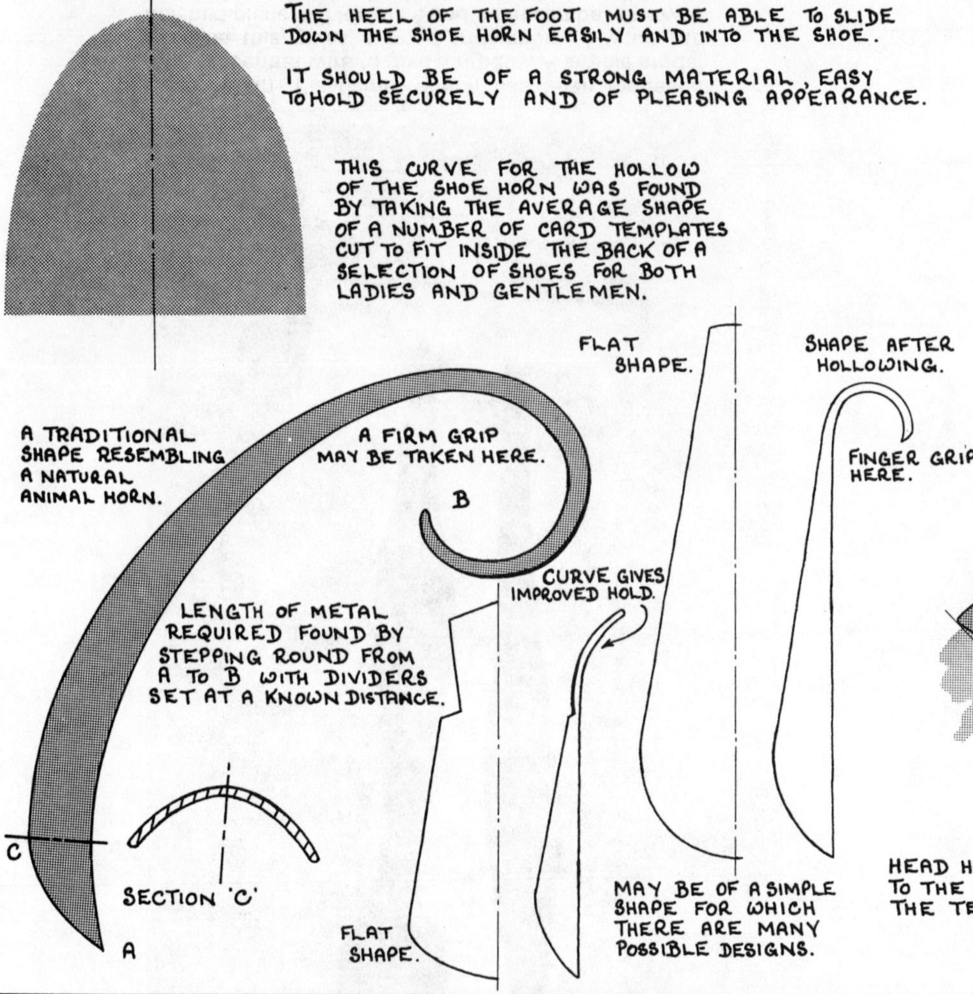
THIS CURVE FOR THE HOLLOW OF THE SHOE HORN WAS FOUND BY TAKING THE AVERAGE SHAPE OF A NUMBER OF CARD TEMPLATES CUT TO FIT INSIDE THE BACK OF A SELECTION OF SHOES FOR BOTH LADIES AND GENTLEMEN.
A TRADITIONAL SHAPE RESEMBLING A NATURAL ANIMAL HORN.
A FIRM GRIP MAY BE TAKEN HERE.
B
LENGTH OF METAL REQUIRED FOUND BY STEPPING ROUND FROM A TO B WITH DIVIDERS SET AT A KNOWN DISTANCE.
C
SECTION 'C'
A
CURVE GIVES IMPROVED HOLD.
FLAT SHAPE.
FLAT SHAPE.
MAY BE OF A SIMPLE SHAPE FOR WHICH THERE ARE MANY POSSIBLE DESIGNS.
SHAPE AFTER HOLLOWING.
FINGER GRIP HERE.

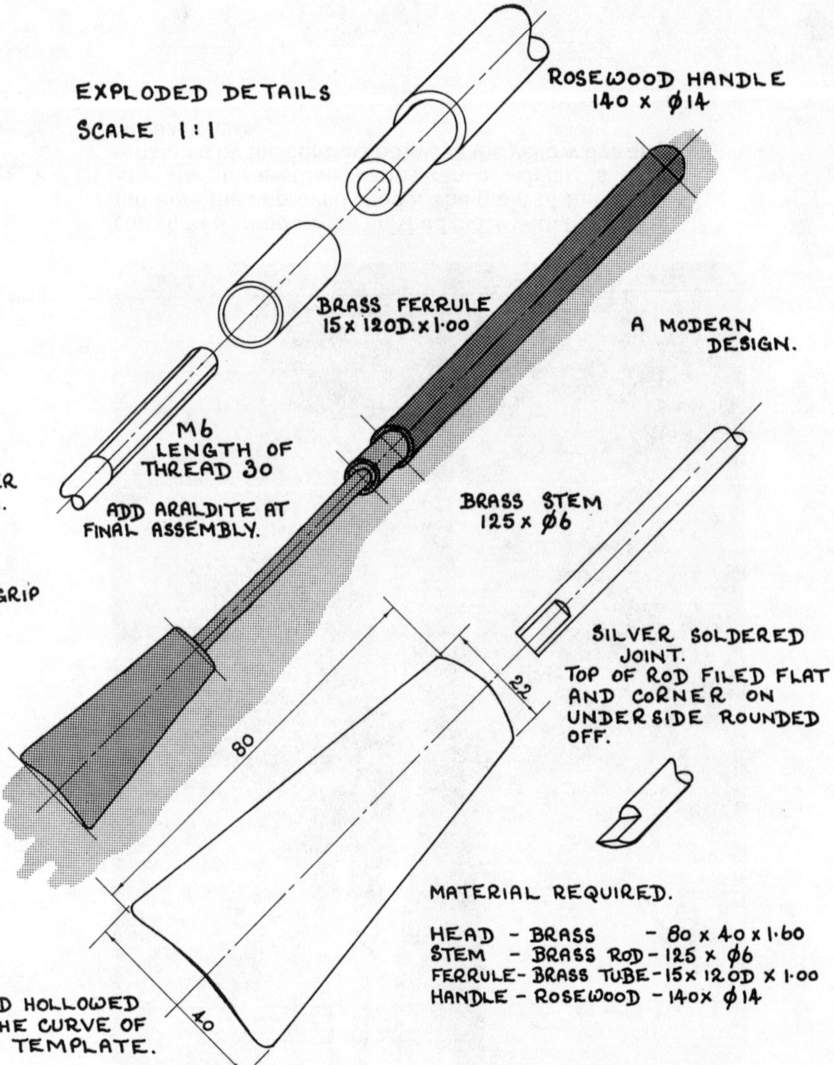
EXPLODED DETAILS
SCALE 1:1
ROSEWOOD HANDLE 140 x ϕ14
BRASS FERRULE 15 x 12OD. x 1·00
A MODERN DESIGN.
M6 LENGTH OF THREAD 30
ADD ARALDITE AT FINAL ASSEMBLY.
BRASS STEM 125 x ϕ6
SILVER SOLDERED JOINT.
TOP OF ROD FILED FLAT AND CORNER ON UNDERSIDE ROUNDED OFF.
22
80
40
HEAD HOLLOWED TO THE CURVE OF THE TEMPLATE.
MATERIAL REQUIRED.
HEAD - BRASS - 80 x 40 x 1·60
STEM - BRASS ROD - 125 x ϕ6
FERRULE - BRASS TUBE - 15 x 12 OD x 1·00
HANDLE - ROSEWOOD - 140 x ϕ14

SHOE-HORNS	DESIGNED BY TREVOR FORD	4G	10:12:71	AIREVILLE SECONDARY

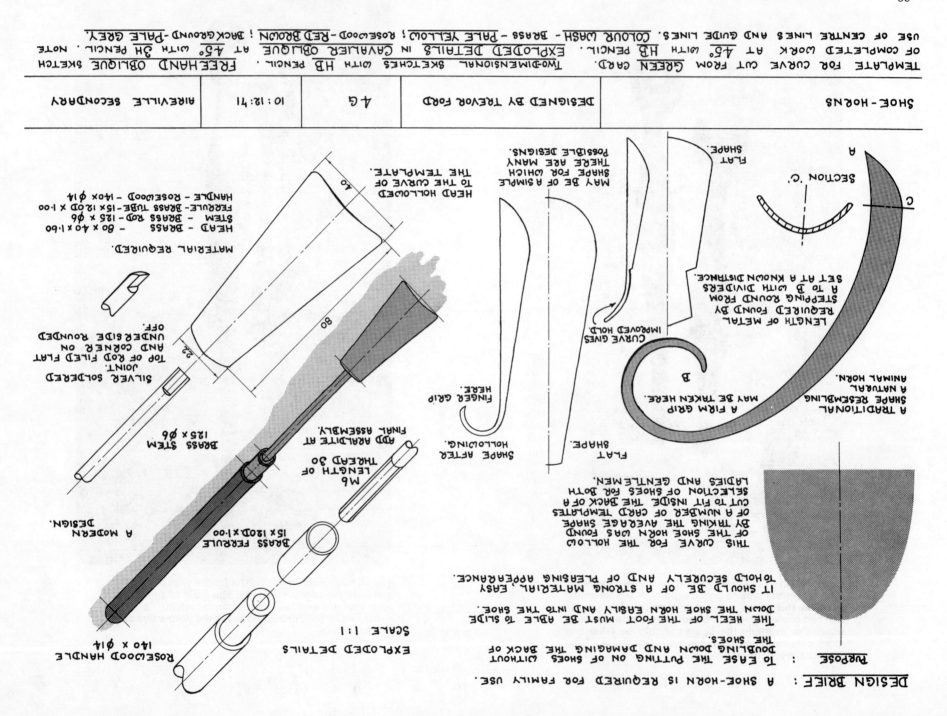

TEMPLATE FOR CURVE CUT FROM GREEN CARD. TWO-DIMENSIONAL SKETCHES WITH HB PENCIL. FREEHAND OBLIQUE SKETCH OF COMPLETED WORK AT 45° WITH HB PENCIL. EXPLODED DETAILS IN CAVALIER OBLIQUE AT 45° WITH 3H PENCIL. NOTE USE OF CENTRE LINES AND GUIDE LINES. COLOUR WASH - BRASS - PALE YELLOW; ROSEWOOD - RED BROWN; BACKGROUND - PALE GREY.

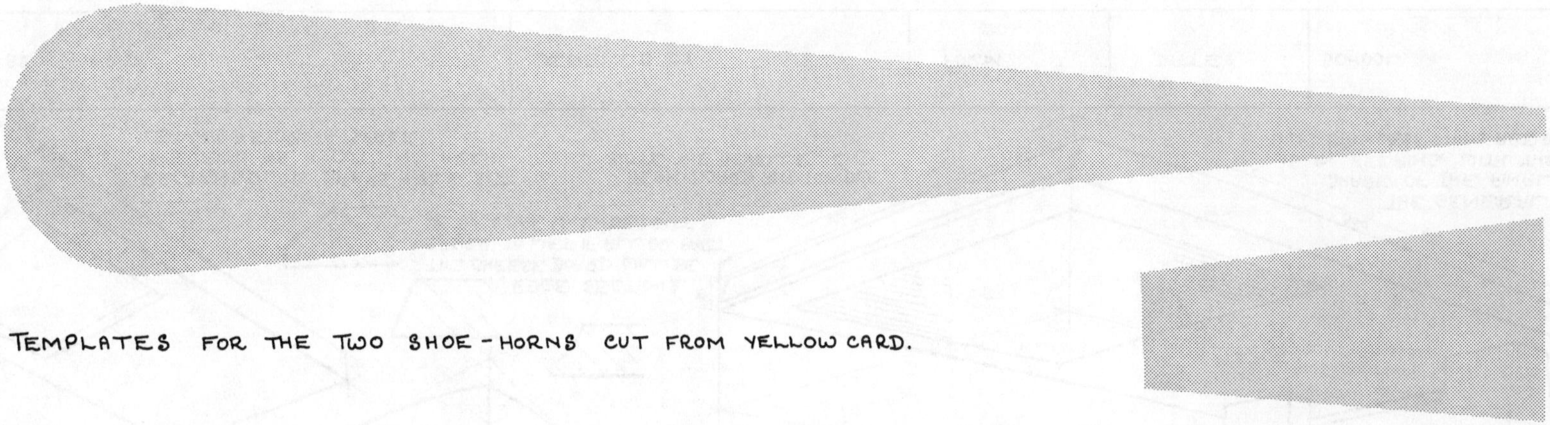

TEMPLATES FOR THE TWO SHOE-HORNS CUT FROM YELLOW CARD.

The pleasing shape and obvious efficiency of the two shoe-horns is apparent from these photographs.

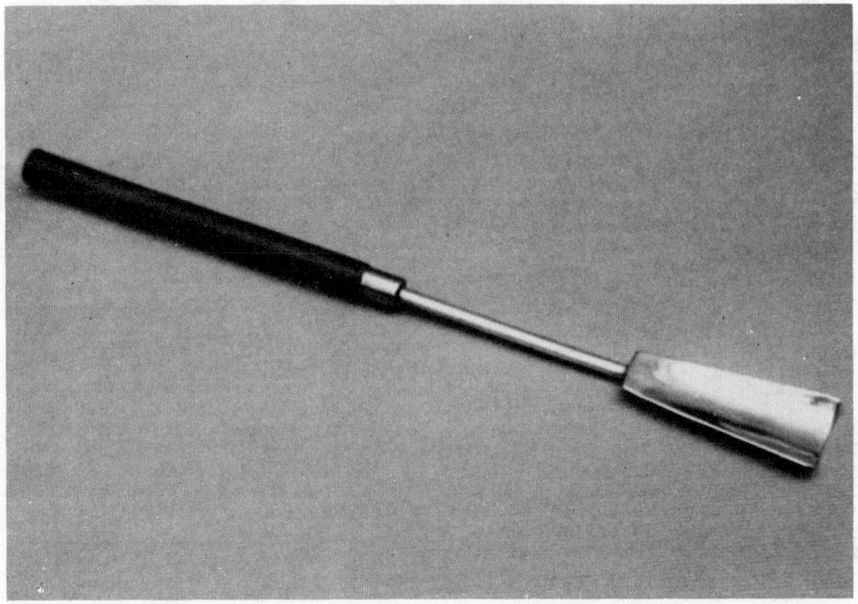

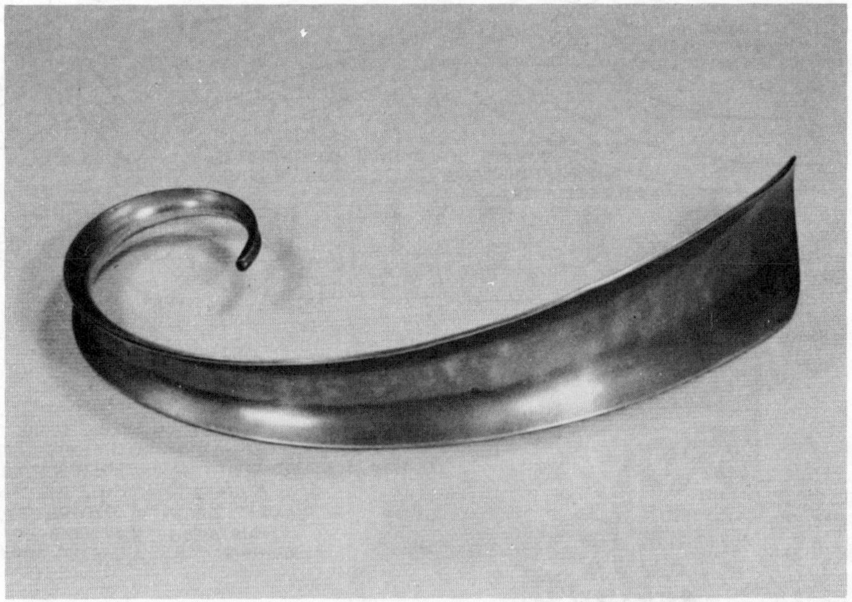

CARD TEMPLATE
152mm SQUARE

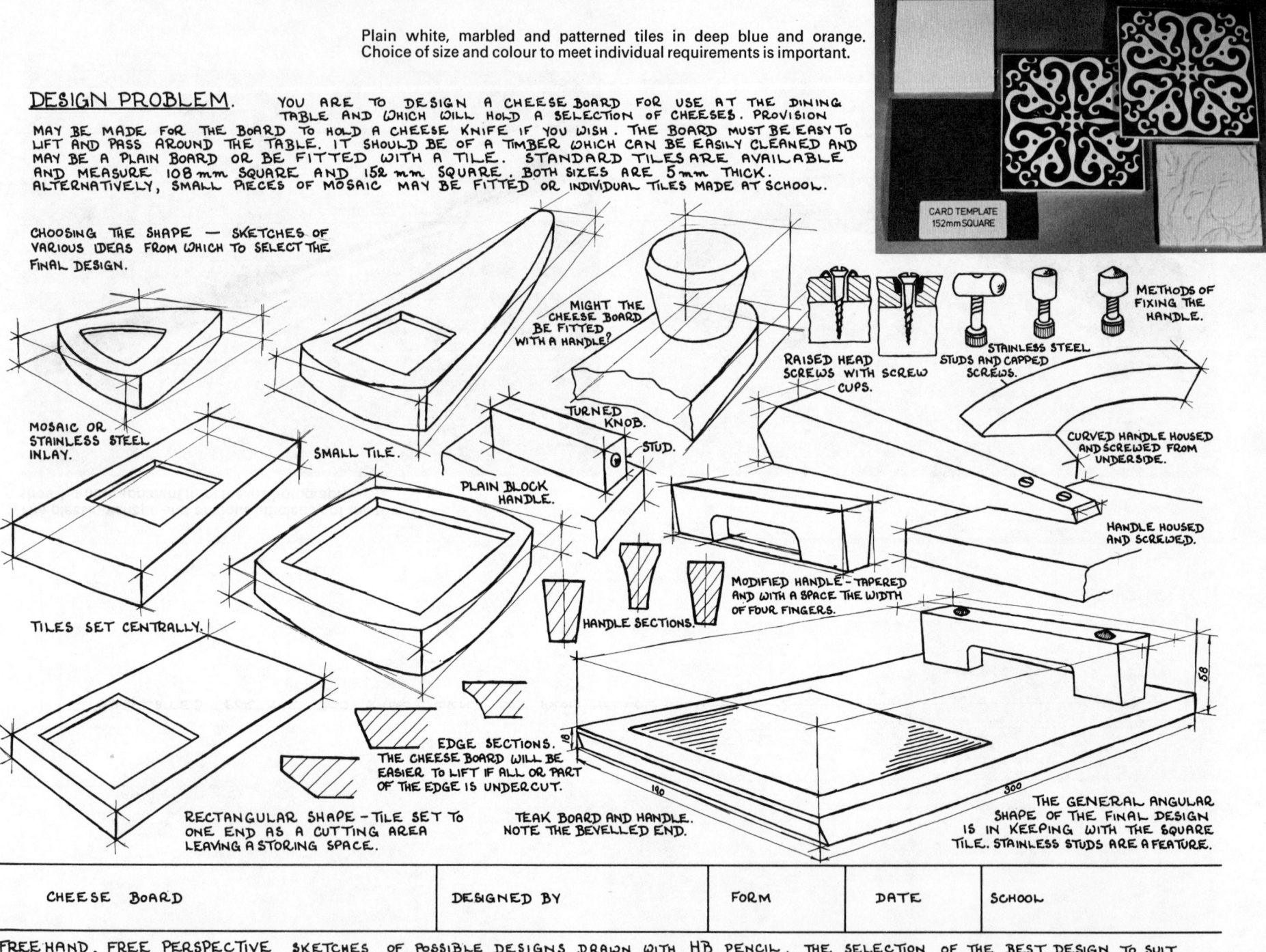

Plain white, marbled and patterned tiles in deep blue and orange. Choice of size and colour to meet individual requirements is important.

DESIGN PROBLEM. YOU ARE TO DESIGN A CHEESE BOARD FOR USE AT THE DINING TABLE AND WHICH WILL HOLD A SELECTION OF CHEESES. PROVISION MAY BE MADE FOR THE BOARD TO HOLD A CHEESE KNIFE IF YOU WISH. THE BOARD MUST BE EASY TO LIFT AND PASS AROUND THE TABLE. IT SHOULD BE OF A TIMBER WHICH CAN BE EASILY CLEANED AND MAY BE A PLAIN BOARD OR BE FITTED WITH A TILE. STANDARD TILES ARE AVAILABLE AND MEASURE 108 mm SQUARE AND 152 mm SQUARE. BOTH SIZES ARE 5 mm THICK. ALTERNATIVELY, SMALL PIECES OF MOSAIC MAY BE FITTED OR INDIVIDUAL TILES MADE AT SCHOOL.

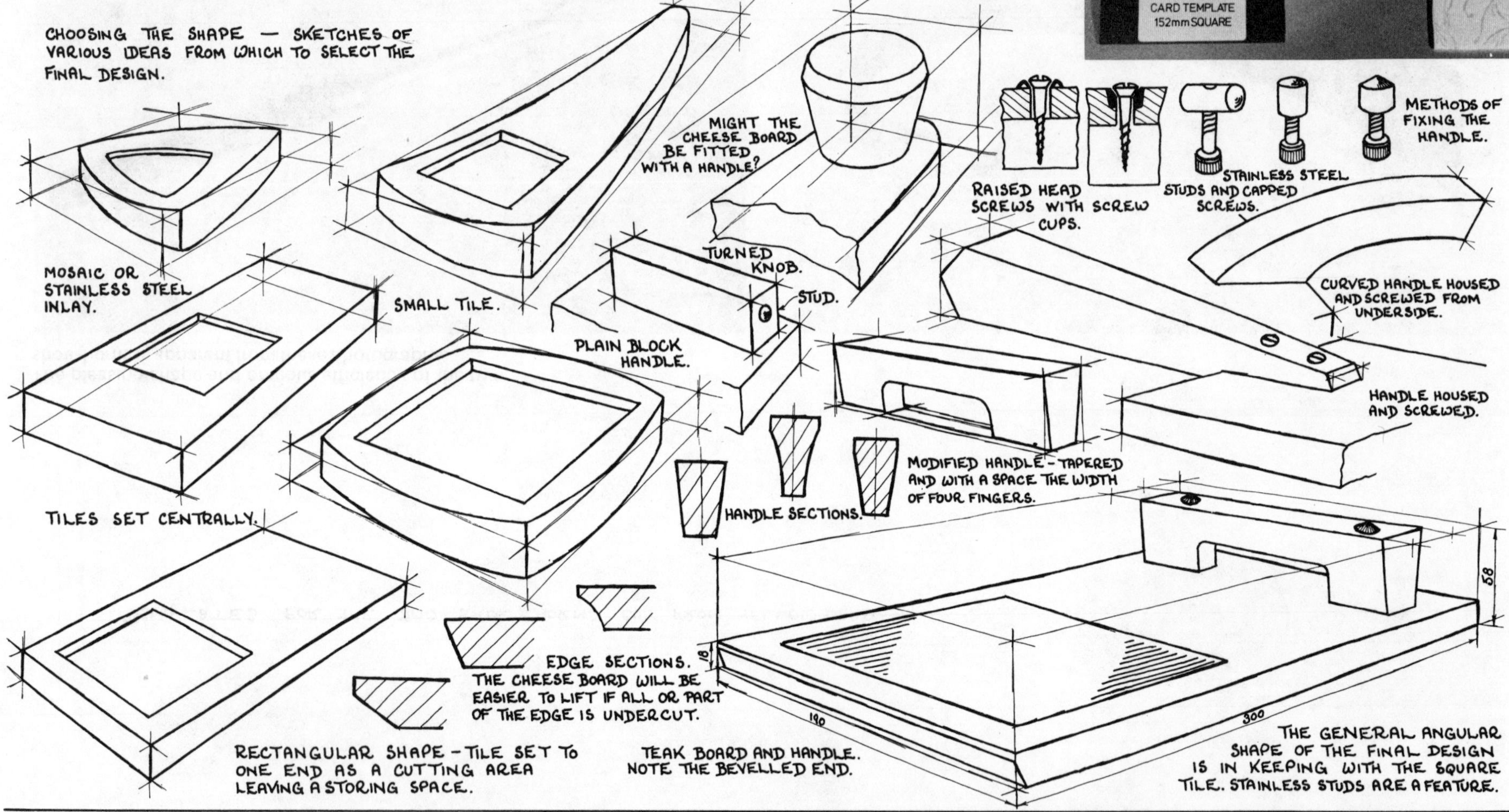
CHOOSING THE SHAPE — SKETCHES OF VARIOUS IDEAS FROM WHICH TO SELECT THE FINAL DESIGN.
MIGHT THE CHEESE BOARD BE FITTED WITH A HANDLE?
METHODS OF FIXING THE HANDLE.
RAISED HEAD SCREWS WITH SCREW CUPS.
STAINLESS STEEL STUDS AND CAPPED SCREWS.
MOSAIC OR STAINLESS STEEL INLAY.
SMALL TILE.
TURNED KNOB.
STUD.
CURVED HANDLE HOUSED AND SCREWED FROM UNDERSIDE.
PLAIN BLOCK HANDLE.
HANDLE HOUSED AND SCREWED.
MODIFIED HANDLE - TAPERED AND WITH A SPACE THE WIDTH OF FOUR FINGERS.
HANDLE SECTIONS.
TILES SET CENTRALLY.
58
18
EDGE SECTIONS.
THE CHEESE BOARD WILL BE EASIER TO LIFT IF ALL OR PART OF THE EDGE IS UNDERCUT.
190
300
THE GENERAL ANGULAR SHAPE OF THE FINAL DESIGN IS IN KEEPING WITH THE SQUARE TILE. STAINLESS STUDS ARE A FEATURE.
RECTANGULAR SHAPE - TILE SET TO ONE END AS A CUTTING AREA LEAVING A STORING SPACE.
TEAK BOARD AND HANDLE. NOTE THE BEVELLED END.

CHEESE BOARD	DESIGNED BY	FORM	DATE	SCHOOL

FREE HAND, FREE PERSPECTIVE SKETCHES OF POSSIBLE DESIGNS DRAWN WITH HB PENCIL. THE SELECTION OF THE BEST DESIGN TO SUIT PERSONAL TASTES AND REQUIREMENTS IS MADE EASIER BY DRAWING A NUMBER OF SOLUTIONS FROM WHICH TO CHOOSE. THE WORKSHOP DRAWING IN THIRD ANGLE PROJECTION ENABLES THE DETAILS TO BE WORKED OUT VERY ACCURATELY. NOTE THE USE OF THE ROTRING Ⅲ 3.5 STENCIL FOR THE PRINTING.

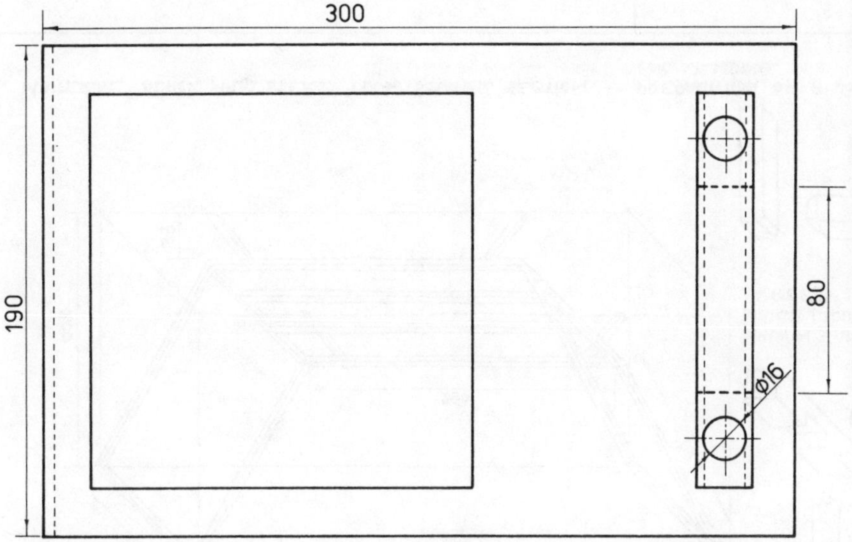
300
190
80
ø16

PLAN

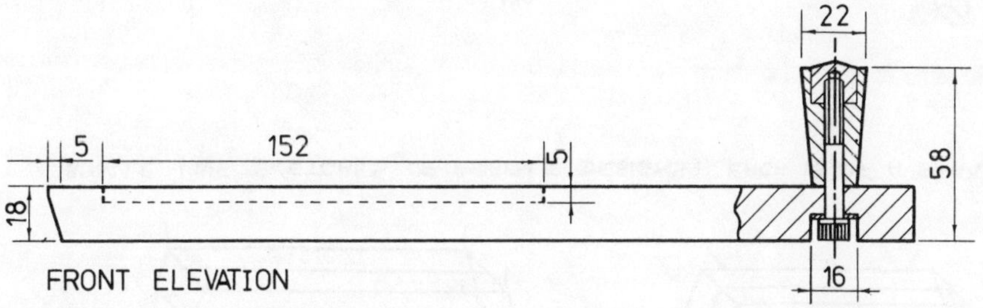
5
152
5
18
22
58
16

FRONT ELEVATION

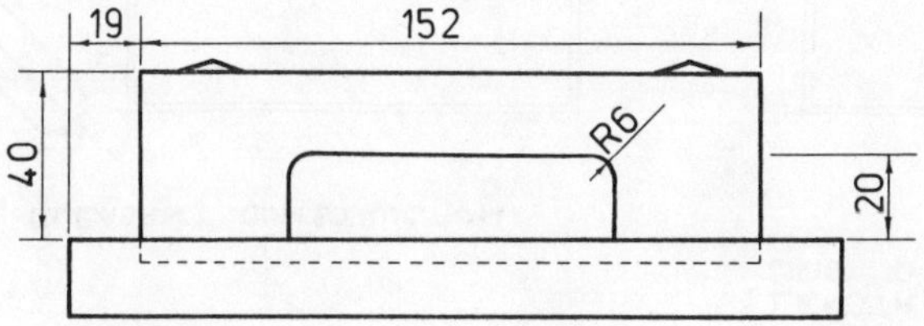
19
152
40
R6
20

END ELEVATION

LACTIC CHEESE SPREAD
FROM SOMERSET

The completed cheese board ready for use at the table.

THIRD ANGLE PROJECTION.

SCALE 1 : 2

ALL DIMENSIONS IN MILLIMETRES.

CUTTING LIST.

TEAK.

BASE	1 OFF	300 × 190 × 18
HANDLE	1 OFF	152 × 40 × 22

DESIGN PROBLEM. TO DESIGN A LOG BASKET TO STAND NEAR TO THE FIREPLACE AND WHICH WILL HOLD ATLEAST AN ARMFUL OF LOGS.
IT IS TO BE CONSTRUCTED OF WROUGHT IRON OR BLACK MILD STEEL AND MAY BE BRAZED OR WELDED TOGETHER. THE BASKET MUST STAND FIRMLY ON THE FLOOR ; IT MUST BE EASY TO CLEAN AND EASY TO PUT LOGS ON OR TO TAKE THEM OFF.

AN ARMFUL OF LOGS. THE SHAPE OF THE BENT ARM SUGGESTS A POSSIBLE DESIGN.

LENGTH OF FOREARM 250 mm
WRIST TO FINGER TIPS 180 mm

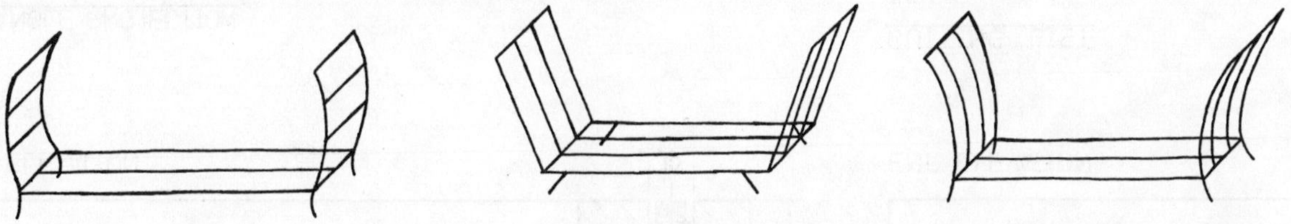

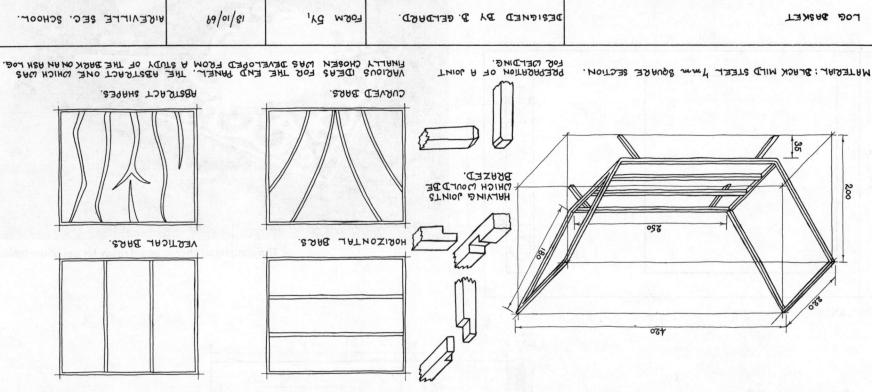

SINGLE LINE SKETCHES OF POSSIBLE DESIGNS. EACH IS OF A SIMPLE, PLEASANT CONSTRUCTION.

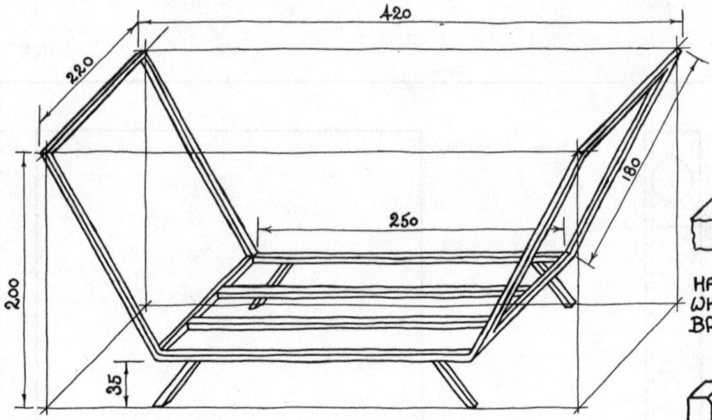
420
220
180
250
200
35

MATERIAL : BLACK MILD STEEL 7mm SQUARE SECTION.

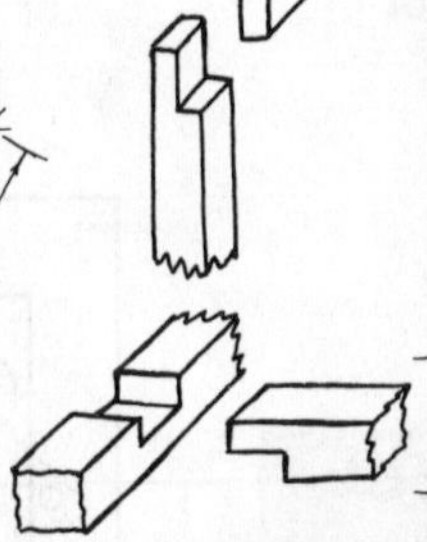

HALVING JOINTS WHICH WOULD BE BRAZED.

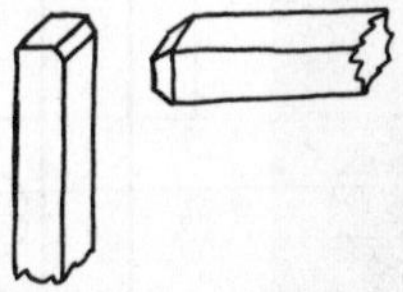

PREPARATION OF A JOINT FOR WELDING.

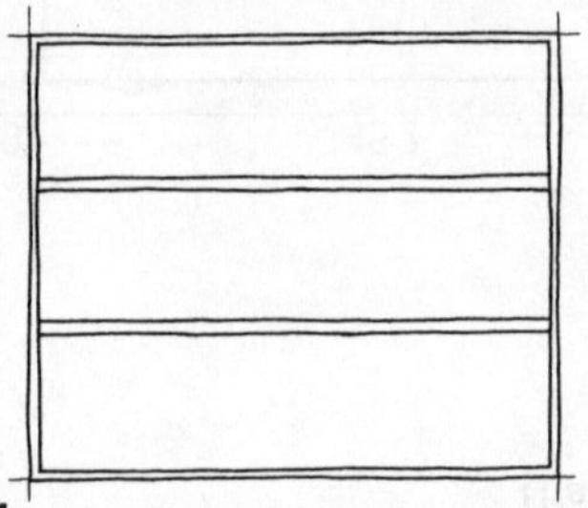

HORIZONTAL BARS.

VERTICAL BARS.

CURVED BARS.

ABSTRACT SHAPES.

VARIOUS IDEAS FOR THE END PANEL. THE ABSTRACT ONE WHICH WAS FINALLY CHOSEN WAS DEVELOPED FROM A STUDY OF THE BARK ON AN ASH LOG.

LOG BASKET	DESIGNED BY B. GELDARD.	FORM 5Y1	13/10/69	AIREVILLE SEC. SCHOOL.

SINGLE LINE SKETCHES AND SKETCH OF COMPLETED FRAME IN FREEHAND CABINET OBLIQUE AT 45° WITH HB PENCIL. PROPOSALS FOR THE END PANEL AND FRAME JOINTS SKETCHED WITH HB PENCIL. PRINTING FOR THESE WITH H PENCIL. ORTHOGRAPHIC PROJECTION WITH 3H PENCIL AND INKED WITH ROTRING 0·5 m PEN. DIMENSION LINES AND CENTRE LINES INKED WITH 0·18 m PEN. DIMENSIONS AND PRINTING WITH ROTRING STENCIL m 3·5 AND 0·35 m PEN. m – NEW PREFERRED SERIES 1 DRAWING STANDARDS.

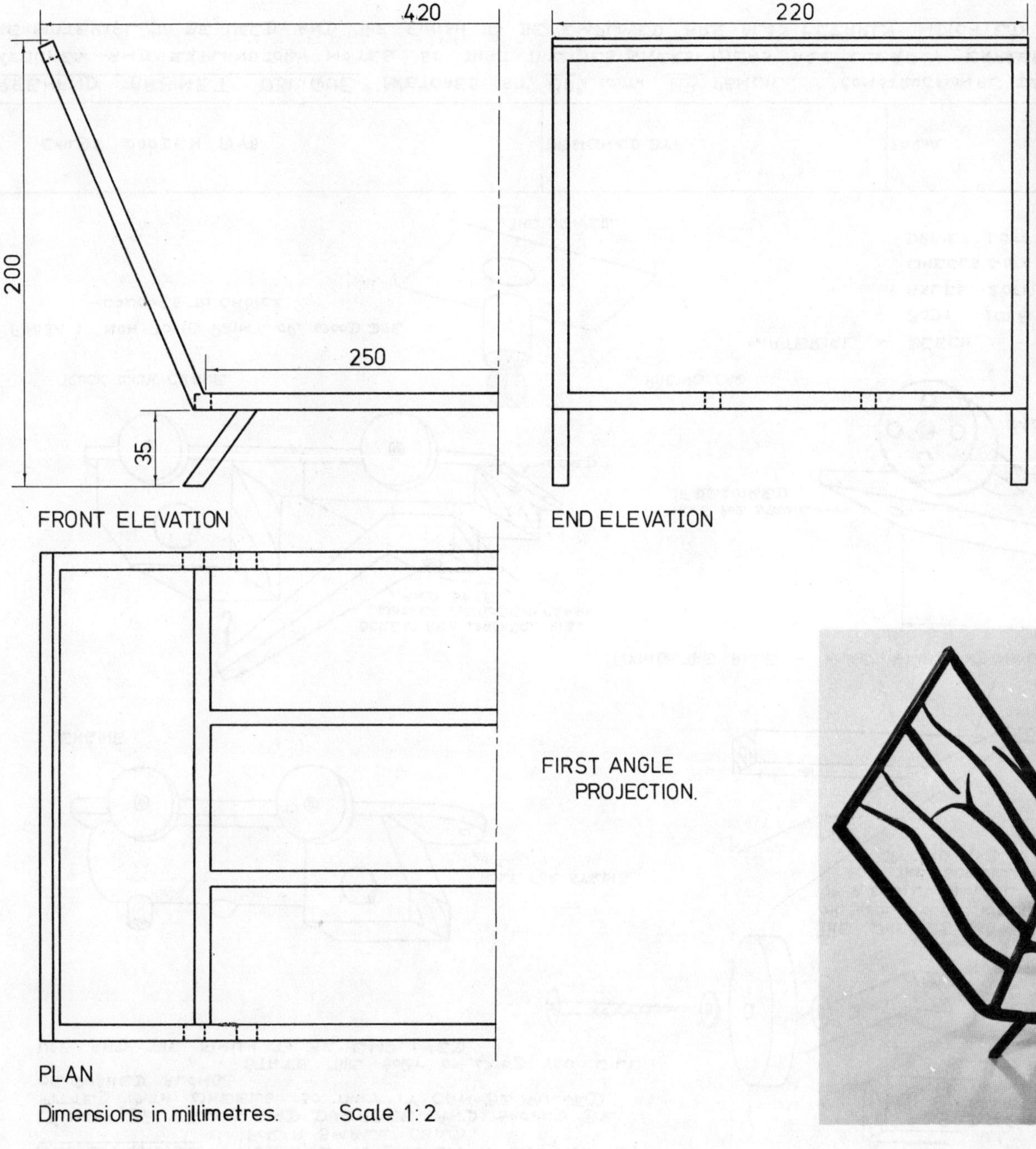
420
220
200
250
35
FRONT ELEVATION
END ELEVATION
FIRST ANGLE PROJECTION.
PLAN
Dimensions in millimetres.
Scale 1: 2

Ash log from which the design of the end panel was developed.

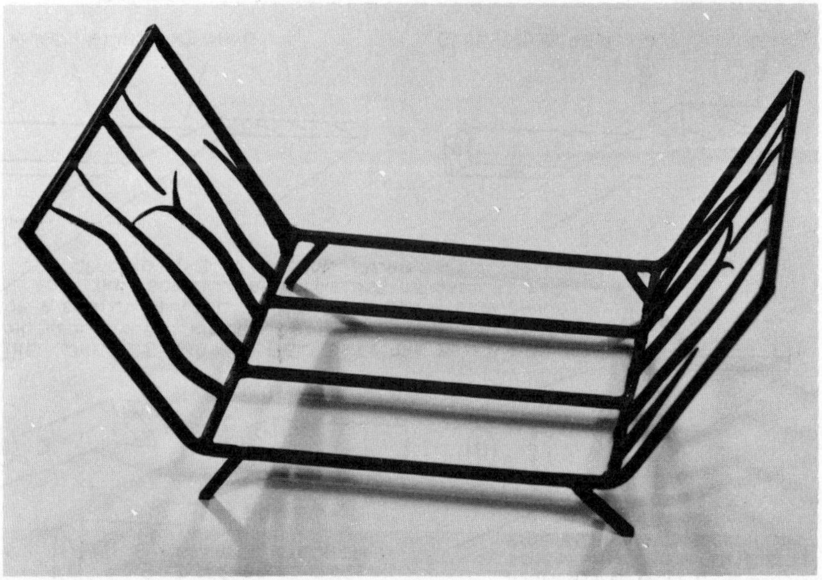

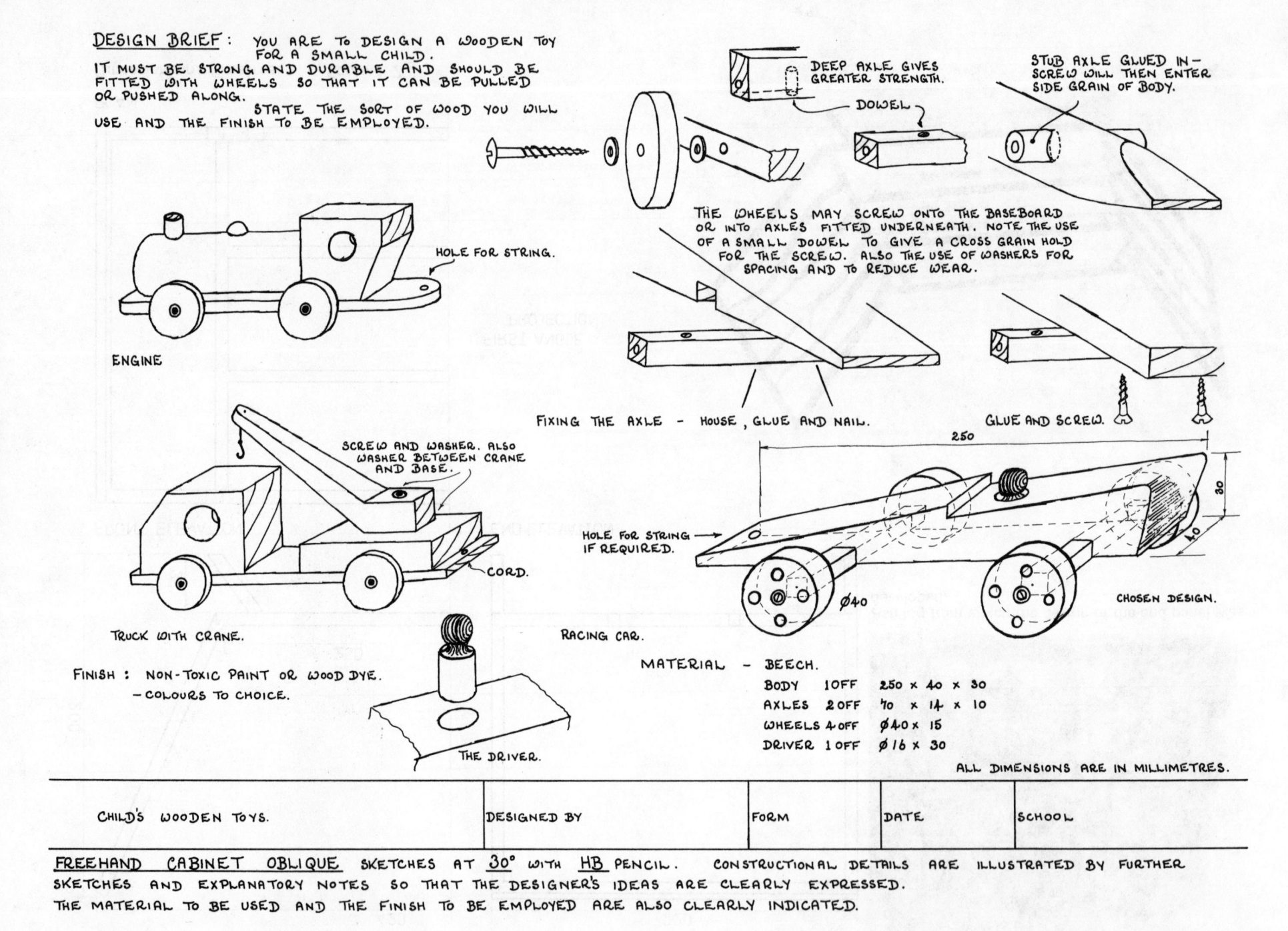

DESIGN BRIEF: YOU ARE TO DESIGN A WOODEN TOY FOR A SMALL CHILD.
IT MUST BE STRONG AND DURABLE AND SHOULD BE FITTED WITH WHEELS SO THAT IT CAN BE PULLED OR PUSHED ALONG.
STATE THE SORT OF WOOD YOU WILL USE AND THE FINISH TO BE EMPLOYED.

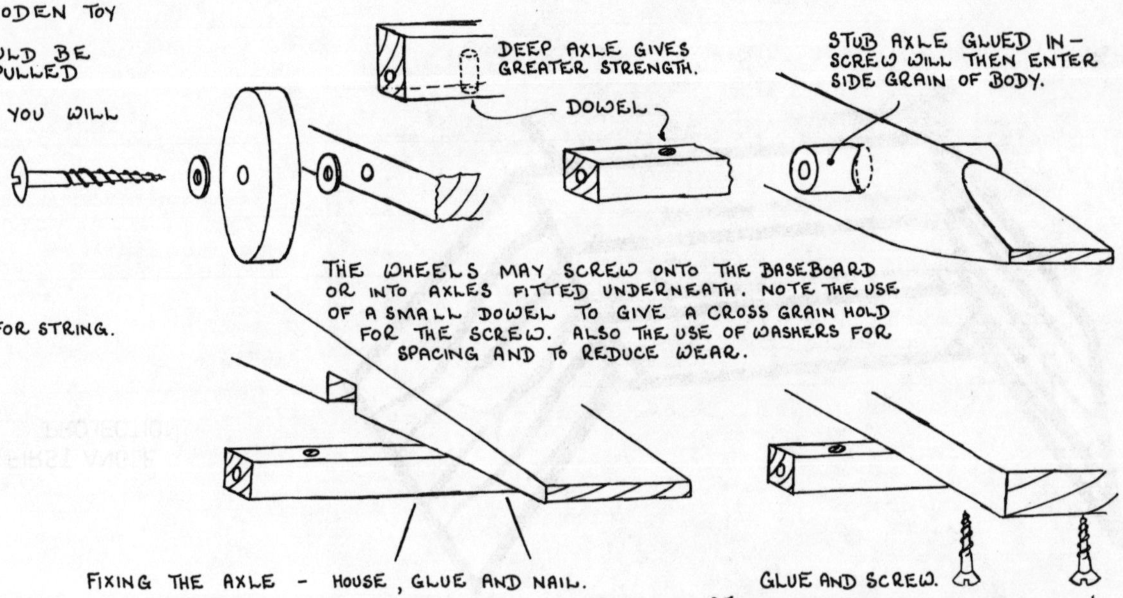
DEEP AXLE GIVES GREATER STRENGTH.
DOWEL
STUB AXLE GLUED IN - SCREW WILL THEN ENTER SIDE GRAIN OF BODY.
THE WHEELS MAY SCREW ONTO THE BASEBOARD OR INTO AXLES FITTED UNDERNEATH. NOTE THE USE OF A SMALL DOWEL TO GIVE A CROSS GRAIN HOLD FOR THE SCREW. ALSO THE USE OF WASHERS FOR SPACING AND TO REDUCE WEAR.
FIXING THE AXLE - HOUSE, GLUE AND NAIL.
GLUE AND SCREW.

HOLE FOR STRING.

ENGINE

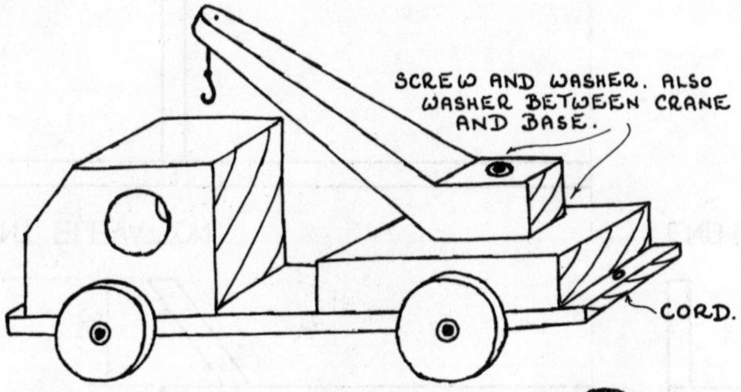
SCREW AND WASHER. ALSO WASHER BETWEEN CRANE AND BASE.
CORD.

TRUCK WITH CRANE.

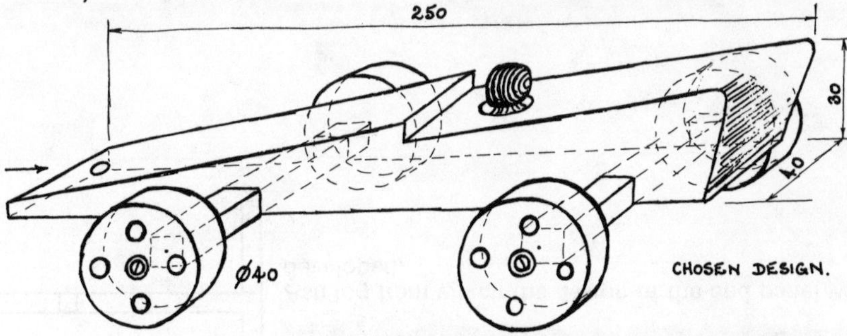
250
30
40
HOLE FOR STRING IF REQUIRED.
Ø40

CHOSEN DESIGN.

RACING CAR.

FINISH : NON-TOXIC PAINT OR WOOD DYE.
- COLOURS TO CHOICE.

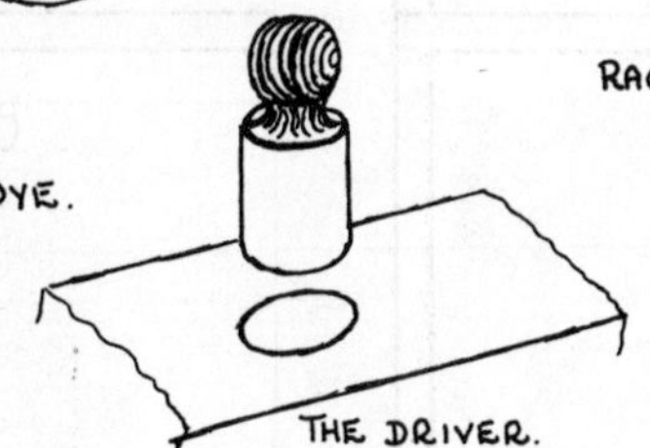

THE DRIVER.

MATERIAL - BEECH.

BODY	1 OFF	250 × 40 × 30
AXLES	2 OFF	70 × 14 × 10
WHEELS	4 OFF	Ø40 × 15
DRIVER	1 OFF	Ø16 × 30

ALL DIMENSIONS ARE IN MILLIMETRES.

CHILD'S WOODEN TOYS.	DESIGNED BY	FORM	DATE	SCHOOL

FREEHAND CABINET OBLIQUE SKETCHES AT 30° WITH HB PENCIL. CONSTRUCTIONAL DETAILS ARE ILLUSTRATED BY FURTHER SKETCHES AND EXPLANATORY NOTES SO THAT THE DESIGNER'S IDEAS ARE CLEARLY EXPRESSED. THE MATERIAL TO BE USED AND THE FINISH TO BE EMPLOYED ARE ALSO CLEARLY INDICATED.

The completed toy.

The wide wheel base makes it stable and the wheels run freely on the screws. There is a washer on each side of each wheel to prevent wear. The toy is attractively finished in yellow and red wood dyes and clear lacquer.

DESIGN PROBLEM.

THE SKETCHES SHOW A TYPICAL SELECTION OF SANDWICHES AND OPEN SAVOURIES. YOU ARE REQUIRED TO DESIGN A TRAY ON WHICH TO SERVE THEM. IT MUST HAVE A PLEASANT APPEARANCE FOR USE AT THE TABLE. IT MUST BE EASY TO HANDLE AND TO CLEAN. THE TRAY SHOULD BE CAPABLE OF HOLDING SUFFICIENT FOR FOUR PEOPLE.

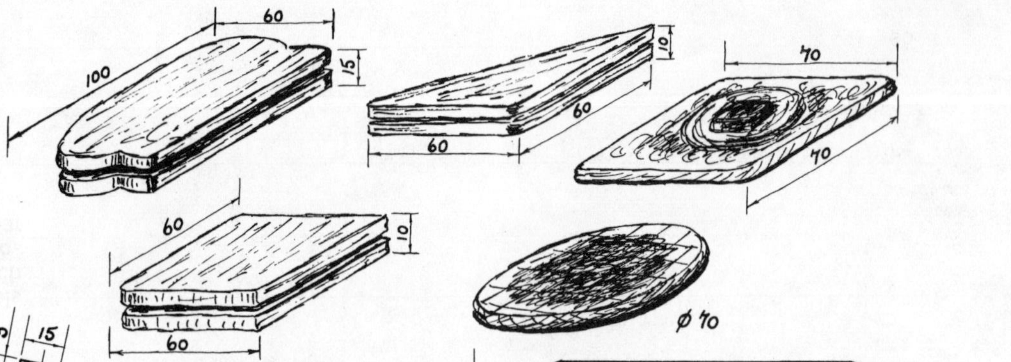
60
100
15
10
60
60
70
70
60
10
60
ϕ 70

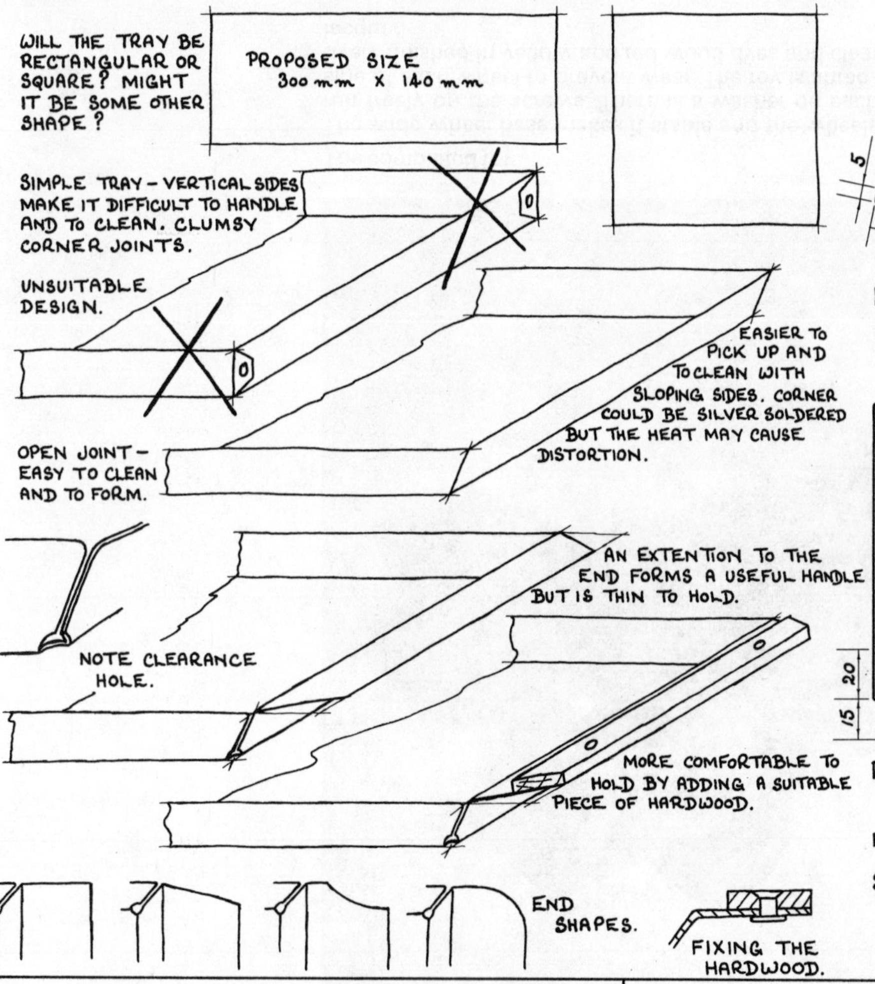
WILL THE TRAY BE RECTANGULAR OR SQUARE? MIGHT IT BE SOME OTHER SHAPE?
PROPOSED SIZE
300 mm x 140 mm
SIMPLE TRAY - VERTICAL SIDES MAKE IT DIFFICULT TO HANDLE AND TO CLEAN. CLUMSY CORNER JOINTS.
UNSUITABLE DESIGN.
EASIER TO PICK UP AND TO CLEAN WITH SLOPING SIDES. CORNER COULD BE SILVER SOLDERED BUT THE HEAT MAY CAUSE DISTORTION.
OPEN JOINT - EASY TO CLEAN AND TO FORM.
AN EXTENTION TO THE END FORMS A USEFUL HANDLE BUT IS THIN TO HOLD.
NOTE CLEARANCE HOLE.
MORE COMFORTABLE TO HOLD BY ADDING A SUITABLE PIECE OF HARDWOOD.
END SHAPES.
FIXING THE HARDWOOD.

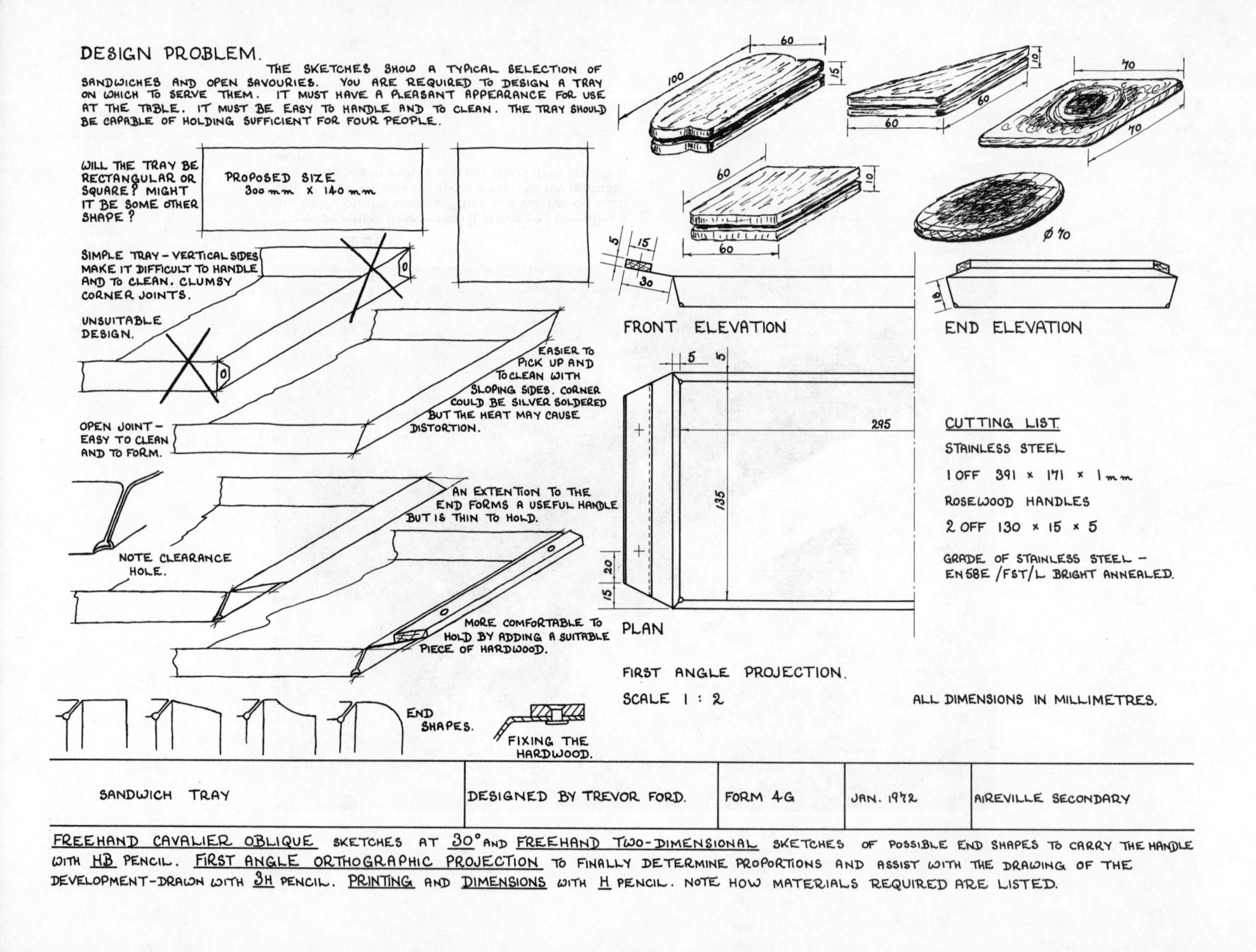

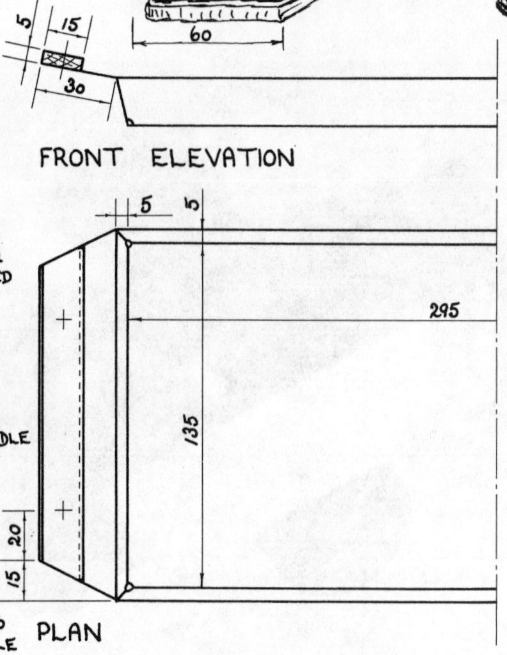
5
15
30
FRONT ELEVATION
5
5
295
135
20
15
PLAN

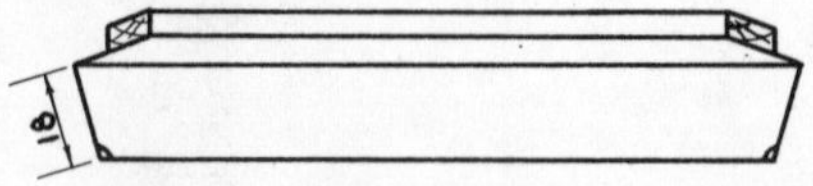
18
END ELEVATION

CUTTING LIST.

STAINLESS STEEL

1 OFF 391 × 171 × 1 mm

ROSEWOOD HANDLES

2 OFF 130 × 15 × 5

GRADE OF STAINLESS STEEL - EN 58E /FST/L BRIGHT ANNEALED.

FIRST ANGLE PROJECTION.

SCALE 1 : 2

ALL DIMENSIONS IN MILLIMETRES.

SANDWICH TRAY	DESIGNED BY TREVOR FORD.	FORM 4G	JAN. 1972	AIREVILLE SECONDARY

FREEHAND CAVALIER OBLIQUE SKETCHES AT 30° AND FREEHAND TWO-DIMENSIONAL SKETCHES OF POSSIBLE END SHAPES TO CARRY THE HANDLE WITH HB PENCIL. FIRST ANGLE ORTHOGRAPHIC PROJECTION TO FINALLY DETERMINE PROPORTIONS AND ASSIST WITH THE DRAWING OF THE DEVELOPMENT-DRAWN WITH 3H PENCIL. PRINTING AND DIMENSIONS WITH H PENCIL. NOTE HOW MATERIALS REQUIRED ARE LISTED.

The development of the shape required from which to make the tray. This was drawn on thin card which was then scored and folded to give a first impression of the finished piece.

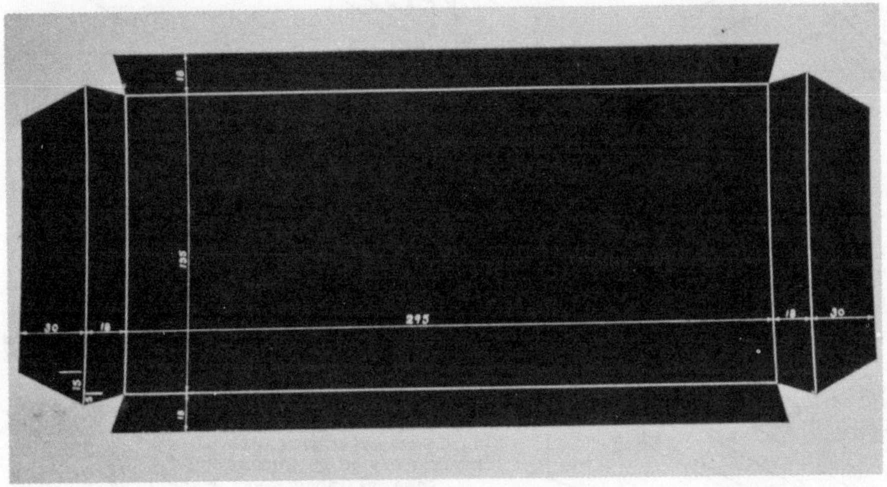
18
135
30
18
295
18
30
15
18

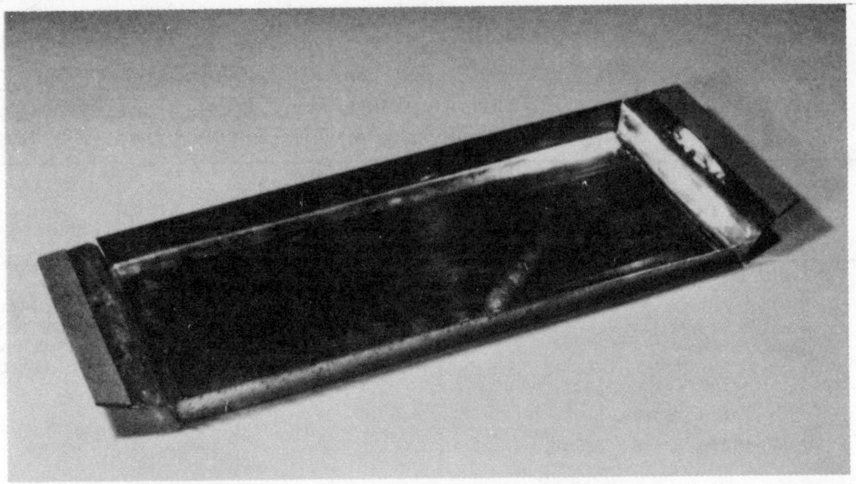

The second stage was to make a mock-up in tinplate. Strawboard was used to represent the rosewood. Being of metal this gave a better idea of how the finished piece would look. Folding the tinplate mock-up at this stage gave valuable experience in the use of techniques required to work the stainless steel into the shape designed.

The completed work. Note how the light shining through the open corner shows its shape in the shadow.

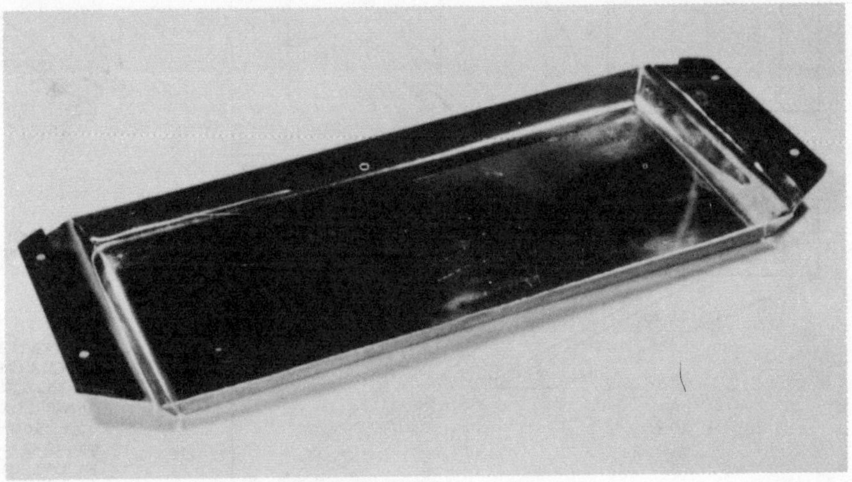

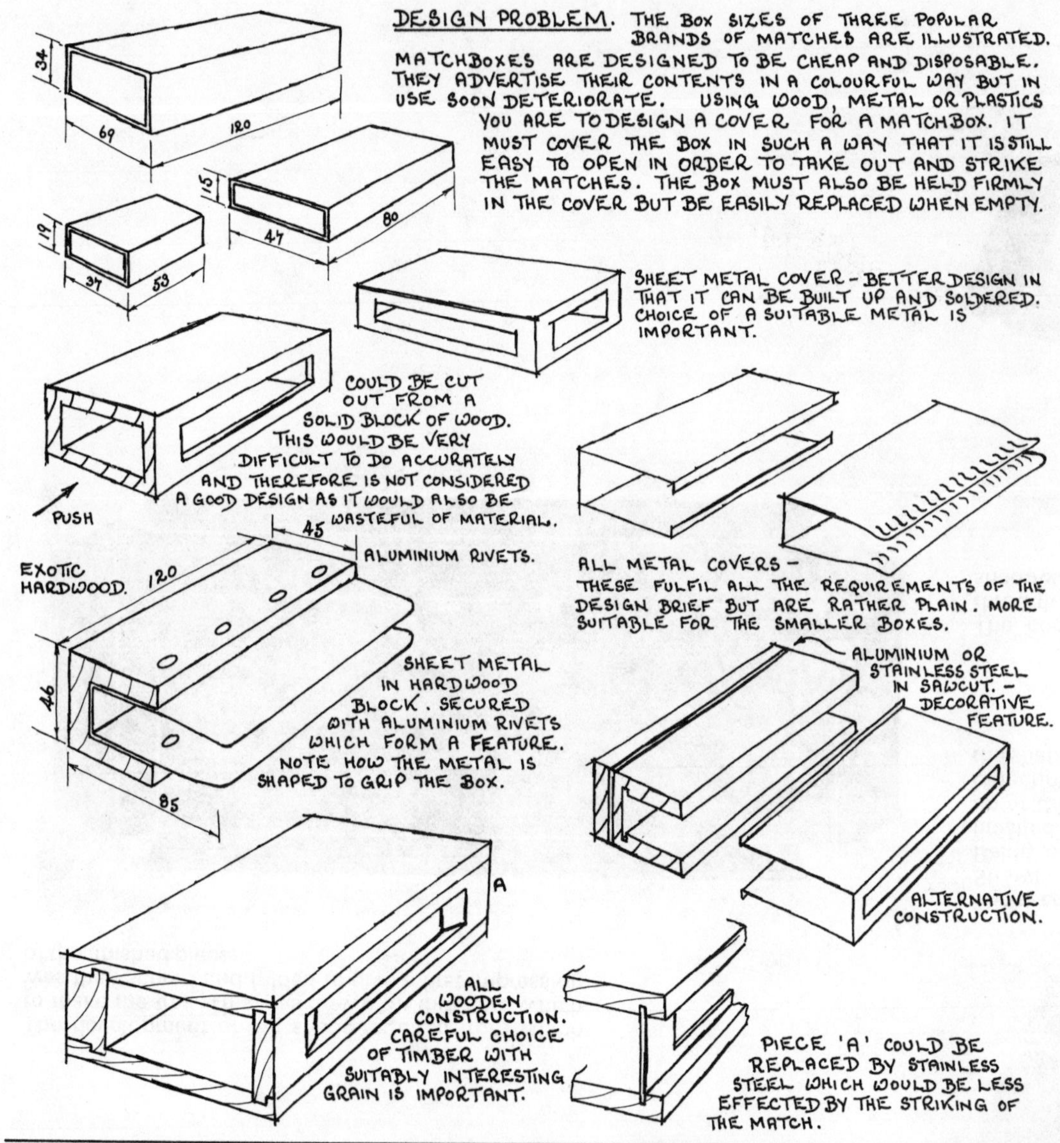
DESIGN PROBLEM. THE BOX SIZES OF THREE POPULAR BRANDS OF MATCHES ARE ILLUSTRATED.
MATCHBOXES ARE DESIGNED TO BE CHEAP AND DISPOSABLE. THEY ADVERTISE THEIR CONTENTS IN A COLOURFUL WAY BUT IN USE SOON DETERIORATE. USING WOOD, METAL OR PLASTICS YOU ARE TO DESIGN A COVER FOR A MATCHBOX. IT MUST COVER THE BOX IN SUCH A WAY THAT IT IS STILL EASY TO OPEN IN ORDER TO TAKE OUT AND STRIKE THE MATCHES. THE BOX MUST ALSO BE HELD FIRMLY IN THE COVER BUT BE EASILY REPLACED WHEN EMPTY.
34
69
120
15
47
80
19
37
53
SHEET METAL COVER - BETTER DESIGN IN THAT IT CAN BE BUILT UP AND SOLDERED. CHOICE OF A SUITABLE METAL IS IMPORTANT.
COULD BE CUT OUT FROM A SOLID BLOCK OF WOOD. THIS WOULD BE VERY DIFFICULT TO DO ACCURATELY AND THEREFORE IS NOT CONSIDERED A GOOD DESIGN AS IT WOULD ALSO BE WASTEFUL OF MATERIAL.
PUSH
45
ALUMINIUM RIVETS.
EXOTIC HARDWOOD.
120
46
85
SHEET METAL IN HARDWOOD BLOCK. SECURED WITH ALUMINIUM RIVETS WHICH FORM A FEATURE. NOTE HOW THE METAL IS SHAPED TO GRIP THE BOX.
ALL METAL COVERS - THESE FULFIL ALL THE REQUIREMENTS OF THE DESIGN BRIEF BUT ARE RATHER PLAIN. MORE SUITABLE FOR THE SMALLER BOXES.
ALUMINIUM OR STAINLESS STEEL IN SAWCUT. - DECORATIVE FEATURE.
ALTERNATIVE CONSTRUCTION.
A
ALL WOODEN CONSTRUCTION. CAREFUL CHOICE OF TIMBER WITH SUITABLY INTERESTING GRAIN IS IMPORTANT.
PIECE 'A' COULD BE REPLACED BY STAINLESS STEEL WHICH WOULD BE LESS EFFECTED BY THE STRIKING OF THE MATCH.

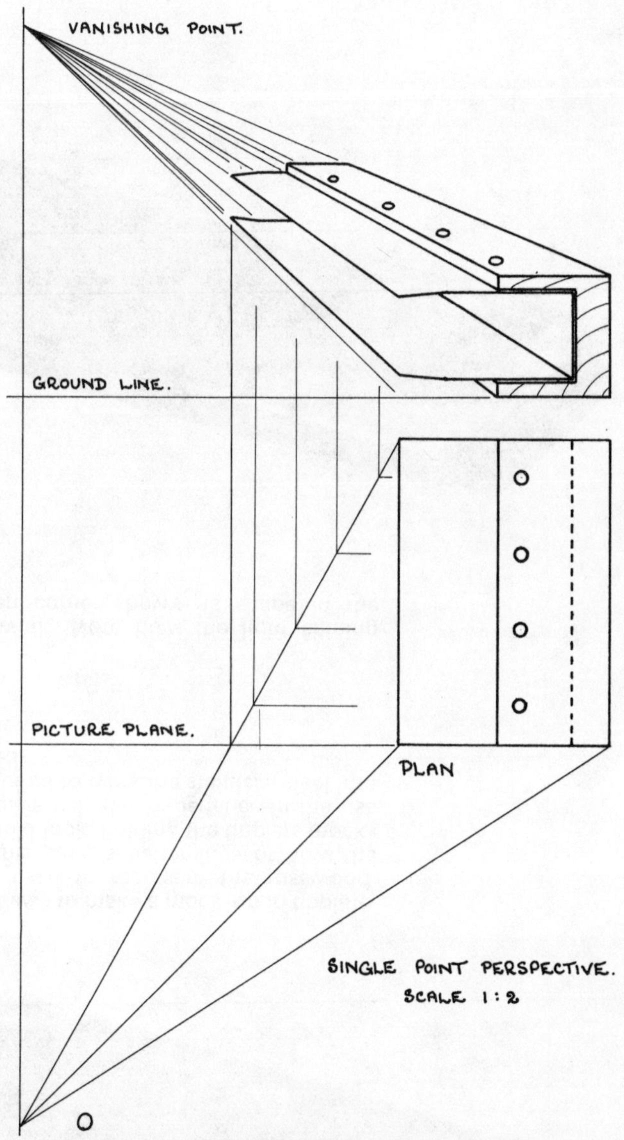
VANISHING POINT.
GROUND LINE.
PICTURE PLANE.
PLAN
O
SINGLE POINT PERSPECTIVE.
SCALE 1:2

MATCH BOX COVER - FOR USE IN THE HOME.	DESIGNED BY	FORM	DATE	SCHOOL

FREEHAND, FREE PERSPECTIVE SKETCHES OF DESIGN POSSIBILITIES DRAWN WITH HB PENCIL AND PRINTING WITH H PENCIL. SINGLE POINT PERSPECTIVE DRAWING OF THE CHOSEN DESIGN PLUS 3RD. ANGLE ORTHOGRAPHIC PROJECTION DRAWN WITH 3H PENCIL. NOTE THE USE OF ROTRING ™ STENCILS FOR DIMENSIONS, NAMES OF VIEWS AND CUTTING LIST.

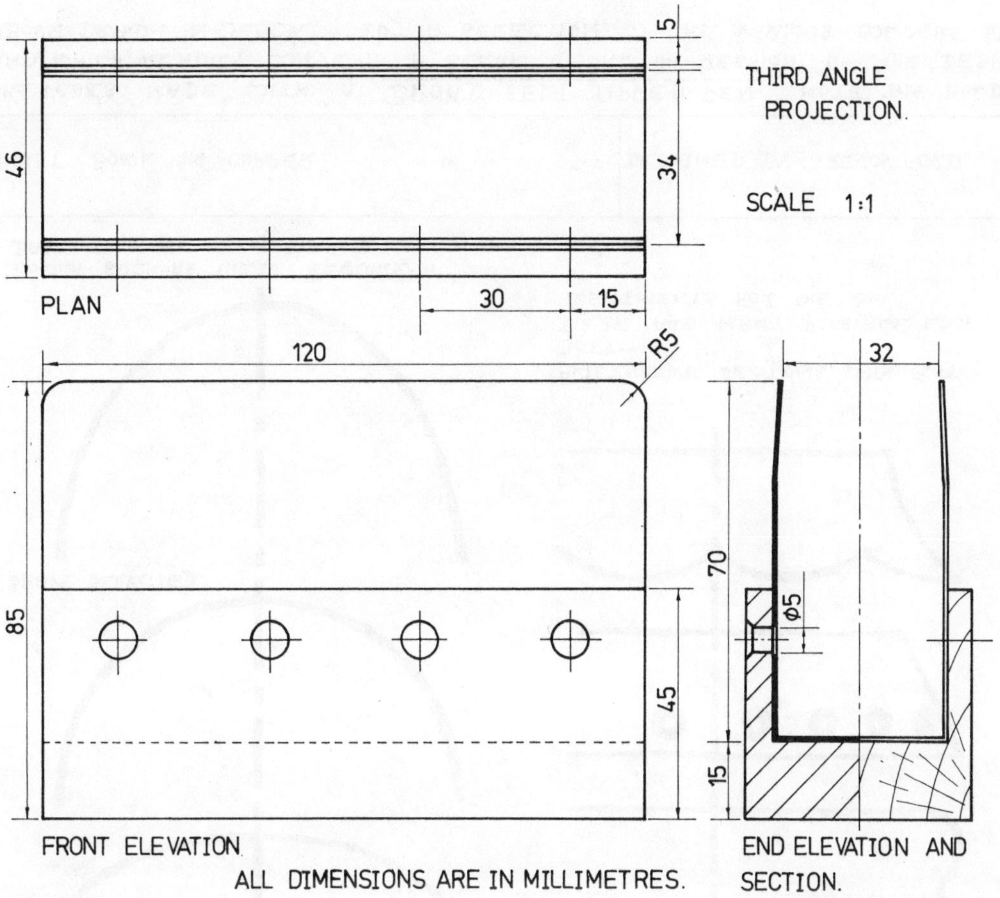
THIRD ANGLE
PROJECTION.
SCALE 1:1
PLAN
5
46
34
30
15
120
R5
32
85
70
⌀5
45
15
FRONT ELEVATION.
END ELEVATION AND
SECTION.
ALL DIMENSIONS ARE IN MILLIMETRES.

PIONEER
HOUSEHOLD
MATCHES
PIONEER HOUSEHOLD
PUNCH
Swan
VESTAS

Examples of boxes of matches in common use. Their sizes are indicated on the sketch sheet.

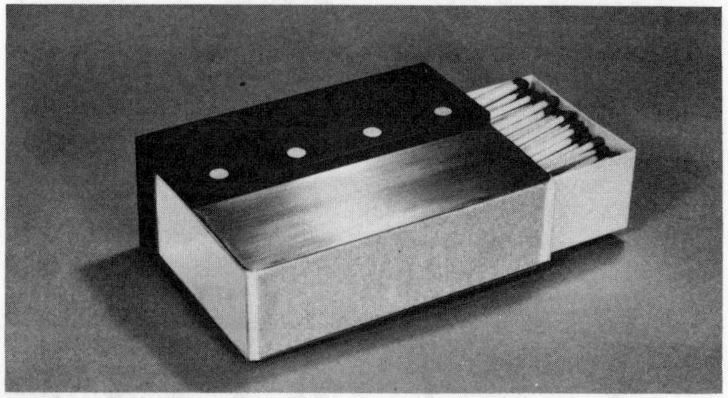

The final design for the cover of the large box. It is interesting to compare the design of this modern piece, employing rosewood and stainless steel in such a pleasing combination, with the cover made by the author's father in 1917.

CUTTING LIST.

ROSEWOOD - 1 OFF / 120 × 46 × 45

STAINLESS STEEL - 1 OFF / 120 × 177 × 1·00

ALUMINIUM RIVETS C/SK HEAD - 8 × ⌀5

FINISH.

STAINLESS STEEL - SATIN FINISH.

ROSEWOOD POLISHED WITH CHILLED WAX.

A cover for a small box of matches, made of brass and intended to be carried in the pocket. Name, address and date have been etched into the metal.

DESIGN BRIEF. A BOWL IS REQUIRED FOR USE IN THE DINING ROOM IN WHICH TO PLACE A SELECTION OF FRESH FRUIT. IT SHOULD BE CAPABLE OF HOLDING SEVERAL APPLES ORANGES, BANANAS AND A BUNCH OF GRAPES.

THERE IS AN INFINITE NUMBER OF POSSIBLE SHAPES FOR BOWLS WITH A CURVED SECTION.
THE SECTION CHOSEN WILL DEPEND UPON INDIVIDUAL TASTE AND REQUIREMENTS.

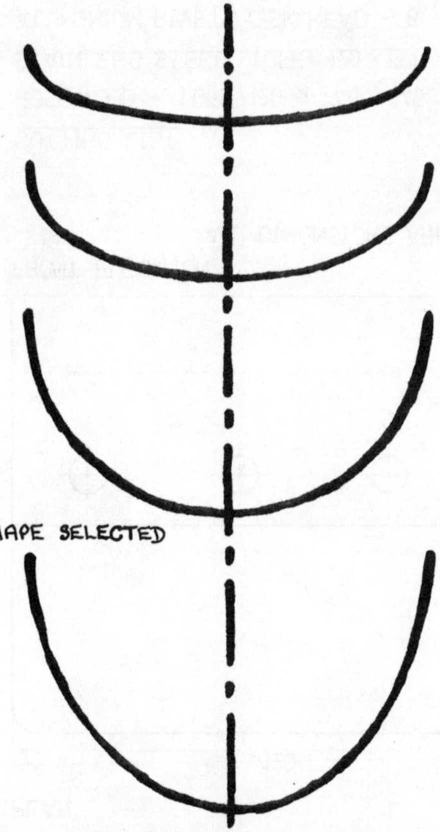

SHAPE SELECTED

BOWLS SUCH AS THESE REQUIRE A BASE TO MAKE THEM STABLE.

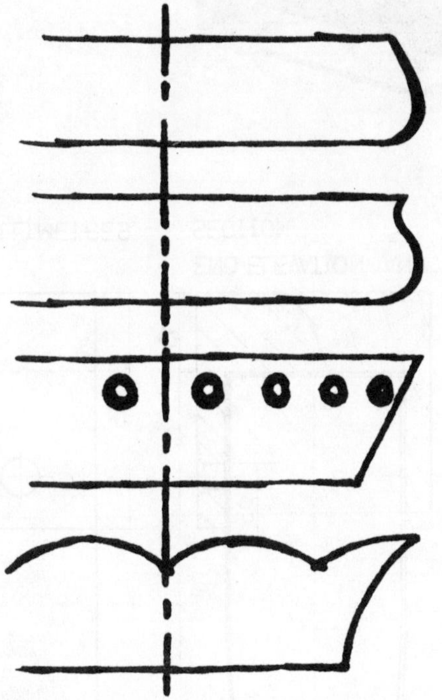

ALTERNATIVE SECTIONS WITH FLAT BOTTOMS.
THERE ARE MANY POSSIBLE EDGE TREATMENTS FOR THE RIM.

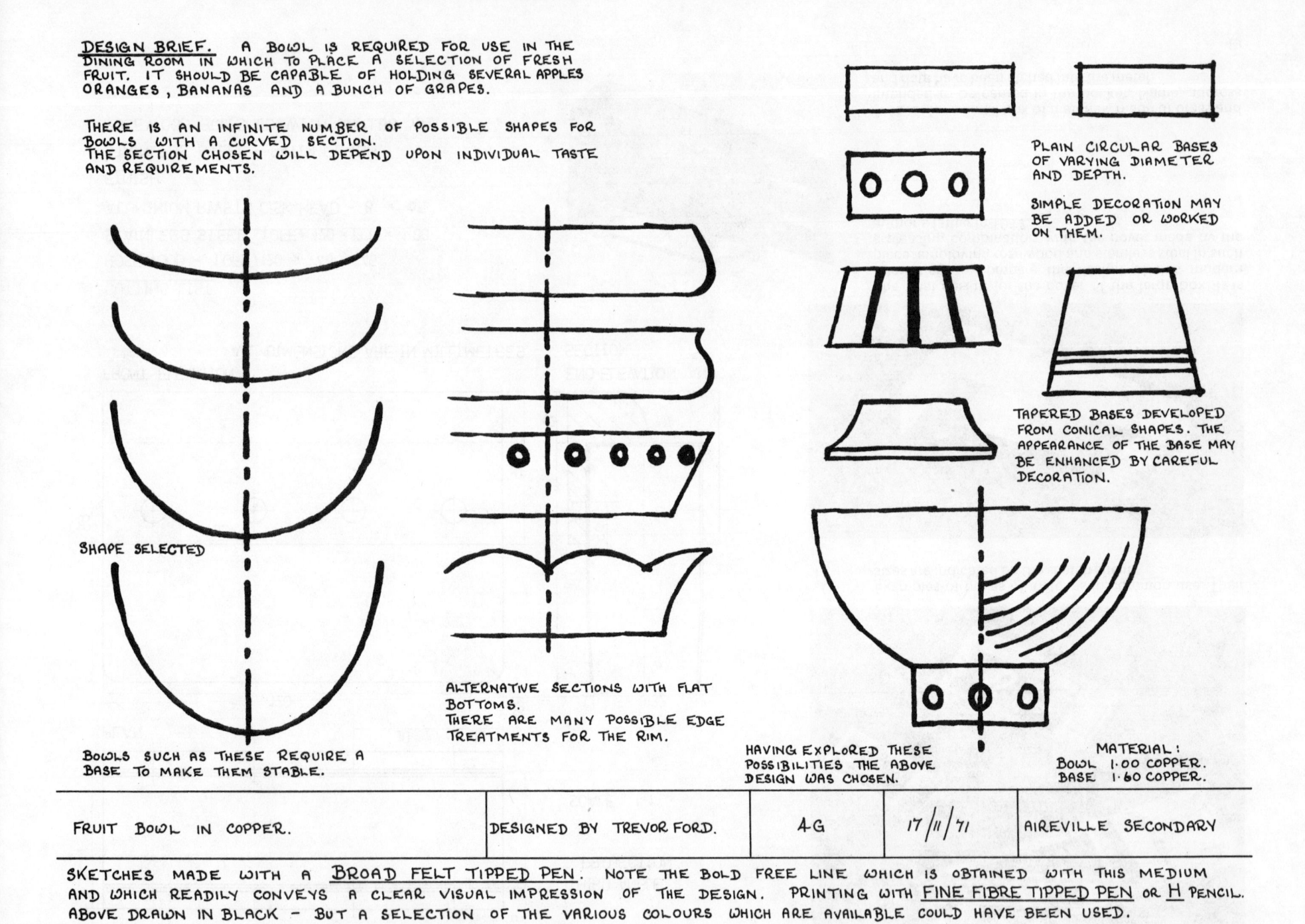

PLAIN CIRCULAR BASES OF VARYING DIAMETER AND DEPTH.

SIMPLE DECORATION MAY BE ADDED OR WORKED ON THEM.

TAPERED BASES DEVELOPED FROM CONICAL SHAPES. THE APPEARANCE OF THE BASE MAY BE ENHANCED BY CAREFUL DECORATION.

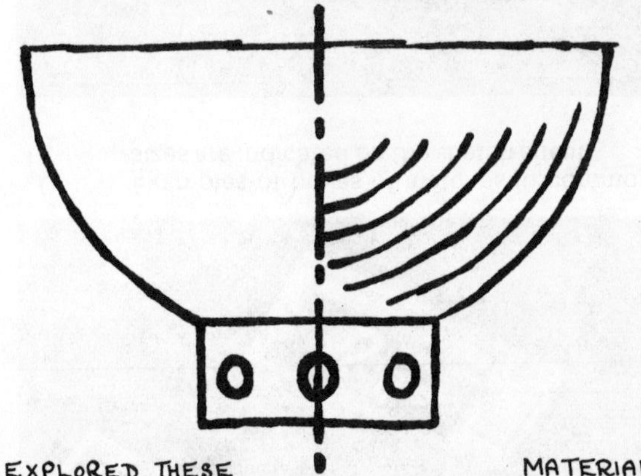

HAVING EXPLORED THESE POSSIBILITIES THE ABOVE DESIGN WAS CHOSEN.

MATERIAL:
BOWL 1·00 COPPER.
BASE 1·60 COPPER.

FRUIT BOWL IN COPPER.	DESIGNED BY TREVOR FORD.	4G	17/11/71	AIREVILLE SECONDARY

SKETCHES MADE WITH A BROAD FELT TIPPED PEN. NOTE THE BOLD FREE LINE WHICH IS OBTAINED WITH THIS MEDIUM AND WHICH READILY CONVEYS A CLEAR VISUAL IMPRESSION OF THE DESIGN. PRINTING WITH FINE FIBRE TIPPED PEN OR H PENCIL. ABOVE DRAWN IN BLACK – BUT A SELECTION OF THE VARIOUS COLOURS WHICH ARE AVAILABLE COULD HAVE BEEN USED.

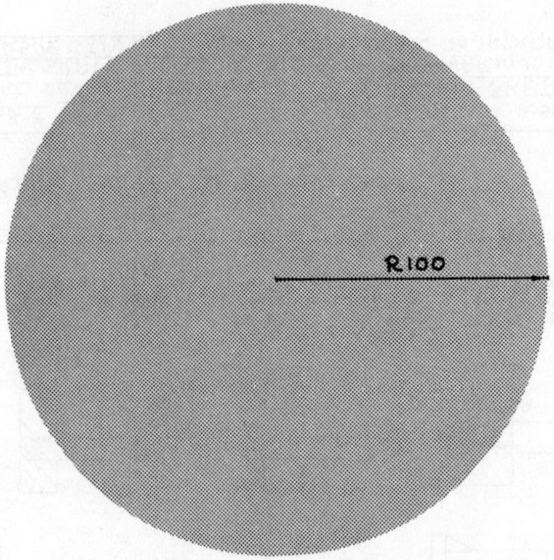
R100

THE DIAMETER OF THE BOWL WAS DETERMINED BY PLACING A SELECTION OF FRUIT TOGETHER AND CUTTING OUT A DISC OF A SUITABLE DIAMETER

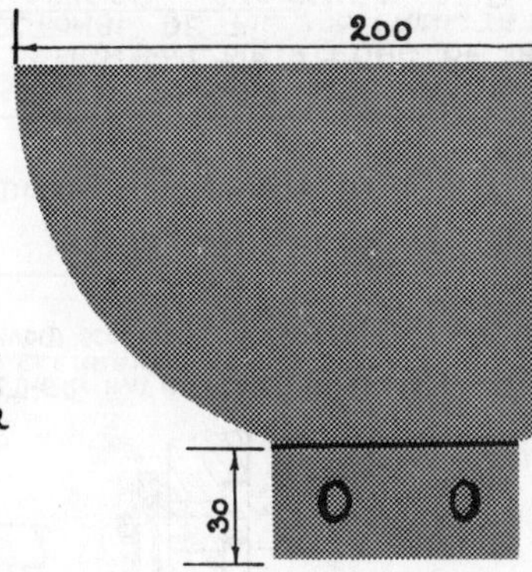
200
30

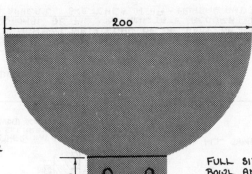

FULL SIZE CARD SILHOUETTE OF BOWL AND BASE. THE CORRECTNESS OF THE PROPORTIONS CAN BE QUICKLY ASSESSED.

INNER AND OUTER TEMPLATES FOR TESTING THE SECTION OF THE BOWL.

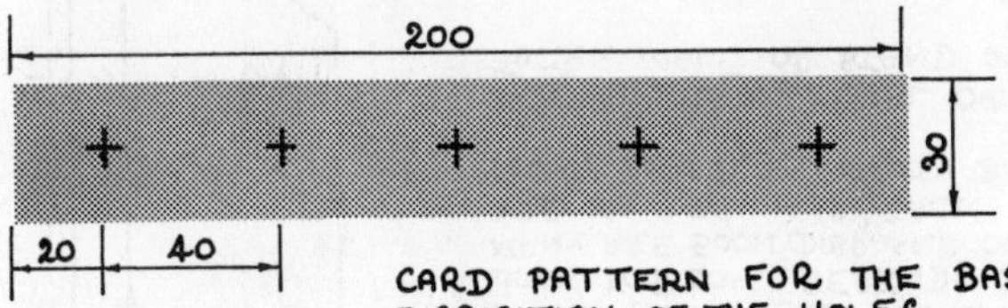
200
30
20
40

CARD PATTERN FOR THE BASE SHOWING THE DISPOSITION OF THE HOLES.

The completed bowl in planished copper.

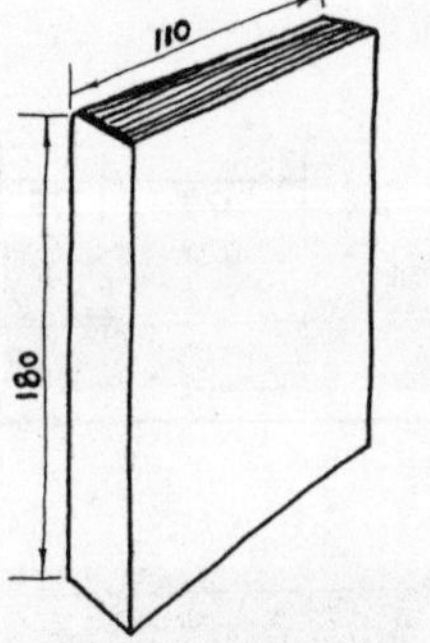
110
180

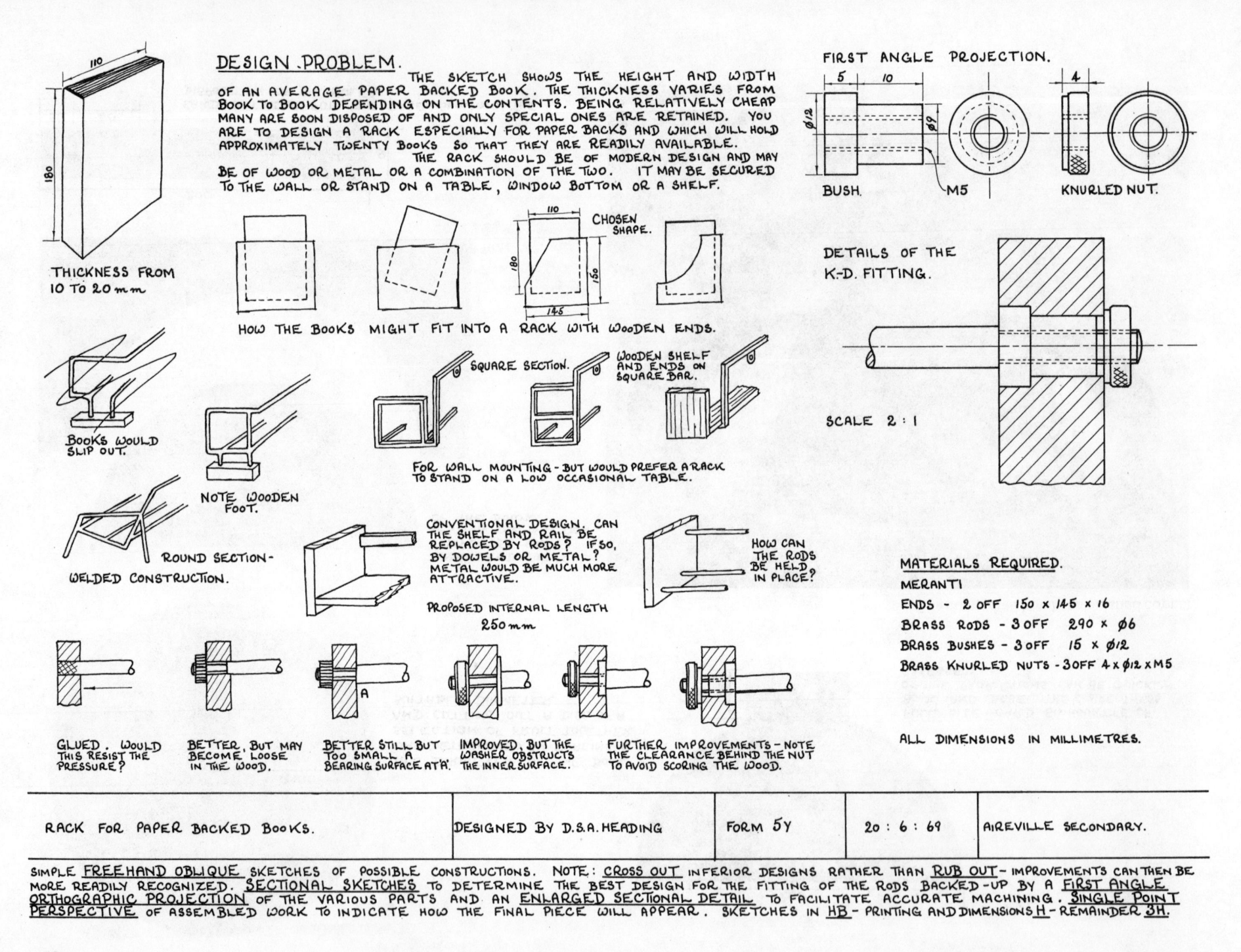

THICKNESS FROM 10 TO 20 mm

DESIGN. PROBLEM.

THE SKETCH SHOWS THE HEIGHT AND WIDTH OF AN AVERAGE PAPER BACKED BOOK. THE THICKNESS VARIES FROM BOOK TO BOOK DEPENDING ON THE CONTENTS. BEING RELATIVELY CHEAP MANY ARE SOON DISPOSED OF AND ONLY SPECIAL ONES ARE RETAINED. YOU ARE TO DESIGN A RACK ESPECIALLY FOR PAPER BACKS AND WHICH WILL HOLD APPROXIMATELY TWENTY BOOKS SO THAT THEY ARE READILY AVAILABLE.

THE RACK SHOULD BE OF MODERN DESIGN AND MAY BE OF WOOD OR METAL OR A COMBINATION OF THE TWO. IT MAY BE SECURED TO THE WALL OR STAND ON A TABLE, WINDOW BOTTOM OR A SHELF.

FIRST ANGLE PROJECTION.

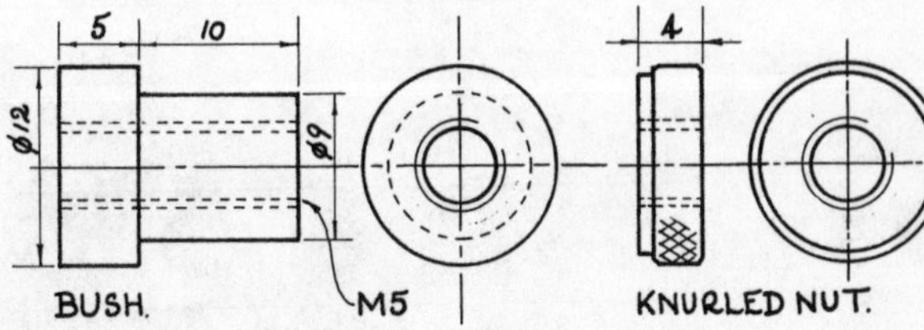
5
10
4
Ø12
Ø9
BUSH.
M5
KNURLED NUT.

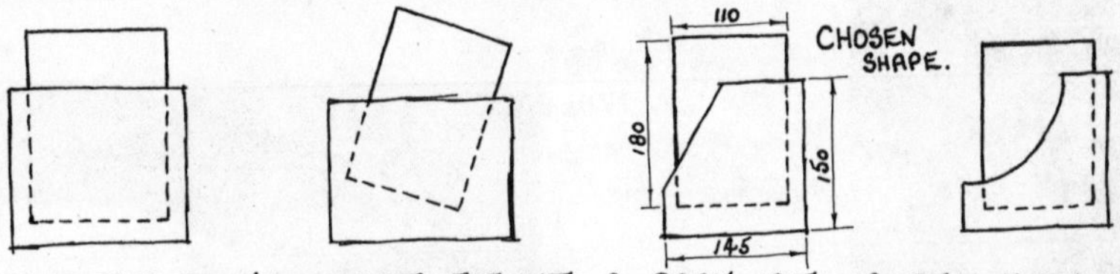
110
CHOSEN SHAPE.
180
150
145

HOW THE BOOKS MIGHT FIT INTO A RACK WITH WOODEN ENDS.

DETAILS OF THE K-D. FITTING.

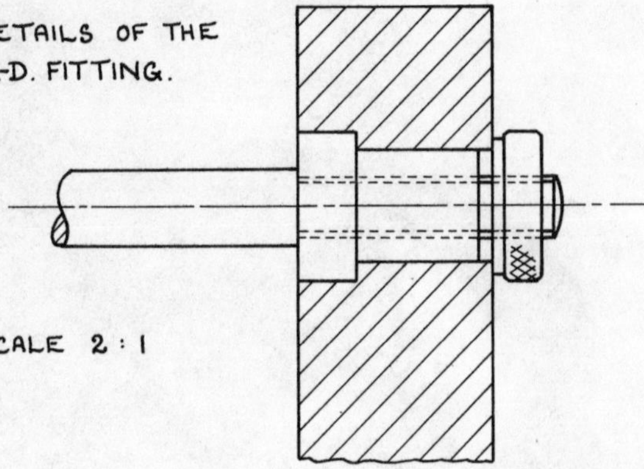

SCALE 2 : 1

BOOKS WOULD SLIP OUT.
SQUARE SECTION.
WOODEN SHELF AND ENDS ON SQUARE BAR.
FOR WALL MOUNTING - BUT WOULD PREFER A RACK TO STAND ON A LOW OCCASIONAL TABLE.

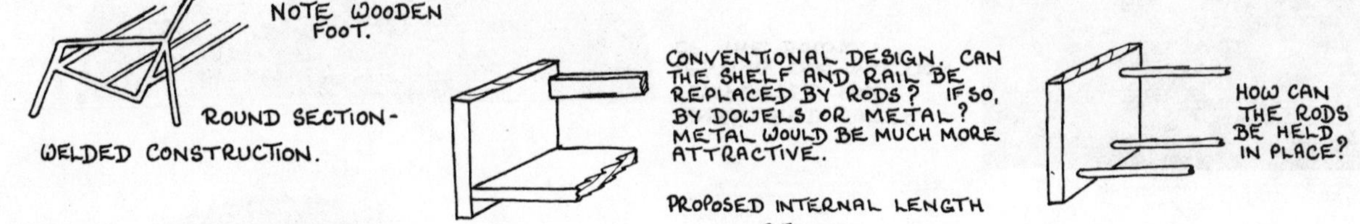
NOTE WOODEN FOOT.
ROUND SECTION-
WELDED CONSTRUCTION.
CONVENTIONAL DESIGN. CAN THE SHELF AND RAIL BE REPLACED BY RODS? IF SO, BY DOWELS OR METAL? METAL WOULD BE MUCH MORE ATTRACTIVE.
HOW CAN THE RODS BE HELD IN PLACE?
PROPOSED INTERNAL LENGTH 250 mm

MATERIALS REQUIRED.

MERANTI

ENDS - 2 OFF 150 x 145 x 16

BRASS RODS - 3 OFF 290 x Ø6

BRASS BUSHES - 3 OFF 15 x Ø12

BRASS KNURLED NUTS - 3 OFF 4 x Ø12 x M5

ALL DIMENSIONS IN MILLIMETRES.

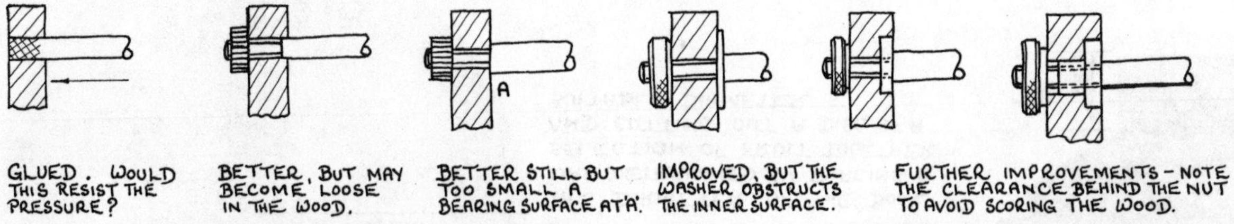
A
GLUED. WOULD THIS RESIST THE PRESSURE?
BETTER, BUT MAY BECOME LOOSE IN THE WOOD.
BETTER STILL BUT TOO SMALL A BEARING SURFACE AT 'A'.
IMPROVED, BUT THE WASHER OBSTRUCTS THE INNER SURFACE.
FURTHER IMPROVEMENTS - NOTE THE CLEARANCE BEHIND THE NUT TO AVOID SCORING THE WOOD.

RACK FOR PAPER BACKED BOOKS.	DESIGNED BY D.S.A. HEADING	FORM 5Y	20 : 6 : 69	AIREVILLE SECONDARY.

SIMPLE FREEHAND OBLIQUE SKETCHES OF POSSIBLE CONSTRUCTIONS. NOTE: CROSS OUT INFERIOR DESIGNS RATHER THAN RUB OUT - IMPROVEMENTS CAN THEN BE MORE READILY RECOGNIZED. SECTIONAL SKETCHES TO DETERMINE THE BEST DESIGN FOR THE FITTING OF THE RODS BACKED-UP BY A FIRST ANGLE ORTHOGRAPHIC PROJECTION OF THE VARIOUS PARTS AND AN ENLARGED SECTIONAL DETAIL TO FACILITATE ACCURATE MACHINING. SINGLE POINT PERSPECTIVE OF ASSEMBLED WORK TO INDICATE HOW THE FINAL PIECE WILL APPEAR. SKETCHES IN HB - PRINTING AND DIMENSIONS H - REMAINDER 3H.

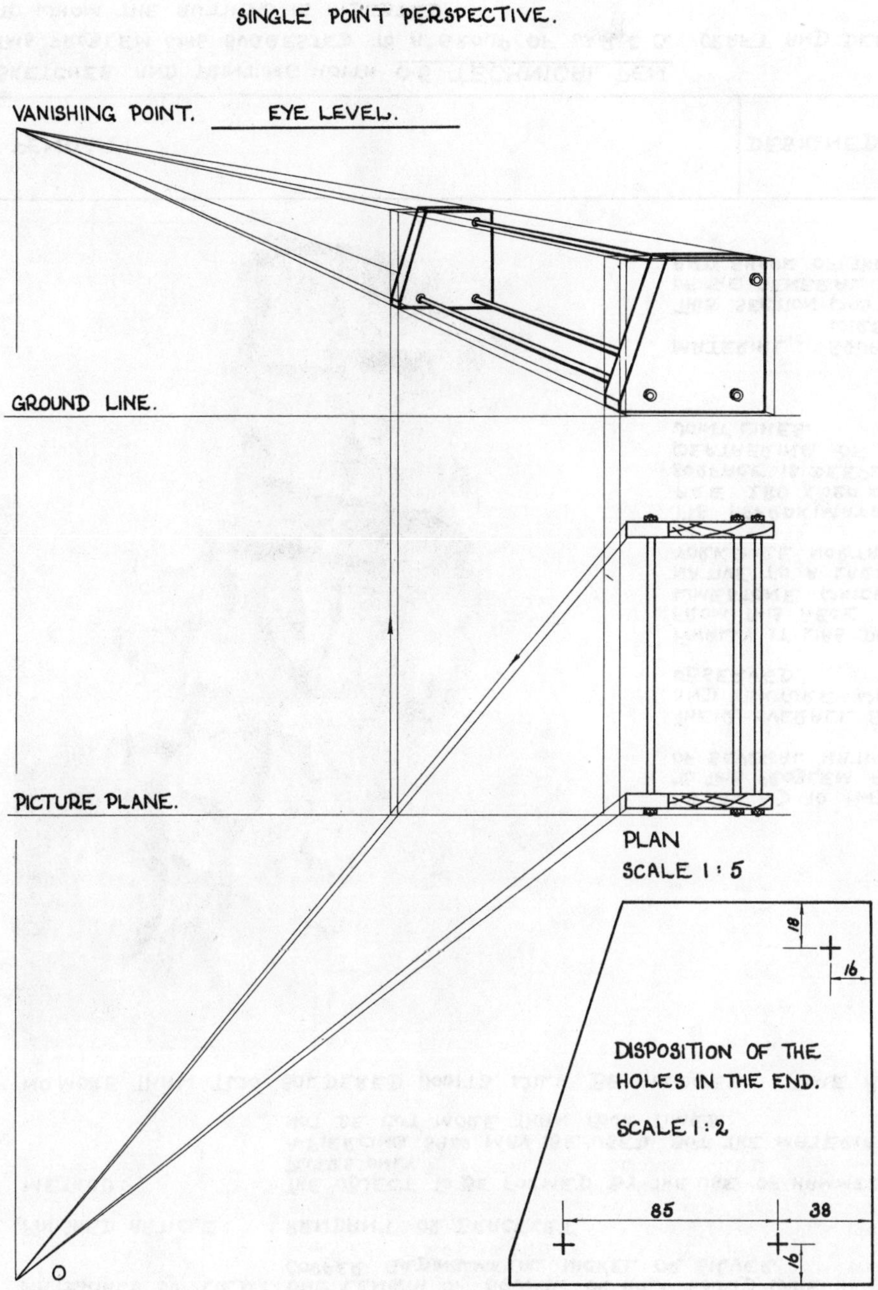
SINGLE POINT PERSPECTIVE.
VANISHING POINT.
EYE LEVEL.
GROUND LINE.
PICTURE PLANE.
PLAN
SCALE 1 : 5
18
16
DISPOSITION OF THE HOLES IN THE END.
SCALE 1 : 2
85
38
16
O

The knock-down fittings.

The sturdy, functional construction of the book rack is quite evident in this photograph of the assembled work. The knock-down fittings become an attractive feature.

'MINI - QUIP' PROJECT.

MATERIALS SUPPLIED : ONE LENGTH OF SQUARE OR HALF ROUND WIRE IN BRASS, COPPER, GILDING METAL, NICKEL OR SILVER.

FINISHED ARTICLE : PENDANT OR BRACELET.

METHOD : THE OBJECT TO BE FORMED BY THE USE OF HAMMERS AND PLIERS ONLY. A PIERCING SAW MAY BE USED BUT THE MATERIAL MUST NOT BE CUT MORE THAN FOUR TIMES.

NO MORE THAN TWO SOLDERED JOINTS WILL BE ALLOWED. TIME 8 HOURS.

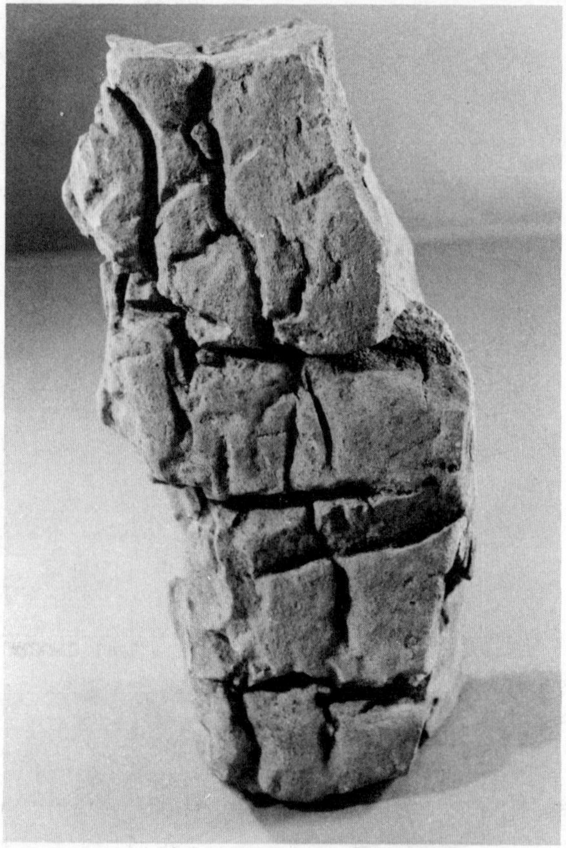

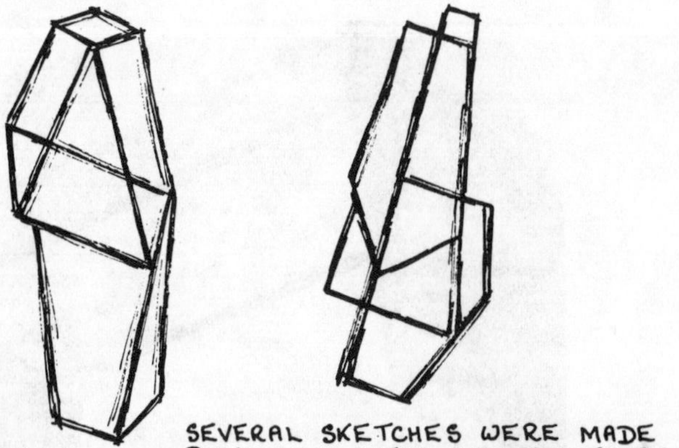

SEVERAL SKETCHES WERE MADE PICKING OUT THE GENERAL SHAPE OF THE ROCK AND THE LINE OF THE TEXTURED SURFACE.

AS AN AID TO FINDING A SOLUTION TO THIS PROBLEM A STUDY WAS MADE OF SEVERAL NATURAL OBJECTS.

THEIR OVERALL SHAPE, STRUCTURE AND TEXTURE WERE CAREFULLY OBSERVED.

FINALLY IT WAS DECIDED TO WORK FROM THIS PIECE OF MOUNTAIN LIMESTONE WHICH IS THE ROCK NATIVE TO A LARGE AREA OF YORKSHIRE NORTH OF SKIPTON.

ITS APPROXIMATE MEASUREMENTS ARE 280 X 120 X 120 AND ITS SURFACE IS DEEPLY DIVIDED BY THE WEATHERING OF THE NATURAL JOINT LINES.

MATERIAL : SQUARE SECTION SILVER WIRE.

THIS SECTION WAS CHOSEN BECAUSE OF THE GENERAL ANGULAR PATTERN AND SHAPE OF THE ROCK.

NOTE HOW THE DESIGN HAS BEEN ALLOWED TO DEVELOP FROM THE FIRST SKETCHES.

AS THE ROCK IS 3-DIMENSIONAL MOCK-UPS WERE THEN MADE TO OBTAIN THIS EFFECT.

PENDANT.	DESIGNED BY T. PETTIT	AIREVILLE SECONDARY SCHOOL, SKIPTON.

SKETCHES AND PRINTING WITH 0·5 TECHNICAL PEN.

THIS PROBLEM WAS SUGGESTED TO A GROUP OF W.R.C.C. CRAFT AND DESIGN TEACHERS BY THEIR JEWELLERY COURSE TUTOR, MRS. JUDITH GUISE, TO WHOM THE AUTHOR IS INDEBTED.

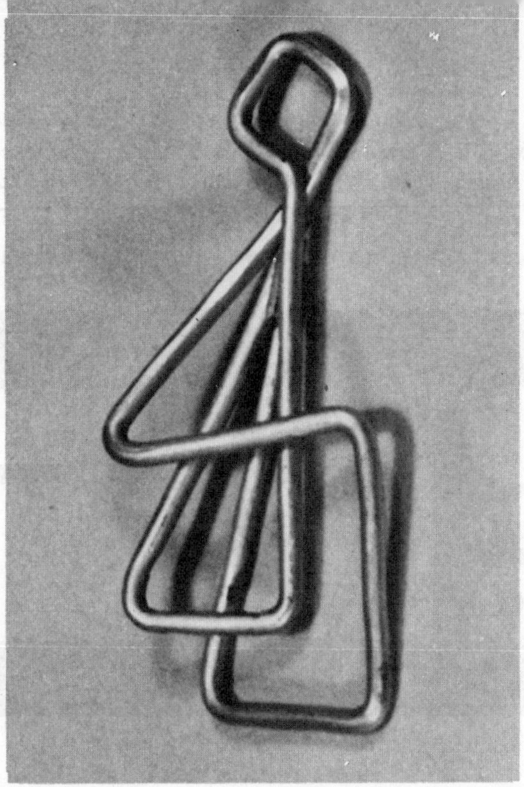

A

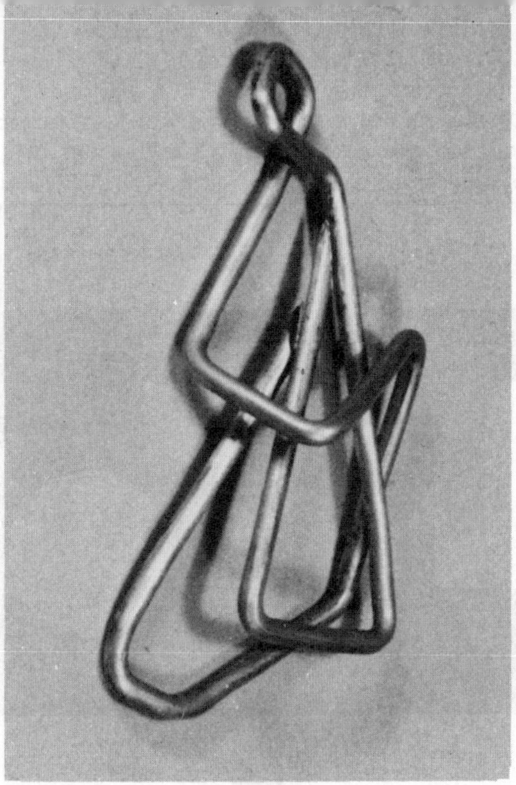

B

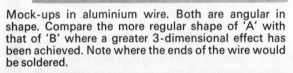

Mock-ups in aluminium wire. Both are angular in shape. Compare the more regular shape of 'A' with that of 'B' where a greater 3-dimensional effect has been achieved. Note where the ends of the wire would be soldered.

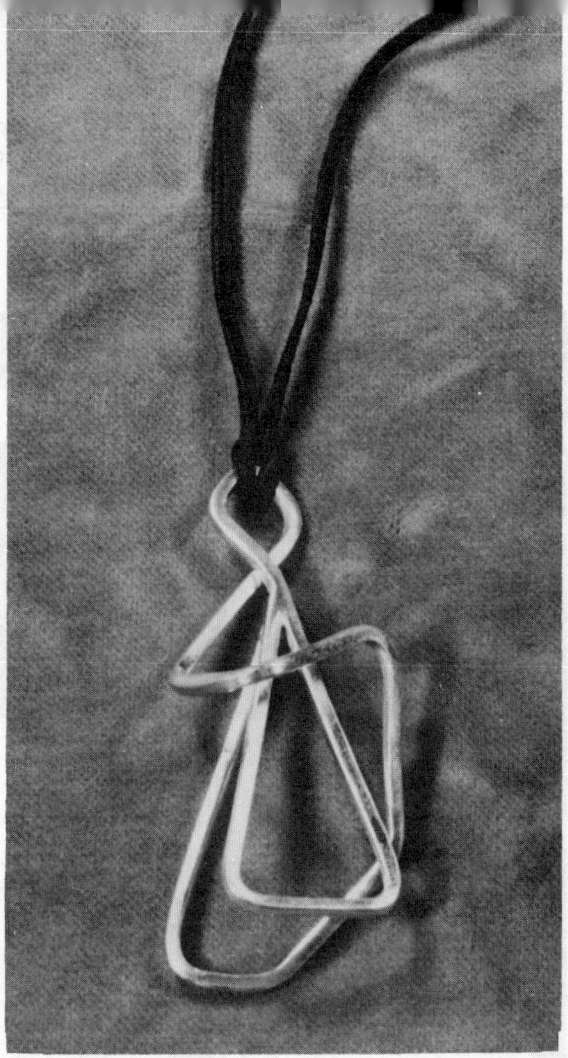

The completed pendant made from silver wire.

The maker's mark and the hallmark of the Sheffield Assay Office 1972. The silver wire used was 2 mm. square in section.

Modern jewellery

Many different pieces of modern jewellery can be designed by the careful arrangement and assembling of repeating units or shapes. The units can be of a very simple regular pattern or be more complex.

The actual joining together of the units into pendants, bracelets and necklaces, etc. requires ingenuity, skill and a sound knowledge of many practical techniques.

It is often possible to design the units so that they can be cut to shape with the minimum of waste and effort.

Designs for work such as this can be illustrated clearly by cutting out the shapes in paper or card and sticking them onto a contrasting paper in various combinations until a suitable arrangement has been found.

This design technique is demonstrated here.

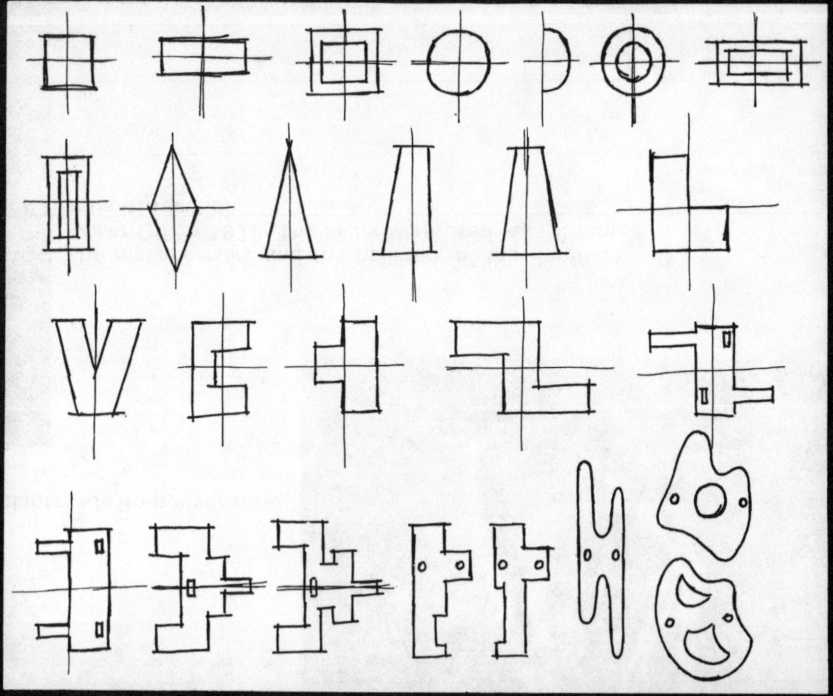

REPEATING UNITS FOR MODERN JEWELLERY.	DESIGNED BY	FORM	DATE	SCHOOL

A NUMBER OF POSSIBLE SHAPES SKETCHED WITH HB PENCIL. NOTE THE USE OF CENTRE LINES.
A SELECTION OF THESE SHAPES CUT OUT FROM WHITE CARD AND STUCK TO A BLACK BACKGROUND. THE POSSIBILITIES OF THE SHAPE THEN BECOME MORE APPARENT.
ARRANGEMENTS OF SHAPES FOR BRACELETS, NECKLACES AND PENDANTS, ETC. AN INFINITE NUMBER OF COMBINATIONS IS POSSIBLE.

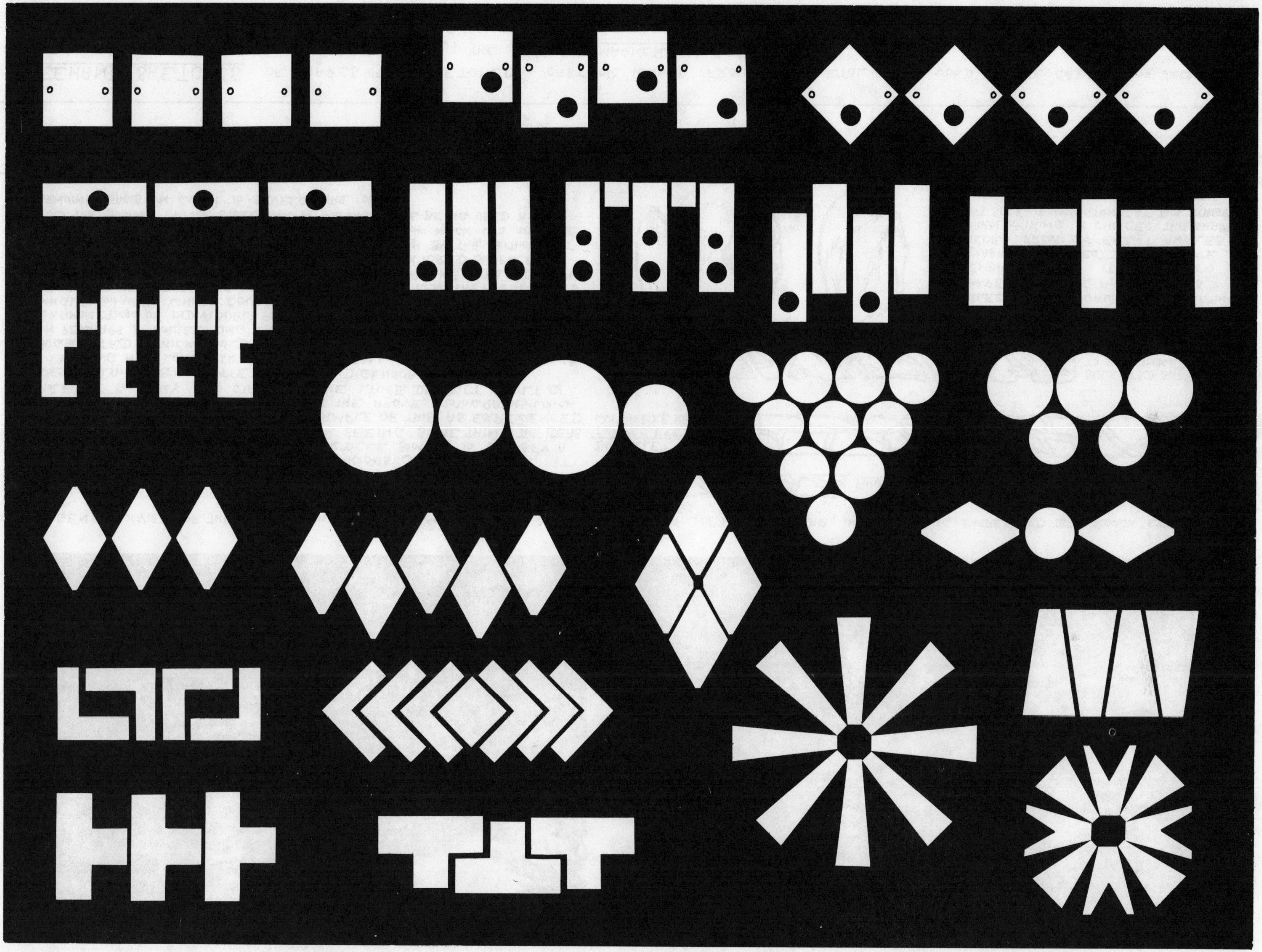

A GENERAL VIEW OF THE AREA WITH THE WALL IN THE FOREGROUND.

DETAIL OF THE IRREGULAR, INTERESTING SHAPES AND THEIR ROUGH TEXTURE.

THE INSPIRATION FOR A PIECE OF WORK, OR THE REALISATION OF DESIGN POSSIBILITIES CAN OCCUR IN VARIOUS CIRCUMSTANCES. IT MAY BE NECESSARY TO MAKE AN ARTICLE SIMPLY TO SATISFY A REQUIREMENT, OR IT MAY BE THAT IN SEEING SOMETHING THE IDEAS FOR A DESIGN COME TO MIND. AN EXAMPLE OF THIS, AS EXPERIENCED BY THE AUTHOR, IS ILLUSTRATED IN THE ABOVE PHOTOGRAPHS WHICH ARE OF A VERY OLD WALL IN THE LAKE DISTRICT BUILT OF WESTMORLAND GREEN SLATE, A ROCK INDIGENOUS TO THE AREA.

LOOKING AT A LONG STRETCH OF THE WALL A RANDOM PATTERN IS SUGGESTED WHICH COULD BE THE BASIS OF AN ETCHED PATTERN ON PERHAPS A FINGER RING OR A BRACELET. ALTERNATIVELY, A CLOSER EXAMINATION OF INDIVIDUAL PIECES OF THE WALL SUGGESTS IDEAS FOR SINGLE SHAPES WHICH COULD BE USED FOR PENDANTS AND BROOCHES, OR LINKED TOGETHER FORMING MORE CONTINUOUS LENGTHS FOR NECKLETS OR BRACLETS. THE RUGGED NATURE OF THE ROCKS AND LANDSCAPE SUGGESTS BOLD PIECES OF WORK WITH HEAVILY TEXTURED SURFACES.

THIS IS SOMETHING STILL BEING WORKED UPON BY THE AUTHOR BUT THE ACCOMPANYING SKETCHES AND PHOTOGRAPHS OF MOCK-UPS INDICATE HOW THE SHAPES OF THE STONEWORK IN THE WALL ARE BEING USED AS A GENUINE BASIS ON WHICH TO DEVELOP THE IDEA.

FINGER RING - ONE OF MANY POSSIBLE COMBINATIONS.

BRACELET - CHOSEN SHAPES RESTRICTED WITHIN SIZE REQUIRED.

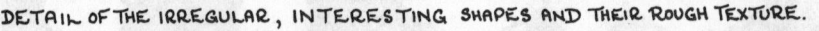

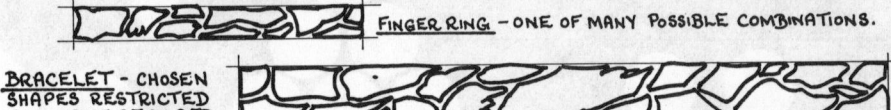

SELECTED SHAPES TO BE LINKED TOGETHER.

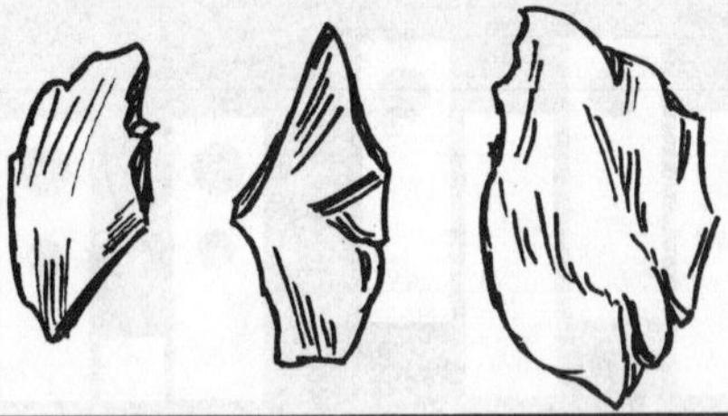

SELECTED INDIVIDUAL PIECES CREATING SHAPES SUITABLE FOR BROOCHES, PENDANTS, ETC. IT IS OFTEN ADVISABLE TO VIEW THE SEPARATE PIECES FROM DIFFERENT ANGLES WHEN MAKING A CHOICE. THE SHAPE, NOT SIZE, IS IMPORTANT AT THIS STAGE.

DESIGNS FOR JEWELLERY.	T. PETTIT	21 : 10 : 72	AIREVILLE SCHOOL.

FREEHAND SKETCHES OF SHAPES TO BE ETCHED, CAST, OR RAISED FROM SHEETMETAL TO BE USED IN THE CREATION OF JEWELLERY. THE SKETCHES WERE DRAWN WITH A FIBRE TIP PEN, THE LAKELAND MARKER 33 FINE - BLACK.

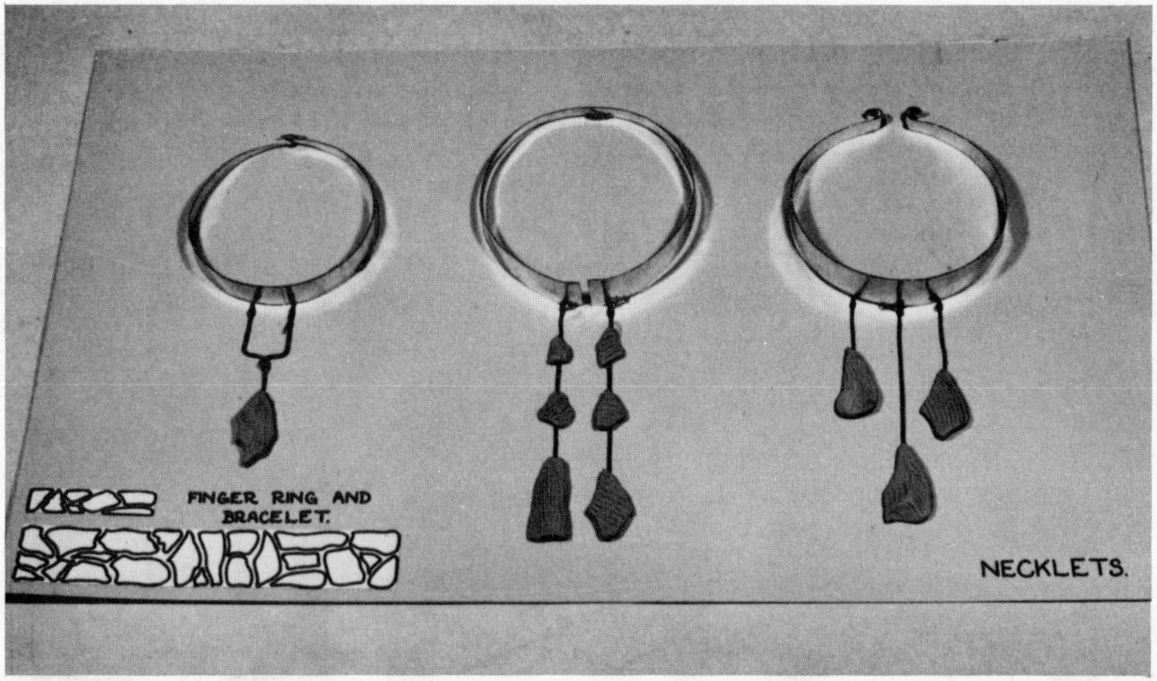
FINGER RING AND
BRACELET.
NECKLETS.

The models of the finger ring and bracelet are of thin card with the proposed etched pattern drawn with a black fibre tip pen. The shapes have been selected from the photographs and fitted together to cover the whole of the required area. The shapes are not necessarily in the same arrangement or the same way up as they appear on the photograph.

The mock-ups for the necklets are of tinplate, soft iron wire and plasticine. The 'drops' could be cast between charcoal blocks suitably hollowed out and wired together, or raised from sheet metal and the texture of the front surface obtained by etching or engraving. The texture reflects the bedded structure of the slate which enables it to be split into thin slabs for facing buildings and for roof tiles.

Work designed in this way, from a simple beginning brought to a successful conclusion, brings great personal satisfaction and a lasting memory of the pleasant circumstances in which it was first conceived.

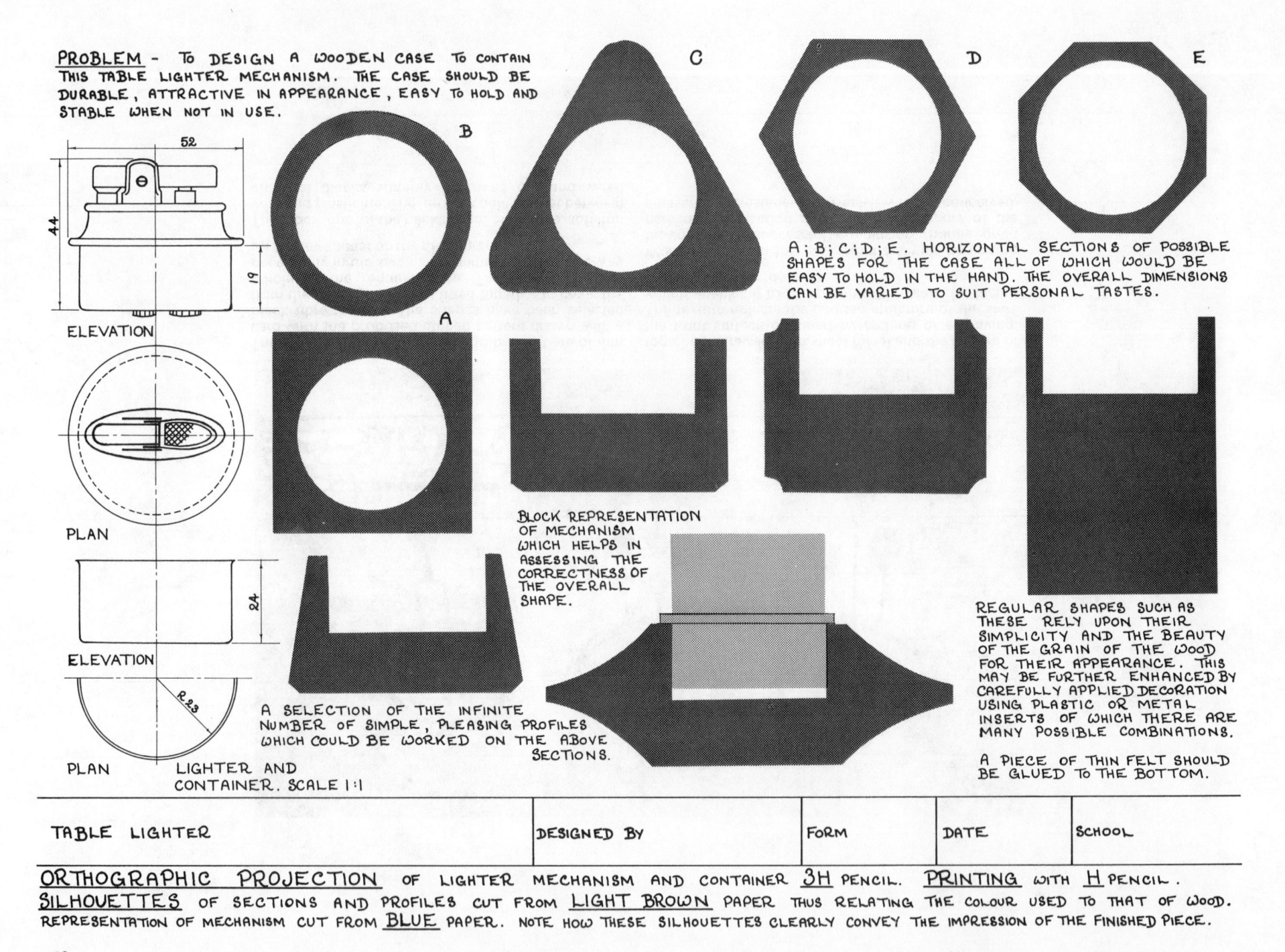

PROBLEM - TO DESIGN A WOODEN CASE TO CONTAIN THIS TABLE LIGHTER MECHANISM. THE CASE SHOULD BE DURABLE, ATTRACTIVE IN APPEARANCE, EASY TO HOLD AND STABLE WHEN NOT IN USE.

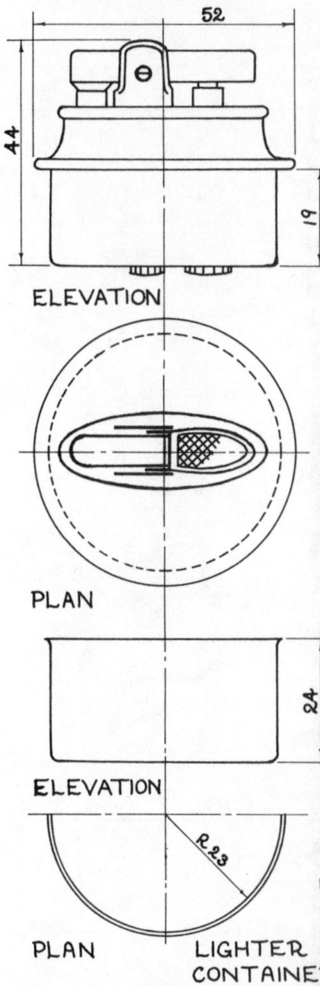

52
44
19
ELEVATION
PLAN
24
ELEVATION
R.23
PLAN
LIGHTER AND CONTAINER. SCALE 1:1

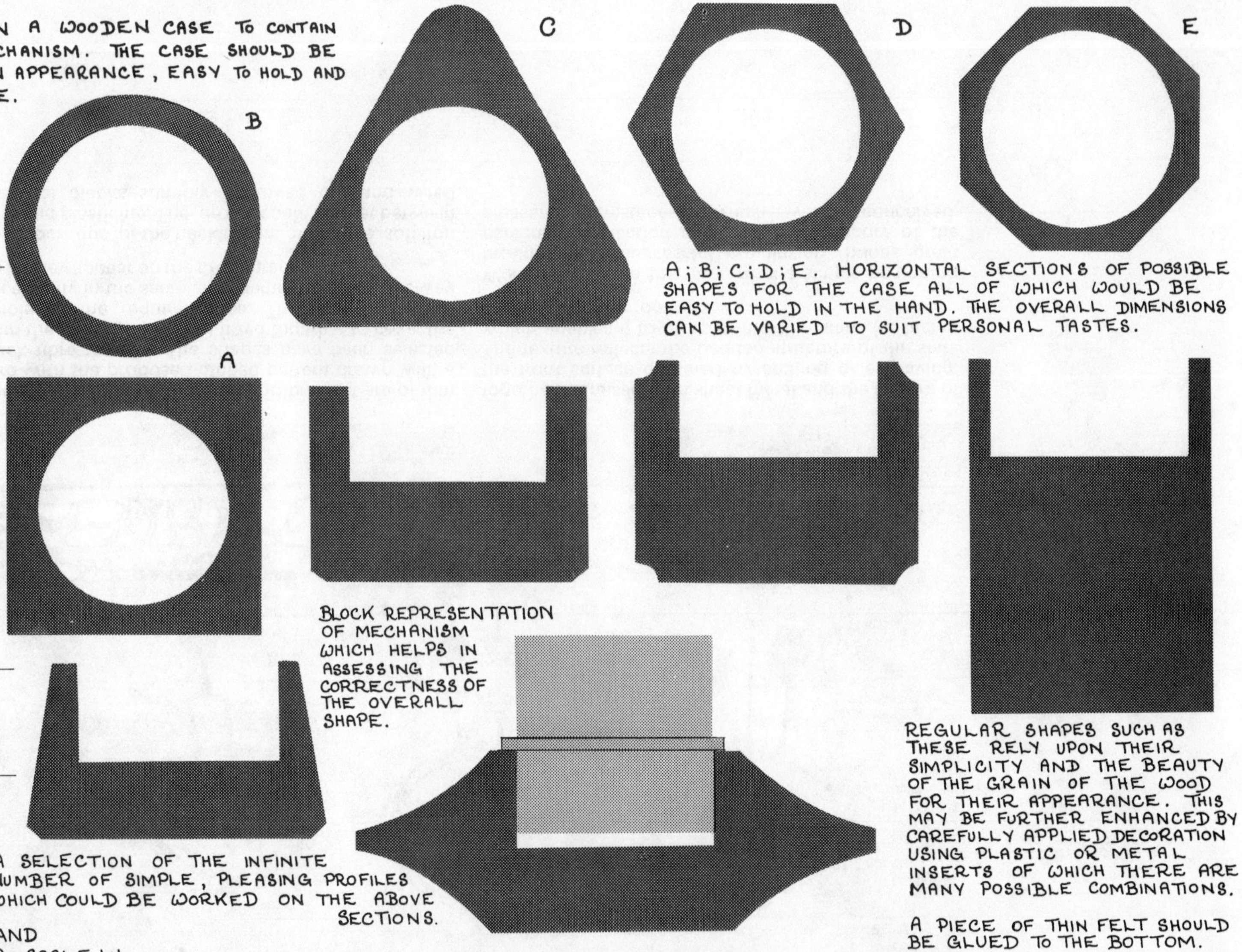

A
B
C
D
E
A; B; C; D; E. HORIZONTAL SECTIONS OF POSSIBLE SHAPES FOR THE CASE ALL OF WHICH WOULD BE EASY TO HOLD IN THE HAND. THE OVERALL DIMENSIONS CAN BE VARIED TO SUIT PERSONAL TASTES.
BLOCK REPRESENTATION OF MECHANISM WHICH HELPS IN ASSESSING THE CORRECTNESS OF THE OVERALL SHAPE.
A SELECTION OF THE INFINITE NUMBER OF SIMPLE, PLEASING PROFILES WHICH COULD BE WORKED ON THE ABOVE SECTIONS.
REGULAR SHAPES SUCH AS THESE RELY UPON THEIR SIMPLICITY AND THE BEAUTY OF THE GRAIN OF THE WOOD FOR THEIR APPEARANCE. THIS MAY BE FURTHER ENHANCED BY CAREFULLY APPLIED DECORATION USING PLASTIC OR METAL INSERTS OF WHICH THERE ARE MANY POSSIBLE COMBINATIONS.
A PIECE OF THIN FELT SHOULD BE GLUED TO THE BOTTOM.

TABLE LIGHTER	DESIGNED BY	FORM	DATE	SCHOOL

ORTHOGRAPHIC PROJECTION OF LIGHTER MECHANISM AND CONTAINER 3H PENCIL. PRINTING WITH H PENCIL.
SILHOUETTES OF SECTIONS AND PROFILES CUT FROM LIGHT BROWN PAPER THUS RELATING THE COLOUR USED TO THAT OF WOOD. REPRESENTATION OF MECHANISM CUT FROM BLUE PAPER. NOTE HOW THESE SILHOUETTES CLEARLY CONVEY THE IMPRESSION OF THE FINISHED PIECE.

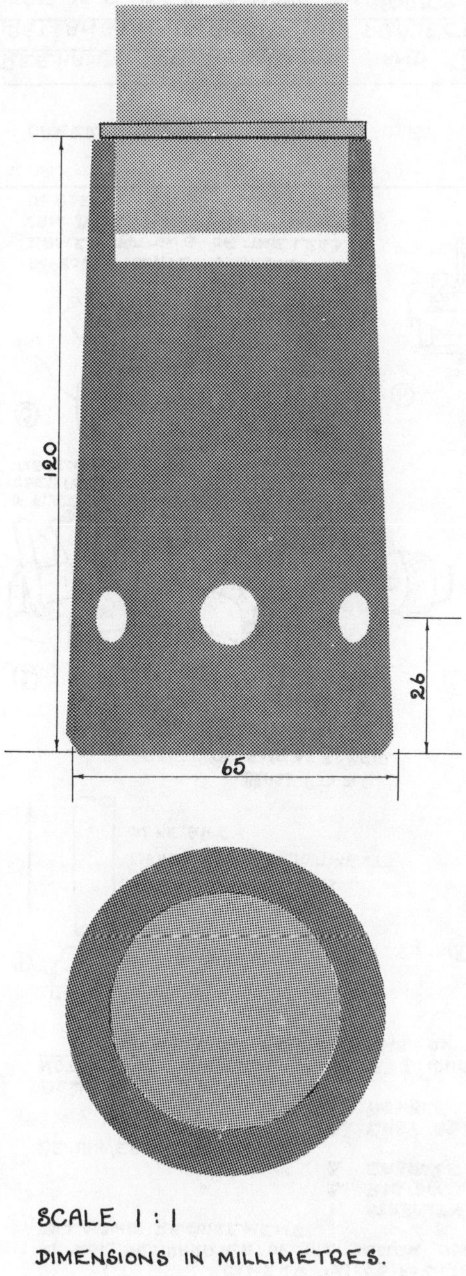
120
26
65
SCALE 1 : 1
DIMENSIONS IN MILLIMETRES.

The lighter mechanism and its container.

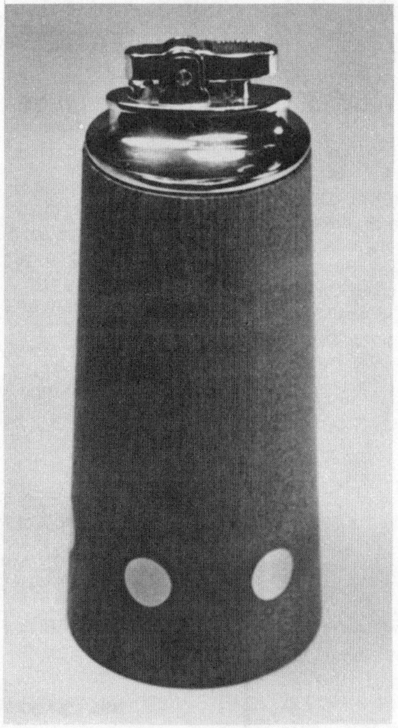

After considering the other ideas this was selected as the final design.

The finished piece is impressive; it can be held firmly due to its height and the base is broad enough to make it very stable.

Material: Teak with aluminium inserts.

DESIGN BRIEF.

CAMERA TRIPOD FOR TABLE USE.

IN YOUR PREPARATION OF THE DESIGN YOU SHOULD OBSERVE THE FOLLOWING REQUIREMENTS.

1. STABILITY.
2. RIGIDITY.
3. EASE OF ADJUSTMENT - WHICH SHOULD BE UNIVERSAL IF POSSIBLE.
4. EASY ADJUSTMENT OF HEIGHT.
5. POSSIBLE USE WITH CINE CAMERA AS WELL AS STILL CAMERA.

NOTE: MOST CAMERAS HAVE A ¼" WHITWORTH SOCKET AS STANDARD IN THE BASE FOR MOUNTING ON TRIPODS.

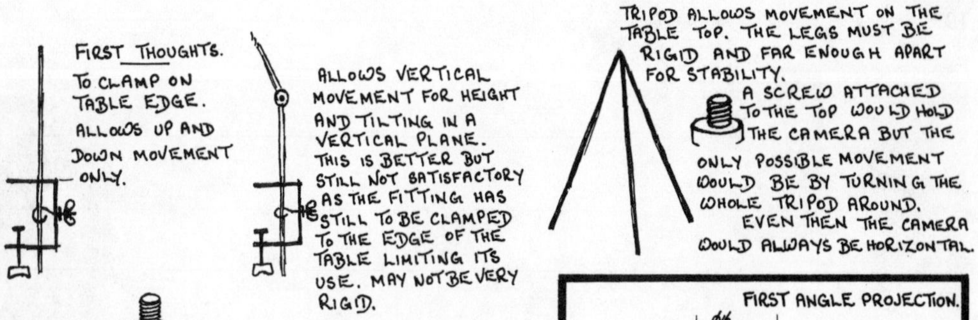
FIRST THOUGHTS.
TO CLAMP ON TABLE EDGE.
ALLOWS UP AND DOWN MOVEMENT ONLY.
ALLOWS VERTICAL MOVEMENT FOR HEIGHT AND TILTING IN A VERTICAL PLANE. THIS IS BETTER BUT STILL NOT SATISFACTORY AS THE FITTING HAS STILL TO BE CLAMPED TO THE EDGE OF THE TABLE LIMITING ITS USE. MAY NOT BE VERY RIGID.
TRIPOD ALLOWS MOVEMENT ON THE TABLE TOP. THE LEGS MUST BE RIGID AND FAR ENOUGH APART FOR STABILITY.
A SCREW ATTACHED TO THE TOP WOULD HOLD THE CAMERA BUT THE ONLY POSSIBLE MOVEMENT WOULD BE BY TURNING THE WHOLE TRIPOD AROUND.
EVEN THEN THE CAMERA WOULD ALWAYS BE HORIZONTAL.

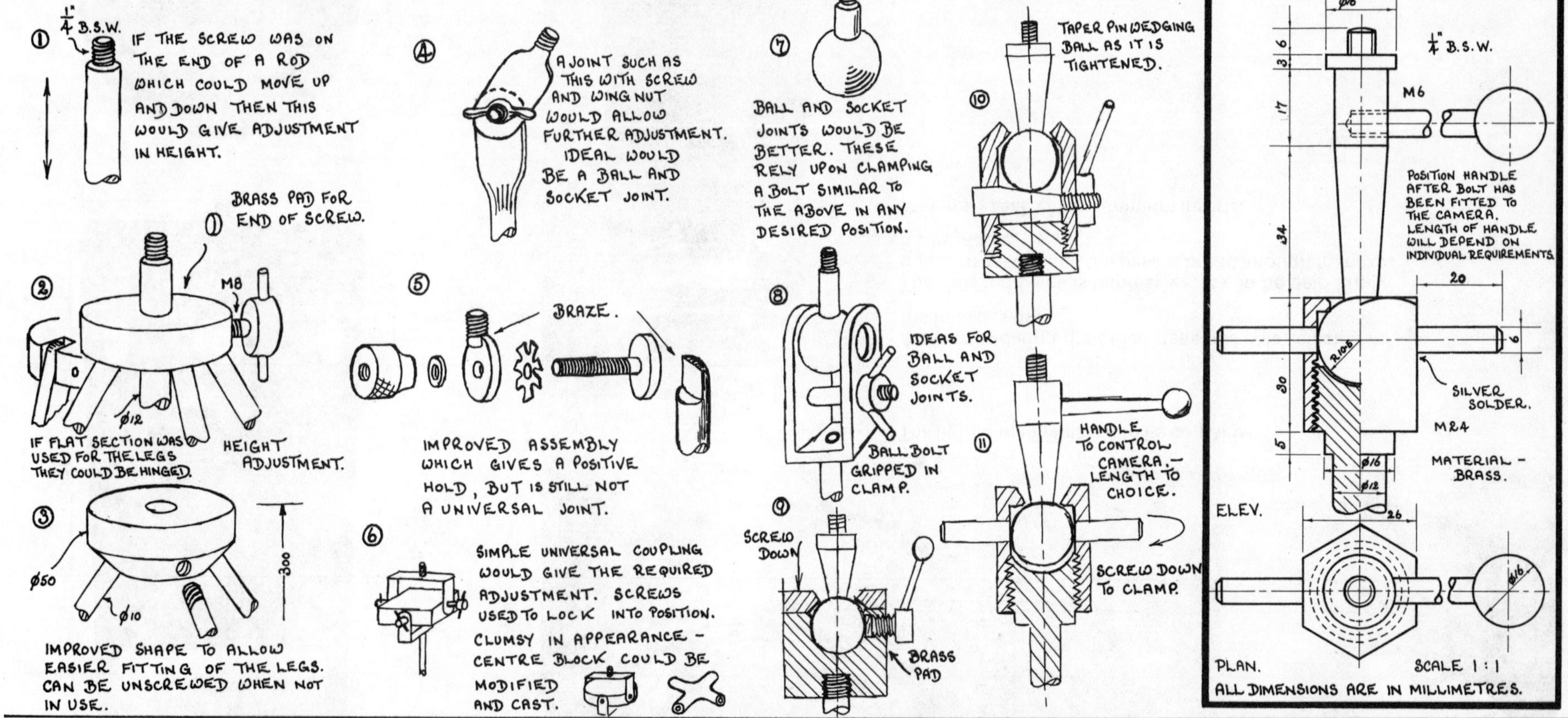
①
¼" B.S.W.
IF THE SCREW WAS ON THE END OF A ROD WHICH COULD MOVE UP AND DOWN THEN THIS WOULD GIVE ADJUSTMENT IN HEIGHT.
②
BRASS PAD FOR END OF SCREW.
M8
ø12
IF FLAT SECTION WAS USED FOR THE LEGS THEY COULD BE HINGED.
HEIGHT ADJUSTMENT.
③
ø50
300
ø10
IMPROVED SHAPE TO ALLOW EASIER FITTING OF THE LEGS. CAN BE UNSCREWED WHEN NOT IN USE.
④
A JOINT SUCH AS THIS WITH SCREW AND WING NUT WOULD ALLOW FURTHER ADJUSTMENT.
IDEAL WOULD BE A BALL AND SOCKET JOINT.
⑤
BRAZE.
IMPROVED ASSEMBLY WHICH GIVES A POSITIVE HOLD, BUT IS STILL NOT A UNIVERSAL JOINT.
⑥
SIMPLE UNIVERSAL COUPLING WOULD GIVE THE REQUIRED ADJUSTMENT. SCREWS USED TO LOCK INTO POSITION.
CLUMSY IN APPEARANCE - CENTRE BLOCK COULD BE MODIFIED AND CAST.
⑦
BALL AND SOCKET JOINTS WOULD BE BETTER. THESE RELY UPON CLAMPING A BOLT SIMILAR TO THE ABOVE IN ANY DESIRED POSITION.
⑧
IDEAS FOR BALL AND SOCKET JOINTS.
BALL BOLT GRIPPED IN CLAMP.
⑨
SCREW DOWN
BRASS PAD
⑩
TAPER PIN WEDGING BALL AS IT IS TIGHTENED.
⑪
HANDLE TO CONTROL CAMERA. - LENGTH TO CHOICE.
SCREW DOWN TO CLAMP.
FIRST ANGLE PROJECTION.
ø16
¼" B.S.W.
6
3
17
M6
34
POSITION HANDLE AFTER BOLT HAS BEEN FITTED TO THE CAMERA. LENGTH OF HANDLE WILL DEPEND ON INDIVIDUAL REQUIREMENTS.
20
R10.5
6
30
SILVER SOLDER.
M24
5
ø16
ø12
MATERIAL - BRASS.
ELEV.
26
ø16
PLAN.
SCALE 1:1
ALL DIMENSIONS ARE IN MILLIMETRES.

CAMERA TRIPOD FOR TABLE USE.	DESIGNED BY	FORM	DATE	SCHOOL.

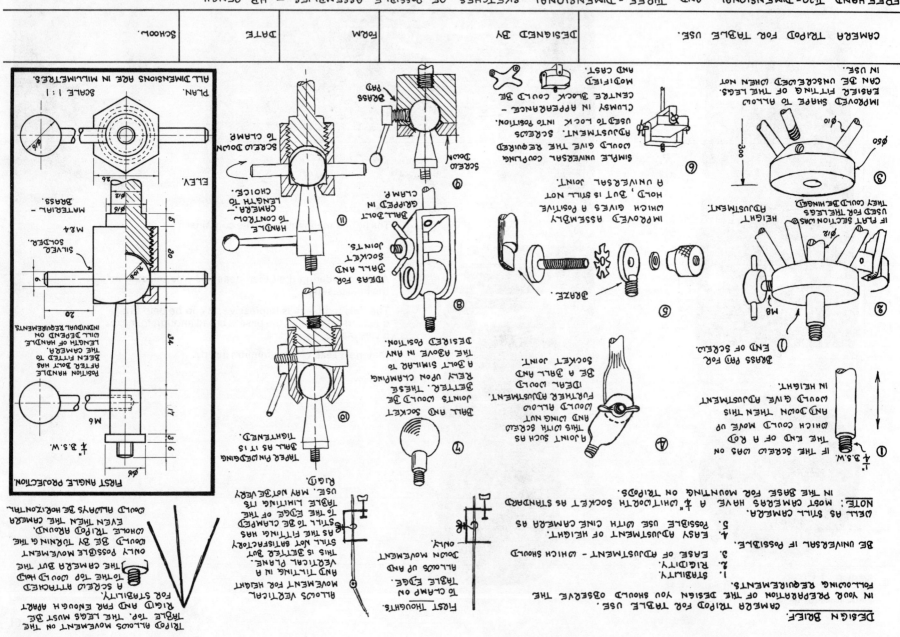

<u>FREEHAND TWO-DIMENSIONAL</u> AND <u>THREE-DIMENSIONAL</u> SKETCHES OF POSSIBLE ASSEMBLIES — <u>HB</u> PENCIL.

<u>FIRST ANGLE ORTHOGRAPHIC PROJECTION</u> WITH <u>SECTIONAL ELEVATION</u> OF THE FINAL DESIGN — <u>3H</u> PENCIL. <u>PRINTING</u> AND <u>DIMENSIONS</u> - <u>H</u> PENCIL.

THERE IS A NEED TO MAKE AN <u>ORTHOGRAPHIC PROJECTION</u> IN SUCH CASES TO ENSURE CORRECT DIMENSIONS AND FITTING.

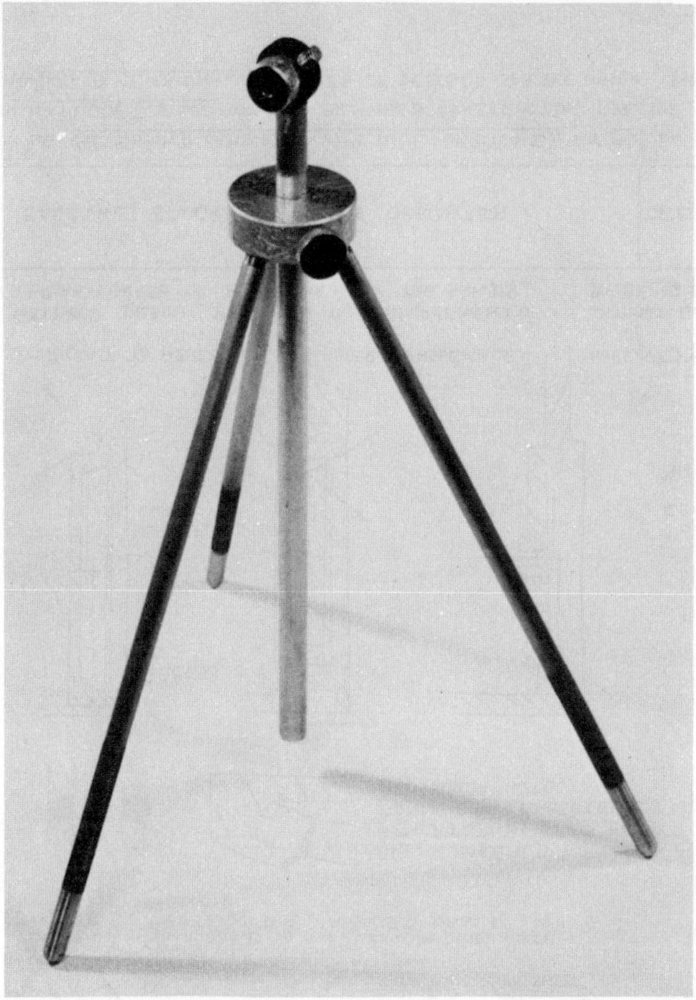

Simple tripod and head as design 5. Adjustment is limited to change in height and camera angle within a vertical plane.

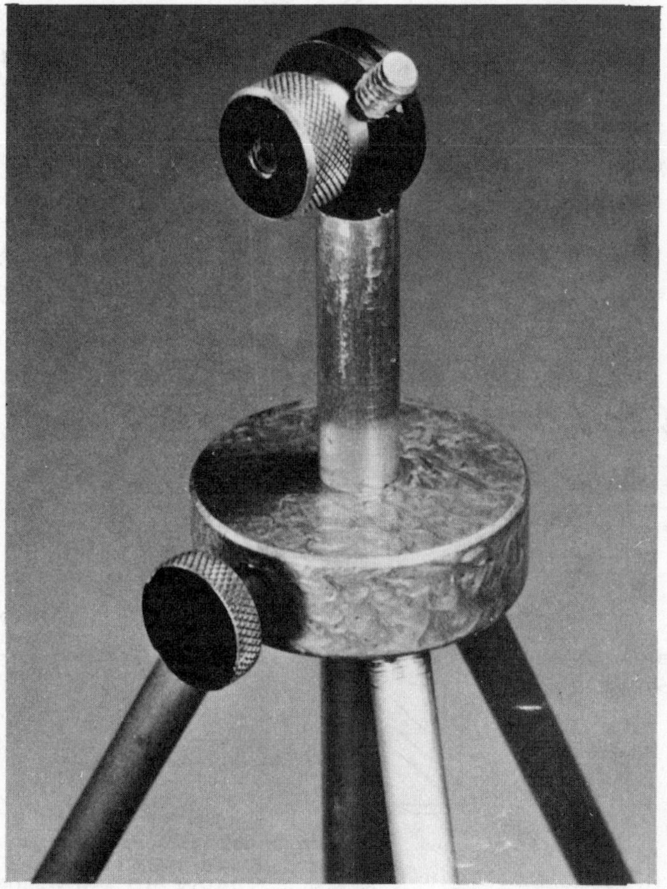

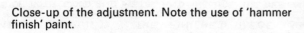

Close-up of the adjustment. Note the use of 'hammer finish' paint.

Ball and socket joint which allows more selective positioning of the camera.

DESIGN BRIEF. YOU ARE TO DESIGN A CLOCK CASE FOR THE BATTERY MOVEMENT SUPPLIED. THE FINISHED PIECE SHOULD BE OF MODERN DESIGN AND MAY BE FREE-STANDING OR WALL MOUNTED. YOUR SOLUTION SHOULD INVOLVE THE USE OF BOTH WOOD AND METAL AND INCLUDE THE DESIGN FOR THE HANDS OF THE CLOCK.

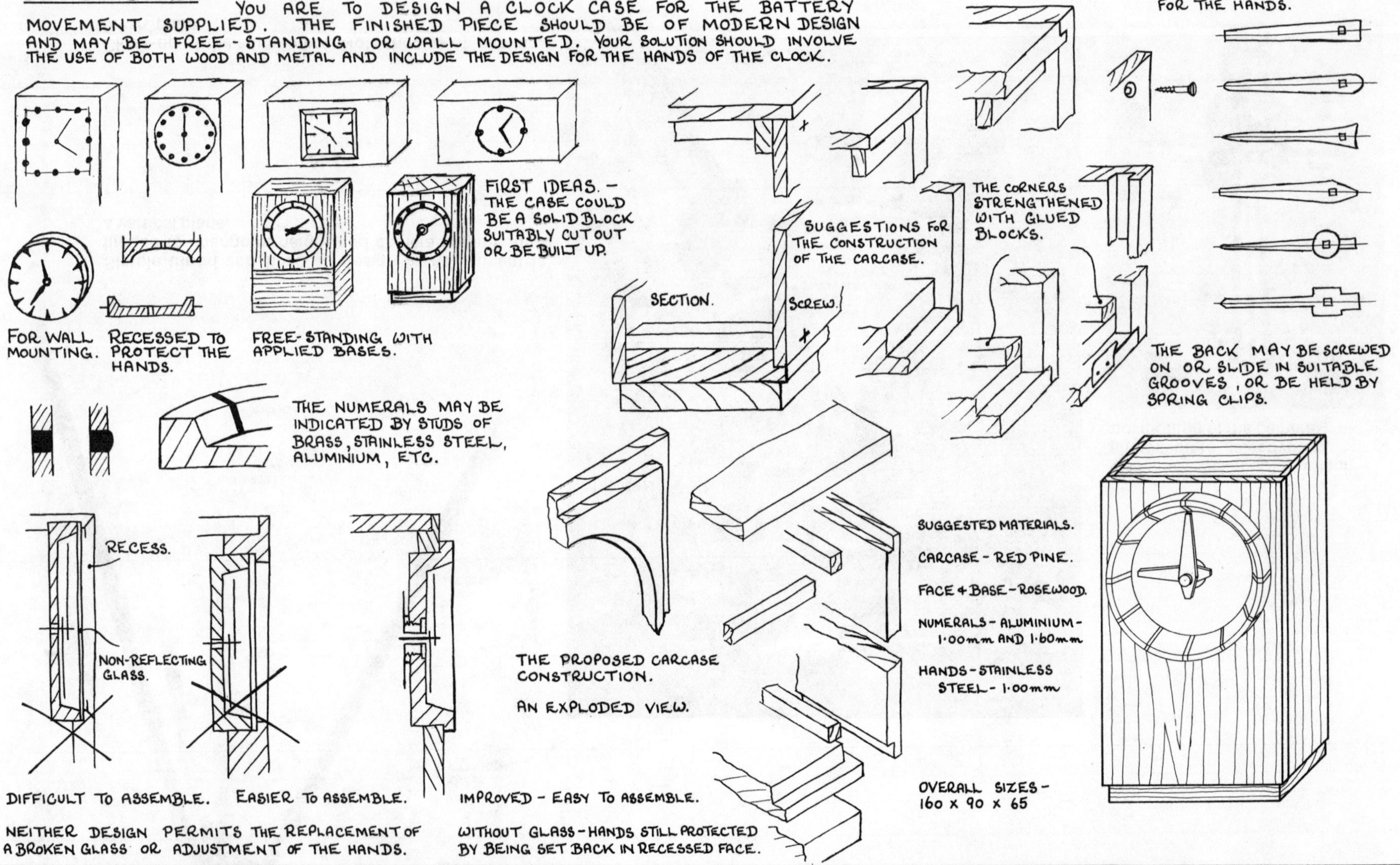
POSSIBLE SHAPES FOR THE HANDS.
FIRST IDEAS. - THE CASE COULD BE A SOLID BLOCK SUITABLY CUT OUT OR BE BUILT UP.
SUGGESTIONS FOR THE CONSTRUCTION OF THE CARCASE.
THE CORNERS STRENGTHENED WITH GLUED BLOCKS.
SECTION.
SCREW.
FOR WALL MOUNTING.
RECESSED TO PROTECT THE HANDS.
FREE-STANDING WITH APPLIED BASES.
THE BACK MAY BE SCREWED ON OR SLIDE IN SUITABLE GROOVES, OR BE HELD BY SPRING CLIPS.
THE NUMERALS MAY BE INDICATED BY STUDS OF BRASS, STAINLESS STEEL, ALUMINIUM, ETC.
RECESS.
NON-REFLECTING GLASS.
THE PROPOSED CARCASE CONSTRUCTION.
AN EXPLODED VIEW.
SUGGESTED MATERIALS.
CARCASE - RED PINE.
FACE + BASE - ROSEWOOD.
NUMERALS - ALUMINIUM - 1·00mm AND 1·60mm
HANDS - STAINLESS STEEL - 1·00mm
OVERALL SIZES - 160 x 90 x 65
DIFFICULT TO ASSEMBLE.
EASIER TO ASSEMBLE.
IMPROVED - EASY TO ASSEMBLE.
NEITHER DESIGN PERMITS THE REPLACEMENT OF A BROKEN GLASS OR ADJUSTMENT OF THE HANDS.
WITHOUT GLASS - HANDS STILL PROTECTED BY BEING SET BACK IN RECESSED FACE.

ELECTRIC CLOCK - BATTERY OPERATED.	DESIGNED BY	FORM	DATE	SCHOOL

SIMPLE FREEHAND CABINET OBLIQUE SKETCHES AT 45° OF POSSIBLE DESIGNS. SECTIONAL DETAILS OF THE SELECTED DESIGN ALSO IN CABINET OBLIQUE PLUS AN EXPLODED VIEW OF THE PROPOSED CONSTRUCTION FOR THE CASE IN FREEHAND ISOMETRIC. TWO-DIMENSIONAL SECTIONAL SKETCHES OF THE FACE ASSEMBLY AND TWO-DIMENSIONAL SKETCHES OF DESIGNS FOR THE HANDS. THE FINAL DESIGN DRAWN WITH INSTRUMENTS IN CABINET OBLIQUE AND 1ST. ANGLE ORTHOGRAPHIC.

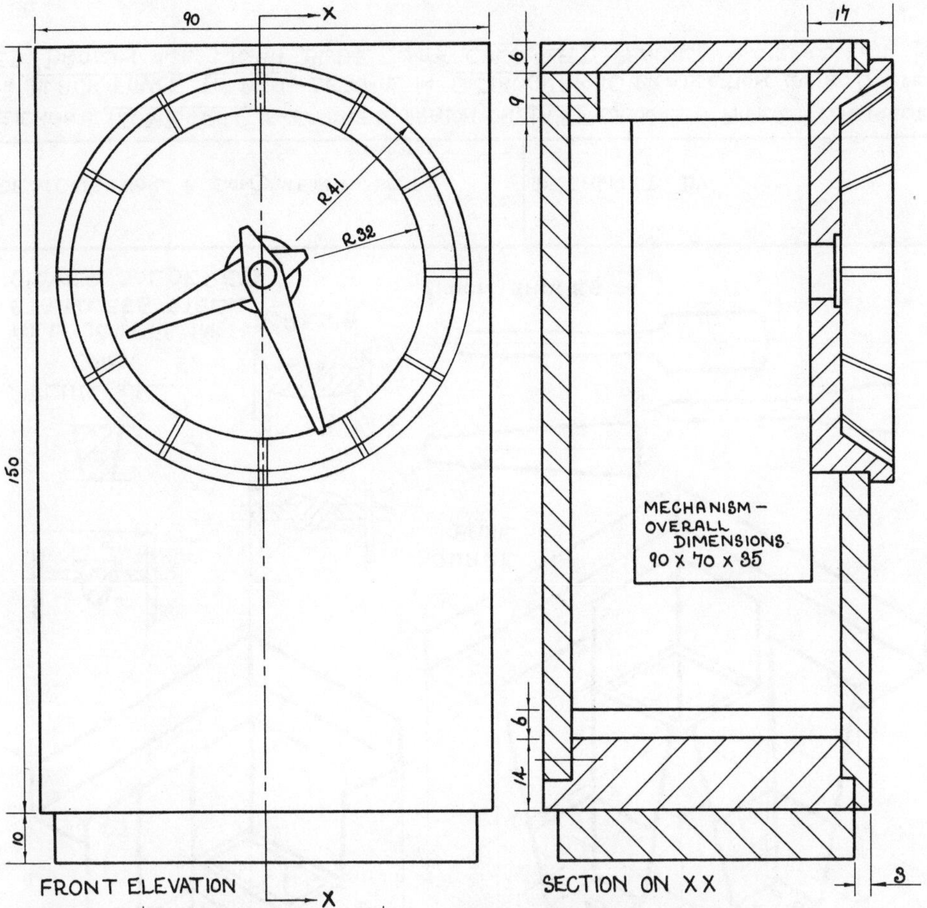
90
X
17
6
9
R41
R32
150
10
MECHANISM – OVERALL DIMENSIONS 90 X 70 X 35
6
14
3
X

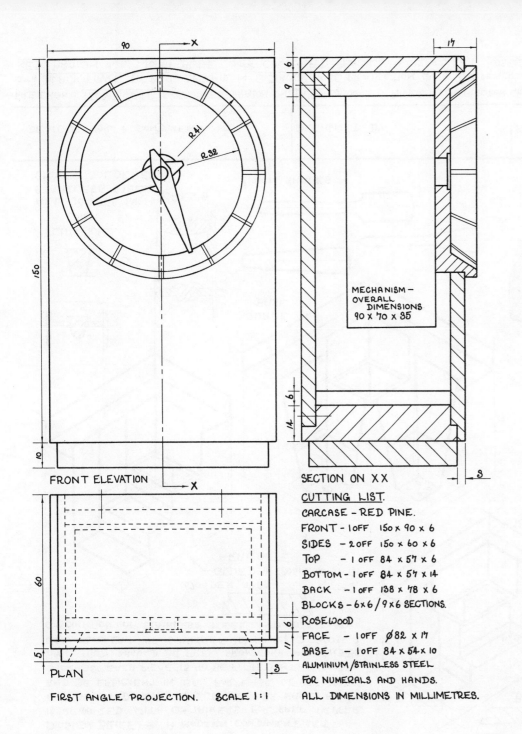

FRONT ELEVATION

SECTION ON XX

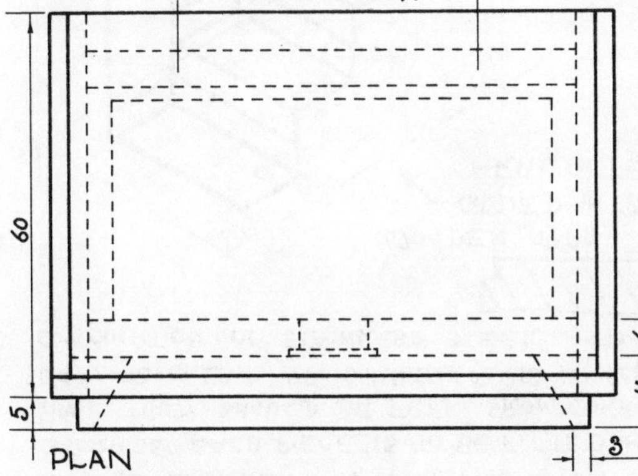
60
5
6
11
3

PLAN

FIRST ANGLE PROJECTION. SCALE 1:1

CUTTING LIST.

CARCASE – RED PINE.

FRONT – 1 OFF 150 x 90 x 6

SIDES – 2 OFF 150 x 60 x 6

TOP – 1 OFF 84 x 57 x 6

BOTTOM – 1 OFF 84 x 57 x 14

BACK – 1 OFF 138 x 78 x 6

BLOCKS – 6x6 / 9x6 SECTIONS.

ROSEWOOD

FACE – 1 OFF Ø82 x 17

BASE – 1 OFF 84 x 54 x 10

ALUMINIUM / STAINLESS STEEL FOR NUMERALS AND HANDS.

ALL DIMENSIONS IN MILLIMETRES.

EVER READ
SUPER
SP2

The clock mechanism and battery.

The completed clock. You can trace its development from the first simple sketches. The contrasting woods and metals combine to give a pleasing design.

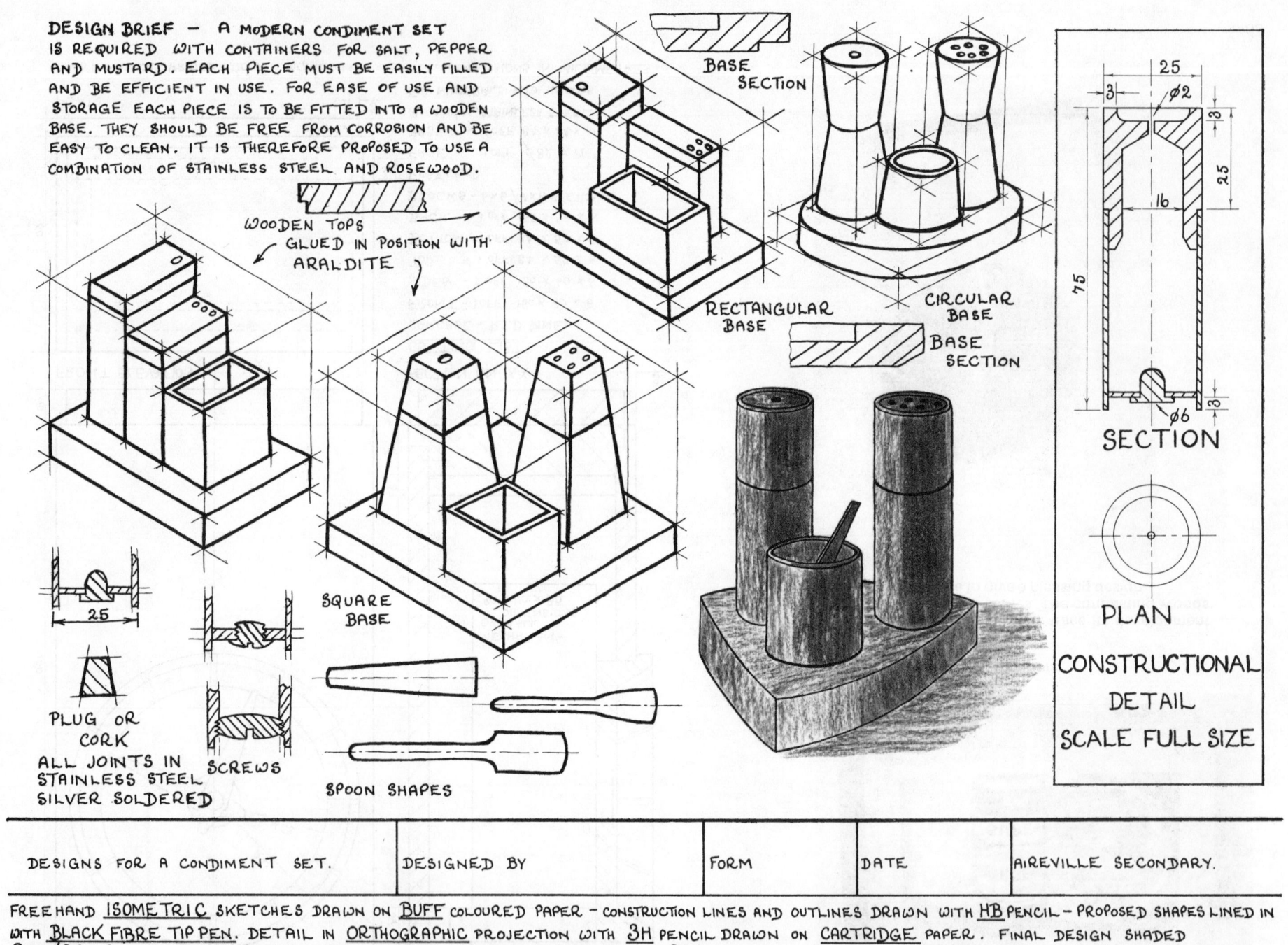

DESIGN BRIEF – A MODERN CONDIMENT SET IS REQUIRED WITH CONTAINERS FOR SALT, PEPPER AND MUSTARD. EACH PIECE MUST BE EASILY FILLED AND BE EFFICIENT IN USE. FOR EASE OF USE AND STORAGE EACH PIECE IS TO BE FITTED INTO A WOODEN BASE. THEY SHOULD BE FREE FROM CORROSION AND BE EASY TO CLEAN. IT IS THEREFORE PROPOSED TO USE A COMBINATION OF STAINLESS STEEL AND ROSEWOOD.

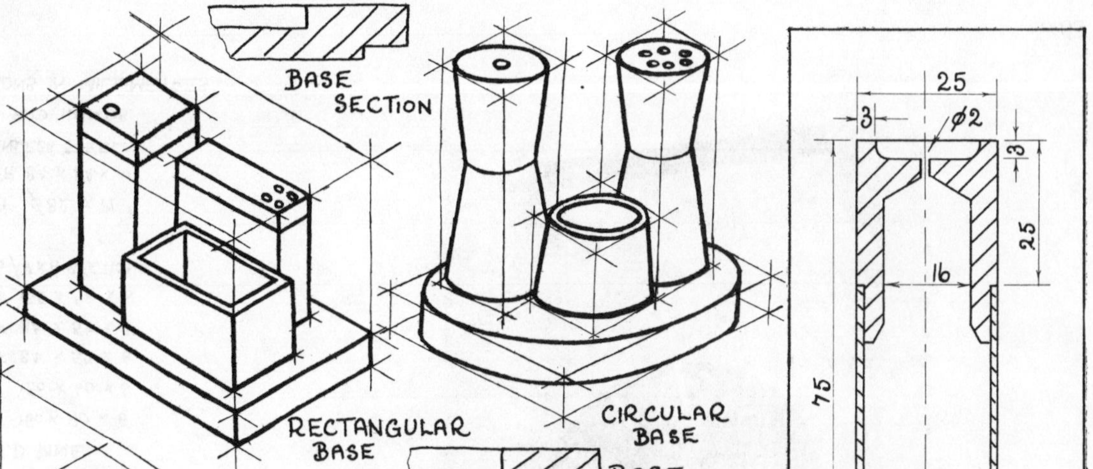
BASE
SECTION
RECTANGULAR
BASE
CIRCULAR
BASE

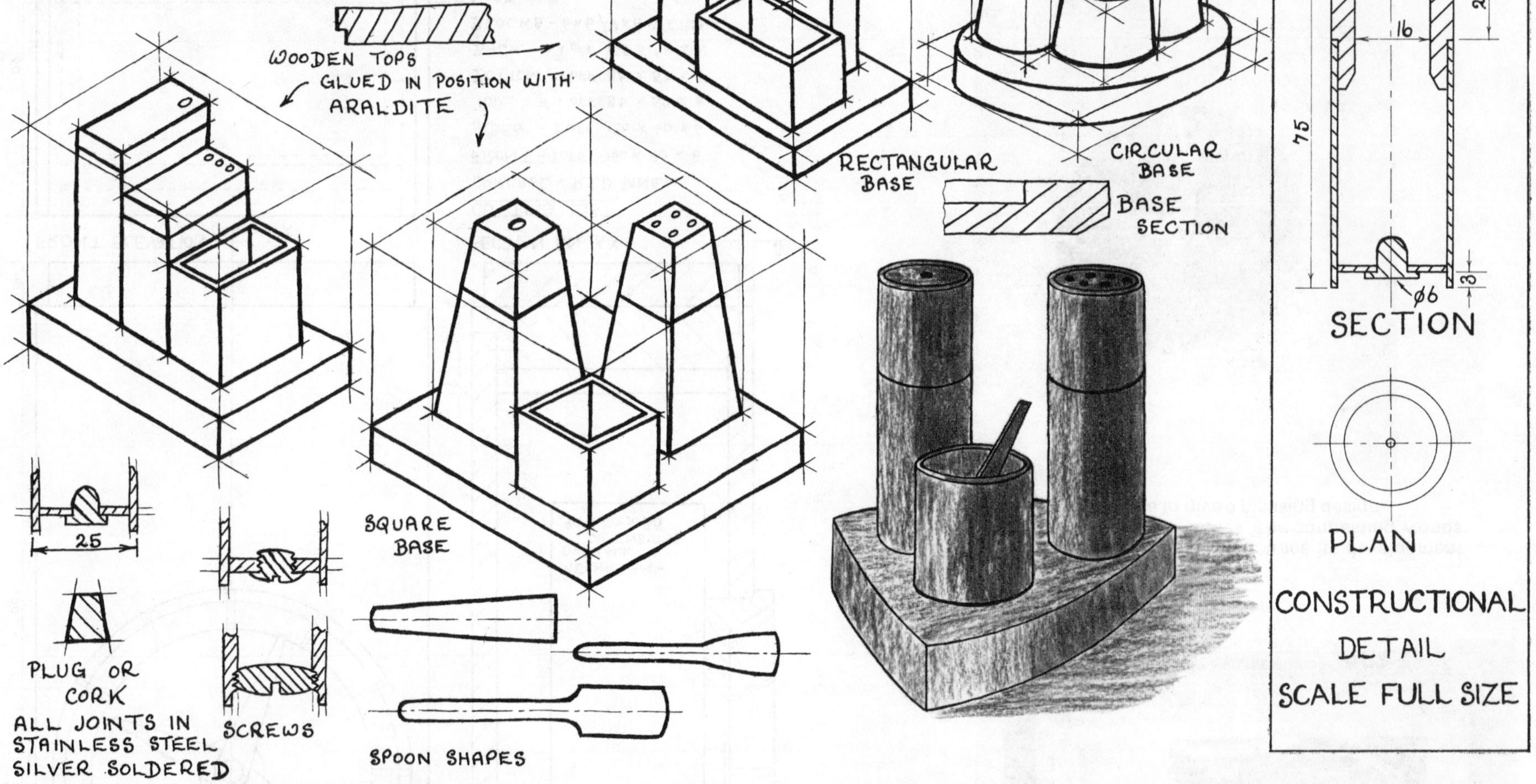
WOODEN TOPS
GLUED IN POSITION WITH
ARALDITE
BASE
SECTION
25
3
ϕ2
3
25
16
75
3
ϕ6
SECTION
PLAN
CONSTRUCTIONAL
DETAIL
SCALE FULL SIZE
25
SQUARE
BASE
PLUG OR
CORK
ALL JOINTS IN
STAINLESS STEEL
SILVER SOLDERED
SCREWS
SPOON SHAPES

DESIGNS FOR A CONDIMENT SET.	DESIGNED BY	FORM	DATE	AIREVILLE SECONDARY.

FREEHAND ISOMETRIC SKETCHES DRAWN ON BUFF COLOURED PAPER – CONSTRUCTION LINES AND OUTLINES DRAWN WITH HB PENCIL – PROPOSED SHAPES LINED IN WITH BLACK FIBRE TIP PEN. DETAIL IN ORTHOGRAPHIC PROJECTION WITH 3H PENCIL DRAWN ON CARTRIDGE PAPER. FINAL DESIGN SHADED RED/BROWN AND LIGHT BLUE WITH COLOURED PENCILS TO REPRESENT ROSEWOOD AND STAINLESS STEEL.

Full size mock-up of each member in softwood. This indicates how well each piece is proportioned in relation to one another and to the base. At this stage it is possible to see whether or not the final overall shape will be of good appearance.

A more realistic impression has been gained by adding colour. The proportions of the wooden and metal parts can be seen clearly.
Aluminium paint was used to give the effect of stainless steel and (red/brown) poster colour for the rosewood.

This is the realization of the design. The work can be evaluated easily by comparing it with the design sheet and the mock-ups.

DESIGN BRIEF - YOU ARE REQUIRED TO DESIGN A PEPPER MILL. THE MECHANISM HAS BEEN PURCHASED AND ITS DESIGN AND DIMENSIONS ARE AS SHOWN. MINOR MODIFICATIONS TO THE MECHANISM MAY BE MADE IF YOU CONSIDER THIS TO BE NECESSARY.

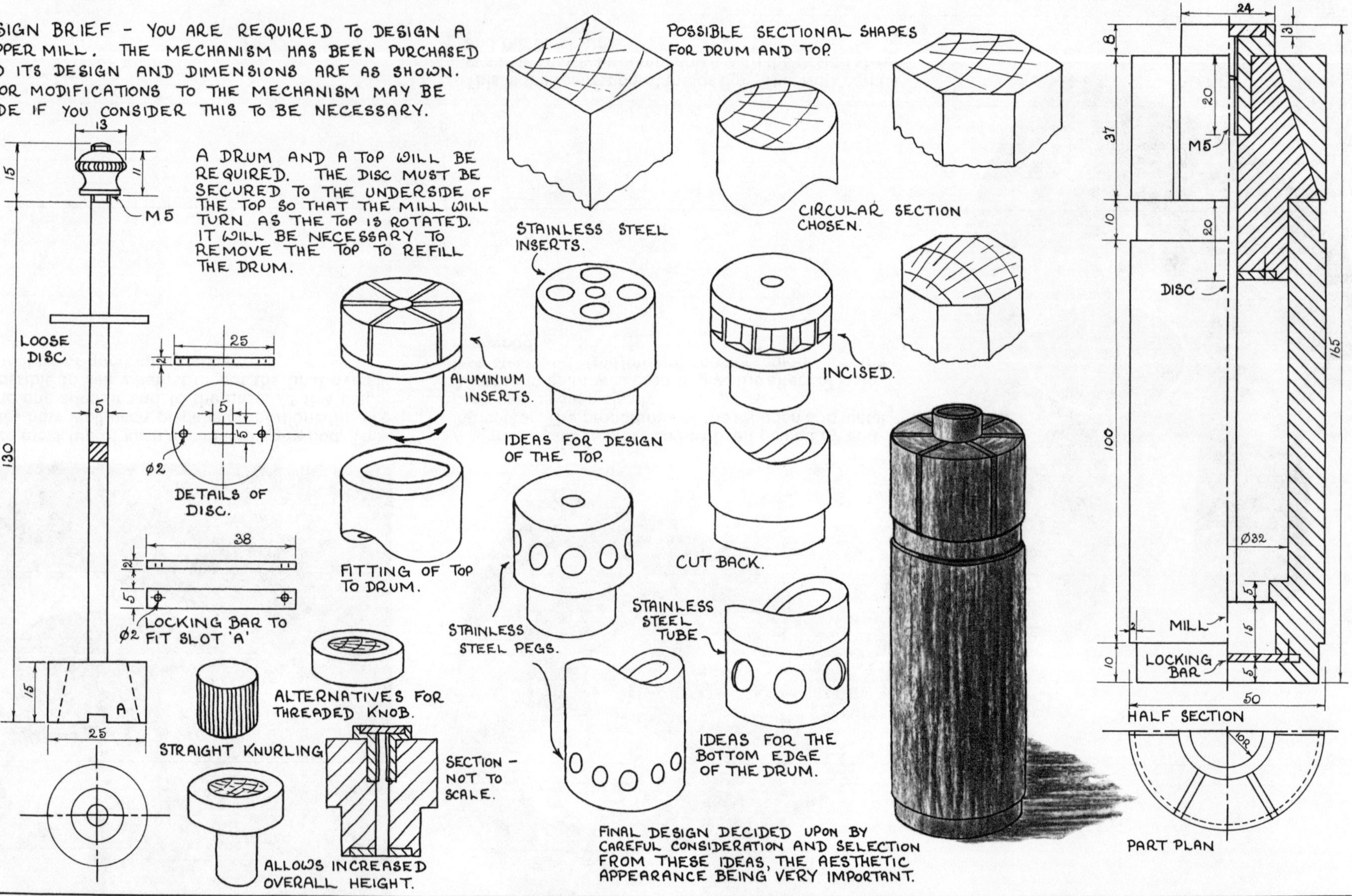

A DRUM AND A TOP WILL BE REQUIRED. THE DISC MUST BE SECURED TO THE UNDERSIDE OF THE TOP SO THAT THE MILL WILL TURN AS THE TOP IS ROTATED. IT WILL BE NECESSARY TO REMOVE THE TOP TO REFILL THE DRUM.
M5
LOOSE DISC
DETAILS OF DISC.
Ø2
LOCKING BAR TO FIT SLOT 'A'
A
STRAIGHT KNURLING
ALTERNATIVES FOR THREADED KNOB.
SECTION - NOT TO SCALE.
ALLOWS INCREASED OVERALL HEIGHT.
POSSIBLE SECTIONAL SHAPES FOR DRUM AND TOP.
CIRCULAR SECTION CHOSEN.
STAINLESS STEEL INSERTS.
ALUMINIUM INSERTS.
INCISED.
IDEAS FOR DESIGN OF THE TOP.
FITTING OF TOP TO DRUM.
CUT BACK.
STAINLESS STEEL PEGS.
STAINLESS STEEL TUBE
IDEAS FOR THE BOTTOM EDGE OF THE DRUM.
FINAL DESIGN DECIDED UPON BY CAREFUL CONSIDERATION AND SELECTION FROM THESE IDEAS, THE AESTHETIC APPEARANCE BEING VERY IMPORTANT.
M5
DISC
Ø32
MILL
LOCKING BAR
HALF SECTION
10R
PART PLAN

PEPPER MILL	DESIGNED BY	FORM	DATE	SCHOOL

DETAIL OF MECHANISM - SCALE FULL SIZE - ORTHOGRAPHIC PROJECTION-3H PENCIL AND INK. FREEHAND ISOMETRIC SKETCHES AND LETTERING DRAWN WITH HB PENCIL AND INKED IN WITH A TECHNICAL PEN. COMPLETED DESIGN IN ORTHOGRAPHIC PROJECTION - NOTE SECTION TO SHOW INNER DETAIL - EXPOSED SURFACES INDICATED BY 'HATCHING' AT 45° - 3H PENCIL AND INK. SKETCH RED/BROWN AND BLUE - ROSEWOOD AND STAINLESS STEEL.

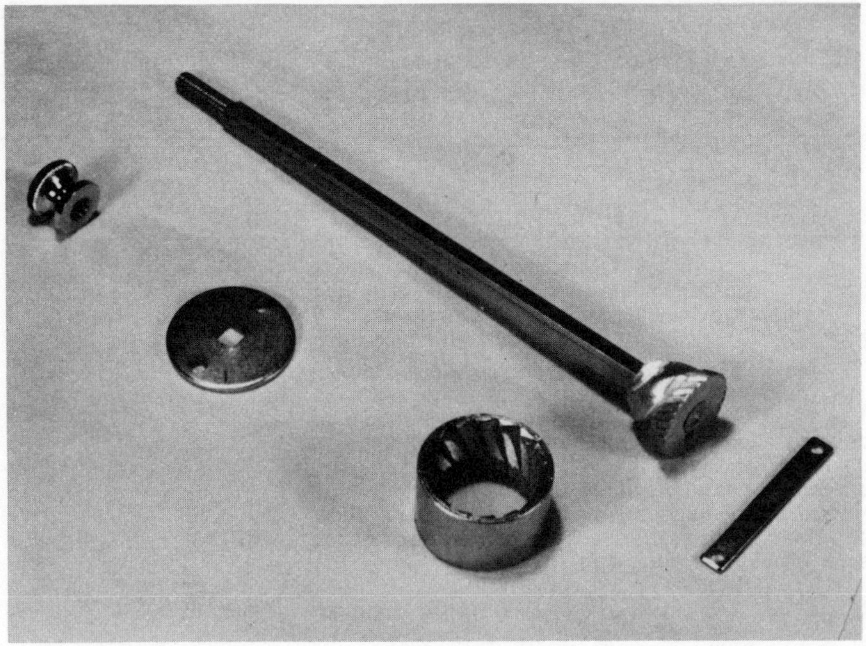

The mechanism of the mill.
Threaded knob – M5.
Disc to fit square spindle.
Outer casing of the mill.
Rotating grinder and square spindle.
Locking bar to secure outer casing.

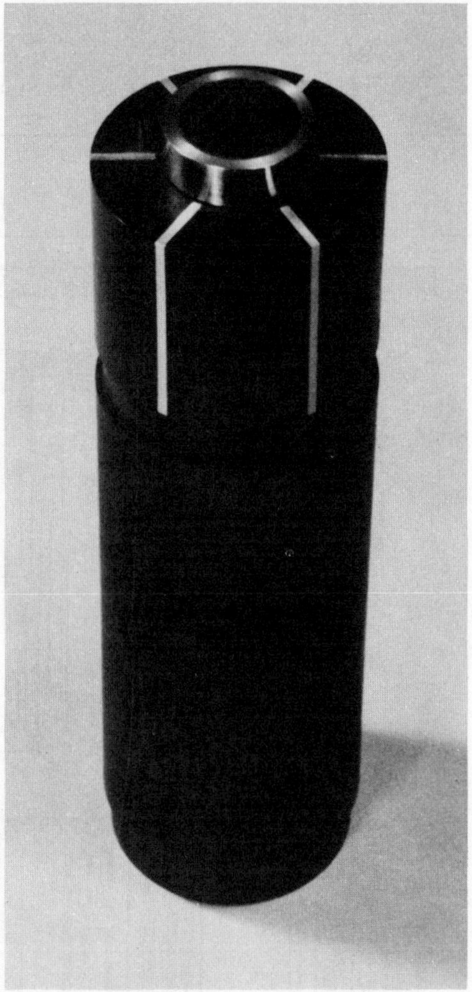

The pepper mill assembled.

Note: the clean modern lines giving an aesthetically pleasing appearance, and the deep drum which will hold a good quantity of pepper-corns and can be held firmly, the satisfying blend of wood and metal for the top and knob, and the radial lines creating a wheel effect which invites you to turn it.

The three parts of the pepper mill ready for assembling.
The drum.
The top with aluminium inserts glued in.
Stainless steel knob with inlay of wood.
Timber – Rosewood (Rio).

Polystyrene is a modern material with which everyone is now familiar. Very many uses have been found for it as an insulating and packing medium. In the workshop it can be used for making patterns from which to make castings. It is ideal for 'one off' as it can be easily fashioned with a sharp knife and/or a hot wire cutter which can be made from resistance wire and run from the *low voltage* supply in the science department, or from a battery. Placed in moulding sand and properly vented the pattern of polystyrene is burnt away as the metal is poured.

Note: *The fumes are toxic so there should be maximum ventilation.* If the patterns are very complex dry silver sand can be used in the moulding box. Tapping the box lightly packs the sand tightly round the pattern. In some cases the sprues can be of polystyrene glued in suitable positions to the pattern.

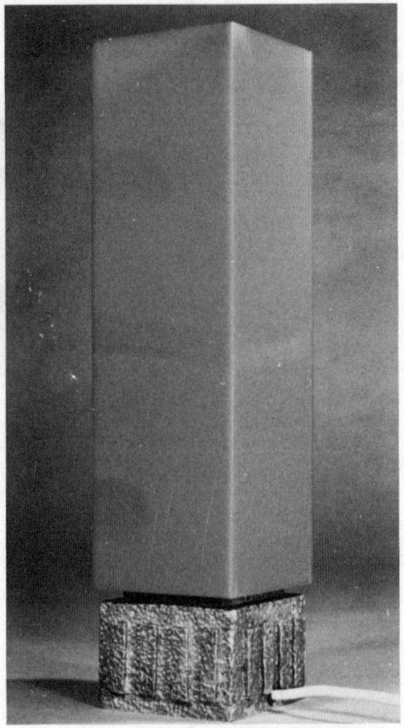

DESIGN BRIEF

The above illustration is of a lamp designed to give background lighting, the base was made using the method described above; the accompanying photographs show various stages in its production. You are to design a lamp base to be made in this way for which a conventional shade may be used or one built up from perspex as in the example.

In your design consideration should be given to:

1 Stability.
2 Provision for wiring, including an earthwire.
3 Bulb to be used. Wattage and overall size.
4 Shape and type of shade.

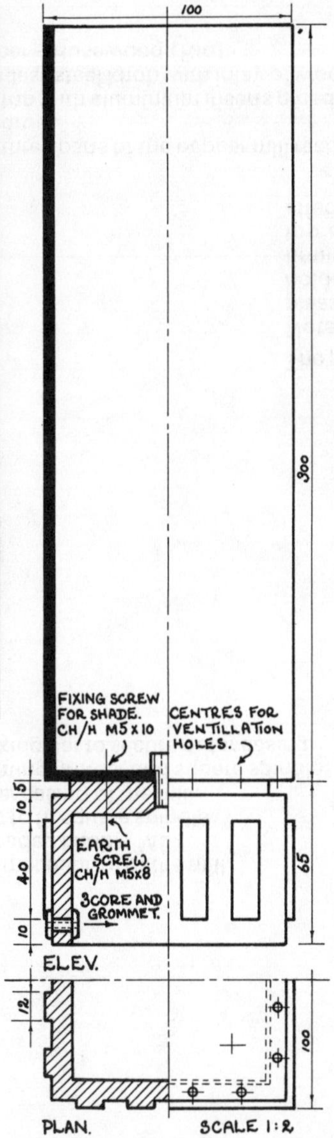

100
300
FIXING SCREW FOR SHADE. CH/H M5x10
CENTRES FOR VENTILLATION HOLES.
EARTH SCREW CH/H M5x8
SCORE AND GROMMET.
10.5
40
10
65
ELEV.
12
100
PLAN.
SCALE 1:2

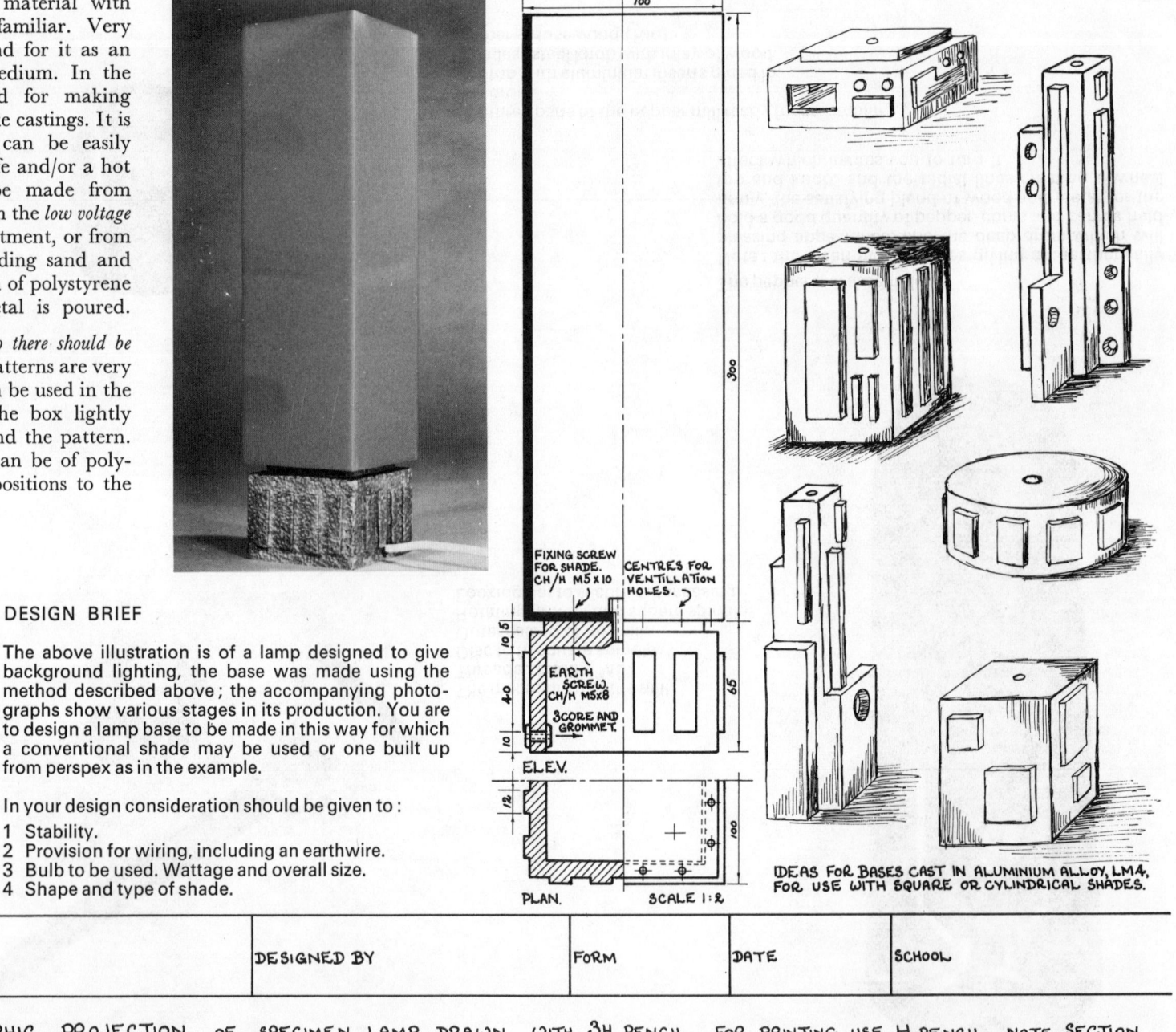

IDEAS FOR BASES CAST IN ALUMINIUM ALLOY, LM4, FOR USE WITH SQUARE OR CYLINDRICAL SHADES.

LAMP	DESIGNED BY	FORM	DATE	SCHOOL

1ST. ANGLE ORTHOGRAPHIC PROJECTION OF SPECIMEN LAMP DRAWN WITH 3H PENCIL. FOR PRINTING USE H PENCIL. NOTE SECTION. FREEHAND CABINET OBLIQUE SKETCHES AT APPROXIMATELY 30° AND 45° DRAWN WITH HB PENCIL.

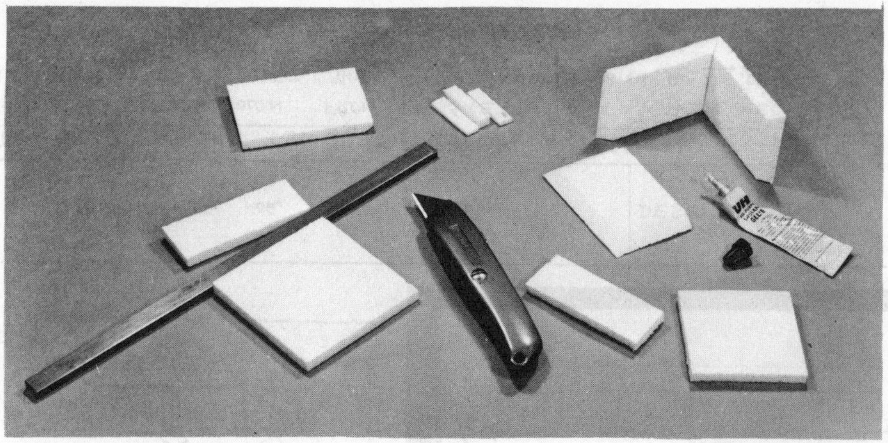

Making up the polystyrene pattern.

Practice joints made on off-cuts of acrylic sheet to test the efficiency of the technique used. The edge of one piece was dipped into *Ethyene Dichloride,* the recommended solvent, until it began to dissolve and felt slippery to the touch. At this stage it was then pressed lightly against the second piece, the surface of which was in turn dissolved by the wet edge of the first piece. This forms a 'cemented' or 'solvent welded' joint which could be handled after 15-20 minutes, and was completely hardened after four hours when all the solvent had evaporated.

The casting produced from the pattern. Note how the texture of the polystyrene has been picked up by the metal which gives a pleasing surface finish. Tapered sprues were positioned where the wire was to be run to avoid disfiguring the surface.

A view of the wiring of the lamp. The flex is white plastic covered 3-core and is fed in through a rubber grommet set into the side of the base. The positive and negative leads are taken to the bulb holder and the earth wire to one of the two screws securing the shade.

DESIGN BRIEF

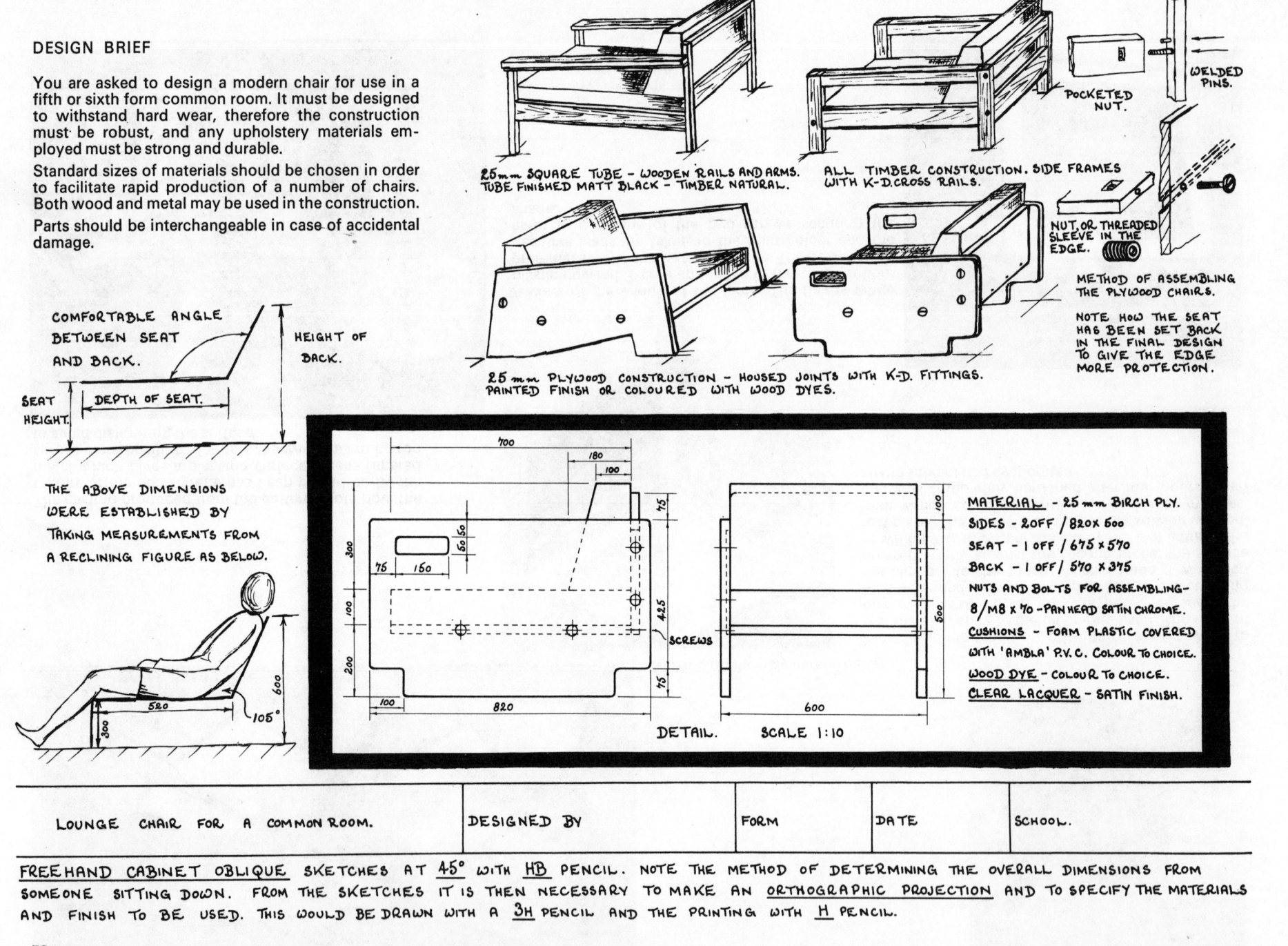

You are asked to design a modern chair for use in a fifth or sixth form common room. It must be designed to withstand hard wear, therefore the construction must be robust, and any upholstery materials employed must be strong and durable.

Standard sizes of materials should be chosen in order to facilitate rapid production of a number of chairs. Both wood and metal may be used in the construction.

Parts should be interchangeable in case of accidental damage.

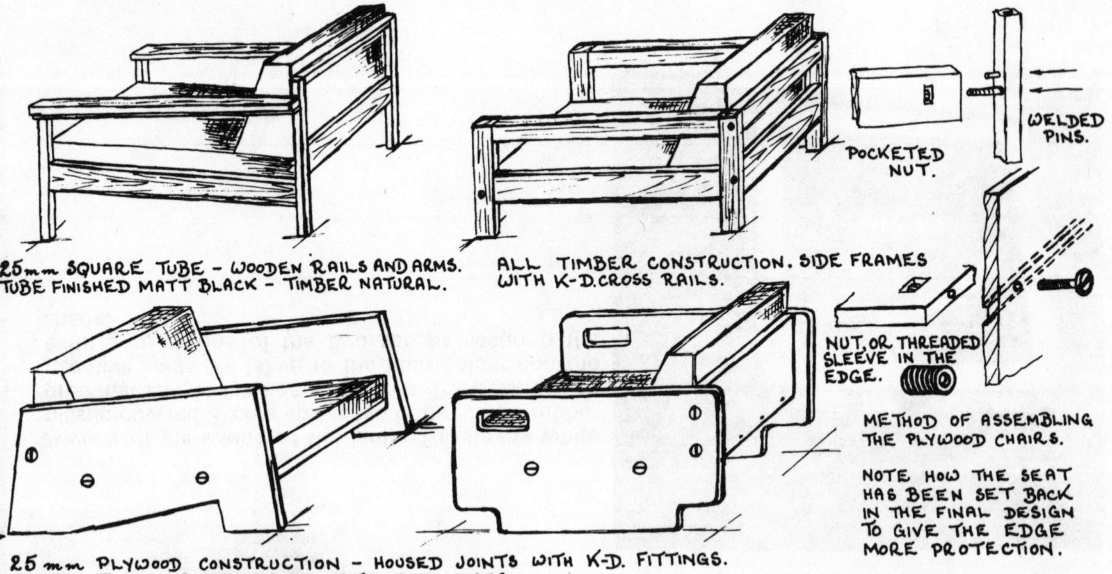
25mm SQUARE TUBE - WOODEN RAILS AND ARMS. TUBE FINISHED MATT BLACK - TIMBER NATURAL.
ALL TIMBER CONSTRUCTION. SIDE FRAMES WITH K-D. CROSS RAILS.
POCKETED NUT.
WELDED PINS.
NUT, OR THREADED SLEEVE IN THE EDGE.
METHOD OF ASSEMBLING THE PLYWOOD CHAIRS.
NOTE HOW THE SEAT HAS BEEN SET BACK IN THE FINAL DESIGN TO GIVE THE EDGE MORE PROTECTION.
25 mm PLYWOOD CONSTRUCTION - HOUSED JOINTS WITH K-D. FITTINGS. PAINTED FINISH OR COLOURED WITH WOOD DYES.

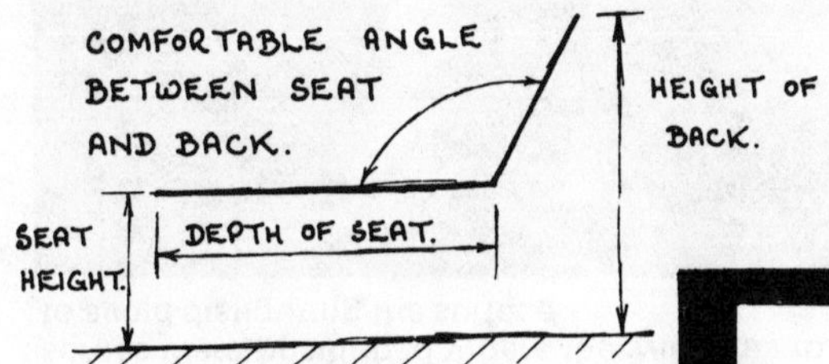
COMFORTABLE ANGLE BETWEEN SEAT AND BACK.
HEIGHT OF BACK.
SEAT HEIGHT.
DEPTH OF SEAT.

THE ABOVE DIMENSIONS WERE ESTABLISHED BY TAKING MEASUREMENTS FROM A RECLINING FIGURE AS BELOW.

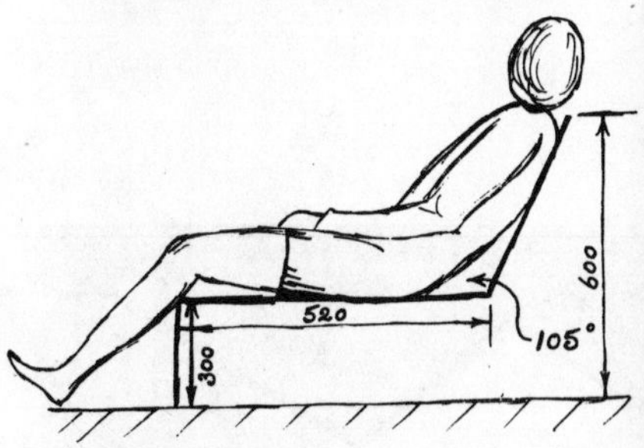
520
600
300
105°

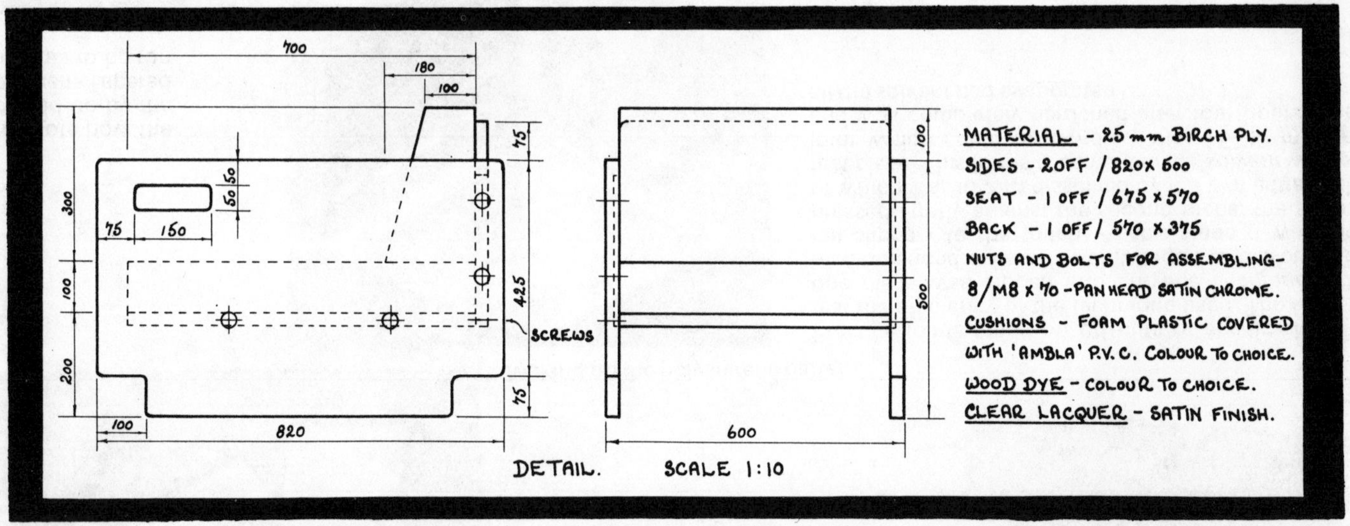
700
180
100
300
50
50
75
150
100
200
425
75
75
SCREWS
100
820
100
500
600
DETAIL. SCALE 1:10
MATERIAL - 25 mm BIRCH PLY.
SIDES - 2 OFF / 820 x 600
SEAT - 1 OFF / 675 x 570
BACK - 1 OFF / 570 x 375
NUTS AND BOLTS FOR ASSEMBLING - 8/M8 x 70 - PAN HEAD SATIN CHROME.
CUSHIONS - FOAM PLASTIC COVERED WITH 'AMBLA' P.V.C. COLOUR TO CHOICE.
WOOD DYE - COLOUR TO CHOICE.
CLEAR LACQUER - SATIN FINISH.

LOUNGE CHAIR FOR A COMMON ROOM.	DESIGNED BY	FORM	DATE	SCHOOL.

FREEHAND CABINET OBLIQUE SKETCHES AT 45° WITH HB PENCIL. NOTE THE METHOD OF DETERMINING THE OVERALL DIMENSIONS FROM SOMEONE SITTING DOWN. FROM THE SKETCHES IT IS THEN NECESSARY TO MAKE AN ORTHOGRAPHIC PROJECTION AND TO SPECIFY THE MATERIALS AND FINISH TO BE USED. THIS WOULD BE DRAWN WITH A 3H PENCIL AND THE PRINTING WITH H PENCIL.

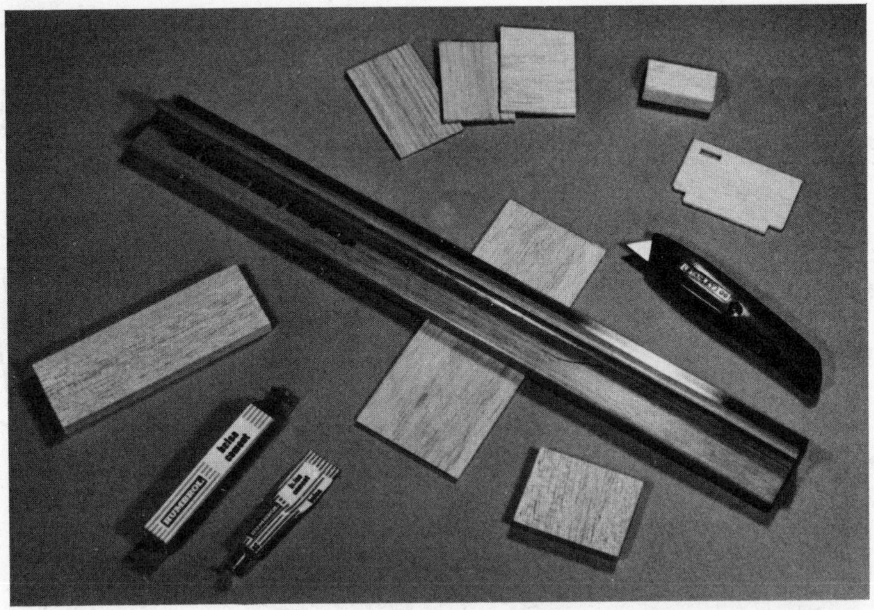

Cutting 'Solarbo' balsa wood from which to make a scale model of the chair. A knife with a very sharp, slim, firm blade is required, a suitable straight edge and a firm surface on which to cut. Thicker pieces of wood may have to be cut with a fine-toothed saw. The balsa wood can be stuck together quickly with balsa cement.

The scale model is finished in red and white 'Cotman' water-colour paints. The features of the chair can be more readily seen from the model than from the original drawing.

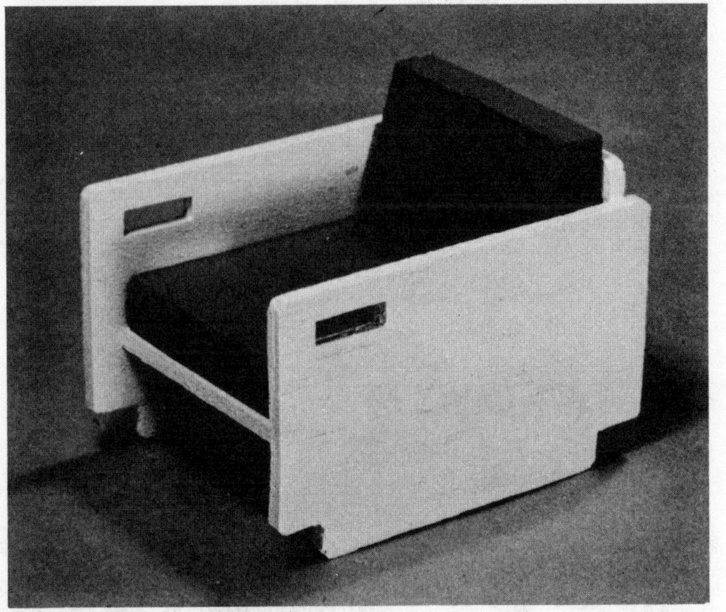

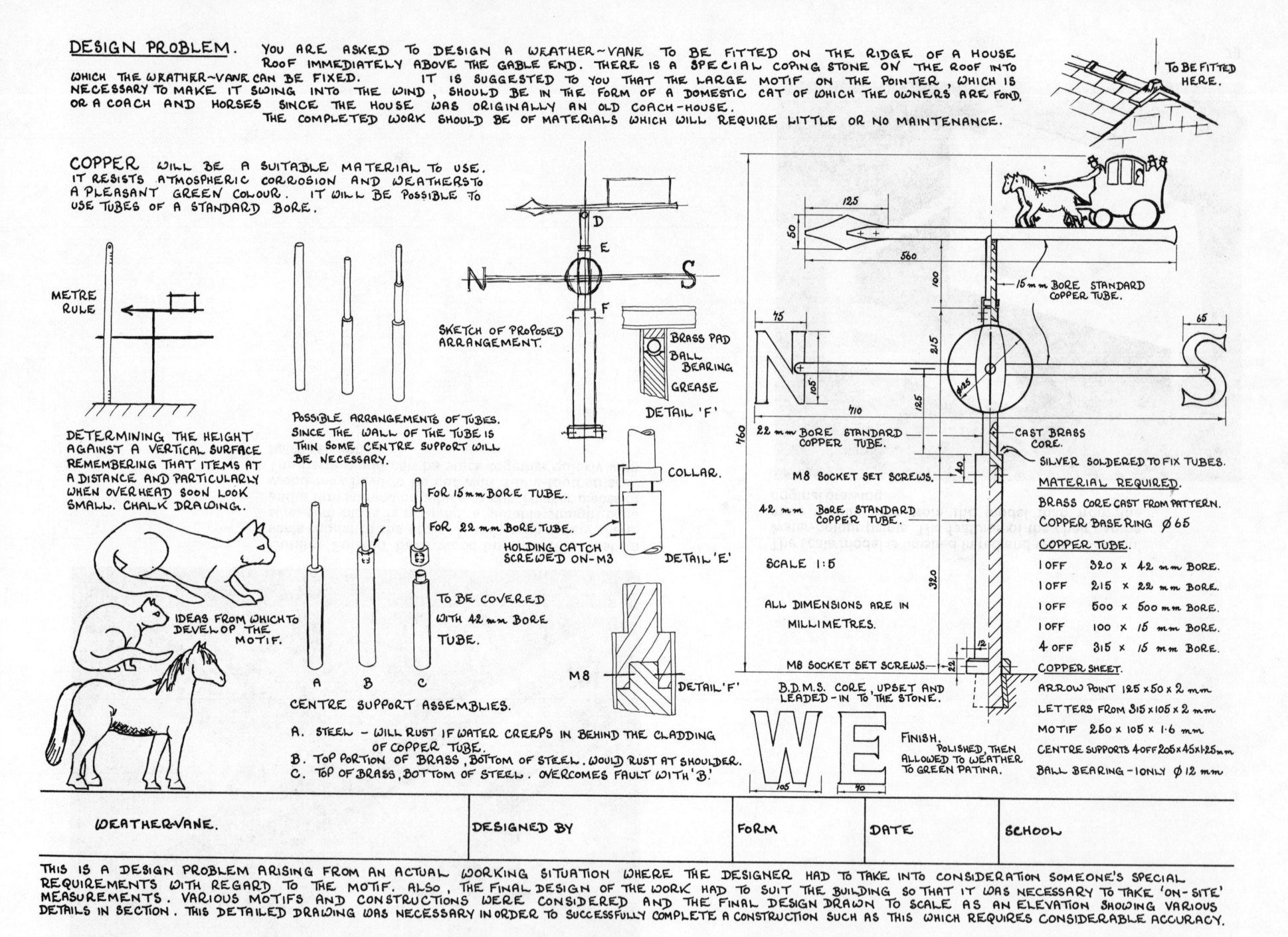

DESIGN PROBLEM. YOU ARE ASKED TO DESIGN A WEATHER~VANE TO BE FITTED ON THE RIDGE OF A HOUSE ROOF IMMEDIATELY ABOVE THE GABLE END. THERE IS A SPECIAL COPING STONE ON THE ROOF INTO WHICH THE WEATHER~VANE CAN BE FIXED. IT IS SUGGESTED TO YOU THAT THE LARGE MOTIF ON THE POINTER, WHICH IS NECESSARY TO MAKE IT SWING INTO THE WIND, SHOULD BE IN THE FORM OF A DOMESTIC CAT OF WHICH THE OWNERS ARE FOND, OR A COACH AND HORSES SINCE THE HOUSE WAS ORIGINALLY AN OLD COACH-HOUSE.

THE COMPLETED WORK SHOULD BE OF MATERIALS WHICH WILL REQUIRE LITTLE OR NO MAINTENANCE.

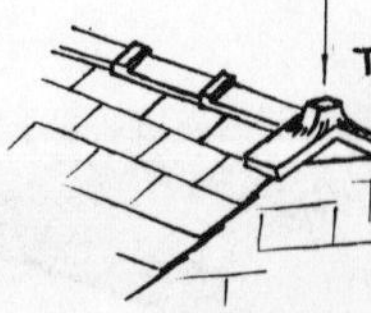
TO BE FITTED HERE.

COPPER WILL BE A SUITABLE MATERIAL TO USE. IT RESISTS ATMOSPHERIC CORROSION AND WEATHERS TO A PLEASANT GREEN COLOUR. IT WILL BE POSSIBLE TO USE TUBES OF A STANDARD BORE.

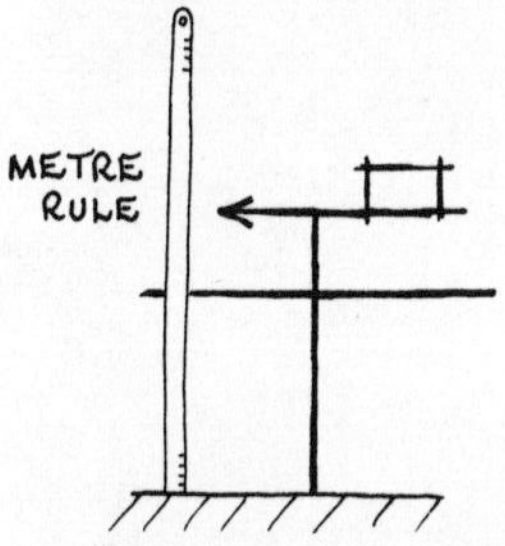
METRE
RULE

DETERMINING THE HEIGHT AGAINST A VERTICAL SURFACE REMEMBERING THAT ITEMS AT A DISTANCE AND PARTICULARLY WHEN OVERHEAD SOON LOOK SMALL. CHALK DRAWING.

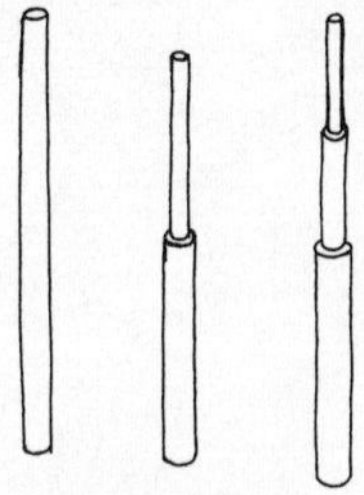

POSSIBLE ARRANGEMENTS OF TUBES. SINCE THE WALL OF THE TUBE IS THIN SOME CENTRE SUPPORT WILL BE NECESSARY.

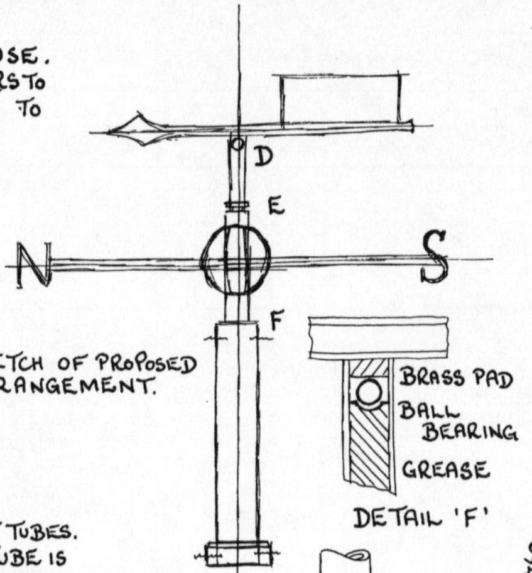
D
E
N
S
F
SKETCH OF PROPOSED ARRANGEMENT.
BRASS PAD
BALL BEARING
GREASE
DETAIL 'F'

IDEAS FROM WHICH TO DEVELOP THE MOTIF.

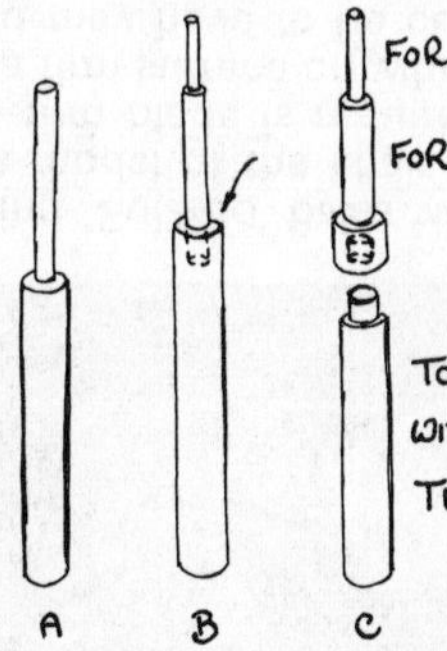
FOR 15 mm BORE TUBE.
FOR 22 mm BORE TUBE.
TO BE COVERED WITH 42 mm BORE TUBE.
A
B
C

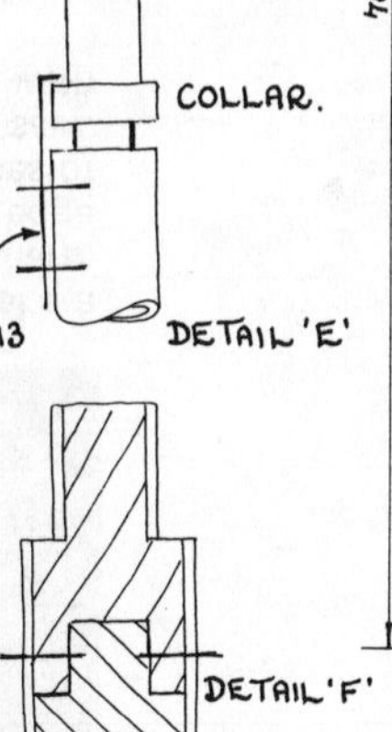
COLLAR.
HOLDING CATCH SCREWED ON-M3
DETAIL 'E'
M8
DETAIL 'F'

CENTRE SUPPORT ASSEMBLIES.

A. STEEL – WILL RUST IF WATER CREEPS IN BEHIND THE CLADDING OF COPPER TUBE.
B. TOP PORTION OF BRASS, BOTTOM OF STEEL. WOULD RUST AT SHOULDER.
C. TOP OF BRASS, BOTTOM OF STEEL. OVERCOMES FAULT WITH 'B'.

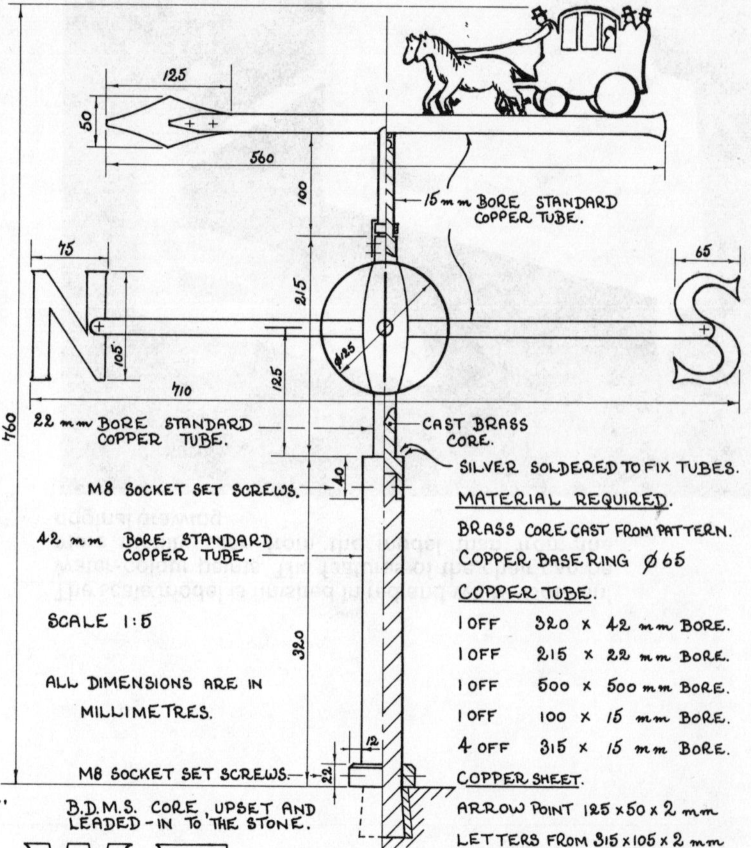
125
50
560
100
15 mm BORE STANDARD COPPER TUBE.
65
75
215
N
S
105
Ø125
410
125
760
22 mm BORE STANDARD COPPER TUBE.
CAST BRASS CORE.
SILVER SOLDERED TO FIX TUBES.
M8 SOCKET SET SCREWS.
40
42 mm BORE STANDARD COPPER TUBE.
SCALE 1:5
320
ALL DIMENSIONS ARE IN MILLIMETRES.
12
22
M8 SOCKET SET SCREWS.
B.D.M.S. CORE, UPSET AND LEADED-IN TO THE STONE.

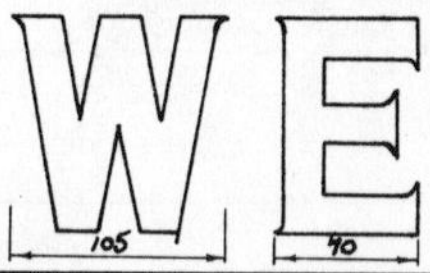
W
E
105
40

FINISH.
POLISHED, THEN ALLOWED TO WEATHER TO GREEN PATINA.

MATERIAL REQUIRED.

BRASS CORE CAST FROM PATTERN.
COPPER BASE RING Ø 65

COPPER TUBE.

1 OFF	320	x	42 mm	BORE.
1 OFF	215	x	22 mm	BORE.
1 OFF	500	x	500 mm	BORE.
1 OFF	100	x	15 mm	BORE.
4 OFF	315	x	15 mm	BORE.

COPPER SHEET.

ARROW POINT 125 x 50 x 2 mm
LETTERS FROM 315 x 105 x 2 mm
MOTIF 250 x 105 x 1·6 mm
CENTRE SUPPORTS 4 OFF 205 x 45 x 1·25 mm
BALL BEARING – 1 ONLY Ø 12 mm

WEATHER-VANE.	DESIGNED BY	FORM	DATE	SCHOOL

THIS IS A DESIGN PROBLEM ARISING FROM AN ACTUAL WORKING SITUATION WHERE THE DESIGNER HAD TO TAKE INTO CONSIDERATION SOMEONE'S SPECIAL REQUIREMENTS WITH REGARD TO THE MOTIF. ALSO, THE FINAL DESIGN OF THE WORK HAD TO SUIT THE BUILDING SO THAT IT WAS NECESSARY TO TAKE 'ON-SITE' MEASUREMENTS. VARIOUS MOTIFS AND CONSTRUCTIONS WERE CONSIDERED AND THE FINAL DESIGN DRAWN TO SCALE AS AN ELEVATION SHOWING VARIOUS DETAILS IN SECTION. THIS DETAILED DRAWING WAS NECESSARY IN ORDER TO SUCCESSFULLY COMPLETE A CONSTRUCTION SUCH AS THIS WHICH REQUIRES CONSIDERABLE ACCURACY.

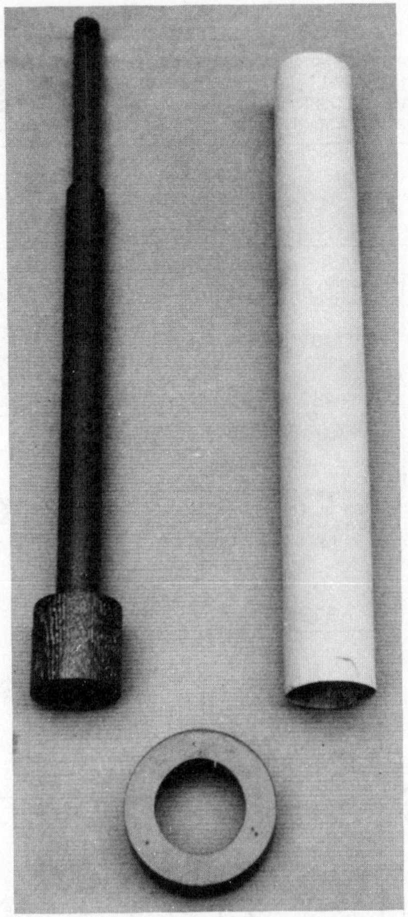

The wooden patterns from which the top and bottom portions of the spindle were cast and a card model of the centre tube.

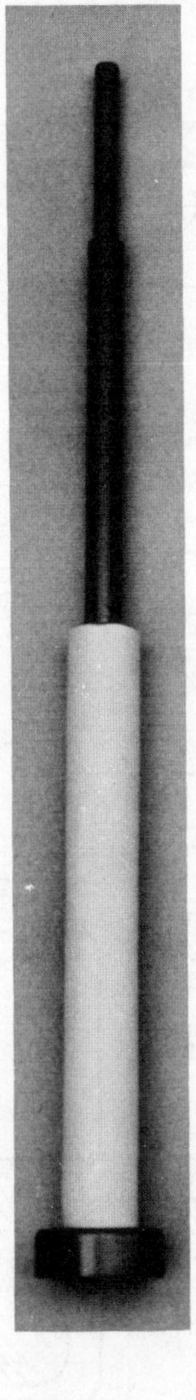

The three assembled as they will be when made in copper.

W
S
E

The final piece assembled before being fixed to the ridge of the roof. To give individuality to his work the author has adopted an oak leaf symbol as his maker's mark. In this case it has been applied in copper near the base.

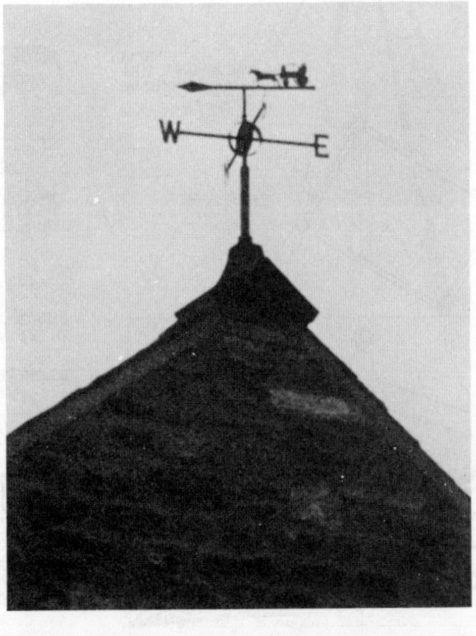

W
E

The weather-vane in position. The wind-direction indicator was lubricated for easy movement and to reduce wear. High melting point grease was used so that it would not run out of the bearing thereby lessening the need for frequent maintenance.

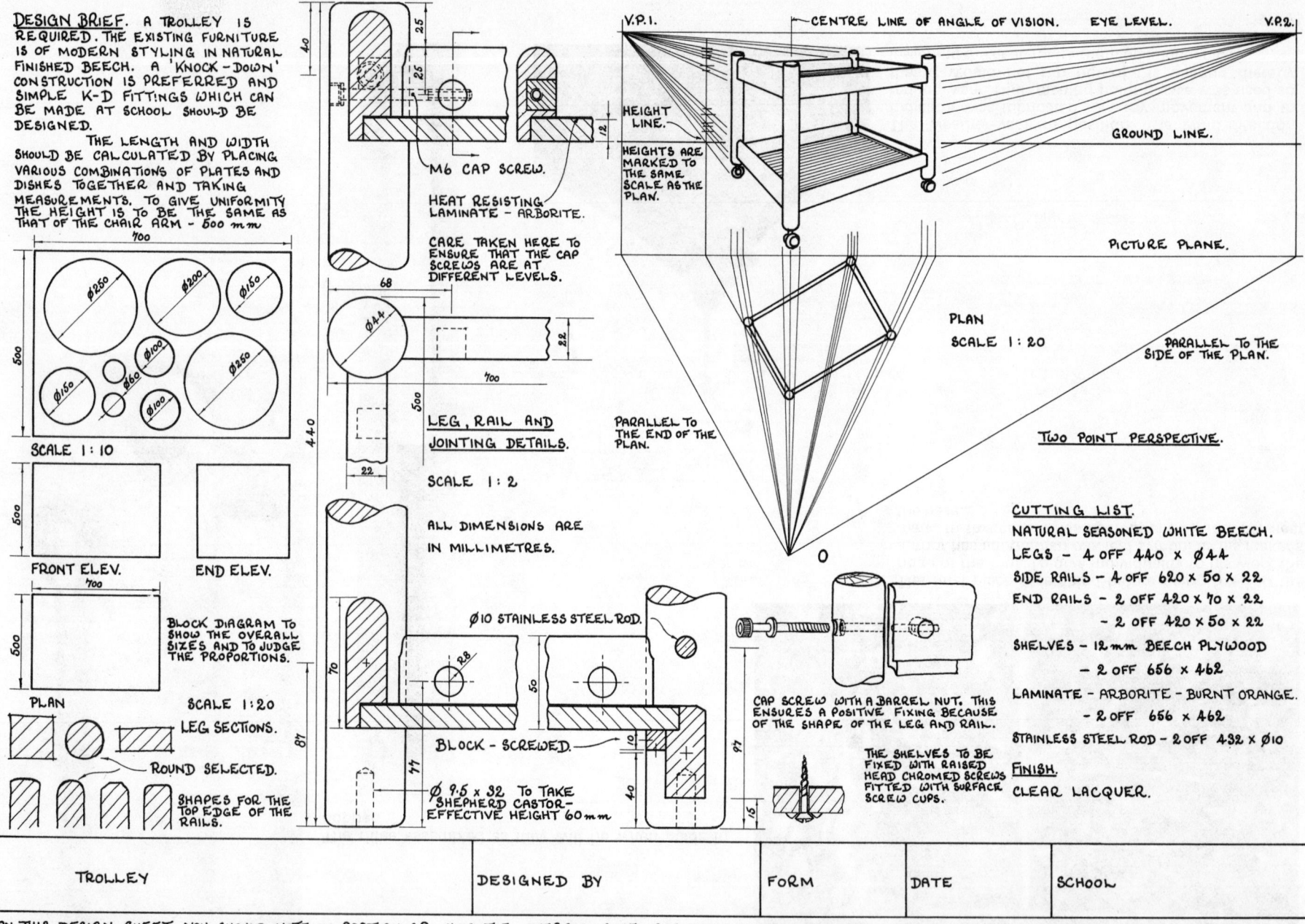

DESIGN BRIEF. A TROLLEY IS REQUIRED. THE EXISTING FURNITURE IS OF MODERN STYLING IN NATURAL FINISHED BEECH. A 'KNOCK-DOWN' CONSTRUCTION IS PREFERRED AND SIMPLE K-D FITTINGS WHICH CAN BE MADE AT SCHOOL SHOULD BE DESIGNED.

THE LENGTH AND WIDTH SHOULD BE CALCULATED BY PLACING VARIOUS COMBINATIONS OF PLATES AND DISHES TOGETHER AND TAKING MEASUREMENTS. TO GIVE UNIFORMITY THE HEIGHT IS TO BE THE SAME AS THAT OF THE CHAIR ARM - 500 mm

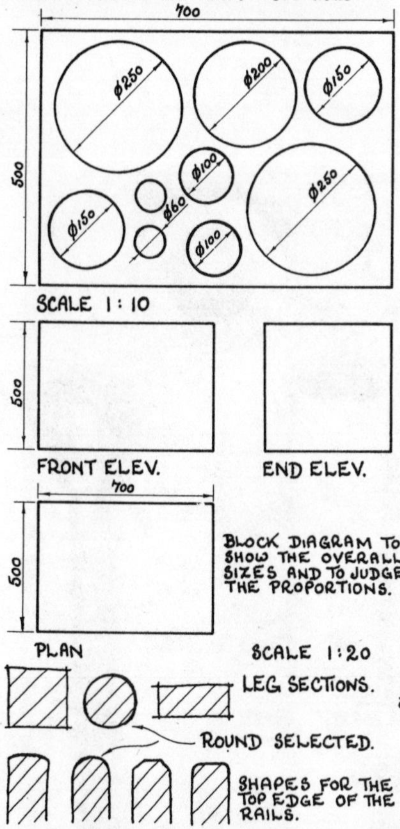

700
Ø250
Ø200
Ø150
Ø100
Ø60
Ø250
Ø150
Ø100
500
SCALE 1:10
500
FRONT ELEV.
END ELEV.
700
500
BLOCK DIAGRAM TO SHOW THE OVERALL SIZES AND TO JUDGE THE PROPORTIONS.
PLAN
SCALE 1:20
LEG SECTIONS.
ROUND SELECTED.
SHAPES FOR THE TOP EDGE OF THE RAILS.

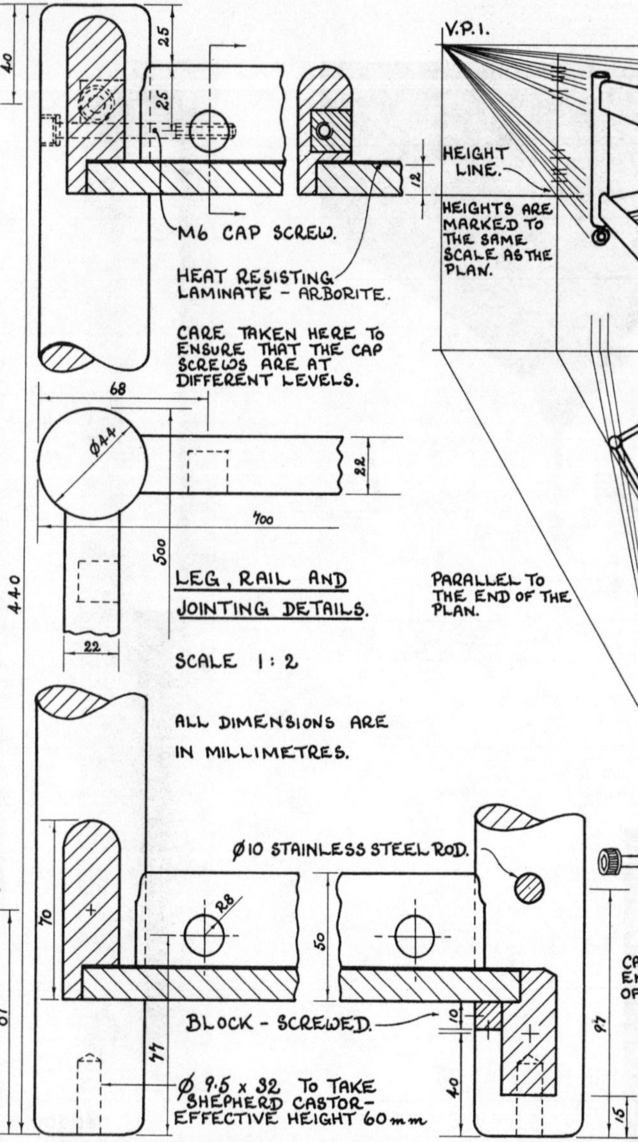

40
25
25
12
M6 CAP SCREW.
HEAT RESISTING LAMINATE - ARBORITE.
CARE TAKEN HERE TO ENSURE THAT THE CAP SCREWS ARE AT DIFFERENT LEVELS.
68
Ø44
22
700
500
440
22
LEG, RAIL AND JOINTING DETAILS.
SCALE 1:2
ALL DIMENSIONS ARE IN MILLIMETRES.
Ø10 STAINLESS STEEL ROD.
70
R8
50
87
44
BLOCK - SCREWED.
10
40
97
15
Ø 9.5 x 32 TO TAKE SHEPHERD CASTOR-EFFECTIVE HEIGHT 60 mm

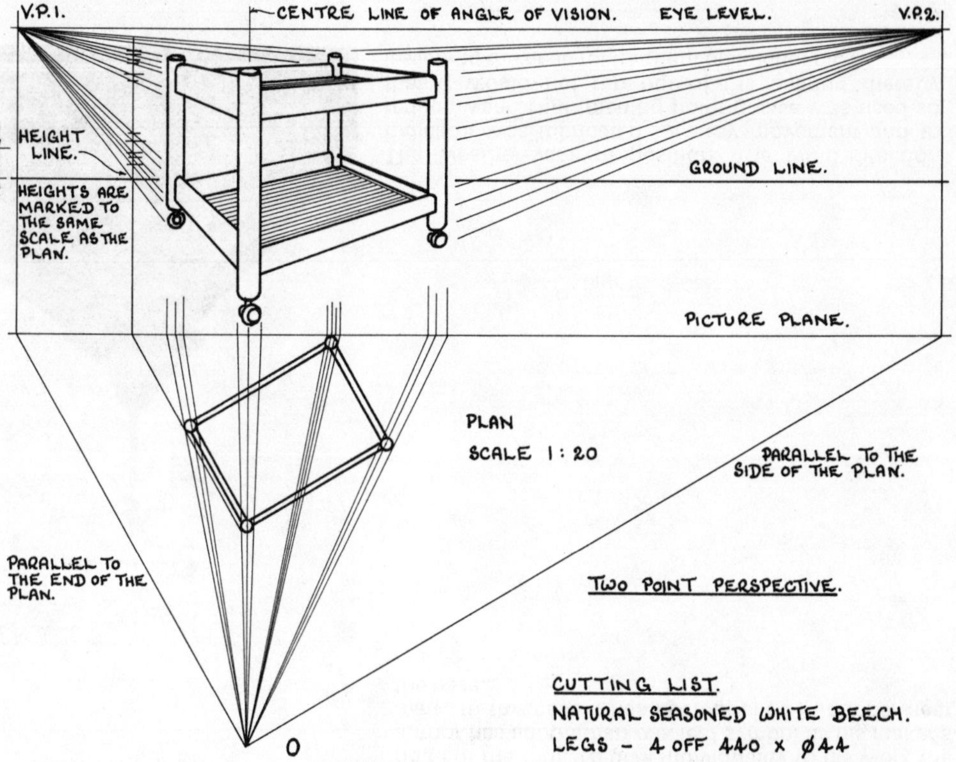

V.P.1.
CENTRE LINE OF ANGLE OF VISION.
EYE LEVEL.
V.P.2.
HEIGHT LINE.
HEIGHTS ARE MARKED TO THE SAME SCALE AS THE PLAN.
GROUND LINE.
PICTURE PLANE.
PLAN
SCALE 1:20
PARALLEL TO THE SIDE OF THE PLAN.
PARALLEL TO THE END OF THE PLAN.
O

TWO POINT PERSPECTIVE.

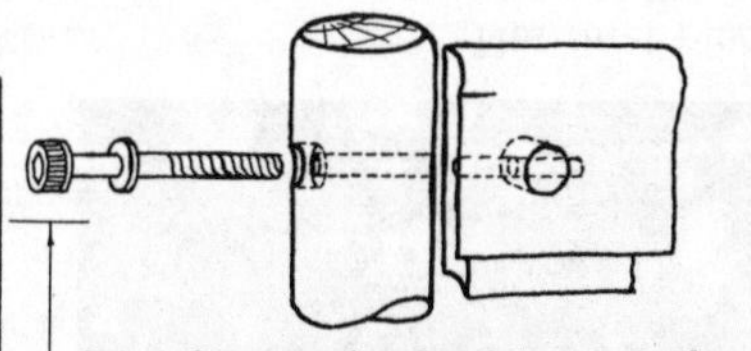

CAP SCREW WITH A BARREL NUT. THIS ENSURES A POSITIVE FIXING BECAUSE OF THE SHAPE OF THE LEG AND RAIL.

THE SHELVES TO BE FIXED WITH RAISED HEAD CHROMED SCREWS FITTED WITH SURFACE SCREW CUPS.

CUTTING LIST.

NATURAL SEASONED WHITE BEECH.

LEGS - 4 OFF 440 x Ø44

SIDE RAILS - 4 OFF 620 x 50 x 22

END RAILS - 2 OFF 420 x 70 x 22

- 2 OFF 420 x 50 x 22

SHELVES - 12 mm BEECH PLYWOOD

- 2 OFF 656 x 462

LAMINATE - ARBORITE - BURNT ORANGE.

- 2 OFF 656 x 462

STAINLESS STEEL ROD - 2 OFF 432 x Ø10

FINISH.

CLEAR LACQUER.

TROLLEY	DESIGNED BY	FORM	DATE	SCHOOL

ON THIS DESIGN SHEET YOU SHOULD NOTE IN PARTICULAR HOW THE OVERALL SIZE WAS DECIDED UPON AND THEN THE IMMEDIATE NECESSITY TO MAKE A WORKSHOP DRAWING IN THE FORM OF A SECTIONAL ELEVATION IN ORDER TO DETERMINE WITH GREAT ACCURACY THE POSITION OF THE RAILS AND THE K-D FITTINGS. PRELIMINARY SKETCHING OF THE STYLING WAS NOT NECESSARY IN THIS CASE AS IT WAS PREDETERMINED BY THE EXISTING FURNITURE. THE PERSPECTIVE DRAWING GIVES A GOOD IMPRESSION OF HOW THE FINISHED PIECE WILL LOOK AND THE CUTTING LIST GIVES COMPLETE DETAILS OF THE MATERIALS REQUIRED.

A rail end showing the machining and rebate for the tray.

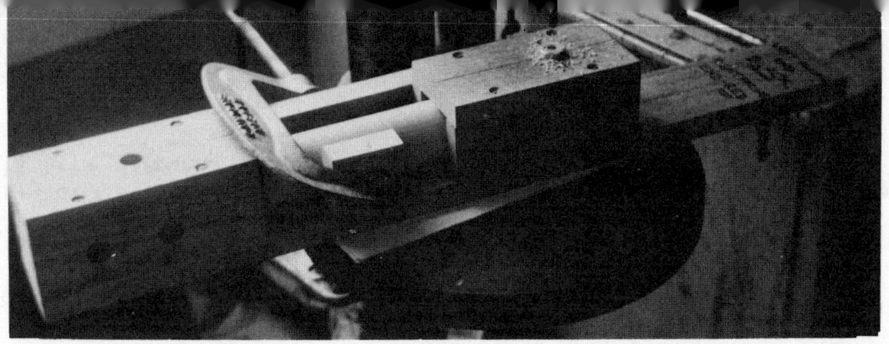

The drilling jig for the legs in use.

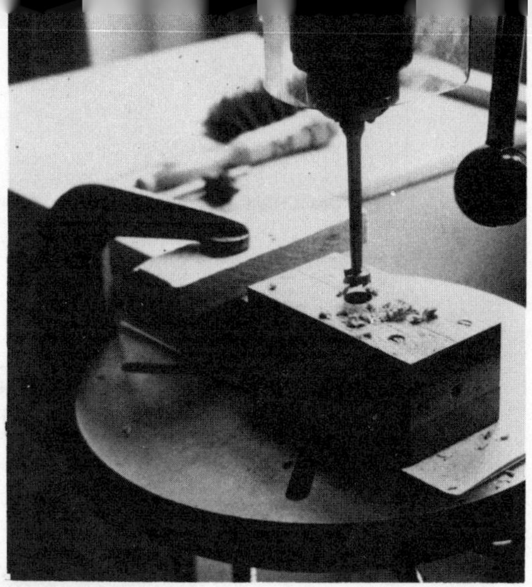

Drilling the rails for the barrel nut. These were all drilled to the same depth using the depth stop on the machine. Note the hole in the end of the jig for positioning the bolt hole in the end of the rail.

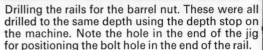

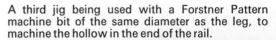

A third jig being used with a Forstner Pattern machine bit of the same diameter as the leg, to machine the hollow in the end of the rail.

The brass bushes used in the drilling jig for the legs. These were to give greater accuracy and to ensure the concentricity of the counter bored holes.

A mock-up in redwood. This was a valuable test piece to check the accuracy of the design of the jigs.

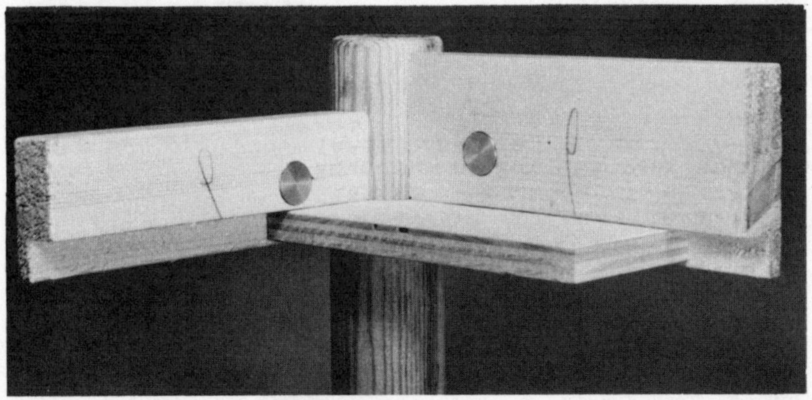

Drilling the end of the leg for the castor. The guide for the drill was a loose block which fitted into the end of the drilling jig.

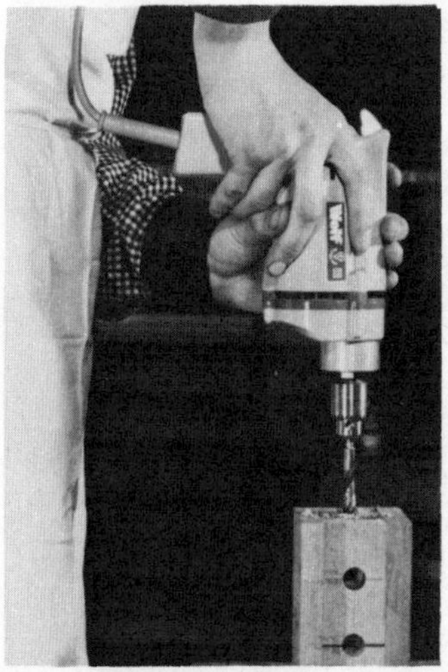

The completed trolley. This was an exercise in what may be termed 'wood engineering'. The design of the jigs to ensure absolute accuracy was an important part of the work.

DESIGN BRIEF FOR SIDEBOARD.

MAXIMUM DIMENSIONS FOR CARCASE ONLY –
1·900 m X 500 X 500

TO STORE :– TABLE MATS AND LINEN.
CUTLERY AND CUTLERY TRAYS.
GLASSES – FOR WATER, WINE, ETC.
SELECTION OF BOTTLES – MAX. HEIGHT 340 mm
TABLE WARE.

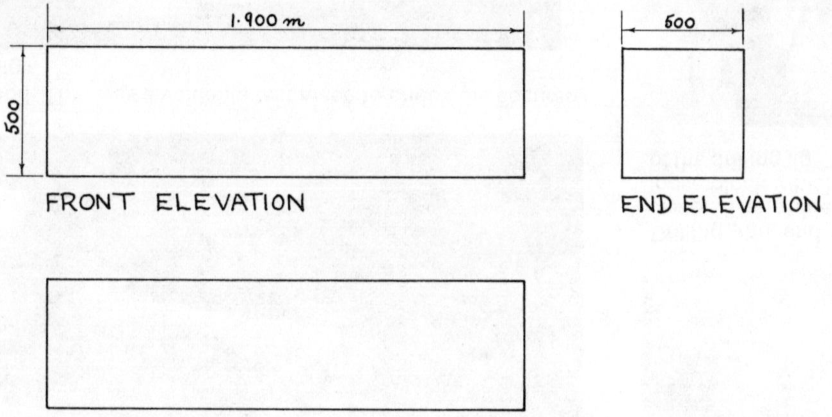
1·900 m
500
600

FRONT ELEVATION

END ELEVATION

PLAN

PROPORTIONS OF THE CARCASE.

IT IS NOW NECESSARY TO ESTABLISH THE HEIGHT OF THE BASE ON WHICH THE CARCASE IS TO BE SUPPORTED.

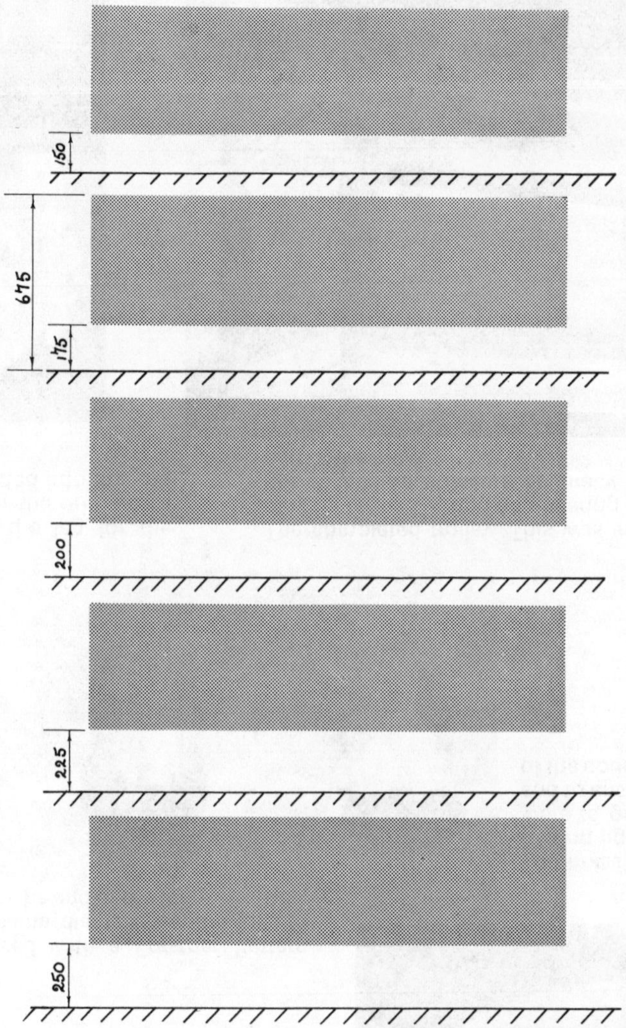
150
675
175
200
225
250

CARCASE AT VARIOUS HEIGHTS ABOVE FLOOR LEVEL. 175 mm CHOSEN – IS IN GOOD PROPORTION – GIVES GOOD OVERALL HEIGHT.

SIDEBOARD – SHEET I – SCALE 1:20	DESIGNED BY	FORM	DATE	SCHOOL

ORTHOGRAPHIC PROJECTION OF CARCASE BLOCK – 3H PENCIL.
CARCASE BLOCKS FOR ASSESSING HEIGHT OF BASE CUT FROM GREY PAPER. A SIMILAR EFFECT COULD BE OBTAINED BY SHADING OR PAINTING.
ALL LETTERING AND DIMENSIONS WITH H PENCIL.

TO MEET THE STORAGE REQUIREMENTS OF THE BRIEF BOTH CUPBOARDS AND DRAWERS WILL BE NECESSARY. IN DECIDING UPON THE SPACING OF THESE CAREFUL THOUGHT MUST BE GIVEN TO THE APPEARANCE OF THE FRONT OF THE SIDEBOARD. SELECTION AND POSITION OF HANDLES, IF NESSARY, IS IMPORTANT.

A

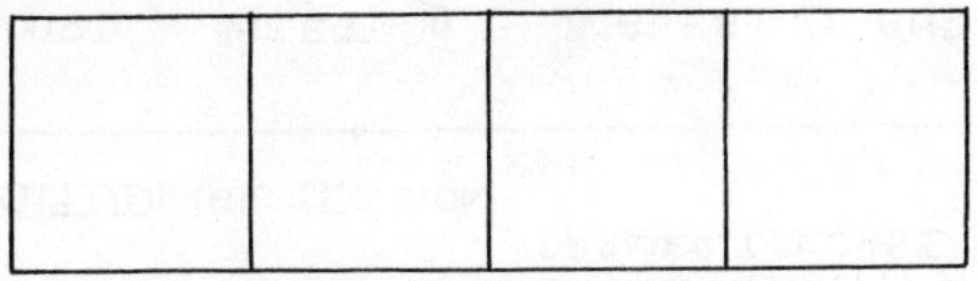

FOUR DOORS WITH DRAWER SPACE BEHIND ONE OR TWO OF THEM.

B

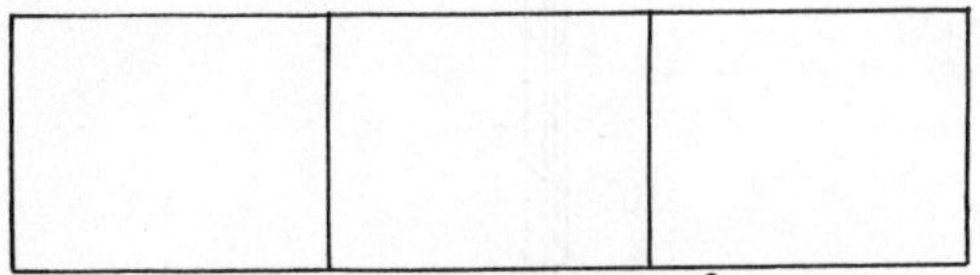

WOULD THREE DOORS BE BETTER? WOULD THEY BE HINGED OR MIGHT THEY SLIDE?

C

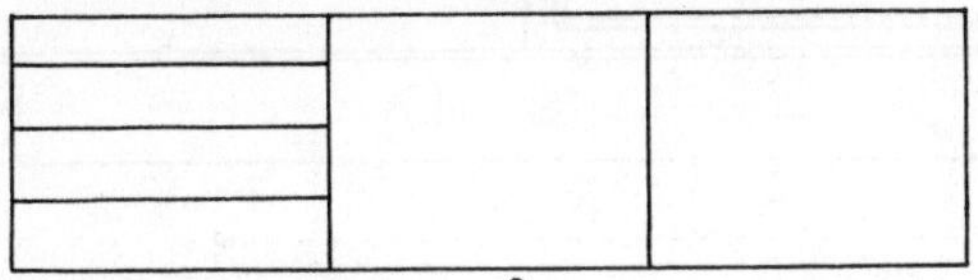

CAN THE DRAWERS SHOW? IF SO, IN WHICH SPACE DO THEY LOOK BEST?

D

THIS ARRANGEMENT GIVES A MORE BALANCED APPEARANCE. ONE DOOR CAN SLIDE ACROSS THE FRONT OF THE DRAWERS. THE OTHER, FOR THE BOTTLE AND GLASSES CUPBOARD CAN BE A DROP DOOR TO FORM A SHELF WHEN OPEN. NOTE CENTRE HANDLES. THE ABOVE DESIGN FULFILS THE NEEDS SPECIFIED, BUT MANY OTHER ALTERNATIVES ARE POSSIBLE.

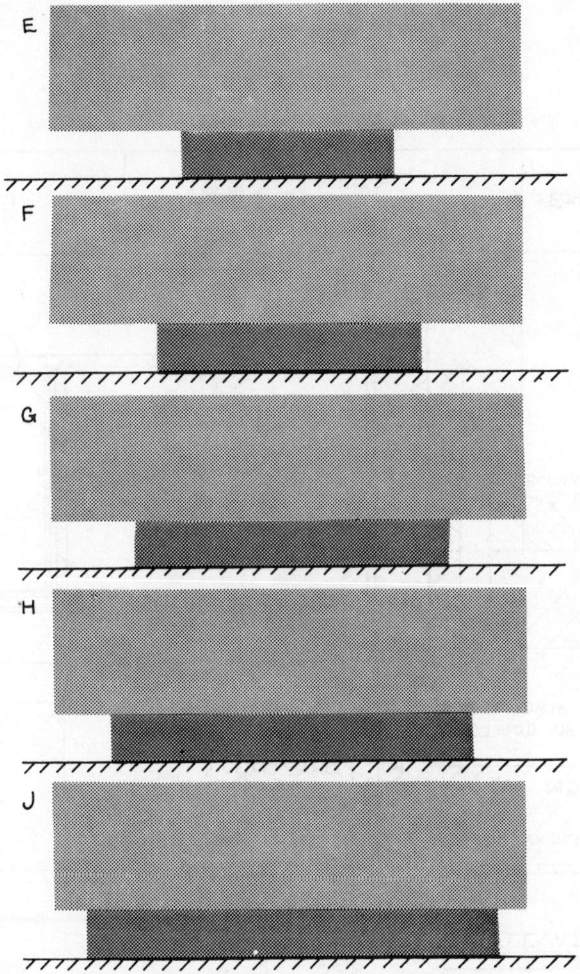
E
F
G
H
J

COLOURED BLOCKS, EACH 175 HIGH, BUT OF VARIOUS LENGTHS TO ASSIST IN DETERMINING THE LENGTH OF THE BASE.

IDEAS FOR THE CONSTRUCTION OF THE BASE; SOME EMPLOYING A COMBINATION OF WOOD AND METAL.

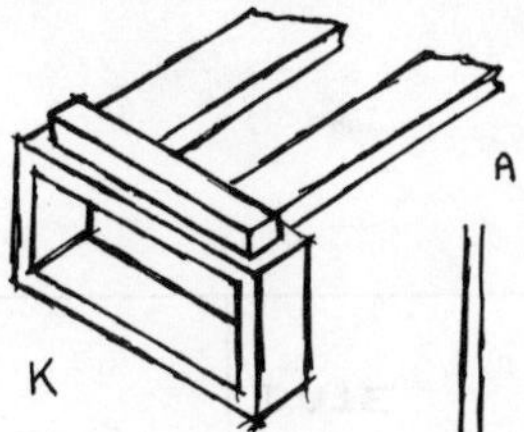

K

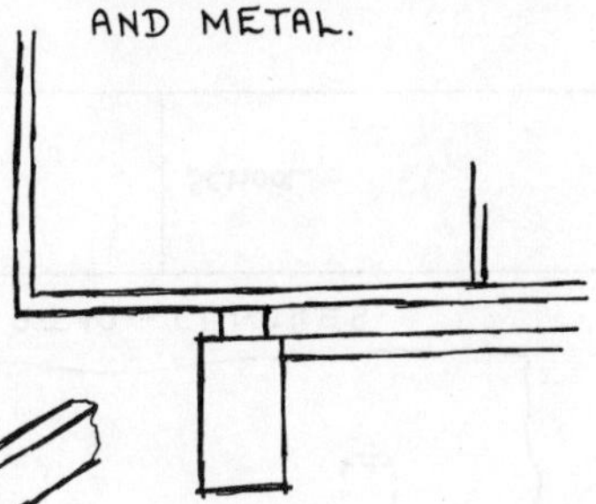

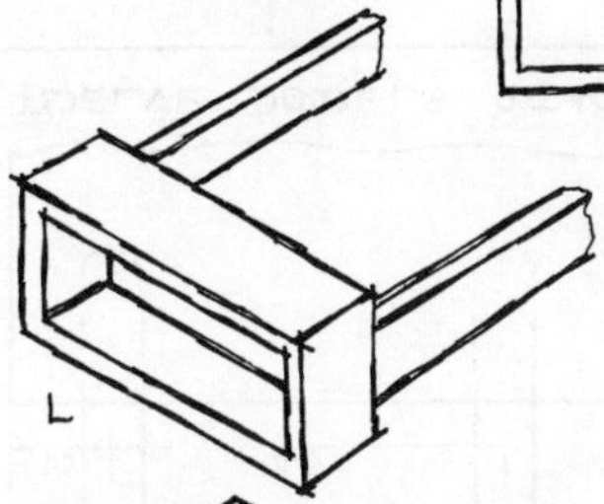

L

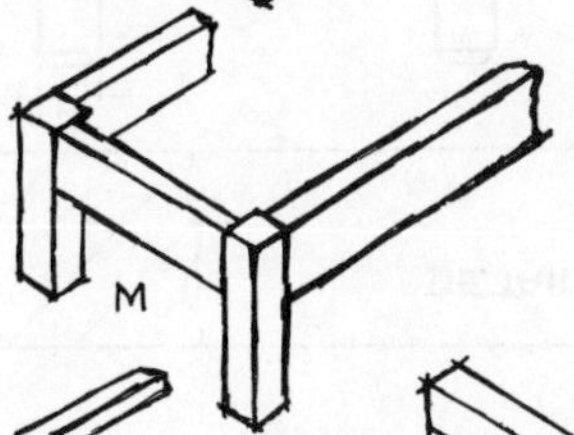

M

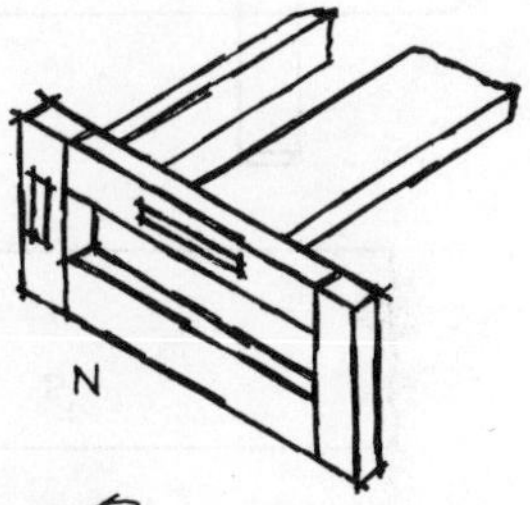

N

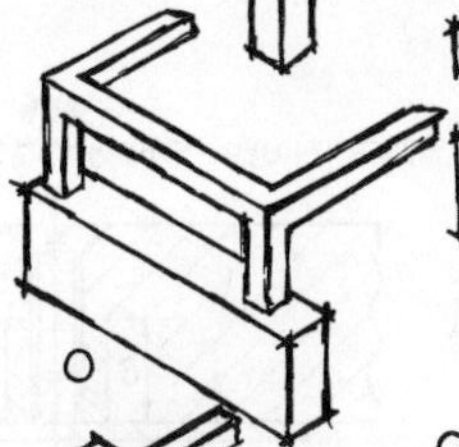

O

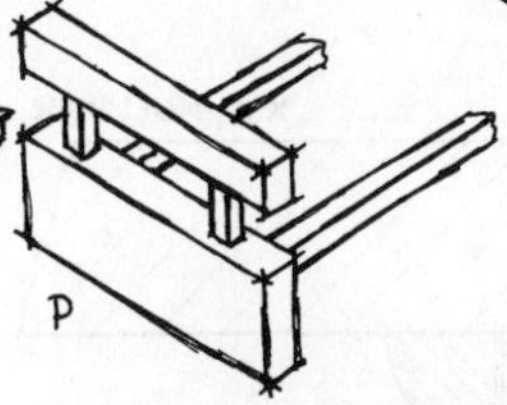

P

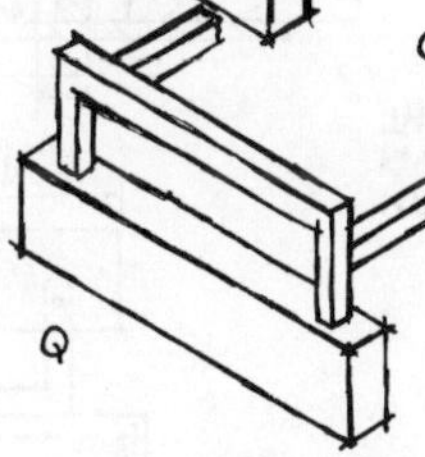

Q

O, P AND Q INVOLVE THE USE OF SQUARE SECTION TUBE.

THE DESIGN TO BE CONTINUED USING A COMBINATION OF FRONT 'D' AND BASE LENGTH 'G' CONSTRUCTED AS AT 'O'

SIDEBOARD - SHEET II - SCALE 1:20	DESIGNED BY	FORM	DATE	SCHOOL

FRONT VIEWS 3H PENCIL, SKETCHES AND LETTERING HB PENCIL AND H PENCIL RESPECTIVELY.
CARCASE BLOCKS CUT FROM GREY PAPER AND BASE BLOCKS FROM BLUE. EASY COMPARISON IS POSSIBLE AND A SUITABLE LENGTH CHOSEN. THE FINAL CHOICE IS OFTEN A MATTER OF PERSONAL PREFERENCE BUT CONSIDERATION MUST BE GIVEN TO STRENGTH OF CONSTRUCTION AS WELL AS TO APPEARANCE.

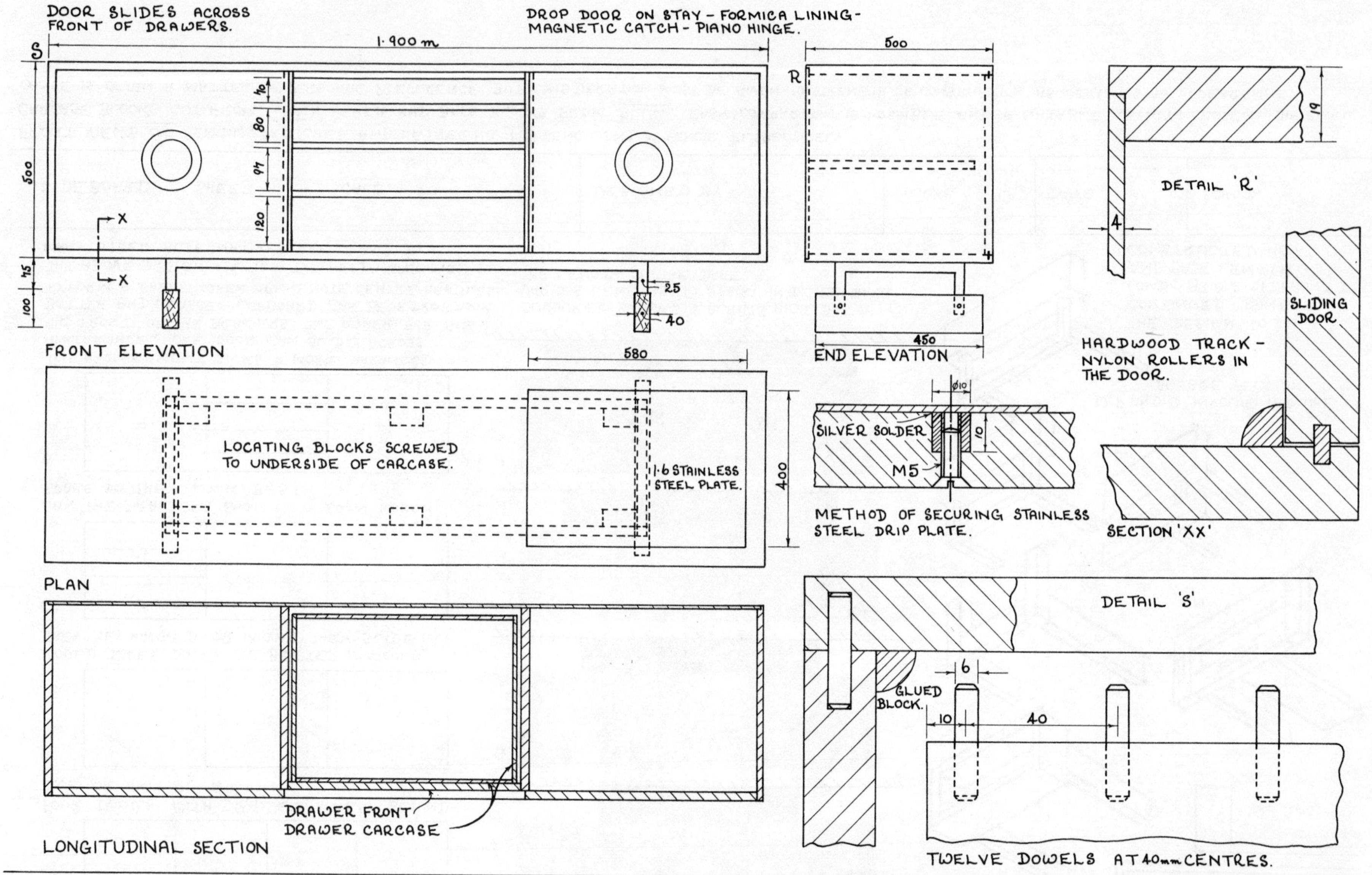
DOOR SLIDES ACROSS FRONT OF DRAWERS.
DROP DOOR ON STAY - FORMICA LINING - MAGNETIC CATCH - PIANO HINGE.
1·900 m
500
S
R
40
80
97
120
45
100
X
25
40
450
FRONT ELEVATION
END ELEVATION
580
400
LOCATING BLOCKS SCREWED TO UNDERSIDE OF CARCASE.
1·6 STAINLESS STEEL PLATE.
PLAN
DRAWER FRONT
DRAWER CARCASE
LONGITUDINAL SECTION
19
DETAIL 'R'
4
SLIDING DOOR
HARDWOOD TRACK - NYLON ROLLERS IN THE DOOR.
SECTION 'XX'
ϕ10
SILVER SOLDER
10
M5
METHOD OF SECURING STAINLESS STEEL DRIP PLATE.
DETAIL 'S'
6
GLUED BLOCK.
10
40
TWELVE DOWELS AT 40mm CENTRES.

SIDEBOARD - SHEET III - SCALES 1:10 AND 1:1 | DESIGNED BY | FORM | DATE | SCHOOL

ORTHOGRAPHIC PROJECTION - 3H PENCIL.
FULL SIZE DETAILS - 3H PENCIL.
PRINTING AND DIMENSIONS - H PENCIL.

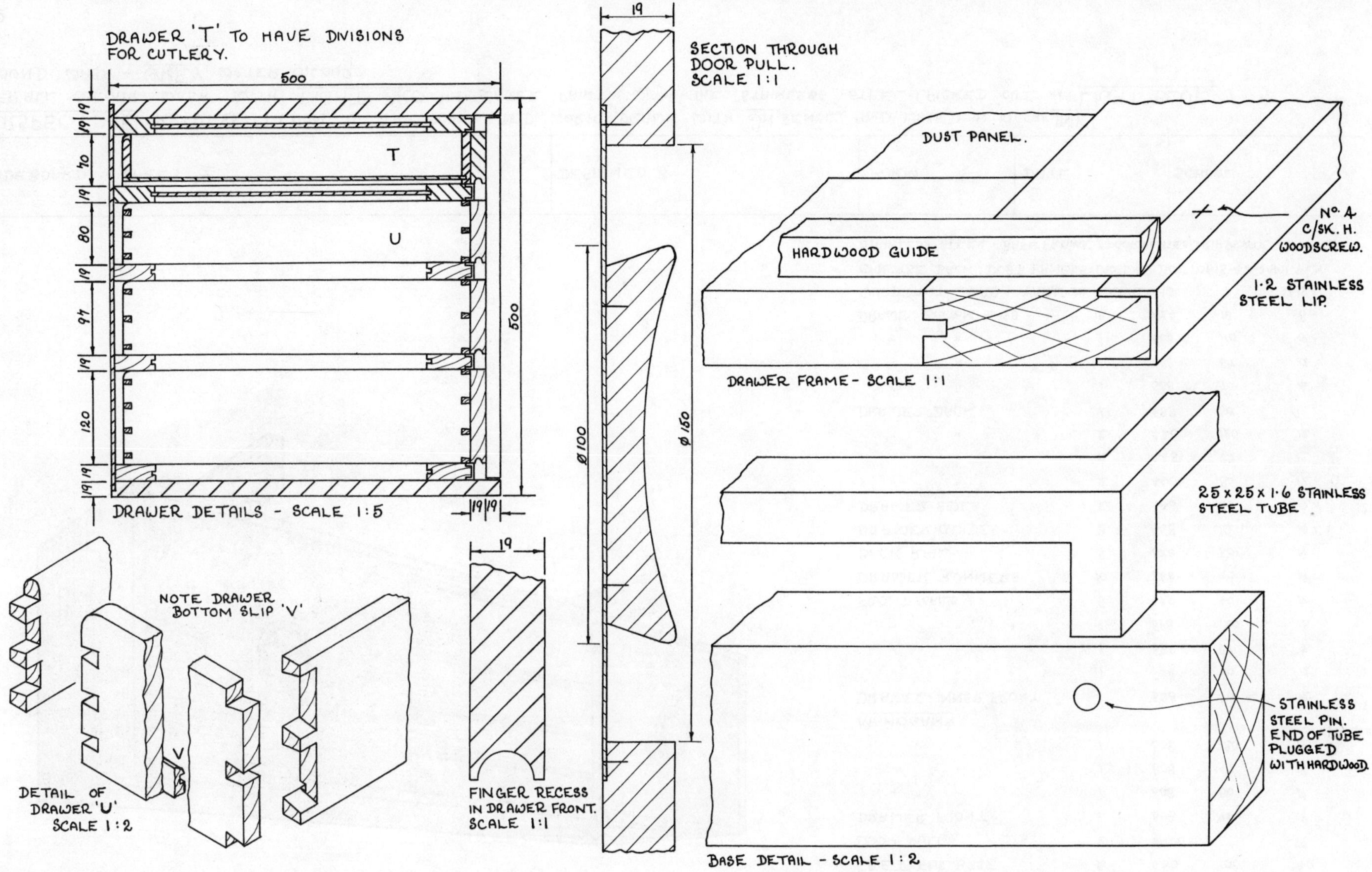
DRAWER 'T' TO HAVE DIVISIONS FOR CUTLERY.
500
19
19
19
40
19
80
19
94
19
120
19
19
T
U
500
19
19
DRAWER DETAILS - SCALE 1:5
19
SECTION THROUGH DOOR PULL. SCALE 1:1
Ø 100
Ø 150
DUST PANEL.
HARDWOOD GUIDE
No. 4 C/SK. H. WOODSCREW.
1·2 STAINLESS STEEL LIP.
DRAWER FRAME - SCALE 1:1
25 x 25 x 1·6 STAINLESS STEEL TUBE
STAINLESS STEEL PIN. END OF TUBE PLUGGED WITH HARDWOOD.
BASE DETAIL - SCALE 1:2
NOTE DRAWER BOTTOM SLIP 'V'
V
DETAIL OF DRAWER 'U' SCALE 1:2
19
FINGER RECESS IN DRAWER FRONT. SCALE 1:1

SIDEBOARD - SHEET IV - SCALES AS SHOWN.	DESIGNED BY	FORM	DATE	SCHOOL

SECTION SHOWING DRAWER DETAILS : DRAWER CONSTRUCTION : DOOR PULL : DRAWER FRAMES AND BASE DRAWN WITH 3H PENCIL.
PRINTING WITH H PENCIL.
EXPLODED DETAIL OF DRAWER IN ISOMETRIC PROJECTION . DRAWER FRAME AND BASE DETAILS IN OBLIQUE PROJECTION. - 3H PENCIL.

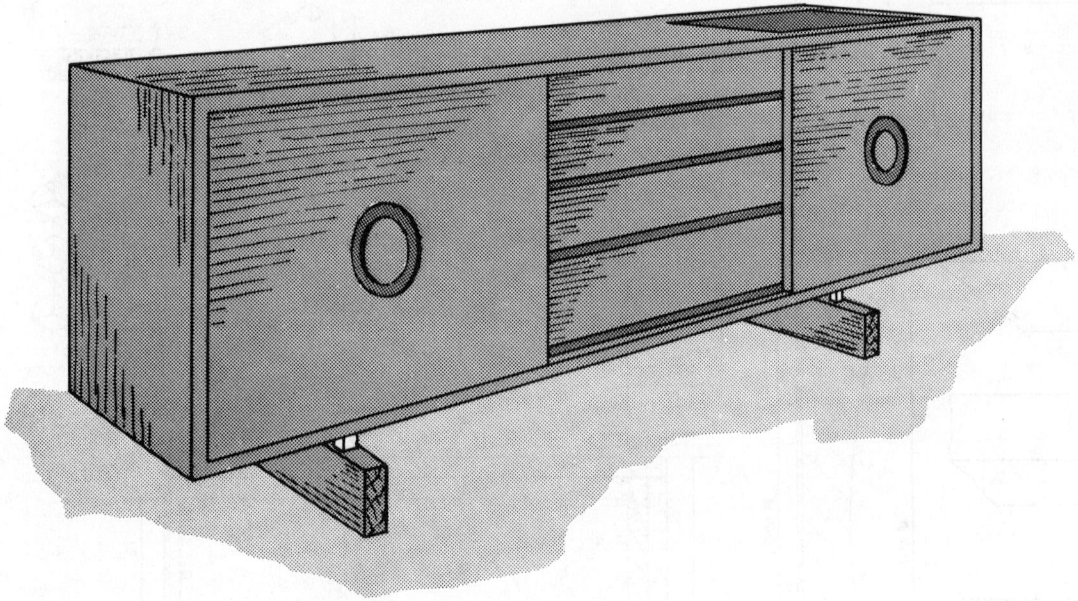

MATERIAL REQUIRED - FINISHED SIZES.

SIZES IN MILLIMETRES	No. OFF	LENGTH	WIDTH	THICKNESS
CARCASE				
TEAK VENEERED CHIPBOARD.				
TOP/BOTTOM	2	1900	600	19
ENDS/DIVISIONS	4	500	500	19
DOORS	2	620	462	19
SHELVES	2	630	430	19
TEAK				
FEET FOR BASE	2	450	100	40
DOOR PULLS	2	ϕ100		19
DRAWER FRONT	1	608	70	19
" "	1	608	80	19
" "	1	608	97	19
" "	1	608	120	19
MAHOGANY				
DRAWER-INNER FRONT	1	588	70	12
" " "	1	588	80	12
" " "	1	588	97	12
" " "	1	588	120	12
FRONT RAILS	5	620	60	19
DRAWER RUNNERS	10	360	40	19
BACK RAIL	5	620	50	19
DRAWER GUIDES	8	458	10	10
DRAWER SIDES	2	448	70	12
" "	2	448	80	12
" "	2	448	97	12
" "	2	448	120	12
DRAWER BACK	1	588	60	12
" "	1	588	70	12
" "	1	588	87	12
" "	1	588	110	12
DRAWER BOTTOM SLIPS	8	424	18	8
QUADRANT BEAD - VARIOUS LENGTHS				R12

CARCASE BACK : DUST PANELS: DRAWER BOTTOMS-4mm MAH. PLY.

STAINLESS STEEL - BASE FRAME / DOOR PLATES / DRIP PLATE / LIPPING.

SIDEBOARD - SHEET V	DESIGNED BY	FORM	DATE	SCHOOL

PERSPECTIVE REPRESENTATION OF THE COMPLETED WORK DRAWN WITH 3H PENCIL AND LINED IN WITH INK.
OVERALL COLOUR WASH WITH LIGHT BROWN WATER PAINT WITH THE STAINLESS STEEL PICKED OUT IN LIGHT BLUE.
GROUND WASH - GREY WATER COLOUR.

A scale model made quickly from a block of softwood. The features were drawn in with soft pencil. Grey paper was used to represent the drip plate and door-pulls. The feet were pegged on with matchsticks and glued with balsa cement.

This 3-dimensional model was made in a few minutes and readily gave an idea of whether the proportions chosen were correct.

This carefully made scale model took much longer to assemble but this was justifiable before beginning such a large piece of work. It is possible to see how satisfactory the design preparation has been and whether or not it is aesthetically acceptable. The model is veneered in teak. Aluminium foil was used to represent the stainless steel on the doors, rails and top. A square section of aluminium was used for the base frame and glued in position with 'Araldite'.

Drawing and Modelling Equipment

Drawing equipment

The purpose of this chapter is to give an indication of the wide variety of drawing aids and media which are available to facilitate design presentation which the author has used in his everyday work at school and in the preparation of this book. The items illustrated form a basis from which to make a selection to be included in the resources of the school's design area. Good quality should be a deciding factor in making a choice, since just as good quality materials lead to good practical work, so does good quality drawing equipment lead to good drawing and design. This is equally true of materials used for mock-ups and model making.

The pencil is the most common medium used for visual expression and may be of conventional construction or the more modern clutch pattern.

FABER-CASTELL
TK
10 Minen Leads
9071
H

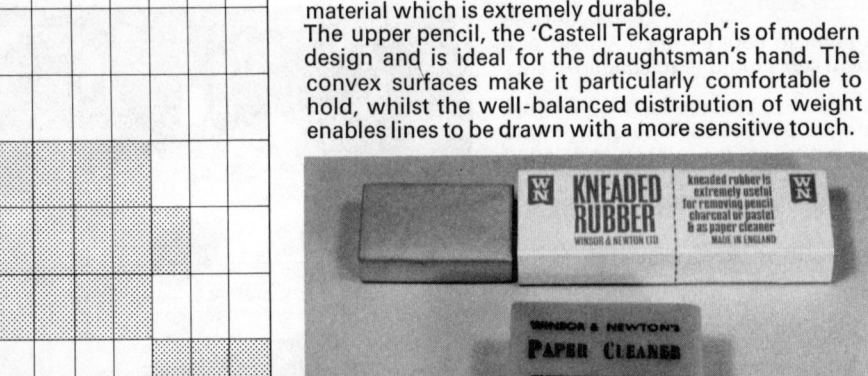

Clutch pencils with a box of leads and a lead sharpener. The body of the pencils is of 'Cellidor', a plastic material which is extremely durable.
The upper pencil, the 'Castell Tekagraph' is of modern design and is ideal for the draughtsman's hand. The convex surfaces make it particularly comfortable to hold, whilst the well-balanced distribution of weight enables lines to be drawn with a more sensitive touch.

Castell Degree Chart

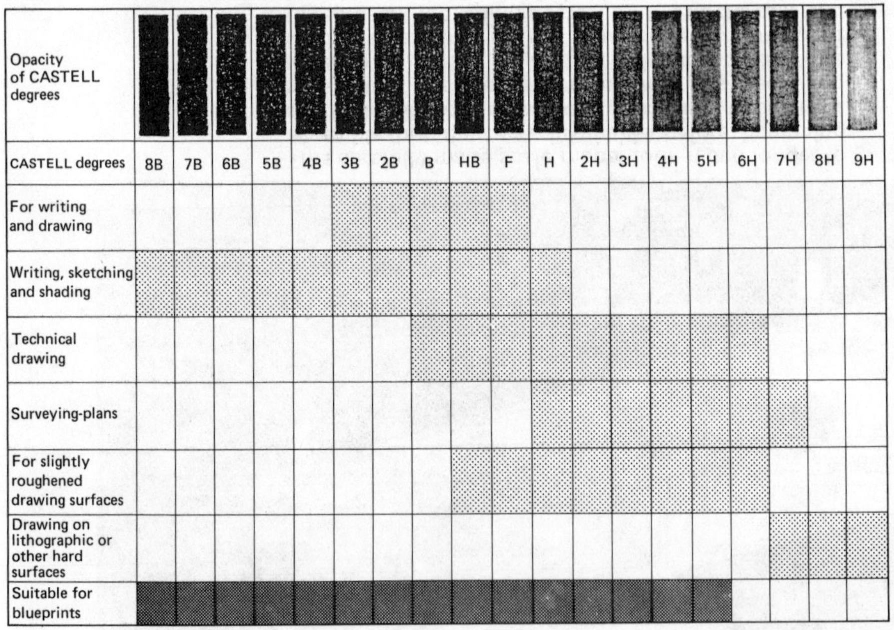

Opacity of CASTELL degrees
CASTELL degrees
8B 7B 6B 5B 4B 3B 2B B HB F H 2H 3H 4H 5H 6H 7H 8H 9H
For writing and drawing
Writing, sketching and shading
Technical drawing
Surveying-plans
For slightly roughened drawing surfaces
Drawing on lithographic or other hard surfaces
Suitable for blueprints

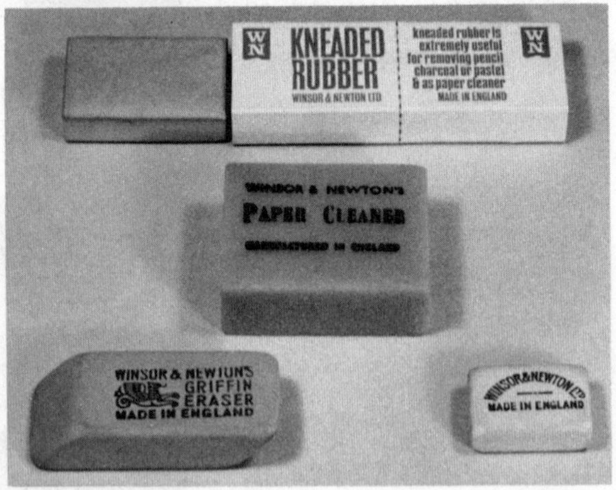

KNEADED RUBBER
WINSOR & NEWTON LTD
kneaded rubber is extremely useful for removing pencil charcoal or pastel & as paper cleaner
MADE IN ENGLAND
WINSOR & NEWTON'S
PAPER CLEANER
WINSOR & NEWTONS GRIFFIN ERASER
MADE IN ENGLAND
WINSOR&NEWTON LTD
MADE IN ENGLAND

Erasers. Good quality erasers are essential pieces of drawing equipment.
Illustrated : a 'Kneaded Rubber' which is sometimes known as 'Plastic' or 'Putty' and which can be moulded to a fine point for minute erasures ; a general 'Paper Cleaner' ; a 'Griffin' green, double-wedged-shaped eraser made to a special non-smear formula ; and a 'Best Soft White Rubber'.

The 'TK-Plast' plastic eraser for quick and clean corrections. It is encased in a durable plastic sleeve.

'British Thornton' timber faced drawing board and tee square. The tee square has a parallel blade which means that full board coverage is available for both right and left hand use. The blade is made from a mica-type material which completely eliminates problems of warp and twist and has a much longer working life than the traditional timber type. It is screwed securely to a beechwood stock.

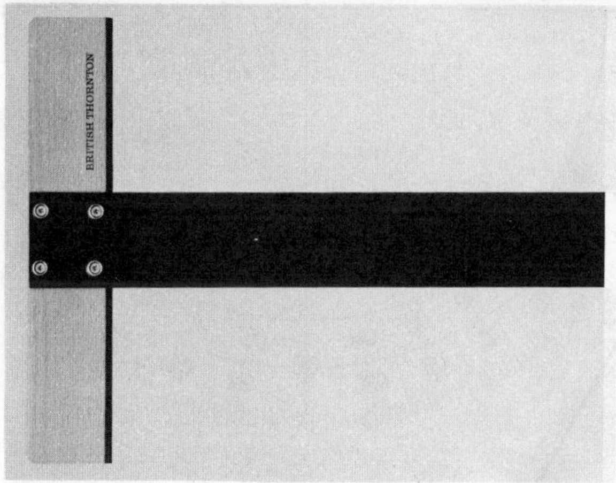
BRITISH THORNTON

In schools free hand sketching and technical drawing are done on cartridge paper of which there are a number of different weights and textures. Four of these, stocked by Windsor and Newton Ltd., are Educational, Collegiate, School of Art and Engineer's. The first two are light-weight and suitable for general use; for more serious or permanent work the heavier ones would be more suitable. For freehand sketching the paper should be left loose, but for mechanical drawing it should be held firmly to the drawing board which in turn can be a separate item or part of a drawing unit.

Metric Paper Size

AO	1189 x 841	A4	297 x 210
A1	841 x 594	A5	210 x 148
A2	594 x 420	A6	148 x 105
A3	420 x 297	A7	105 x 74

British Thornton work station RA 020 fitted with A2 drafting unit.

The drawing board and parallel motion can be used in specialised subjects like technical drawing, craft and design, art, and in ordinary subjects like maths, history and geography – subjects which have not traditionally involved drawing. This may be for the production of maps, diagrams or charts. The top panel of the unit can be reversed to make a desk for ordinary written work.

Detail design, both ergonomics and mechanics, has been considered. The general dimensions are based on the recommendations of the British Standards Institution plus independent research. The drawing board is adjustable to four specific working angles, and a parallel motion rule is fitted.

Prime quality steamed beech is used for the structure. The joints on the end frames are of mortise and tenon construction, pegged and glued for extra strength, and the top frame is comb jointed. Top surfaces are laminated with a very tough, hard-wearing plastics material.

The drawing board is also faced with a plastics laminate, but this time of a firmly resilient nature which eliminates the need for backing paper. Overall, the construction is firm and stable, the working parts smooth and precise.

Having illustrated the drawing board and tee square it is logical to show the next most simple and very necessary instruments – the set squares and protractor – before leading on to the more sophisticated items. Many children experience great difficulty in appreciating the real value of these and it is for this reason that they have been included here.

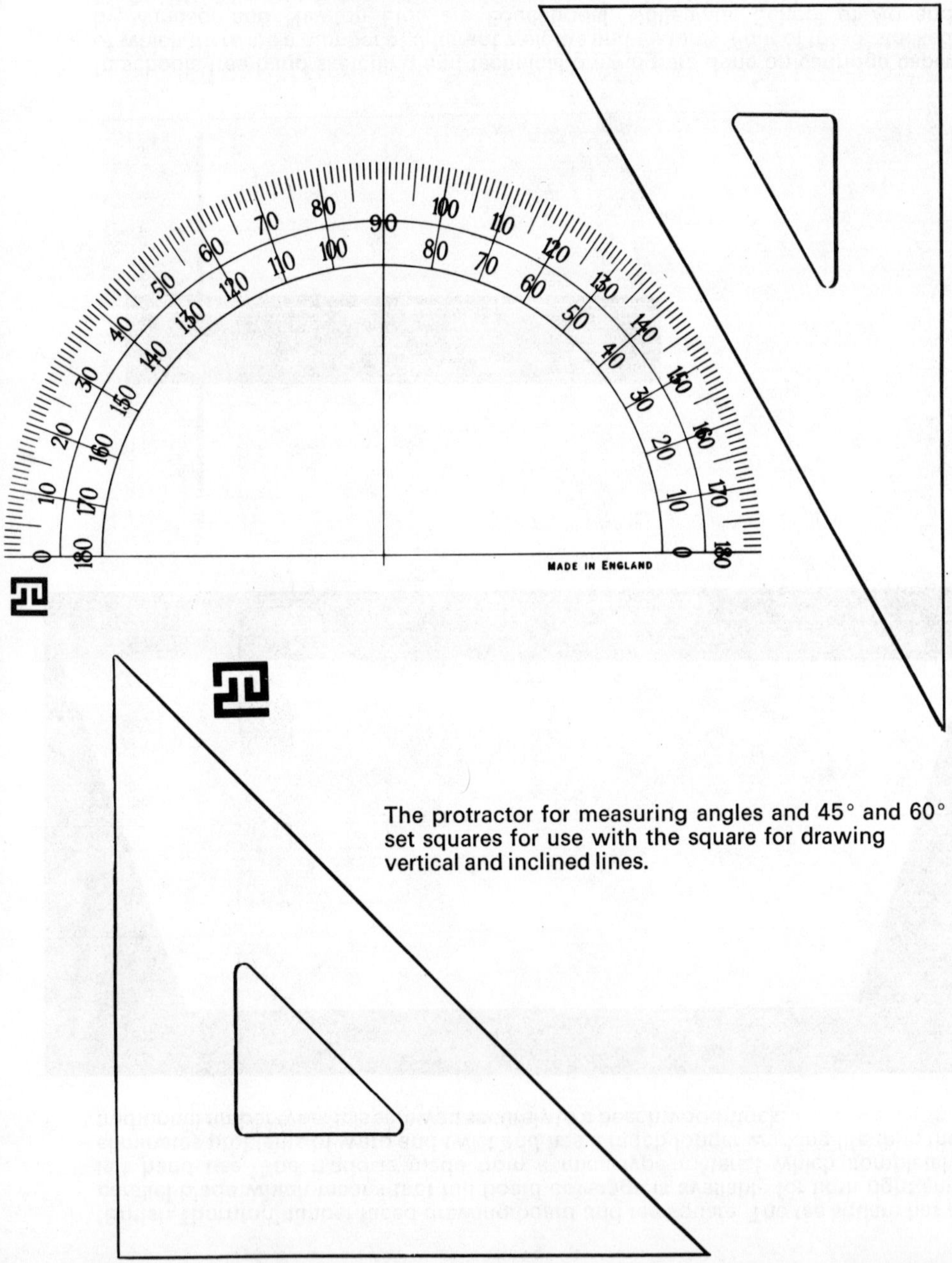
MADE IN ENGLAND

The protractor for measuring angles and 45° and 60° set squares for use with the square for drawing vertical and inclined lines.

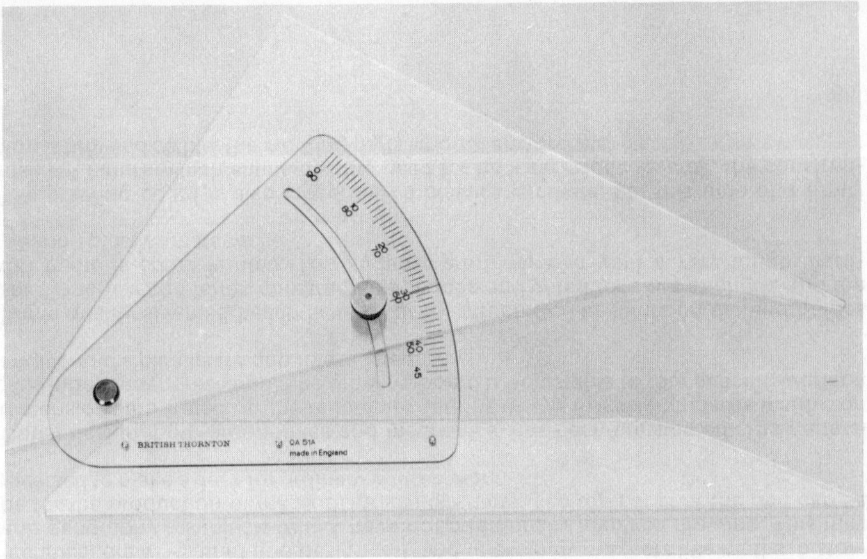
BRITISH THORNTON
made in England

The adjustable triangle used in conjunction with the tee square will do the work of the protractor and 45° and 60° set squares. It can be used above or below the tee square blade as indicated below.

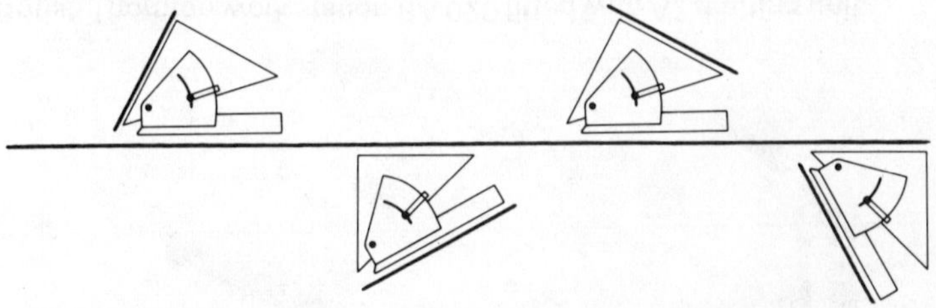

The 'Unique' draft square is similar in principle to the adjustable triangle. The arms are fixed at 90° to each other and sweep any angle over the 180° between the horizontal arms.

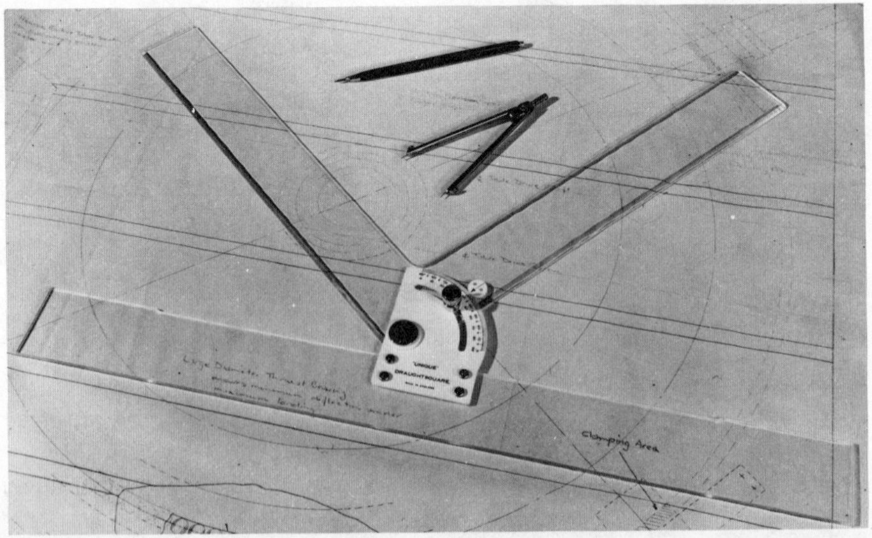

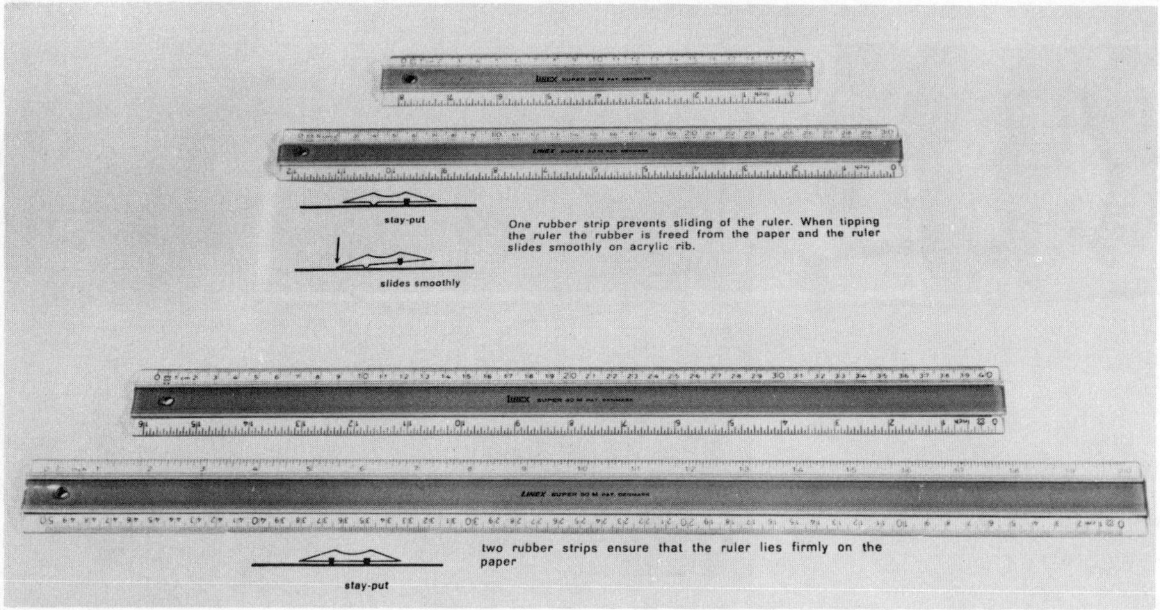
stay-put
One rubber strip prevents sliding of the ruler. When tipping the ruler the rubber is freed from the paper and the ruler slides smoothly on acrylic rib.
slides smoothly
two rubber strips ensure that the ruler lies firmly on the paper
stay-put

'Super' rulers by 'Linex'. Made from crystal-clear acrylic with green centre. With bevels on both edges they may be used for tracing.

These metric scales which are oval in section are made from 'Dunirit' – an exceptionally hard-wearing plastic. It is inert and consequently will not be affected by fluctuations in temperature and humidity. At the same time the plastic is flexible which helps to prevent chipping and scratching and is easily cleaned with warm soapy water.

Those illustrated are:
B.S. 1347 No. 1 1 : 1 : 2 : 5 : 10
B.S. 1347 No. 2 1 : 5 : 50 : 10 : 100 : 20 : 200 : 500 : 1000

METRIC
DISTRIBUTED BY EAGLE PENCIL CO. LTD. LONDON
LINEX 601 DENMARK
BS.1347 NO.1

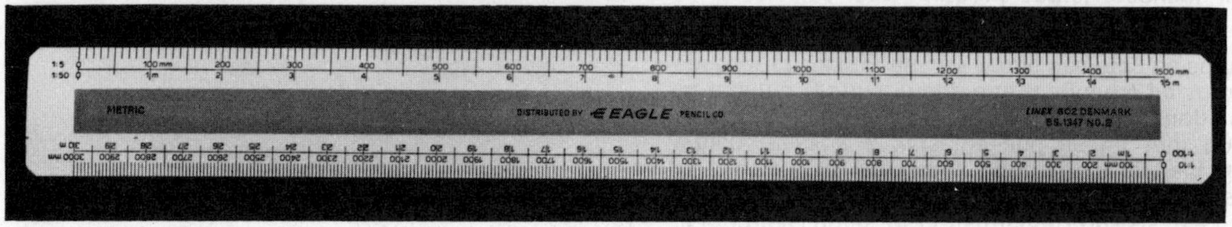
METRIC
DISTRIBUTED BY EAGLE PENCIL CO
LINEX 602 DENMARK
BS.1347 NO.2

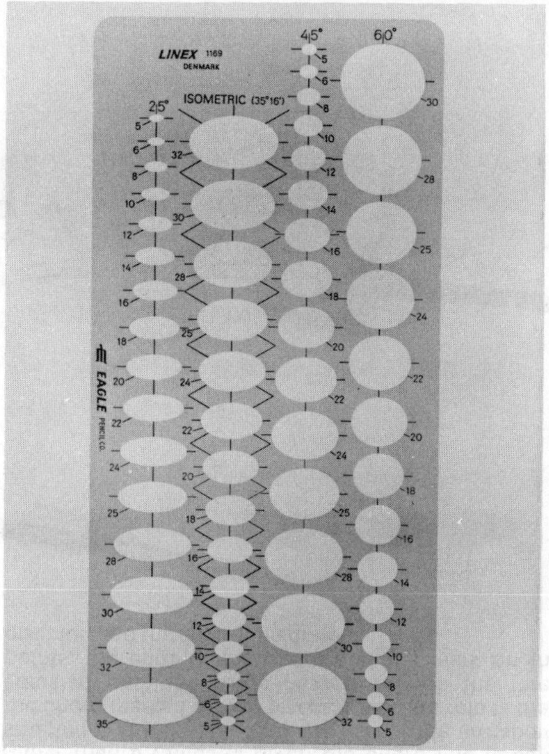
LINEX 1169
DENMARK
ISOMETRIC (35°16')
EAGLE

An 'Isometric' template – one of a wide variety ranging from circles to nut and bolt profiles to welding and electrical symbols. Made of transparent green plastic.

The slide rule which enables the designer to make rapid calculations as his work proceeds.

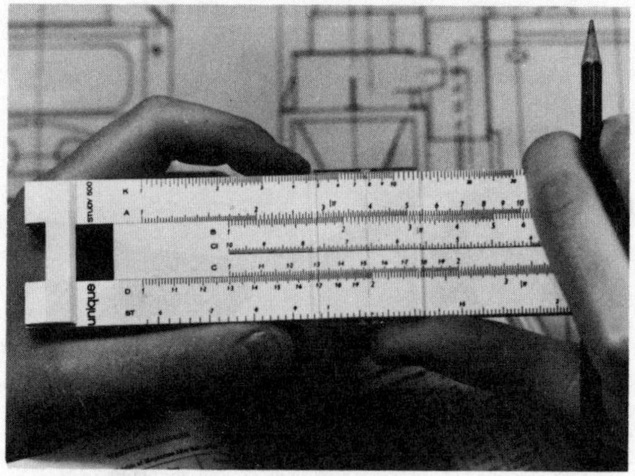

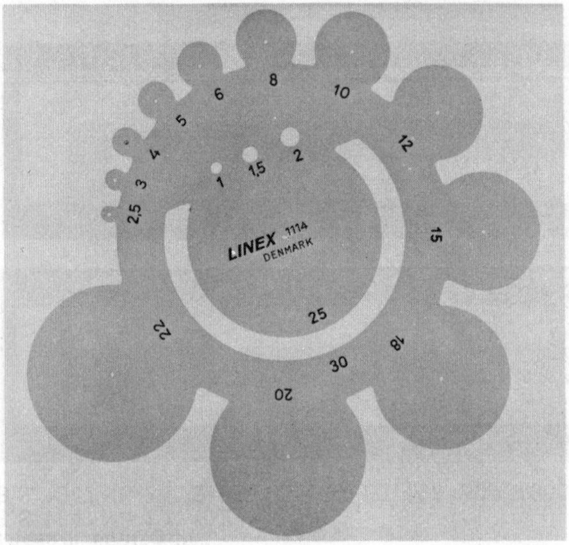
LINEX 1114
DENMARK

'Bow' template for quick drawing of small diameter circles within radii from 1 to 30 mm. In transparent green plastic.

The 'Unique' flexicurve is designed to produce regular or irregular curves. Its construction consists of a P.V.C. outer casing with a core of lead with regulating strips of spring steel on either side. It has characteristics which make it a versatile and useful tool on the drawing board and in many other applications such as making graphs, maps and diagrams, jig forming, contour checking, etc. Its properties may be summed up as follows:

1 It remains inert, without partial recovery, when positioned.
2 Steel springs ensure regular transition from one curve to another.
3 Forms curves as small as 25 mm radius.
4 Bevelled edges give good visibility.
5 Concave base for grip.
6 One edge has a flange for drawing with ink.
7 The other edge is used for pencil.
8 Strong, simple and washable.

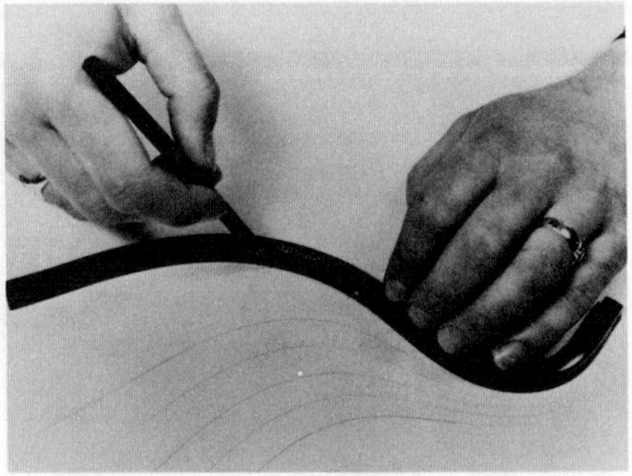

The 'Unique' arc rule is a new development enabling the true arc of any large radius to be drawn accurately. This simple instrument will form an important unit in the range of instruments used by draughtsmen, designers, architects and in workshops for marking out purposes. The micro control is adjusted and the true arc is produced by the stainless steel drawing blade. Small arcs can easily be blended into a large arc by placing the blade at a tangent to the smaller radii after these have been drawn in. Where a camber rather than a radius is given the chord line is constructed and dissected and the rise of the arc above the chord marked on the bisector. The arc rule is then adjusted until the blade passes through the three points, the ends of the chord and the mark on the bisector, and the arc is then drawn.

Curves – English set with bevelled edge in glass-clear 'Dunion'. Used for drawing irregular curves.

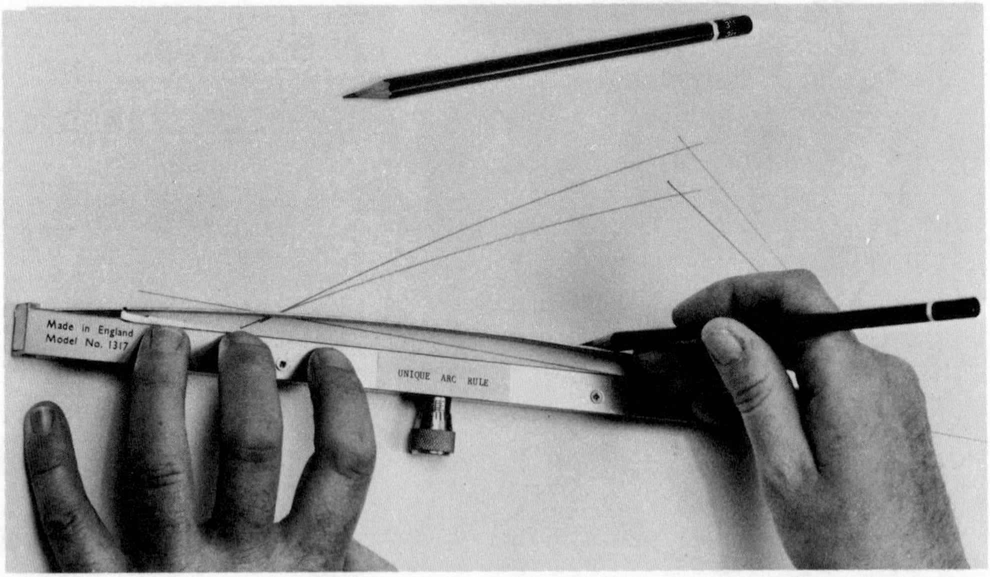
Made in England
Model No. 1317
UNIQUE ARC RULE

'British Thornton' drawing instruments. These are well-made instruments designed to perform their particular function perfectly. Ease of setting has been given careful attention. Certain of the instruments are fitted with a ball-race head and where even greater stability is required the 'C' clamp principle has been adopted, with a centre screw for perfect balance and ease of adjustment. The instruments are exceptionally durable and the 'Lansin' stainless finish (tin-nickel alloy electroplating) is extremely hardwearing and has an attractive appearance.

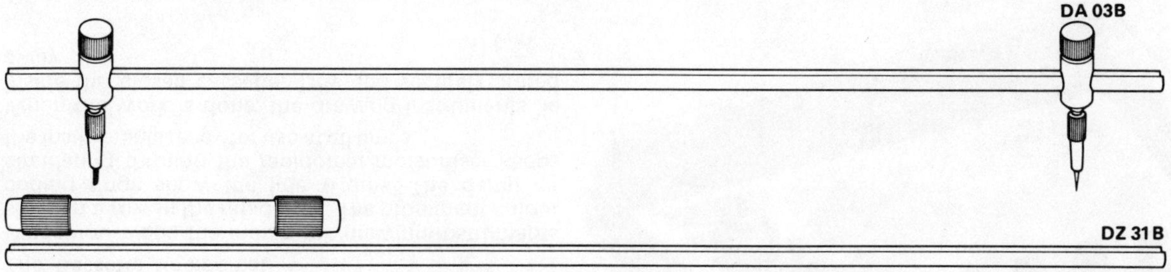
DA 03B
DZ 31B

DA 010 large pencil spring compass 'C' clamp head and centre-screw control with nylon bearings. 'Lansin' stainless finish.
DD 010 pencil compass ball-race head. 'Lansin' stainless finish.
DA 020 pencil spring bow 'C' clamp head and centre-screw control with nylon bearings. 'Lansin' stainless finish.
DD 110 divider ball-race head. 'Lansin' stainless finish.
DA 120 divider spring bow 'C' clamp head and centre-screw control with nylon bearings. 'Lansin' finish.

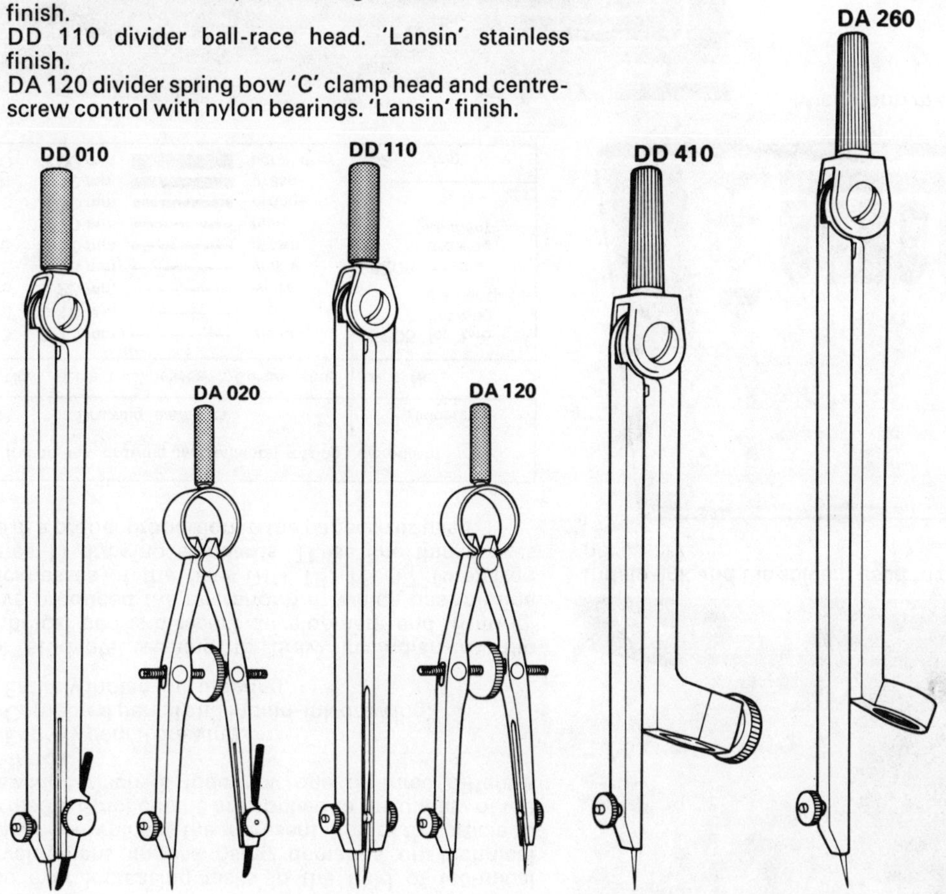
DD 010
DD 110
DD 410
DA 260
DA 020
DA 120

DA 03B pencil beam compass for use up to 250 mm. radius. Stainless steel beam. May be converted to divider with 2 mm. diameter needle, or to technical pen compass with DZ 330 adaptor. Fittings with 'Lansin' stainless finish.

DZ 330

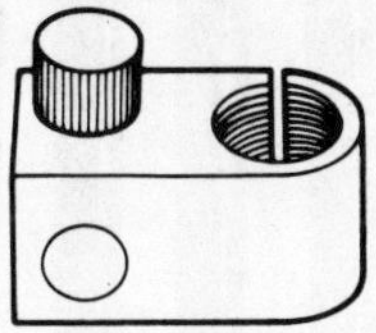

DZ 330 technical pen adaptor for DA 03B. Moulded from nylon with metal screw.
DZ 31B 250 mm. extension beam and connector for DA 03B.

DD 410 pencil compass die-cast construction with ball-race head. Can be used with pencil, ball-pen, fibre-tip pen, etc. An extremely versatile new development.

DA 260 technical pen compass for use with 'Rotring Variant' and 'Varioscript', 'Standardgraph K' and 'Normoscript'. Ball-race head within die-cast head-clip. 'Lansin' stainless finish.

The versatility case in which to store the drawing instruments.

The 'New Indian-ink' drawing and lettering implements.
The ever increasing tasks in the field of technical development impose rising demands on technical drawing – which is the representation of the article to be made. Strict criteria are applied to the quality of the drawing which is today by one of three different methods.
1 Entirely pencil drawing.
2 Combined pencil and indian-ink drawing.
3 Entirely indian-ink drawing.

For students wishing to draw in indian-ink the technical pen is a recent development and 'Rotring' have produced the micronorm *m* which has the line thicknesses of the new DIN 15, 16, 17 (preferred series 1) drawing standards. These line thicknesses are in a proper proportion to the paper sizes used.

Indian-ink drawing instruments rotring micronorm m̅

Drawing elements			Holders	
Art. No.	Line thicknesses	Colour code	Art. No.	
1513	0·13 mm	violet	5205	for two drawing elements
1518	0·18 mm	red		
1525	0·25 mm	white		
1535	0·35 mm	yellow	5206	for one drawing element
1505	0·50 mm	brown		
1507	0·70 mm	blue		
1510	1·00 mm	orange		
1514	1·40 mm	green		
1520	2·00 mm	light grey	5270	Joint

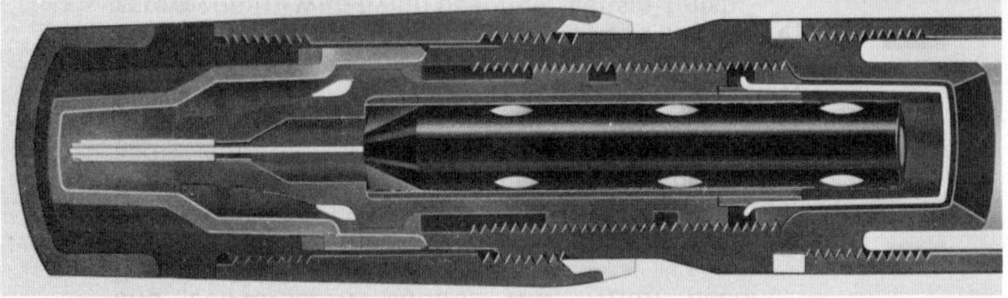

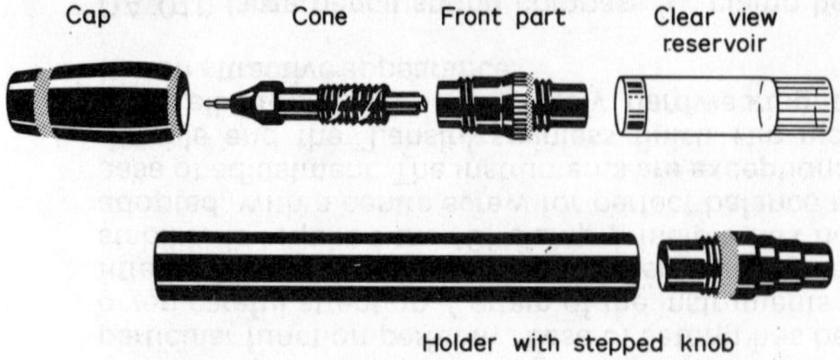
Cap
Cone
Front part
Clear view reservoir
Holder with stepped knob

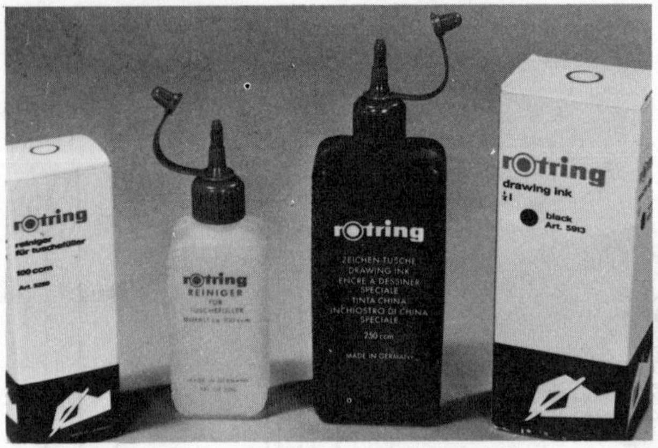
rotring
drawing ink
black
Art. 5913
rotring
REINIGER
rotring

Indian-ink and the solvent used to clean the pen when necessary.

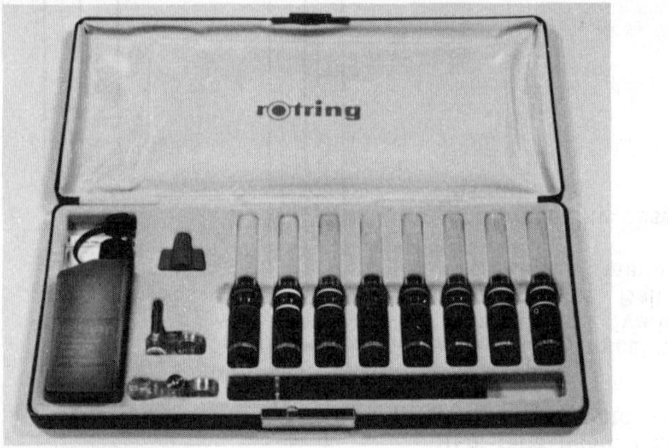
rotring

Micronorm *m* set 0.13 – 2.00 mm.

The 'Cassette-Rapidomat'

While you work, the indian-ink drawing instruments stand in a row in the rapidomat. The prominent colour coding rings show the line widths. The damp air circulating through the rapidomat moisturiser keeps the instruments ready for use at all times.

When the work is done, the drawing instruments lie inside the closed cassette. Tidy and securely stored away.

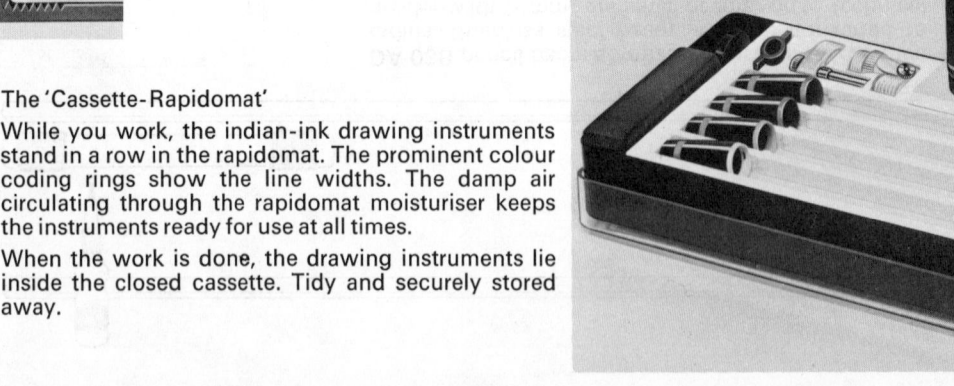

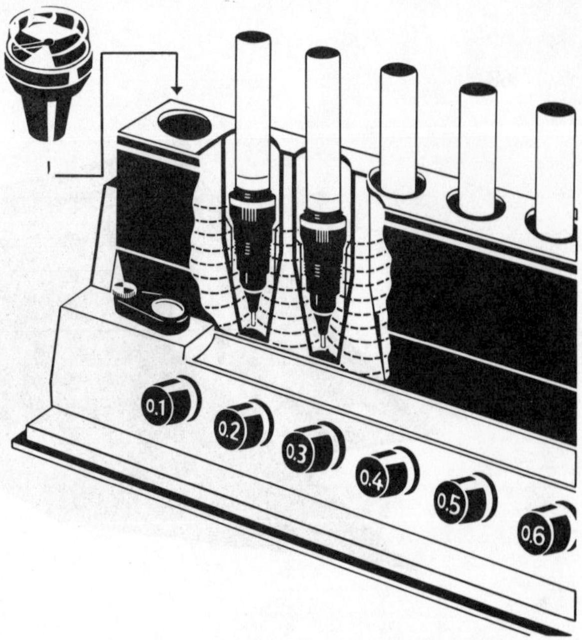
0.1
0.2
0.3
0.4
0.5
0.6

The 'Rotring Rapidomat' and 'Sectional View'. The 'Rapidomat' solves an old problem: dried-up indian-ink. A very simple conception, therefore absolutely safe. The sectional view shows you the functioning of the device. The absorbent material holds water. Humid air circulates around the technical drawing pen thus avoiding drying up of indian-ink. The best check: by means of its three differently coloured sections the hygrometer shows reliably the humidity control of the utensil.

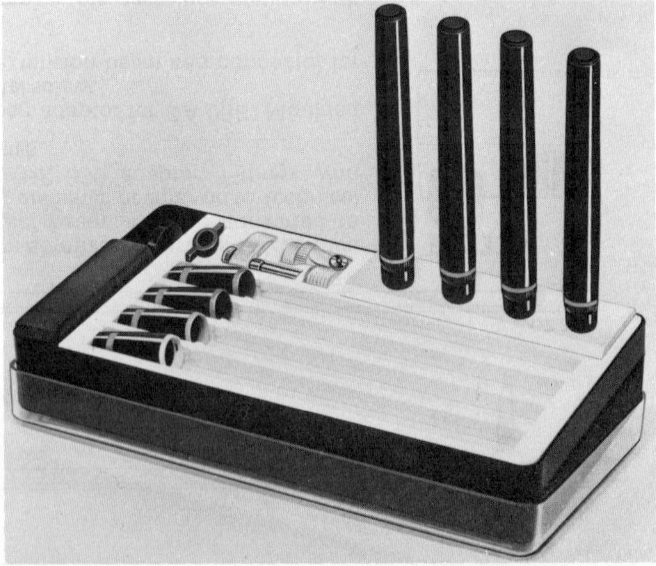

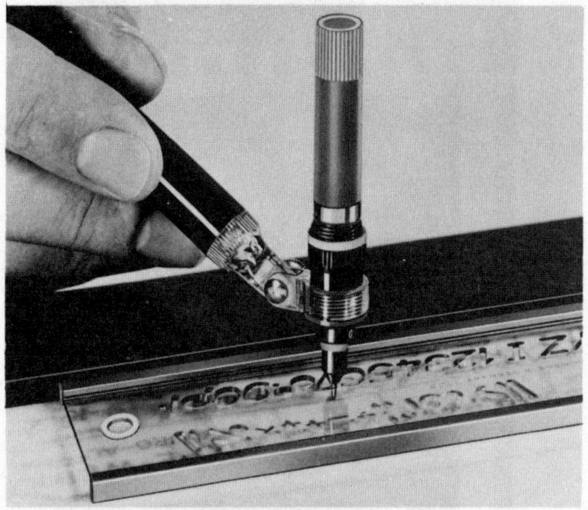

'Rotring' lettering stencils.
Quick and easy lettering with the 'Rotring' lettering stencils.
For lettering you insert a joint between the holder and the drawing element. This gives you an unimpeded view of the lettering point and you can hold the holder as best suits your hand.
The colour markings on the *m* lettering stencil and on the corresponding micronorm *m* indian-ink drawing instrument agree.

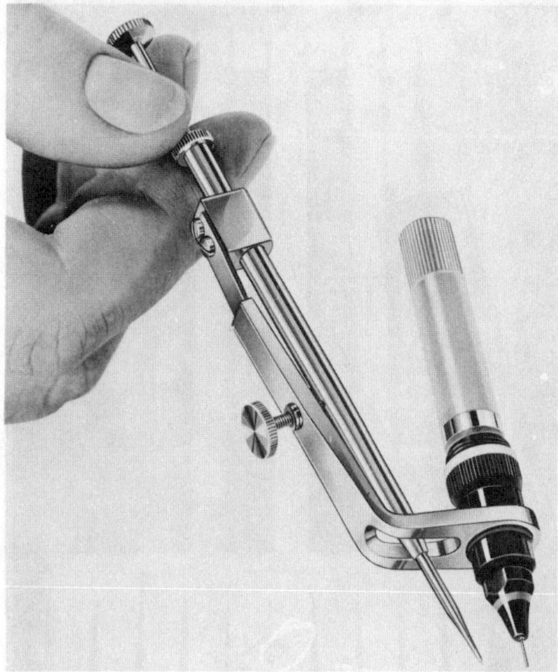

The Rotring pump compass

Z-profile lettering stencils lie flat and level on the sheet – but only where you do not trace. The upper part you are using is safely clear of the paper by about 1 mm. Ink cannot run underneath, characters are not touched, so they cannot smear. 'Rotring' Z-profile stencils are used on both sides. Capital letters are arranged on one side, lower case on the other. Just turn the stencil round and continue to trace. All letters are uniformly spaced. Before writing a letter, align the preceding one on the character last traced.

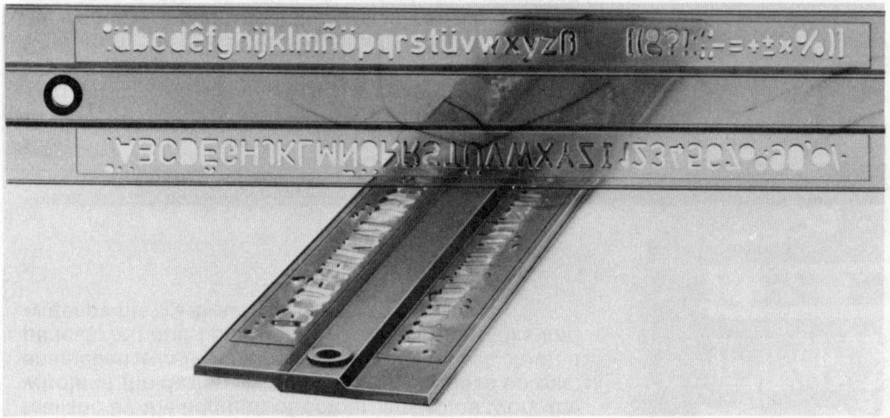

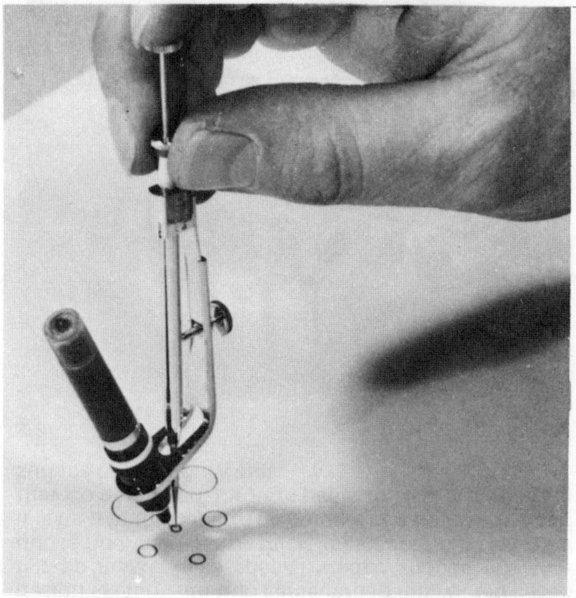

Where many smaller circles of unexcelled precision have to be drawn frequently, the 'Rotring' RP 06 pump compass is the right instrument to use.
The distribution of weight is ideal as the centre of gravity lies on the central axis. Thus this compass enables one to effect the task in hand perfectly.
The strong non-resonant leaf spring ensures the safe and uncomplicated use of this compass. It makes possible the drawing of the smallest circles down to an outside diameter of 0.7 mm.

For erasures on indian-ink drawings. The point can be adjusted as desired being of the propelling type and its very fine glass fibres enable indian-ink drawings to be erased with ease.

GERMANY A.W.FABER 30104

This is a special pencil for writing and marking on a wide variety of materials such as glass, china, transparent film, metals, plastics, leather, glossy card, etc. Useful when model making.
Available in black, red, blue, yellow, green, white.

A.W.FABER-CASTELL
FÜR GLAS, METALL, PLASTIC U.S.W.
2251
GERMANY

Design sketches and drawings in pencil or ink can often be made much more interesting and more realistic by the addition of colour. For some work the whole of the design sketching can be done in colour; enamelled jewellery being a typical example. Coloured pencils, felt and fibre tipped pens, coloured inks and water paints are all available to the designer.

FREXON
NON TOXIC
Crayons
For FREE EXPRESSION in the Classroom or at Home
A Harbutt PRODUCTION
MADE IN ENGLAND

These wax crayons are ideal for drawing large, bold sketches, e.g. designs for ornamental forged ironwork.

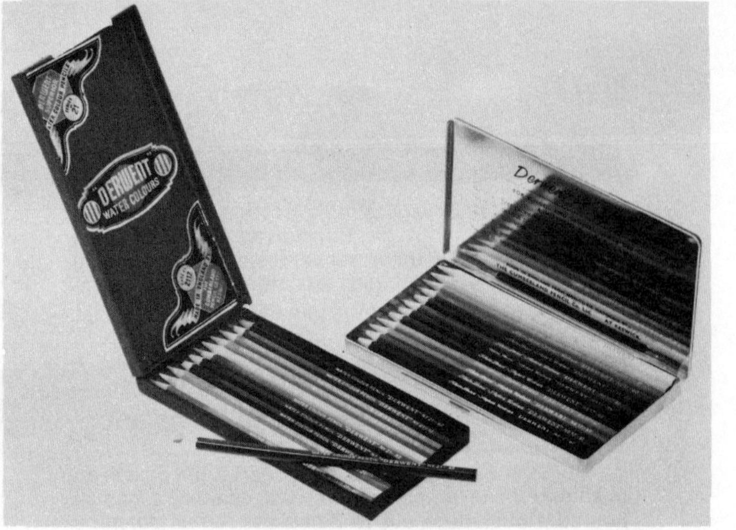
DERWENT
WATER COLOURS

Drawings may be coloured with water colour pencils in the same way as an ordinary pencil. Then, with a brush or a fine wisp of cotton wool, slightly moistened with clean water to dissolve the colour on the paper, spread it as desired. The tones can be varied according to the amount of colour put on with the pencil. Colours may also be blended. The pencil point applied to slightly moistened paper will emphasise details where required.

Colouring can be achieved simply and safely with the common colour pencil. Colours can be blended and the depth of shading varied by increased pressure on the pencil or by further applications. The pencil is easily controlled and therefore the colour can be applied exactly where required. Light tones are generally acceptable on design sketches.

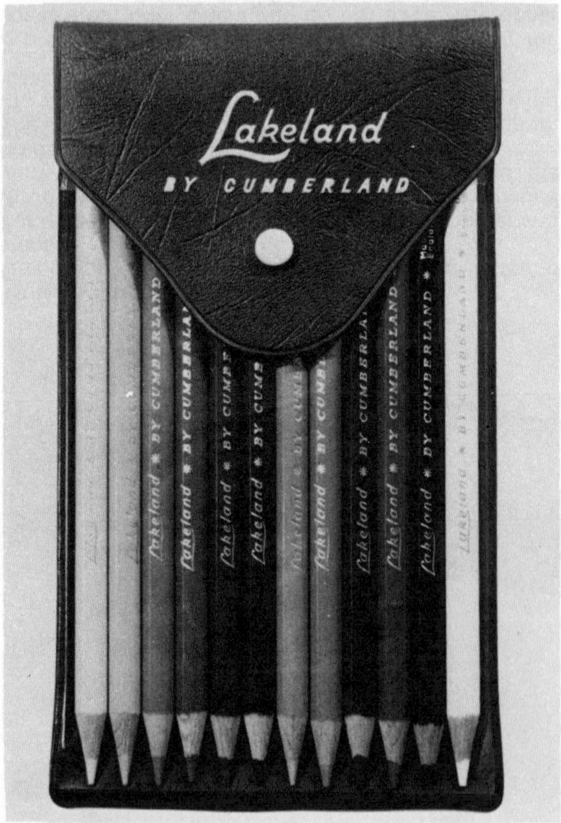
Lakeland
BY CUMBERLAND

As an alternative to coloured pencils fine fibre tips can be used not only for overall coverage but also for sketching outlines as the line produced is firm and clear.

Lakeland
NON-TOXIC
Lakeland MARKER 33 FINE

Colour can be applied quickly and conveniently to a design sketch with the 'Eagle' broad nib, water-based felt-tip marker. The special wedge-shaped nib produces fine, medium or thick lines depending on how it is held to the paper. The colours can be blended and they do not 'bleed' through paper to stain the working surface or other drawings.

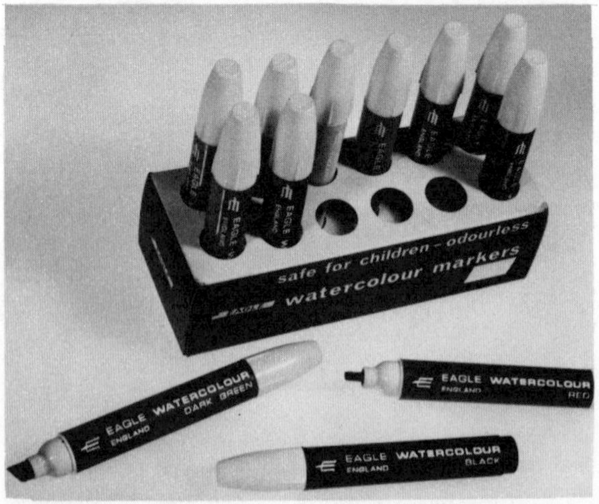
safe for children - odourless
watercolour markers
EAGLE WATERCOLOUR
DARK GREEN
RED
BLACK

Brushes with which to apply inks and water-colours to design sheets should be of good quality and great care should be taken to clean them after use. They should be washed in hot, soapy water and then rinsed thoroughly, the water shaken out and the brush shaped up with the fingers. The brush should then be placed in a pot or jar to dry with bristles uppermost and free from contact with any surface. They should never be left resting on their bristles, if they are to be stored for any length of time they must be perfectly dry to prevent mildew and be placed in a box with a tight fitting lid to protect them from moths.

The ones illustrated and found to be particularly useful are:

A Hand-made, squirrel hair with round wooden handles and seamless aluminium ferrules.

B Hog-hair brush designed particularly for use with powder colours for painting wooden models and mock-ups.

C The 'Cotman' sable which combines large carrying power with the capacity for crisp and delicate finish of edge on line.

Drawing inks can be applied to drawings as a colour wash or to highlight certain features. There are twenty colours in the range; black and white are based on light fast pigments and the remaining colours are based on brilliant dyes. All contain shellac which enables one colour to be superimposed on another.

WINSOR & NEWTON
INK

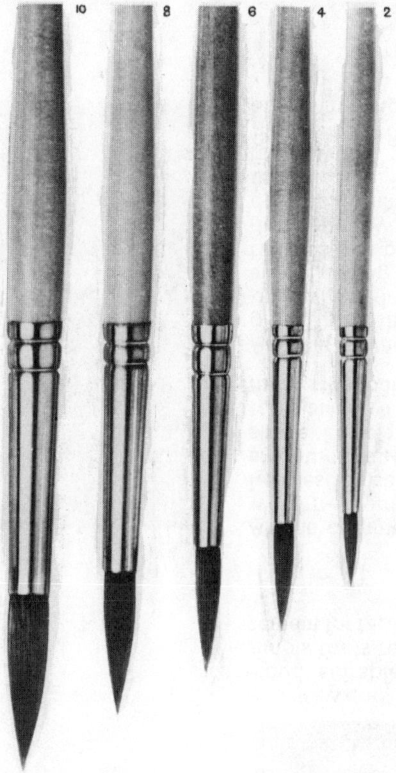
10
8
6
4
2

A

B

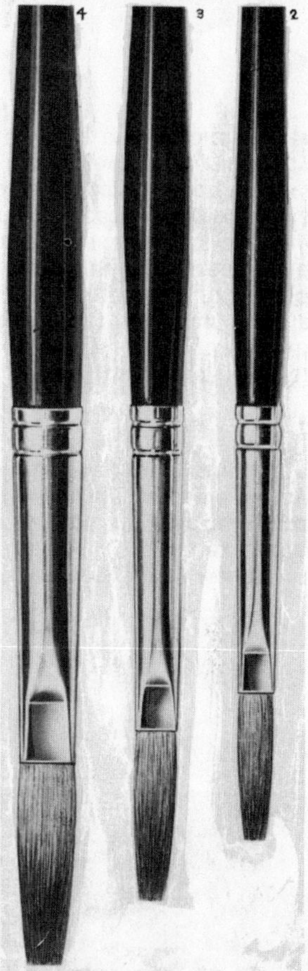
4
3
2

C

If large areas of a drawing are to have an overall colour wash, water colours such as the 'Cotman' range are suitable, being of excellent tinctorial strength and having good working properties.

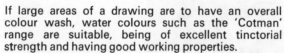

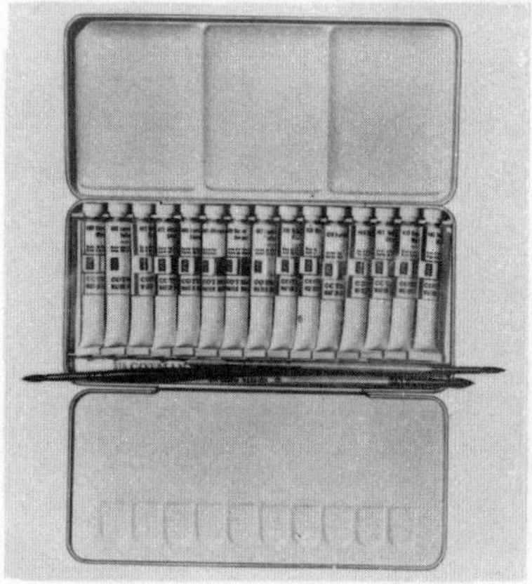

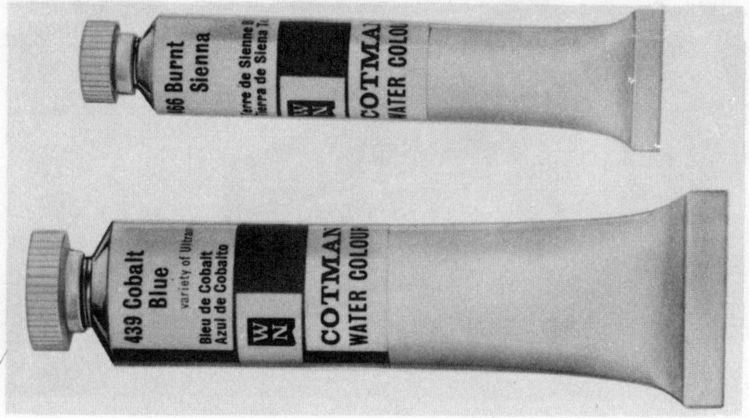
Burnt Sienna
COTMAN
WATER COLOUR
439 Cobalt Blue
Bleu de Cobalt
Azul de Cobalto
COTMAN
WATER COLOUR

Modelling materials

Models and mock-ups can be made from a variety of materials to help you finalize designs. These materials, all of which should be readily available in the design area, can be easily fashioned to shape and joined together and include paper, card, plywood, hardboard, tin plate, wire, plasticine and balsawood.

SOLARBO JUNIOR PAK
OF
BALSA WOOD
READY FOR USE
SOLARBO
ENGLISH ABRASIVES
CEMENT
AVEN JUNIOR HACKSAW

A balsawood pack showing a range of sections of wood suitable for model making. Note also the simple tools required for cutting and shaping and the cement for rapid and easy assembling.

Plasticine is an ideal modelling material as it is non-toxic and can be easily shaped by the fingers or very simple tools. It can be reused indefinitely without deterioration: will maintain the required shape without hardening and will retain the same standard of plasticity.

Examples of modelling in plasticine are illustrated on page 37.

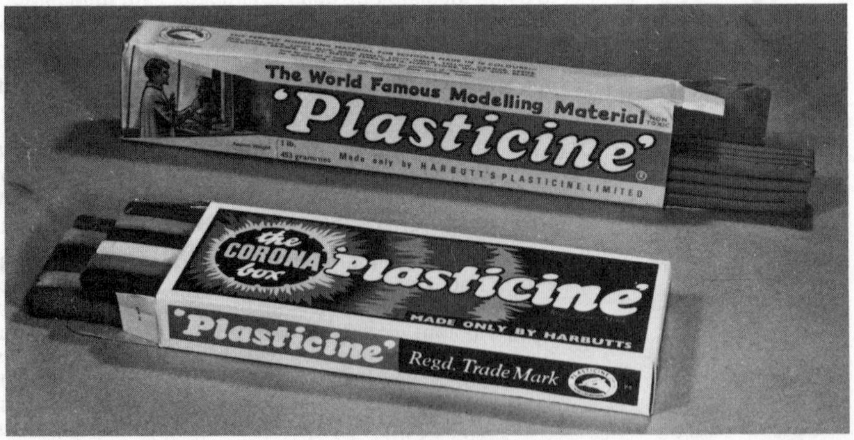
The World Famous Modelling Material
'Plasticine'
Made only by HARBUTT'S PLASTICINE LIMITED
the CORONA box
'Plasticine'
MADE ONLY BY HARBUTTS
'Plasticine' Regd. Trade Mark

All the commercial balsawood comes from Ecuador. Balsawood varies widely in weight – from as little as 64–100 kg./m.^{3} up to 250 kg./m.^{3} or more but even the heaviest balsawood is lightweight compared with other woods. Its lightness and smooth texture make it very easy to cut with a small saw or a knife, or carve to any shape. For elementary work in fact, balsawood can be shaped without using edge tools at all (e.g. by using sanding sticks). It is also strong for its weight – which means that balsawood models are rigid and quite durable.

Another advantage offered by balsawood is that only simple joints are needed, glued up with quick-drying balsa cement. Assemblies can be held together with pins whilst drying, and set hard in ten minutes or so. Finishing in colour, too, is simple, using 'Solarbo' balsa paints or poster colours. Both are non-toxic, and brushes can be cleaned in water after use. Colouring can add further scope to the discipline involved. Selected balsawood is free from knots, shakes, splits and the defects commonly found in other timbers, although the occasional pinhole is unavoidable. This is caused by the Ambrosia (pinhole borer) beetle which attacks green wood, generally recently felled logs. All 'Solarbo' balsawood is sterilised by high temperature kiln-drying, which not only stabilises the wood, but inhibits further attack, making it clean and hygienic to use.

The small backsaw and the junior hacksaw are ideal for general purpose sawing when model making and are very safe in use. The backsaw is particularly suitable for cutting larger sizes of strip and block balsa, 'Obechi' and plywood, or sawing other woods.

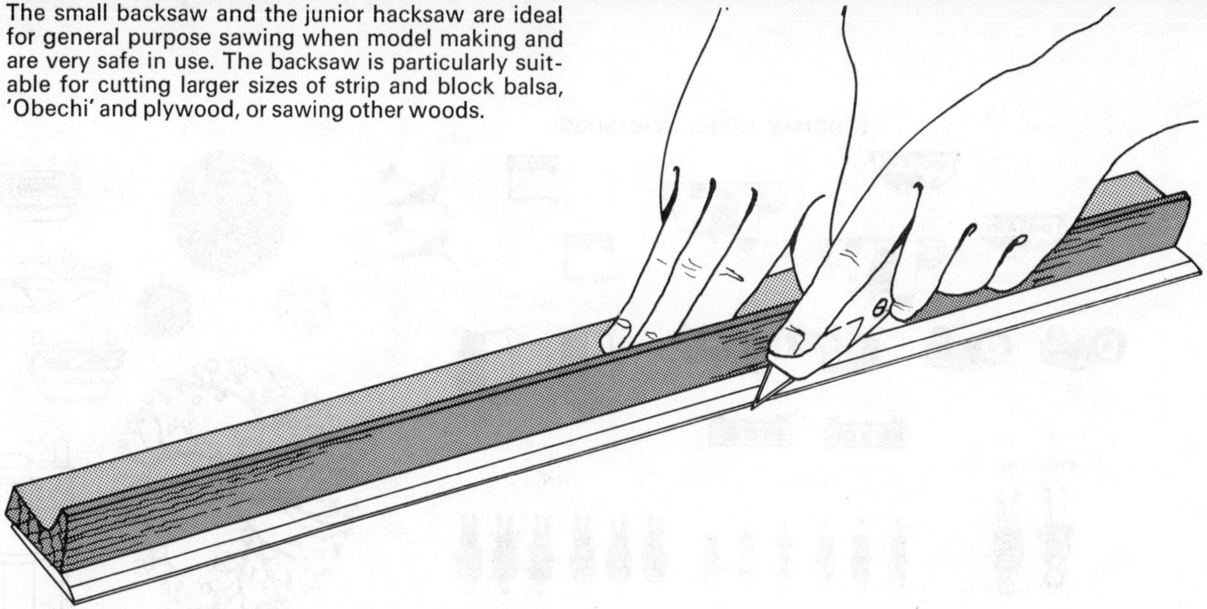

The 'Mousetail' file is a simple little tool which replaces the need for drills to bore holes in balsa. The tip is pushed through and the hole opened up to the required size using the tool as a file. Complete cut-out shapes can also be produced in a similar manner. The teeth are non-clogging and virtually everlasting when used on balsa.

This Safety Straightedge recently introduced by Geliot Whitman Ltd. is an excellent aid for cutting paper, card and thin balsawood when modelling. The rustless-steel straight edge is surmounted with a specially contoured hardwood moulding which ensures that the fingers are always shielded from the knife. Available in lengths of 500 mm, 600 mm, 1000 mm and 1250 mm it is easy to hold firmly in position for accurate cutting.

Glasspaper is an indispensible material for smoothing balsa prior to painting and for cleaning up assemblies after glueing. A selection of three grades should be available.

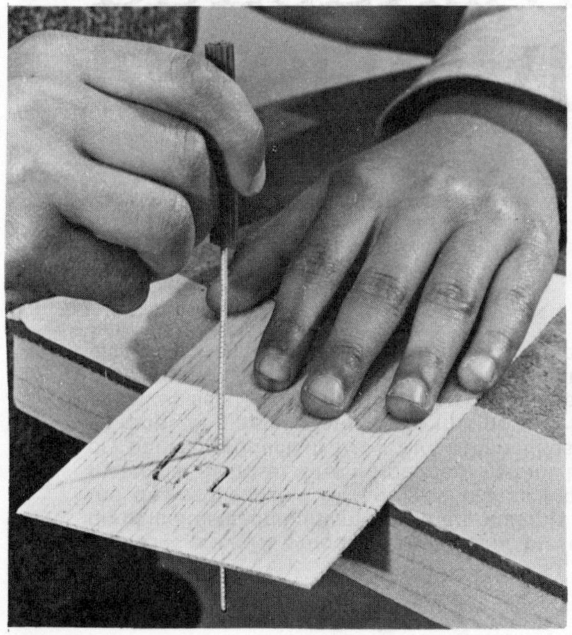

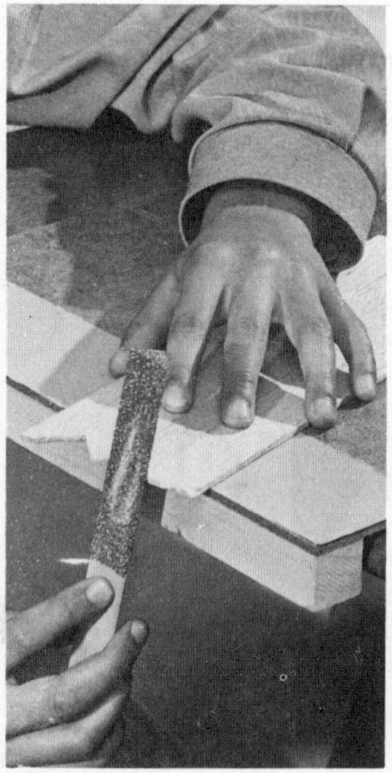

Abrasive sticks made from different-shaped sections of hardwood.

Letraset *instant lettering*
TRADEMARK

'Letraset' provides a modern aid to design presentation. To designers, graphic artists, draughtsmen and art students throughout the world the distinctive name of 'Letraset' means high quality graphic art materials. 'Letraset' first introduced 'Instant Lettering', the original dry transfer product, in 1961. Since then it has consistently added to its range of graphic materials so that now, in addition to a comprehensive selection of instant lettering dry transfer typefaces, art sheets, rub-down textures, shading and colour films, architectural and electronics symbols, etc. are available, some of which are illustrated here.

DRAFTING ARROWS
KEY SYMBOLS
DOTS & SQUARES
ARROWS AND ASTERISKS
REGISTER MARKS

PRESENTATION OF DESIGN — UNIVERS 65

PRESENTATION OF DESIGN — CENTURY SCHOOLBOOK

PRESENTATION OF DESIGN — EUROSTILE MEDIUM EXTENDED

ARCHITECTURAL SYMBOLS 1:100

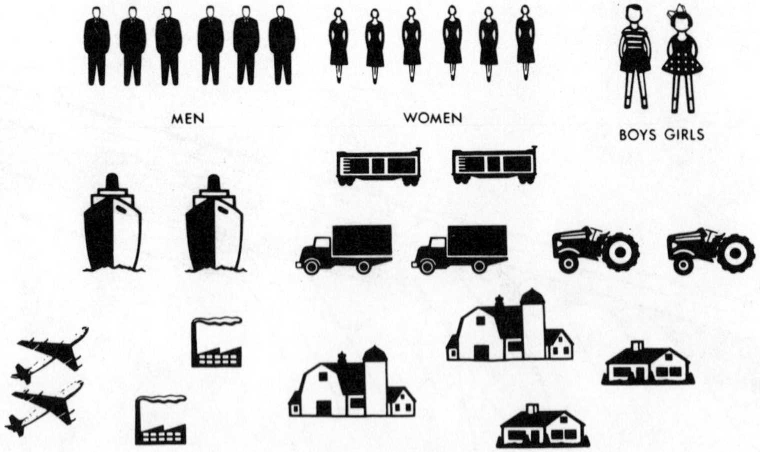
MEN
WOMEN
BOYS GIRLS

INDUSTRIAL CHART SYMBOLS

To provide further stimulation for design ideas the craft and design staff and pupils at the author's school have made a collection of domestic by-gones, small mechanisms, lamps, farm implements and objects of natural history, etc. These are a continual source of interest. Very often design development and improvement can be traced, for example the domestic iron from a flat iron casting to charcoal, to gas and then the modern electric iron.

The collection provides many topics for discussion. Items of interest, many connected with other school subjects, enable the children to see how various materials have been used. The natural-history items in particular offer ideas for shape and surface texture.

Left. A collection of cogwheels, painted in different colours and arranged to form an acceptable panel. *Right.* Car parts welded together and painted black as assemblages.

Collection of domestic items, general ironmongery and small mechanisms.

Clock, small tools, lamps, vintage petrol pump and larger mechanisms.

Bottles and jars of glass and plastic provide an interesting study of shape.

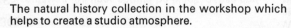

The natural history collection in the workshop which helps to create a studio atmosphere.

British Standard recommendations

British Standard 308, Engineering drawing practice, has been revised under the authority of the Mechanical Engineering Industry Standards Committee principally to bring the standard into line with published Recommendations of the International Organisation for Standardisation (ISO) on engineering drawing practice. The new Standard is in three parts:

BS 308: Part 1: 1972 – General principles.
Part 2: 1972 – Dimensions and tolerancing of size.
Part 3: 1972 – Geometrical tolerancing.

The following extracts from Parts 1 and 2 are reproduced by permission of the British Standards Institution, 2 Park St., London W1A 2BS and will be found to be particularly useful for reference.

BS 308: Part 1: 1972

4.1 Presentation. All lines should be black, dense and bold. It is important that all the lines on a drawing, including those added in any revision, should be of consistent density and reflectance. The lines on any one drawing sheet should preferably be entirely in pencil or entirely in ink. If a mixture of pencil and ink is used, every effort should be made to ensure that uniform density and reflectance are maintained.

4.2.1. Two thicknesses of lines are recommended; the table shows their applications, thicknesses and proportions.

4.2.5 General. All chain lines should start and finish with a long dash and when thin chain lines are used as centre lines they should cross one another at solid portions of the line. Centre lines should extend only a short distance beyond the feature unless required for dimensioning or other purposes. They should not extend through the spaces between views and should not terminate at another line of the drawing.

Where angles are formed in chain lines, long dashes should meet at corners. Arcs should join at tangent points. Dashed lines should also meet at corners and tangent points with dashes.

The figure below illustrates the application of the various types of line.

Lettering

5.1 Introduction. It is important that characters should be uniform and capable of being produced by hand, stencil, machine or other means at reasonable speed. Clarity, style, size and spacing are important, particularly for figures, as unlike letters they rarely fall into identifiable patterns and must be read individually. Characters should be open form and devoid of serifs and other embellishments. All strokes should be black and of consistent density compatible with the line work.

5.2 Style. No particular style for hand lettering is recommended, the aim should be to produce legible and unambiguous characters. Vertical or sloping characters are suitable for general use but the presentation should be consistent on any one drawing, i.e. vertical and sloping letters should not be mixed.

Types of line

Example (letters refer to the figure on this page)	Type of line	Line width mm	Example of application
A	Continuous (thick)	0·7	Visible outlines and edges
B	Continuous (thin)	0·3	Fictitious outlines and edges Dimension and leader lines Hatching Outlines of adjacent parts Outlines of revolving sections
C	Continuous irregular (thin)	0·3	Limits of partial views of sections when the line is not an axis
D	Short dashes (thin)	0·3	Hidden outlines and edges
E	Chain (thin)	0·3	Centre lines Extreme positions of moveable parts
F	Chain (thick at ends and at changes of direction, thin elsewhere)	0·7 0·3	Cutting planes
G	Chain (thick)	0·7	Indication of surfaces which have to meet special requirements

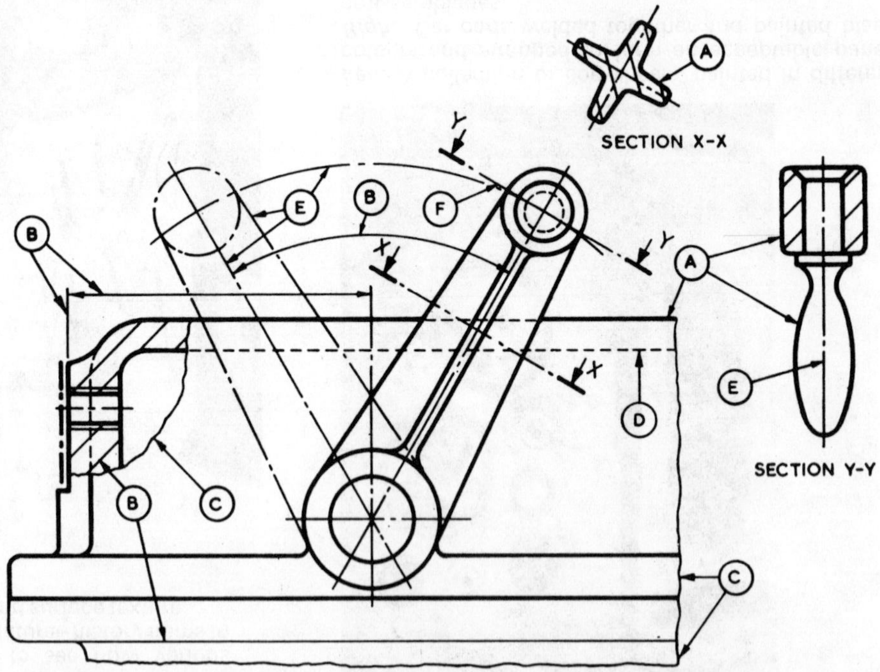
A
B
C
D
E
F
X
Y
SECTION X-X
SECTION Y-Y

9.1 Common features. Conventional representation is adopted in cases where complete delineation of the part would involve unnecessary drawing time or space. Typical examples are shown in the figures below.

Where the conventional representation given is not considered adequate, a more detailed view may be shown.

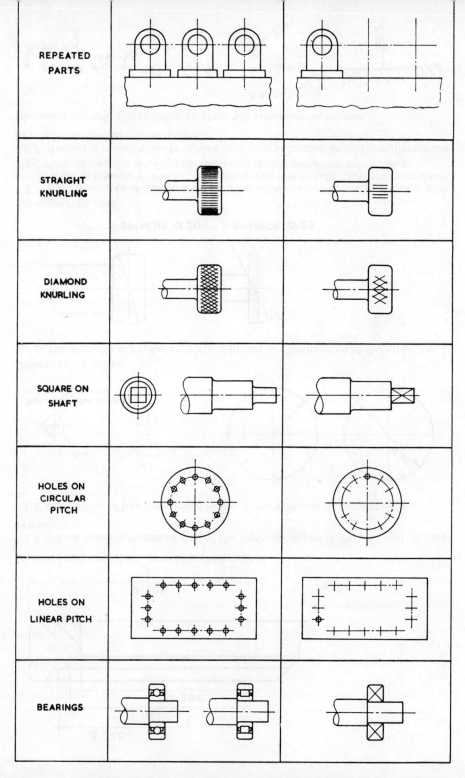

TITLE	SUBJECT	CONVENTION
EXTERNAL SCREW THREADS (DETAIL)	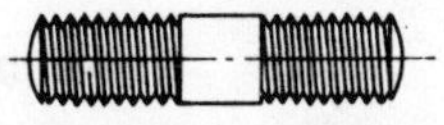	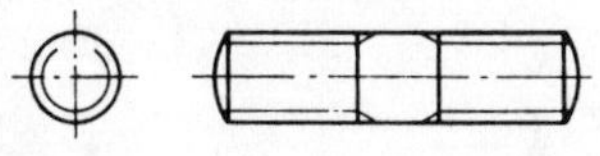
INTERNAL SCREW THREADS (DETAIL)	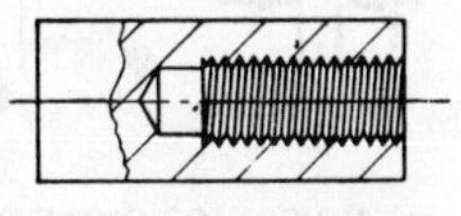	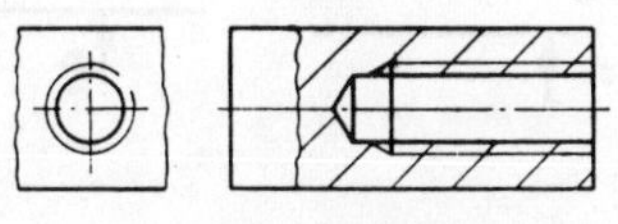
SCREW THREADS (ASSEMBLY)	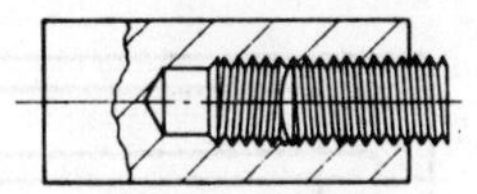	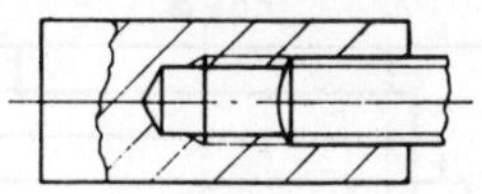
THREAD INSERTS	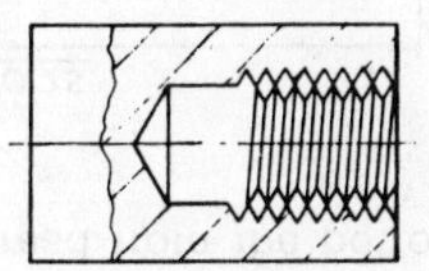	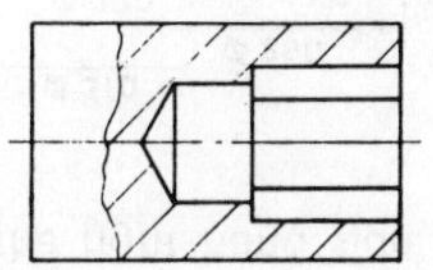
INTERRUPTED VIEWS	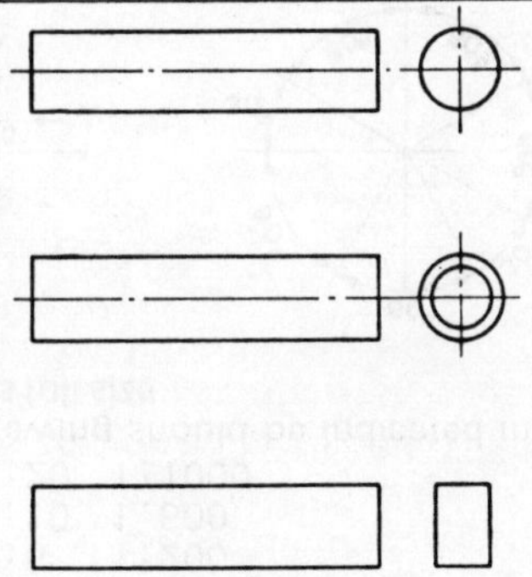	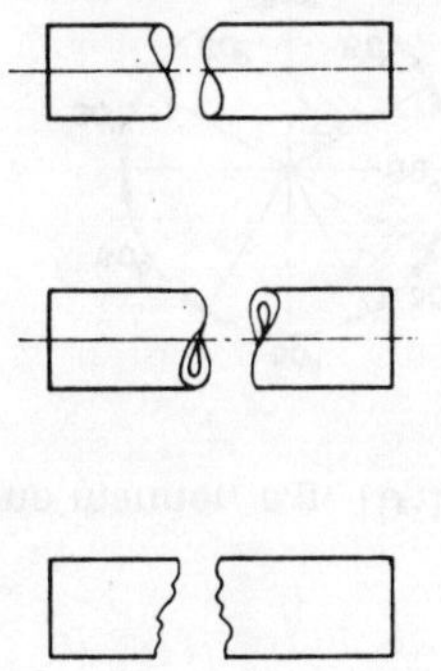
REPEATED PARTS	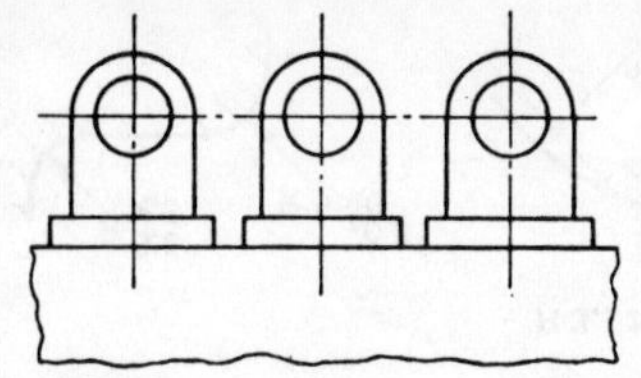	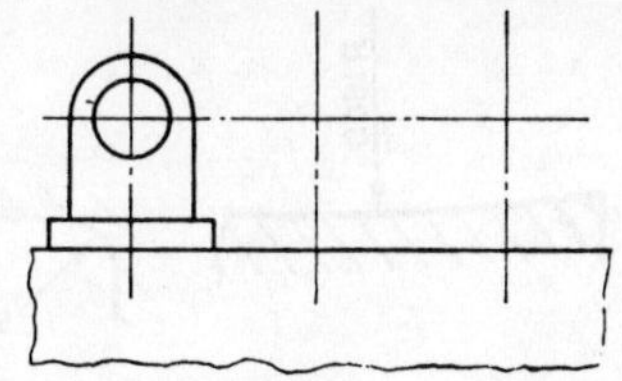
STRAIGHT KNURLING	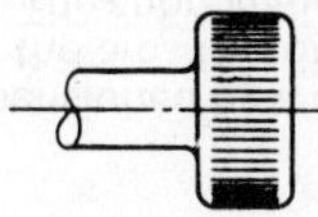	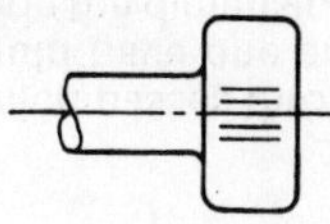
DIAMOND KNURLING	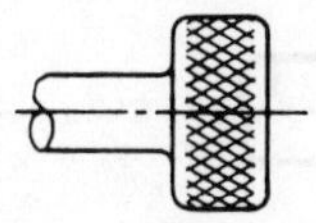	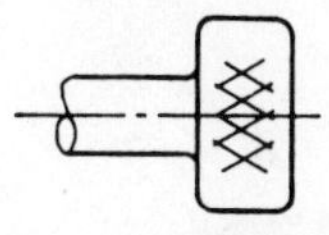
SQUARE ON SHAFT	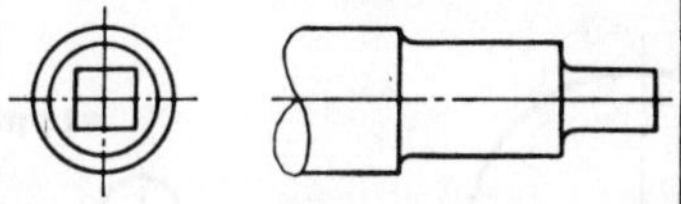	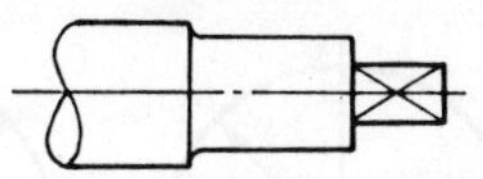
HOLES ON CIRCULAR PITCH	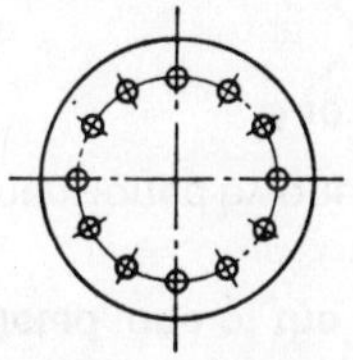	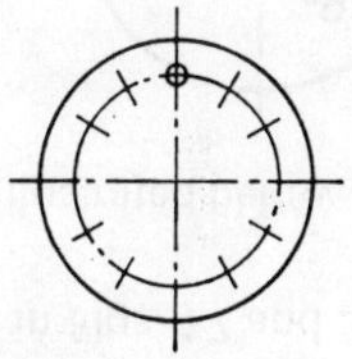
HOLES ON LINEAR PITCH	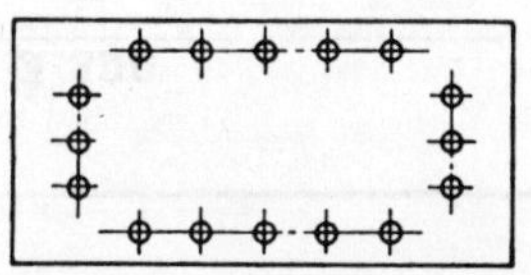	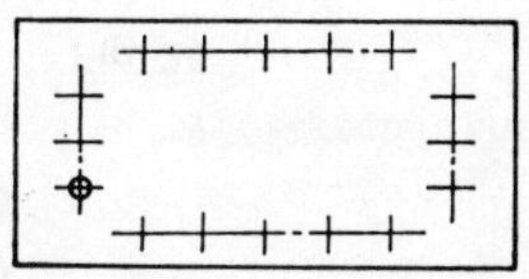
BEARINGS	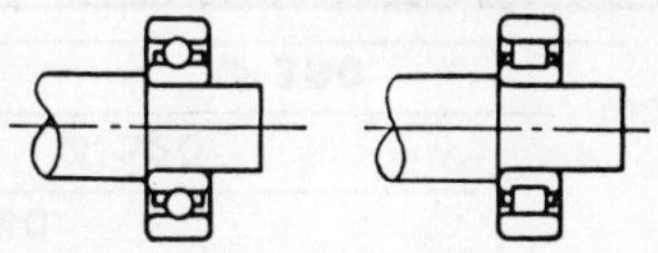	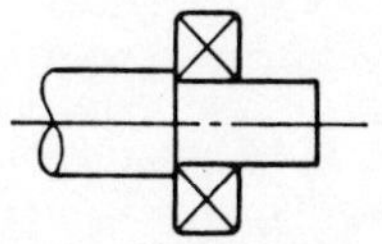

Scale multipliers and divisors of 2 and 5 and 10 are recommended (see BS 1347, Part 3). The resultant representative fractions will be:

1000:1	50:1	1:1	1:50
500:1	20:1	1:2	1:100
200:1	10:1	1:5	1:200
100:1	5:1	1:10	1:500
	2:1	1:20	1:1000

The scale of the drawing should be indicated in the same manner, e.g. 10:1 on a drawing at ten times full size.

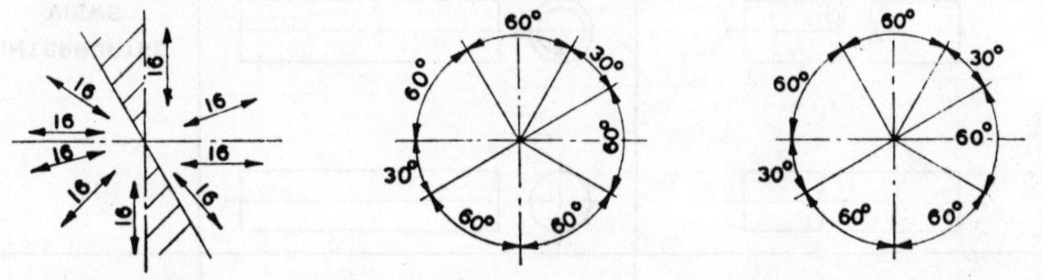

16
60°
30°

Dimensions placed to read from the bottom or from the right-hand side of the drawing

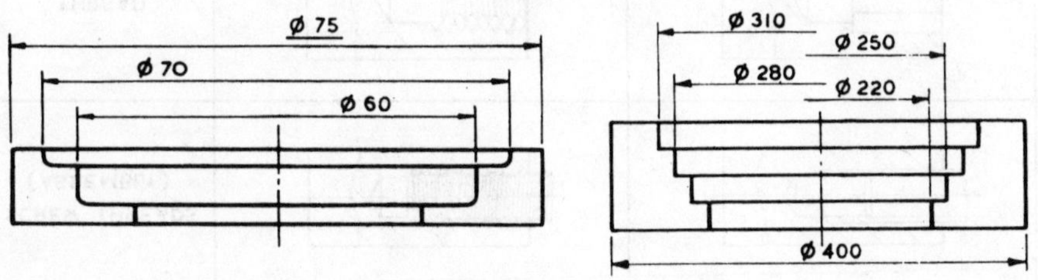

Ø 75
Ø 70
Ø 60
Ø 310
Ø 250
Ø 280
Ø 220
Ø 400

Fig. 17

Dimensions staggered to avoid confusion

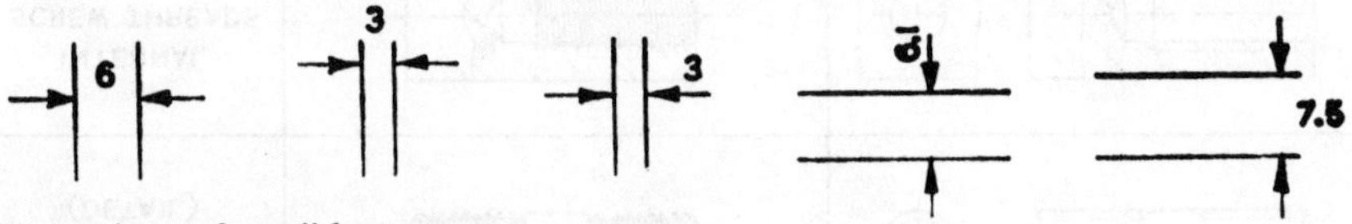

6
3
3
6.1
7.5

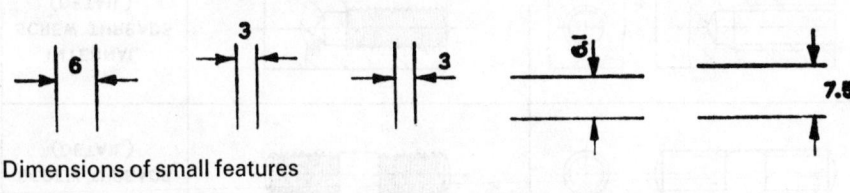

Dimensions of small features

Overall dimensions placed outside intermediate dimensions

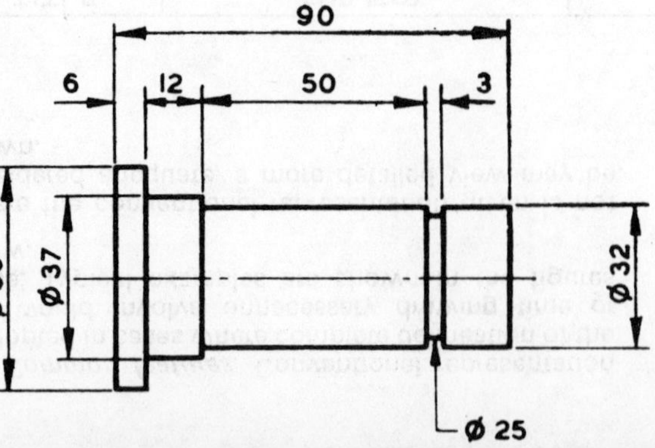

90
6
12
50
3
Ø 50
Ø 37
Ø 32
Ø 25

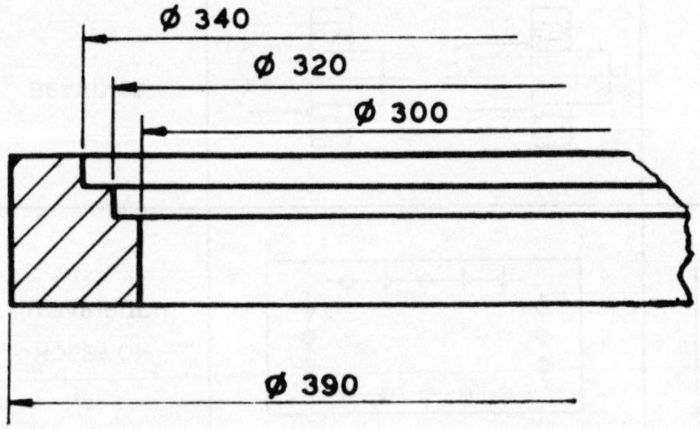

Ø 340
Ø 320
Ø 300
Ø 390

Fig. 26

Dimensioning diameters where space is restricted

6.1.4 Where space is restricted, one of the methods shown in Figs. 17 and 26 may be used.

6.1.5 Circles should be dimensioned by one of the methods illustrated below.

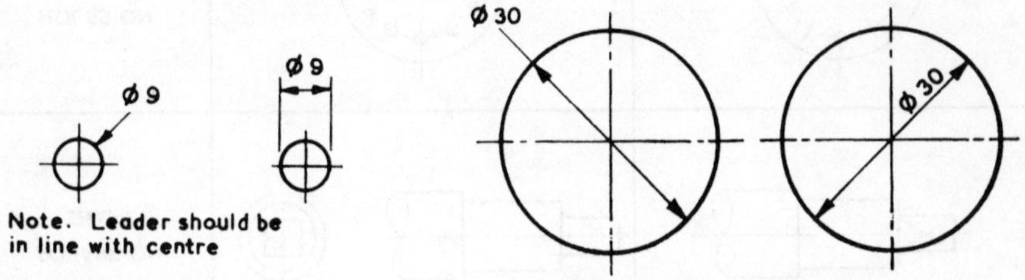

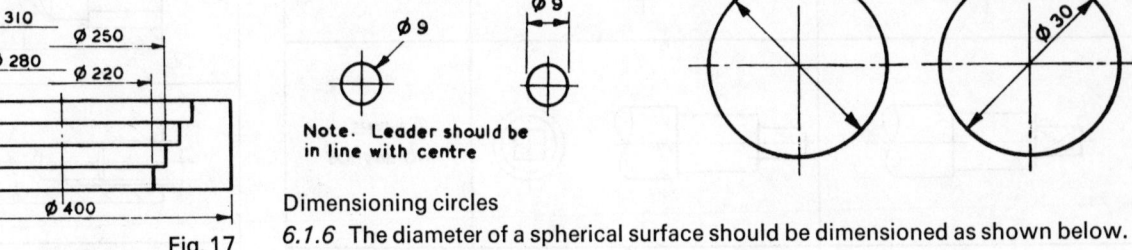

Ø 9
Ø 9
Note. Leader should be in line with centre
Ø 30
Ø 30

Dimensioning circles

6.1.6 The diameter of a spherical surface should be dimensioned as shown below.

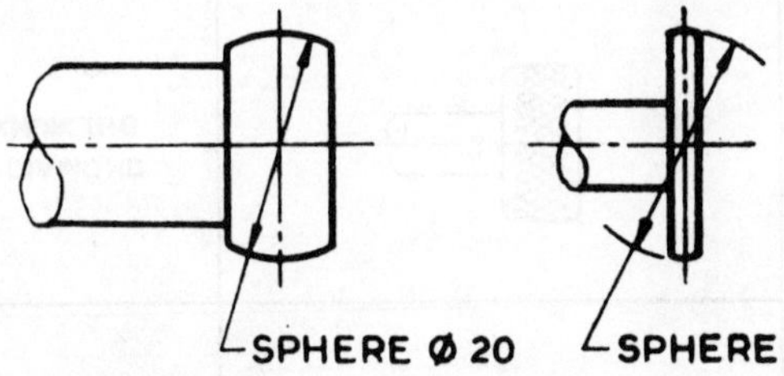

SPHERE Ø 20
SPHERE Ø 20

Spherical diameters

6.2.1 Radii should be dimensioned by a dimension line which passes through, or is in line with, the centre of the arc. The dimension line should have one arrowhead only, that touching the arc. The abbreviation R should precede the dimension.

6.2.2 Radii of arcs which need not have their centres located should be dimensioned by one of the methods shown below.

Dimensioning radii of arcs which need not have their centres located

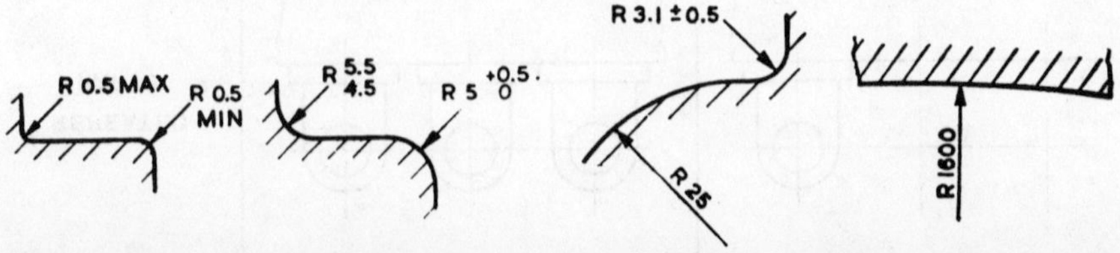

R 0.5 MAX
R 0.5 MIN
R 5.5 4.5
R 5 +0.5 0
R 3.1 ±0.5
R 25
R 1600

USEFUL DEVELOPMENTS WITH FREQUENT WORKSHOP APPLICATIONS.

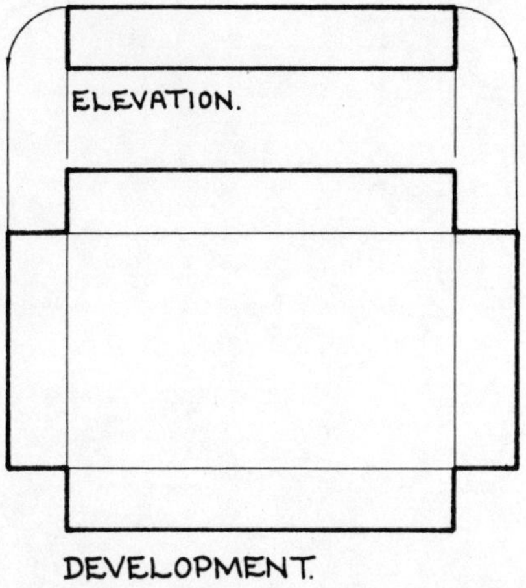
ELEVATION.
DEVELOPMENT.

BOX WITH VERTICAL SIDES.

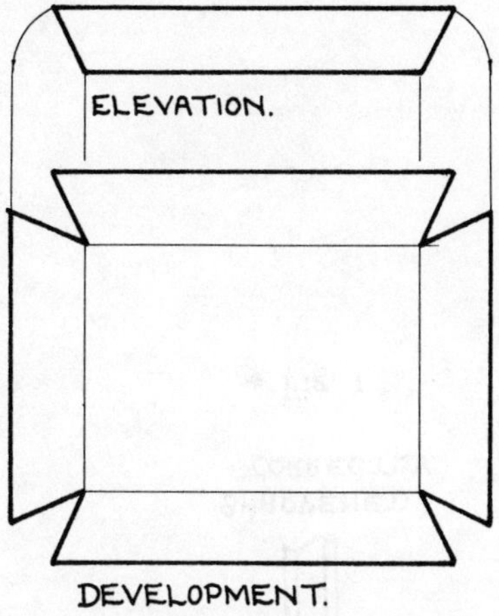
ELEVATION.
DEVELOPMENT.

BOX WITH SLOPING SIDES.

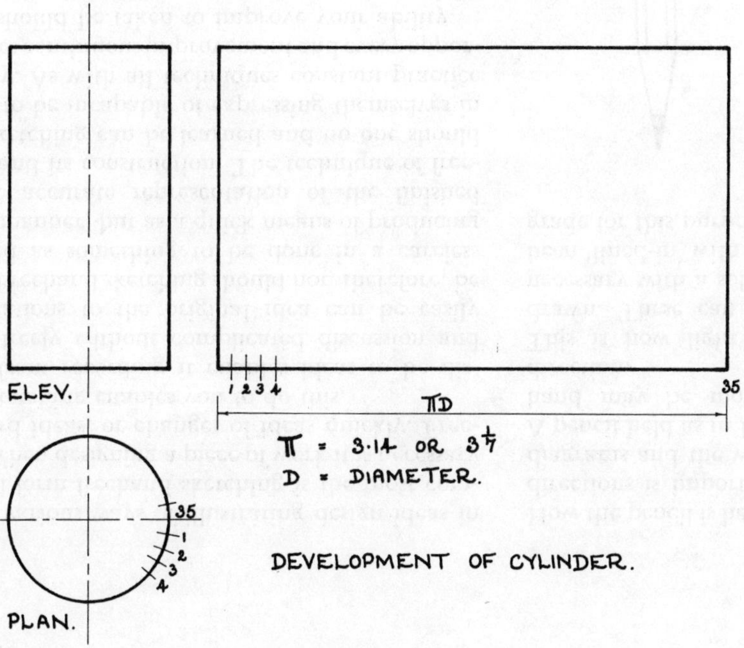
ELEV.
1 2 3 4
35
πD
35
1
2
3
4
PLAN.

$\pi = 3{\cdot}14$ OR $3\frac{1}{7}$

D = DIAMETER.

DEVELOPMENT OF CYLINDER.

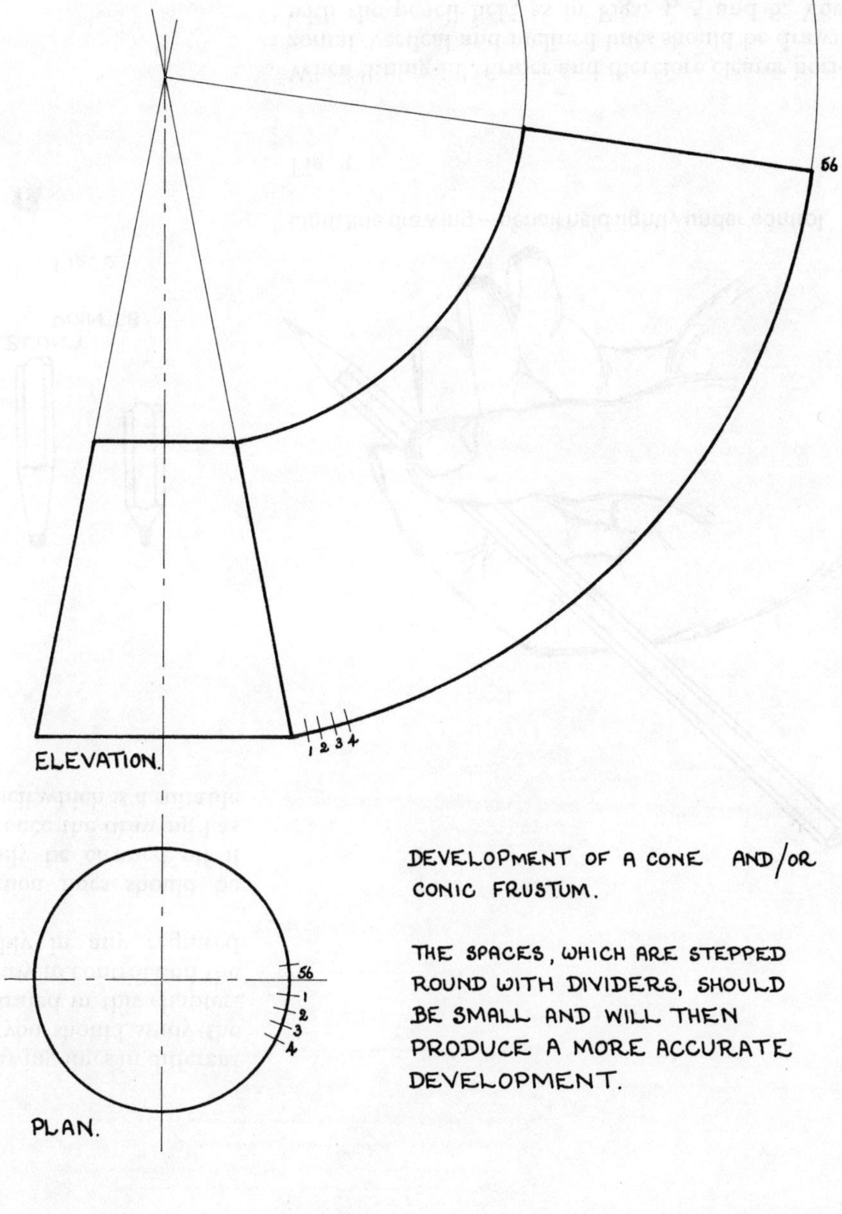
56
ELEVATION.
1 2 3 4
56
1
2
3
4
PLAN.

DEVELOPMENT OF A CONE AND/OR CONIC FRUSTUM.

THE SPACES, WHICH ARE STEPPED ROUND WITH DIVIDERS, SHOULD BE SMALL AND WILL THEN PRODUCE A MORE ACCURATE DEVELOPMENT.

Freehand Sketching

Of the various ways of illustrating design ideas in a visual form freehand sketching is the most common. When designing a piece of work it is necessary to record ideas, or changes of ideas quickly. Freehand sketching enables you to do this.

Apart from recording it enables ideas to be discussed freely without complicated discussion and modifications to the original idea can be easily made. Freehand sketching should not, therefore, be regarded as something to be done in a careless untidy manner, but as a quick means of producing a quite accurate representation of the finished article and its construction. The technique of freehand sketching can be learned and no one should profess to be incapable of expressing themselves in this way. As with all techniques constant practice produces continuous improvement and every opportunity should be taken to improve your ability.

Soft pencils, B or HB, are most frequently used for freehand sketching and should be sharpened to a conical point. (Fig. 1) Blunt pencils – (Fig. 2) will never produce the standard of line required.

How the pencil is held for drawing lines in different directions is important and you should study the diagrams and the ways illustrated in this chapter. A pencil held as in Fig. 3 is easy to control and the hand may be moved readily in any required direction.

This is how light construction lines should be drawn. These can then easily be cleaned off if necessary with a soft rubber once the drawing has been 'lined-in' with an H pencil which is a suitable grade for this purpose.

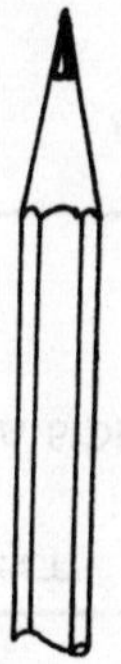
SHARPENED
CORRECTLY.

Fig. 1

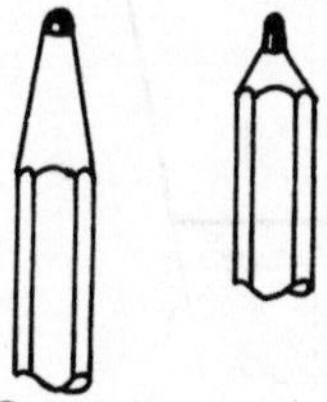
BLUNT
POINTS.

Fig. 2

Light line drawing – pencil held lightly under control.

Fig. 3

When 'lining-in', firmer and therefore clearer horizontal, vertical and inclined lines should be drawn with the pencil held as in Figs. 4, 5 and 6. You should note that the pencil is held approximately at right angles to the line being drawn and at about 40 mm from the point.

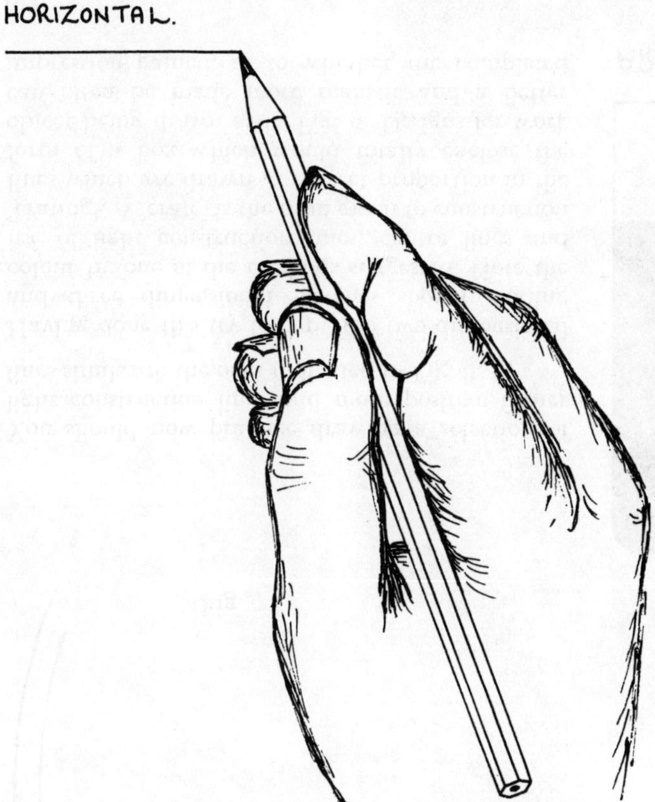
HORIZONTAL.

Fig. 4

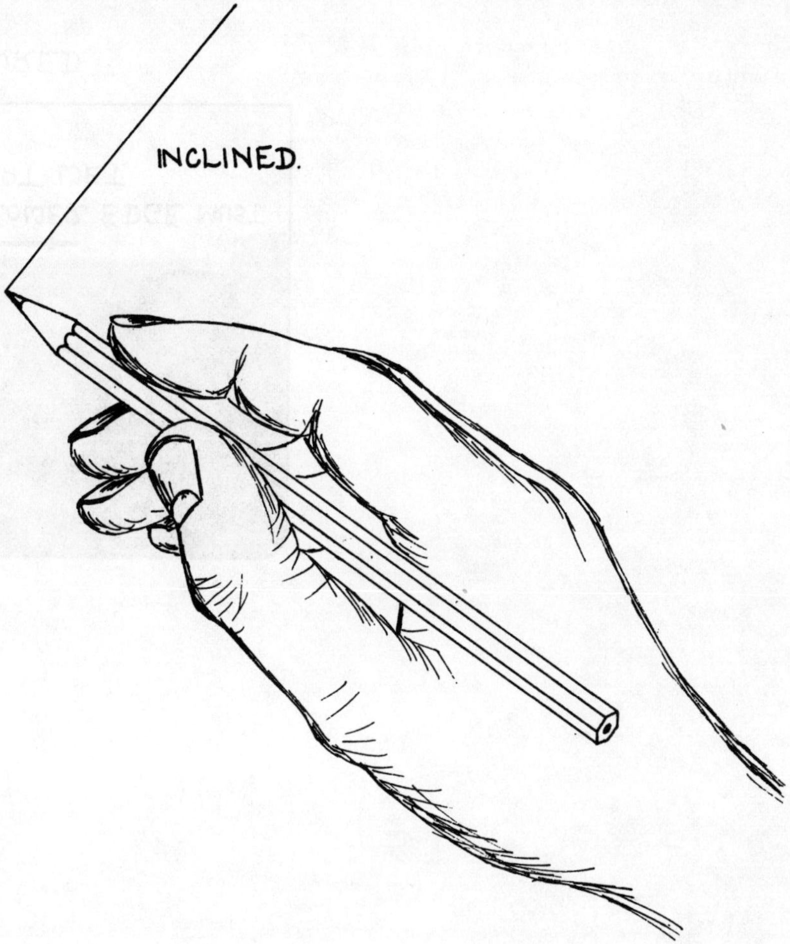
INCLINED.

Fig. 6

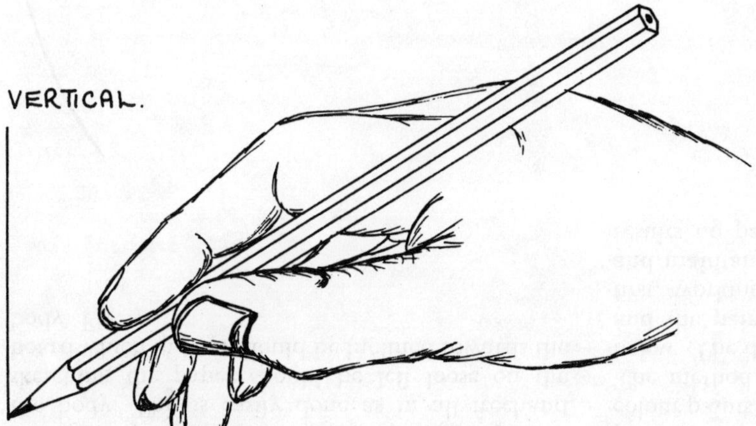
VERTICAL.

Fig. 5

The pencil should be held more firmly and the fingers drawn tightly together. Note the change in the position of the hand and fingers for drawing each line. There will be some individual variation.

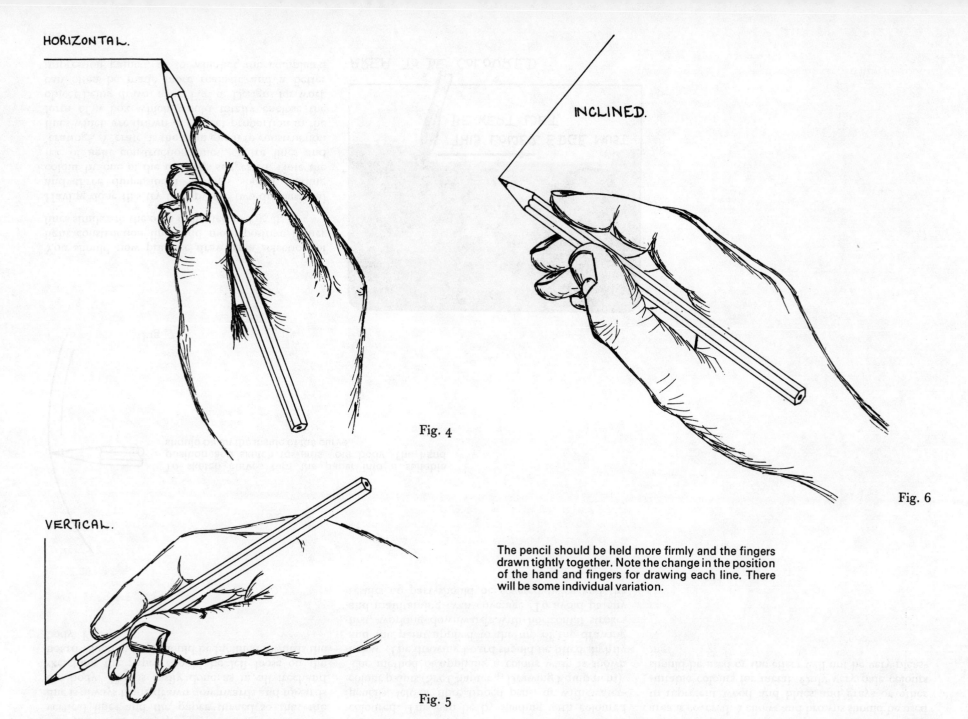

For curved lines the pencil should be held as for vertical lines and the paper turned so that the line is always being drawn downwards and towards the body. This is easily done as in all freehand sketching the paper should be left loose on the board which in turn should be inclined towards the body. Fig. 7

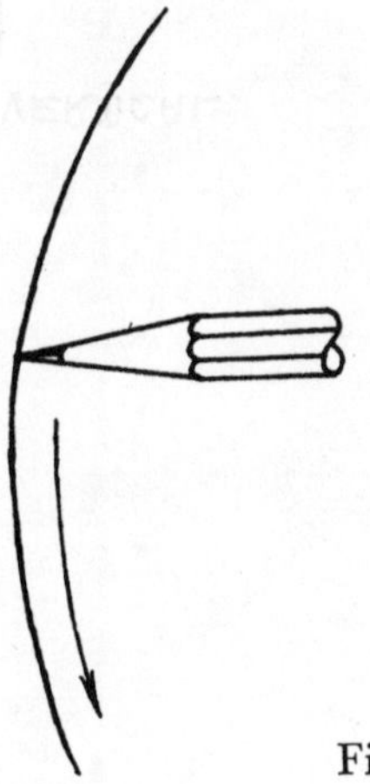

To sketch curves turn the paper into a suitable position and sketch towards your body. The hand should be on the inside of the curve.

Fig. 7

You should now practice drawing a selection of light construction lines and more positive firmer lines similar to the ones indicated in Fig. 8.

Having done this try to copy the two dimensional and three dimensional sketches shown, adding colour by one of the methods suggested. Note the use of light construction lines, centre lines and 'crating'. A 'crate' is the term given to construction lines which are drawn in correct proportion in the form of a box which would totally enclose the object being drawn as in Fig. 9. Designs for work can often be made more realistic and a better impression gained, as to whether the completed article will be satisfactory, if the final sketch is coloured. This can be by shading with coloured pencils, felt or fibre tipped pens, or with water-colour paints (See Chapter 4, Drawing Equipment). The method of applying a colour wash is shown below. The drawing board should be tilted slightly and the paint applied to the top of the drawing first, working downwards with horizontal strokes and maintaining even coverage. To avoid patchy results no part should be covered twice and the bottom edge of the wash kept wet until the whole area is covered. Yellows and browns should be used to represent wood and blues and greys or other suitable colours for metal. Only very pale colours should be used or the effect will not be very pleasing.

THIS LOWER EDGE MUST
BE KEPT WET.
AREA TO BE COLOURED.

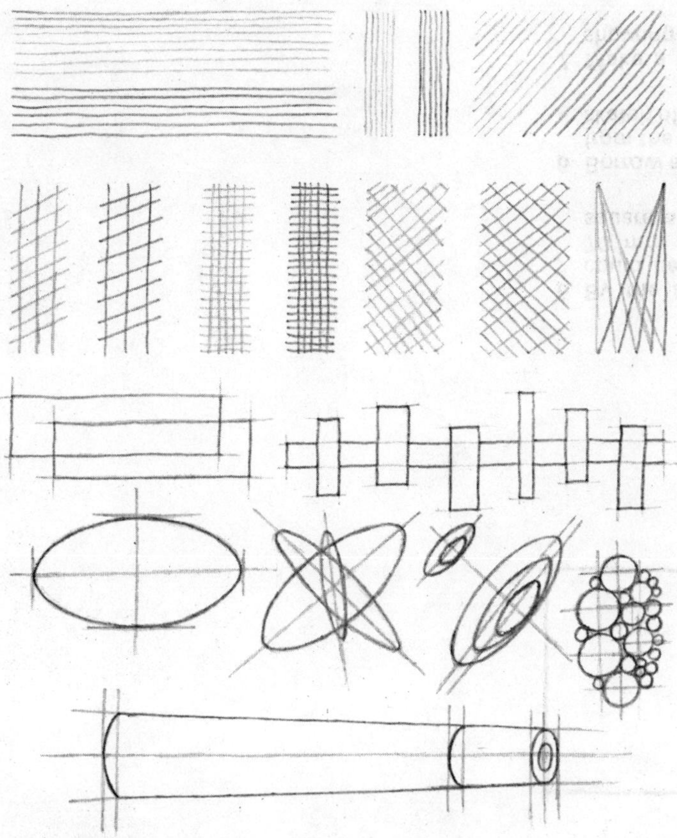

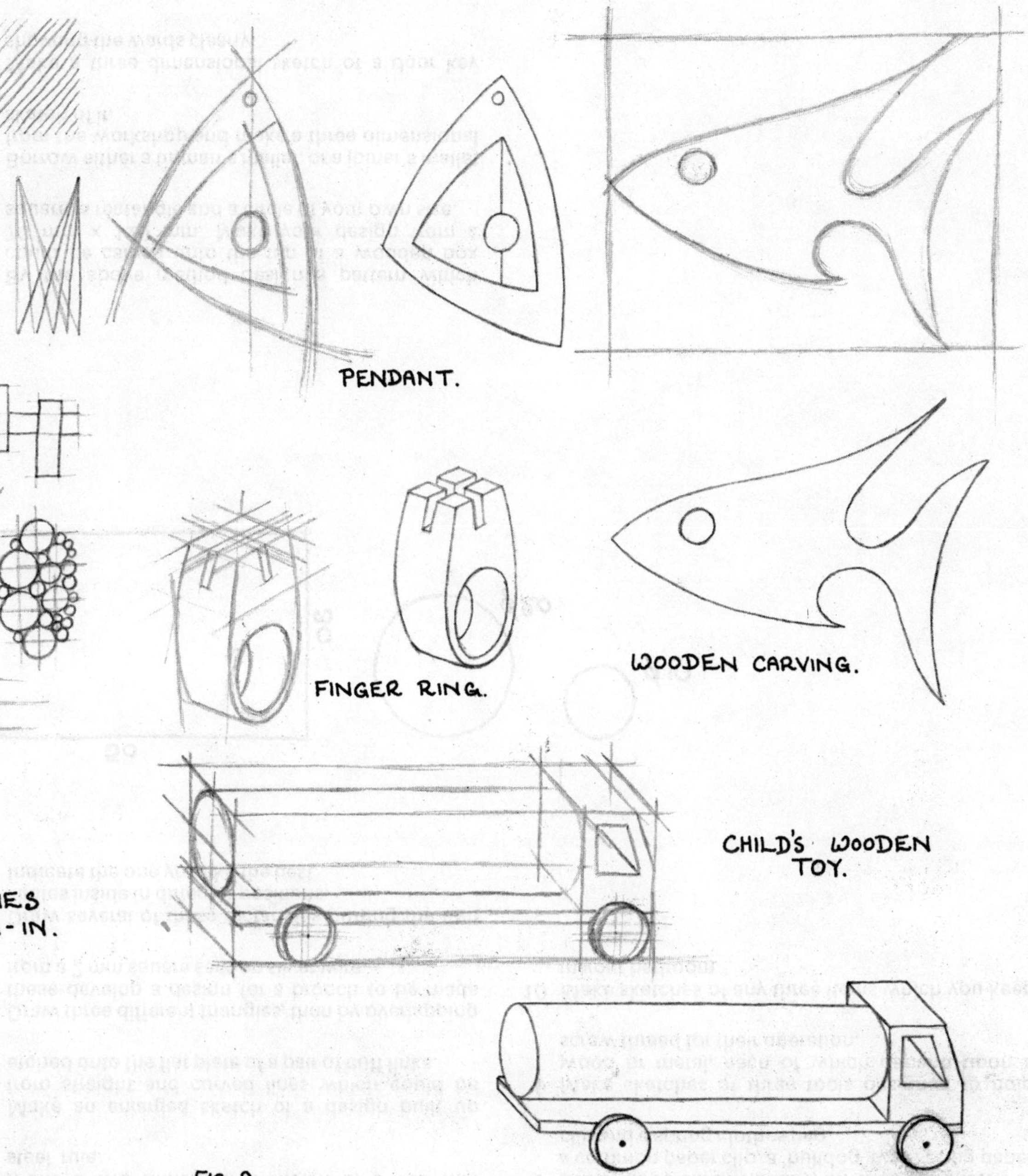
PENDANT.
FINGER RING.
WOODEN CARVING.
CHILD'S WOODEN TOY.

EXAMPLES OF LIGHT CONSTRUCTION LINES AND FIRMER OUTLINES AFTER LINING-IN.

NOTE THE USE OF THE 'CRATE' FOR DRAWING THE WOODEN TOY.

FIG. 8

FIG. 9

Freehand sketching exercises

Having made your own copy of the examples shown, sketch your answers to the following exercises. Apply colour to your finished sketches where appropriate, using the media which suits you best.

1 Make a two dimensional sketch of a 150 mm steel rule.

2 Make an enlarged sketch of a design built up from straight and curved lines which could be etched onto the flat plate of a pair of cuff links.

3 Draw three different triangles, then by overlapping these develop a design for a brooch to be made from a 2 mm square section silver wire.

4 Draw several of these rectangles putting the two circles inside in different positions. Indicate the one you like the best.

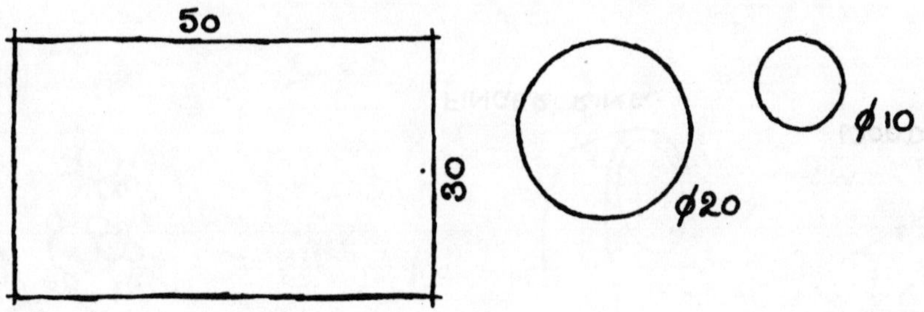
50
30
ϕ20
ϕ10

5 By the above method design a pattern which could be carved onto the top of a wooden box 70 mm x 120 mm. Make your design from a square, a rectangle and a circle of your own size.

6 Borrow either a tinman's mallet, or a joiner's mallet from the workshop and make a three dimensional sketch of it.

7 Make a three dimensional sketch of a door key showing the wards clearly.

8 Draw, three dimensionally, an enlarged sketch of a common paper clip, a 'bulldog' type spring paper clip and a spring clothes peg.

9 Make sketches of three tools designed to hold wood or metal, each of which depend upon a screw thread for their operation.

10 Make sketches of any three items which you keep in your bedroom.

Isometric Drawing

Instruments required

Drawing board, tee square, 30°–60° set square. Compasses to draw 'given circles' and dividers for transferring lengths.

Several examples of Isometric Drawing are illustrated. Isometric means 'equal measure' and the drawing is measured evenly on each side of a vertical line. It is based on three axes – or lines – inclined at 120° to one another.

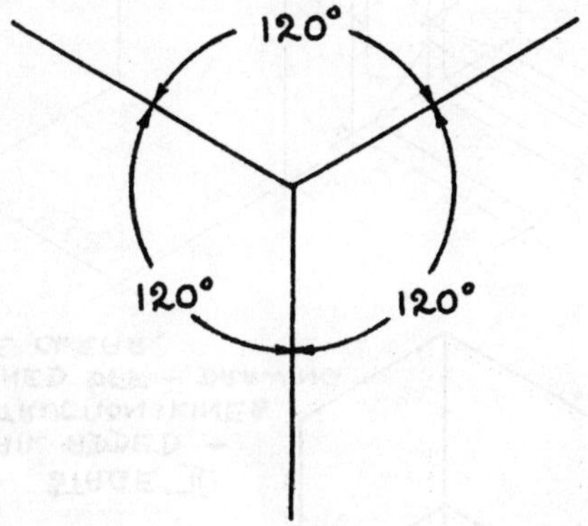
120°
120°
120°

The lines are drawn as shown, one being vertical and the two others going in opposite directions at 30° to the horizontal. These lines are drawn with the 30°–60° set square and for practical purposes the true length, width and height are measured along them. From these points lines parallel to the axes are drawn to complete the view. Any other measurements of the work must also be made along the axes or on lines parallel to them.

It is not usual to show hidden edges in Isometric Drawing unless they are required for some specific reason.
The advantages of this type of pictorial drawing are immediately obvious.

a) Generally one view is sufficient to show the shape clearly.

b) The three main dimensions, length, width and height are shown in relation to one another giving a clear indication of proportions.

c) True lengths are measured off quickly from an ordinary ruler.

EXAMPLES OF ISOMETRIC DRAWING.

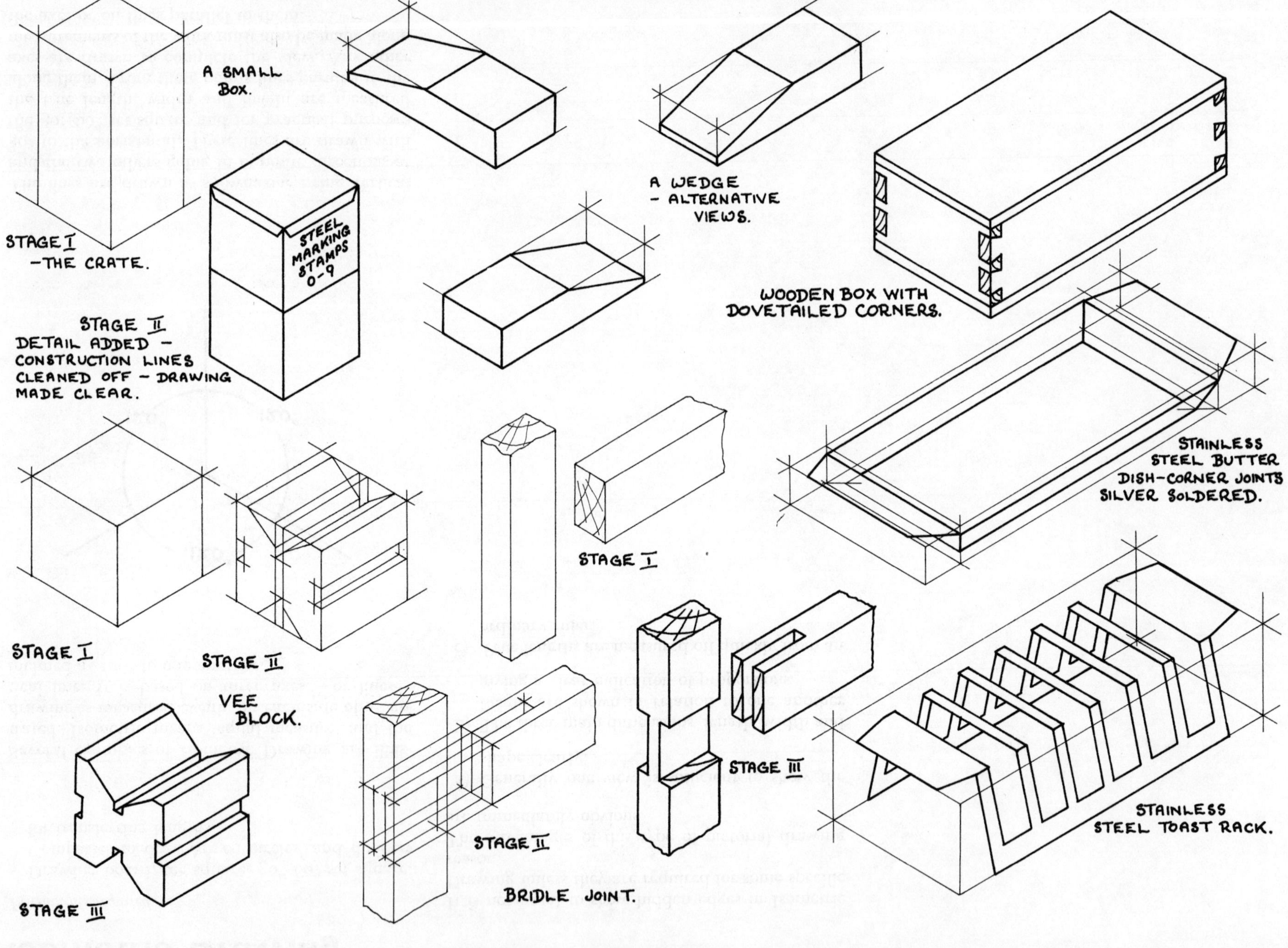
A SMALL BOX.
STAGE I
-THE CRATE.
STEEL MARKING STAMPS 0-9
STAGE II
DETAIL ADDED - CONSTRUCTION LINES CLEANED OFF - DRAWING MADE CLEAR.
A WEDGE - ALTERNATIVE VIEWS.
WOODEN BOX WITH DOVETAILED CORNERS.
STAINLESS STEEL BUTTER DISH-CORNER JOINTS SILVER SOLDERED.
STAGE I
STAGE II
VEE BLOCK.
STAGE III
STAGE I
STAGE II
STAGE III
BRIDLE JOINT.
STAINLESS STEEL TOAST RACK.

EXAMPLES OF ISOMETRIC DRAWING.

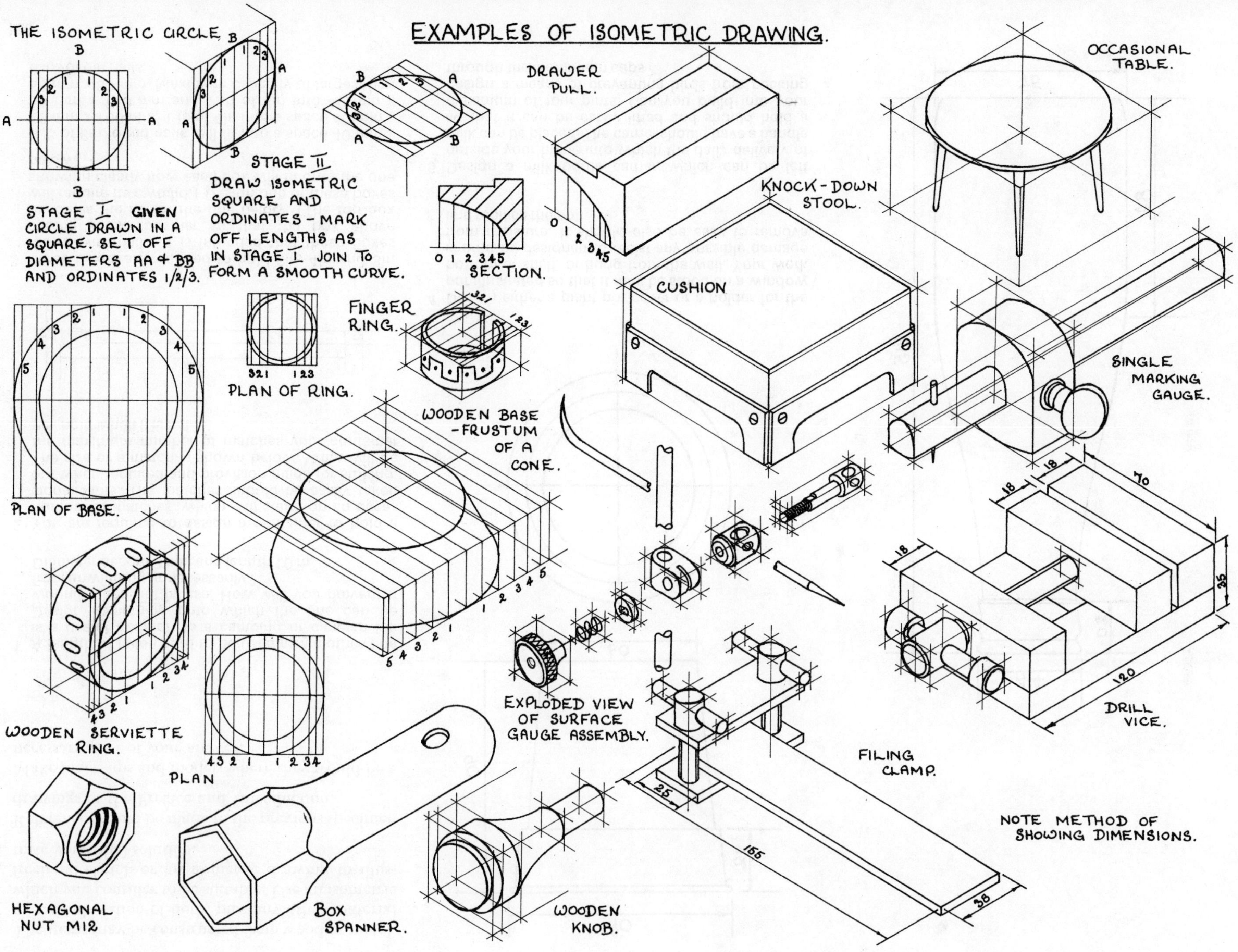

THE ISOMETRIC CIRCLE.
STAGE I GIVEN CIRCLE DRAWN IN A SQUARE. SET OFF DIAMETERS AA & BB AND ORDINATES 1/2/3.
STAGE II
DRAW ISOMETRIC SQUARE AND ORDINATES - MARK OFF LENGTHS AS IN STAGE I JOIN TO FORM A SMOOTH CURVE.
DRAWER PULL.
SECTION.
KNOCK-DOWN STOOL.
CUSHION
OCCASIONAL TABLE.
FINGER RING.
PLAN OF RING.
PLAN OF BASE.
WOODEN BASE - FRUSTUM OF A CONE.
SINGLE MARKING GAUGE.
WOODEN SERVIETTE RING.
PLAN
EXPLODED VIEW OF SURFACE GAUGE ASSEMBLY.
DRILL VICE.
FILING CLAMP.
NOTE METHOD OF SHOWING DIMENSIONS.
HEXAGONAL NUT M12
BOX SPANNER.
WOODEN KNOB.
18
18
70
18
35
120
25
155
38

Isometric design problems

The items may be constructed from wood or metal, or a combination of both, plus any other material which you consider to be suitable. Use an isometric freehand sketch or an isometric drawing to illustrate your final solution.

Reference should be made to the previous specimen drawings in the Preface and Introduction.

Make mock-ups and models where they would be a necessary part of your answer.

1 A length of nylon cord to be used as a clothes line is a useful addition to a camping or caravan kit. Design something onto which the line can be wound when not in use. How will you prevent it from unwinding unnecessarily?
Diameter of cord 3 mm and length 10 m.

2 You are required to design a container to hold a number of matches, which will stand on an occasional table. The matches should be easily taken out when required and provision made for striking. The size of a match is shown below. What will be the maximum number of matches your container will hold when it is full?

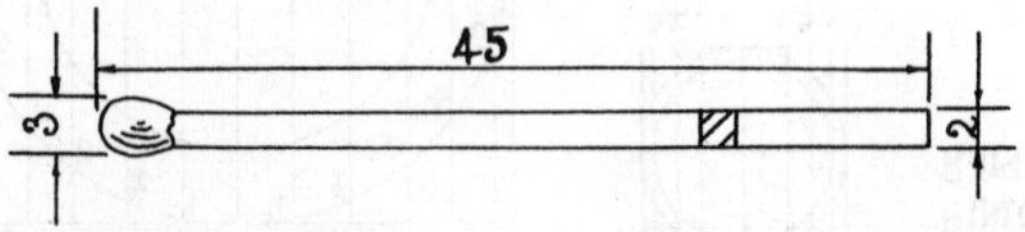

45
3
2

3 Three boxes are required to hold 6in, 4in and 3in round wire nails. It is intended that these boxes should stack together so that the box above becomes the lid for the one below. (The top box will require its own lid.) Design one of these boxes showing clearly how each box will fit onto the one below.

1 lb of 6in round nails will fit into a space 40 mm x 20 mm x 160 mm. 1 lb of 4in into a space 40 mm x 30 mm x 110 mm and 1 lb of 3in into 40 mm x 60 mm x 80 mm. Maximum capacity of largest box 6 lbs of 6in nails.

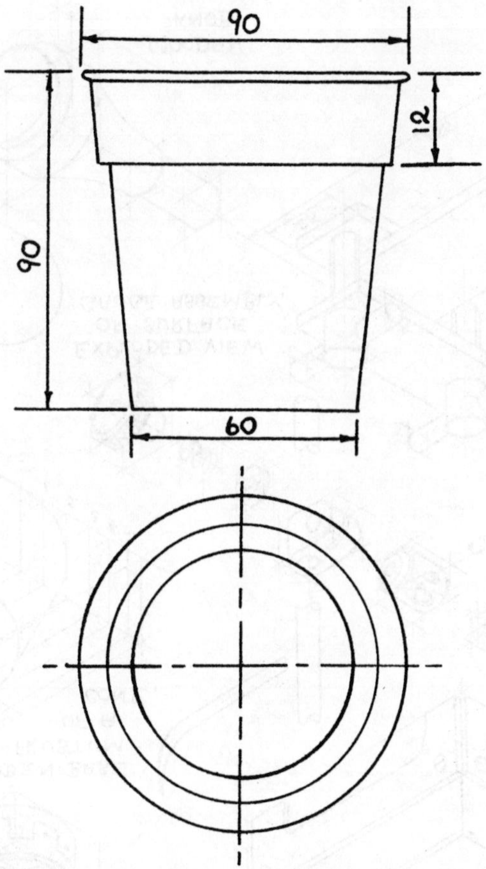

90
12
90
60

4 Design either a plant pot cover or a holder for the pot illustrated so that it may be stood on a window bottom or shelf, or hung from the wall. Your work should be designed to resist any possible damage from moisture. It should also be easy to remove and replace the pot.

5 Design a milk bottle carrier, which can be left outside your home into which the daily delivery of milk can be placed. The carrier should have a handle so that it can be easily lifted and should hold a maximum of four pints. Can you build into your design a means of preventing birds from pecking through the aluminium caps?

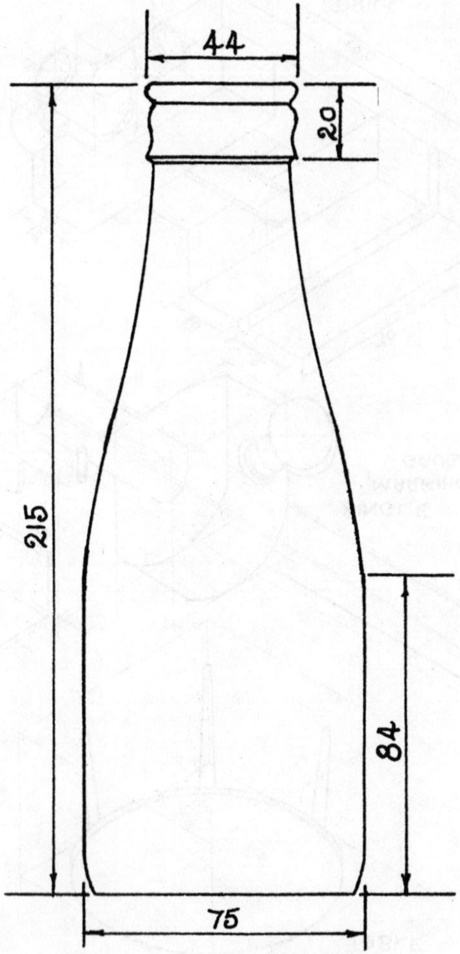

44
20
215
84
75

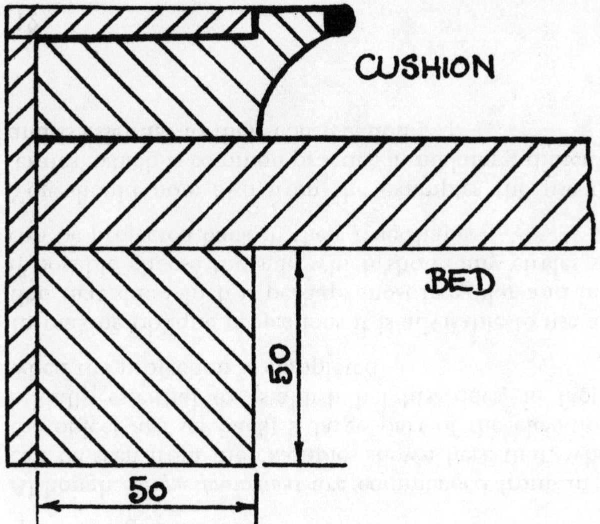

CUSHION
BED
50
50

6 The diagram shows the section through a billiards table which is designed to fit onto the top of a dining table. Design one of four feet which can be fitted into this framework and by which the table can be levelled. How will you prevent the feet from marking the table top?

7 A standard honey jar as used by bee keepers is shown in the illustration. Design a suitable cover into which the jar will fit in order to improve its appearance when used at the breakfast table.

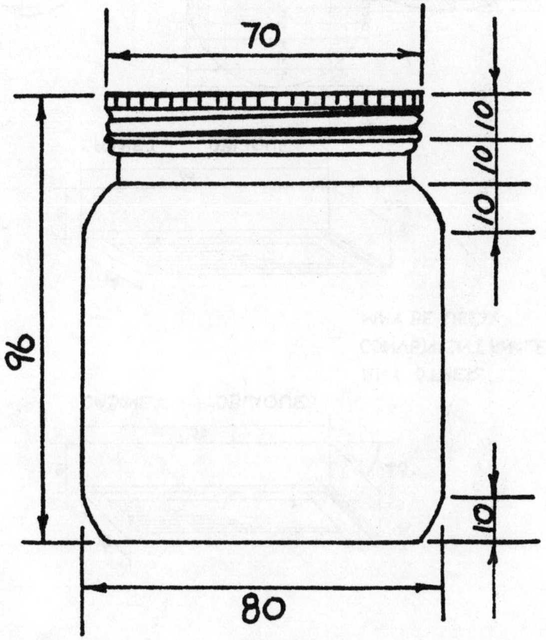

70
10
10
10
10
96
10
80

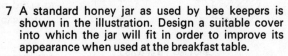

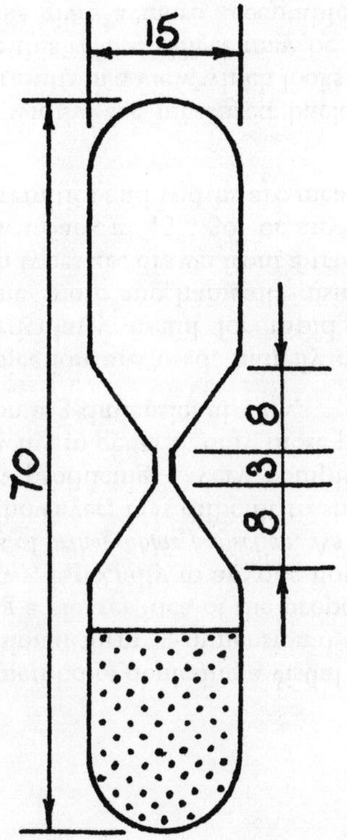

15
70
8
3
8

8 Timing devices as illustrated may be purchased. Design a suitable mounting for this so that it can be placed near to a telephone to enable you to assess the time being spent on a call. The mounting should allow the sand glass to be easily turned over. If you have a phone at home its position and its surroundings, such as furniture, etc., may influence your design.

Oblique Projection

Oblique projection is a method of depicting a visual impression of an object in a 3-dimensional form. 3-dimensional views have the advantage of conveying a clearer idea of the proposed design than do 2-dimensional views, especially to anyone not fully conversant with the principles of *orthographic projection*. As with other 3-dimensional projections however, it is difficult to show hidden details accurately without producing a very complicated and confused drawing. This is why, in general, only those parts which can be seen are depicted on a 3-dimensional view.

Two styles of oblique projection are used, namely *cavalier* and *cabinet*. Each style is particularly useful for rapid free hand sketching or may be done more mechanically using the tee square and set square. Both types are drawn from a true elevation of one side. Lines are drawn back at 45°; 30° or any other convenient angle from the extremities and widths are measured back along these lines.

In *cavalier oblique* the full widths are measured back along the lines but which sometimes results in a view which looks very much distorted and to overcome this *cabinet oblique* may be used when the widths are halved. This gives a more acceptable view, but there are times when in halving the widths, the construction of the completed view becomes more difficult due to restricting the space being used.

Although *oblique projections* are commenced from an elevation it can be seen from the examples shown here that, where parts of the object are set back, a large part of the elevation, which is initially essential to establish heights, does, in fact, disappear when the projection is completed.

In making oblique projections it is advisable to use as the elevation that side which is perhaps most irregular and in particular, if possible choose the side which shows any circles so that they can be projected back in their true shape.

You should note also from the examples the use of enclosing 'crates' which is common practice in making 3-dimensional views and is essential to their construction.

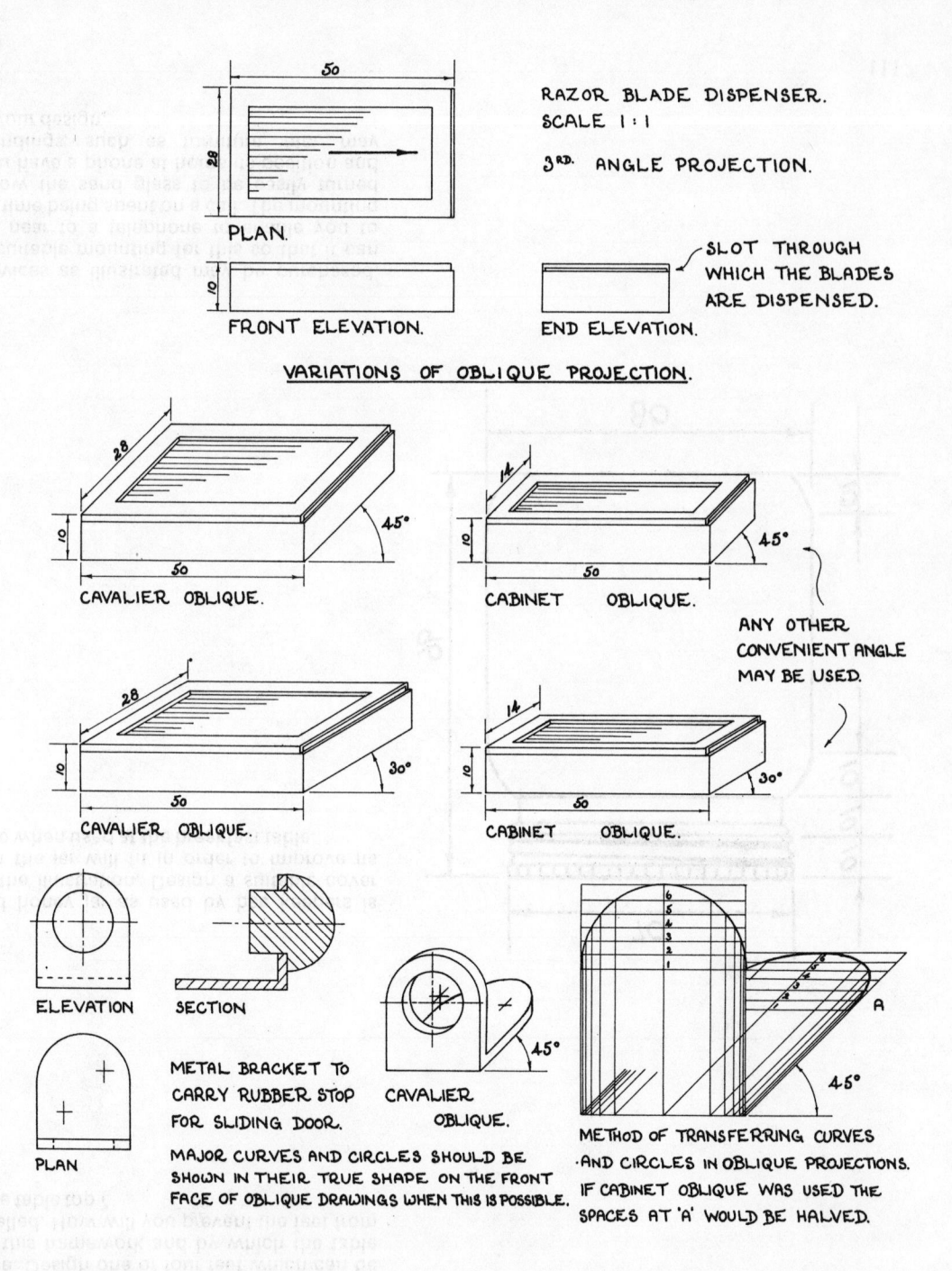

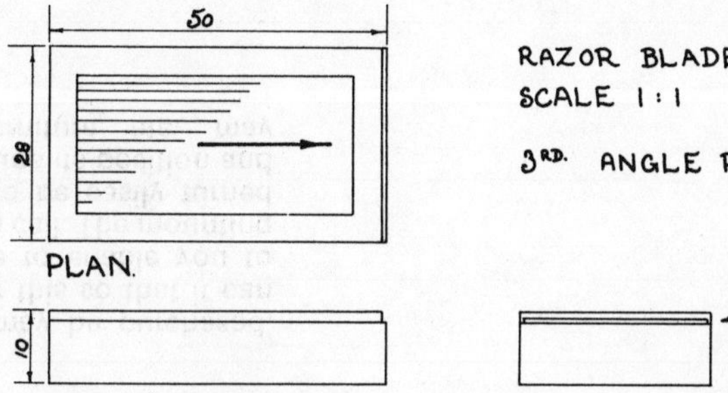

50
28
10
PLAN.
FRONT ELEVATION.
END ELEVATION.
SLOT THROUGH WHICH THE BLADES ARE DISPENSED.

RAZOR BLADE DISPENSER.
SCALE 1:1
3RD. ANGLE PROJECTION.

VARIATIONS OF OBLIQUE PROJECTION.

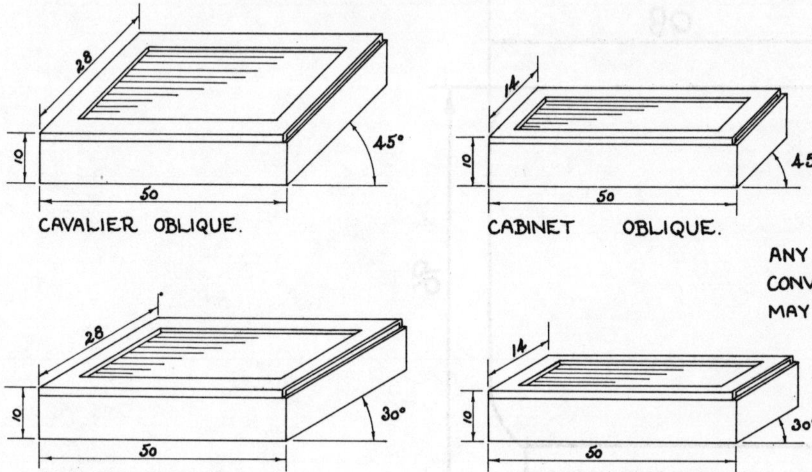

28
10
50
45°
CAVALIER OBLIQUE.
14
CABINET OBLIQUE.
30°
ANY OTHER CONVENIENT ANGLE MAY BE USED.

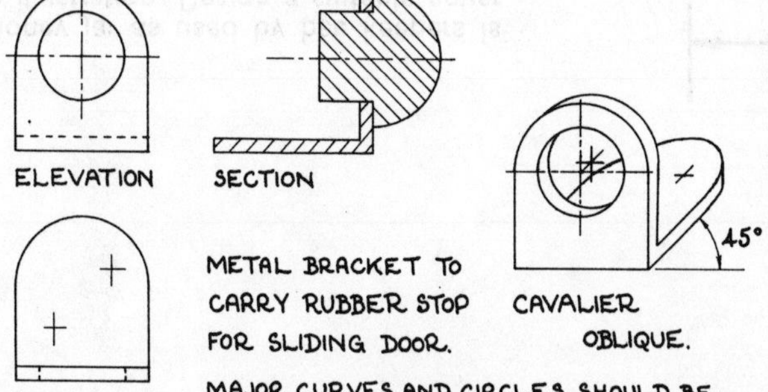

ELEVATION
SECTION
PLAN
45°
CAVALIER OBLIQUE.

METAL BRACKET TO CARRY RUBBER STOP FOR SLIDING DOOR.

MAJOR CURVES AND CIRCLES SHOULD BE SHOWN IN THEIR TRUE SHAPE ON THE FRONT FACE OF OBLIQUE DRAWINGS WHEN THIS IS POSSIBLE.

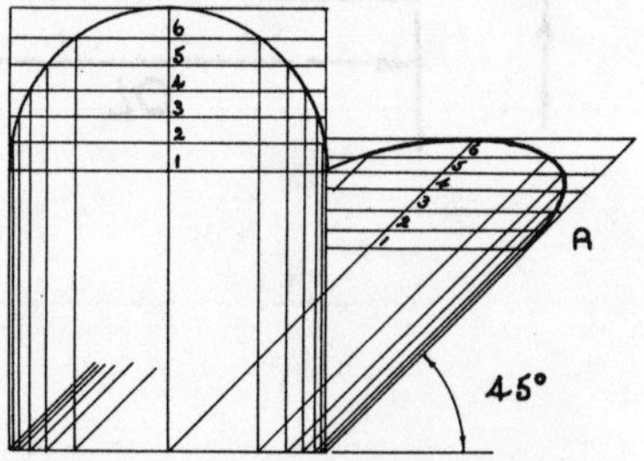

A
45°

METHOD OF TRANSFERRING CURVES AND CIRCLES IN OBLIQUE PROJECTIONS. IF CABINET OBLIQUE WAS USED THE SPACES AT 'A' WOULD BE HALVED.

EXAMPLES OF OBLIQUE PROJECTION.

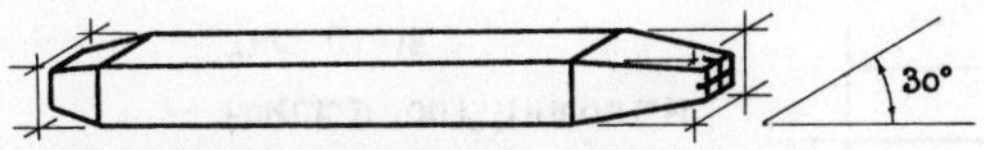
30°

PUNCH FOR DECORATIVE WORK.
CAVALIER OBLIQUE.

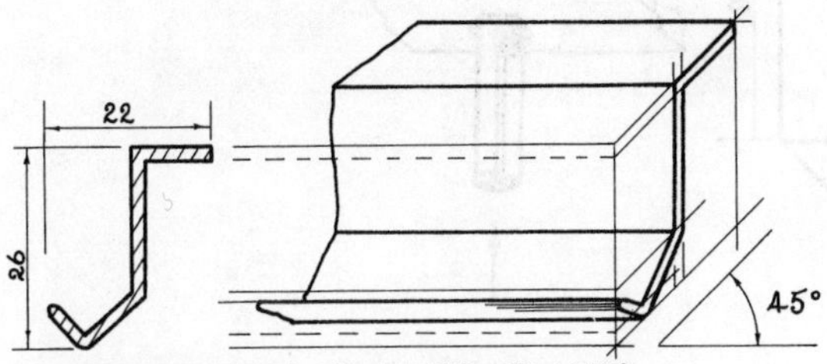
22
26
45°

SECTION OF TRACK FOR SLIDING DOOR. CAVALIER OBLIQUE.

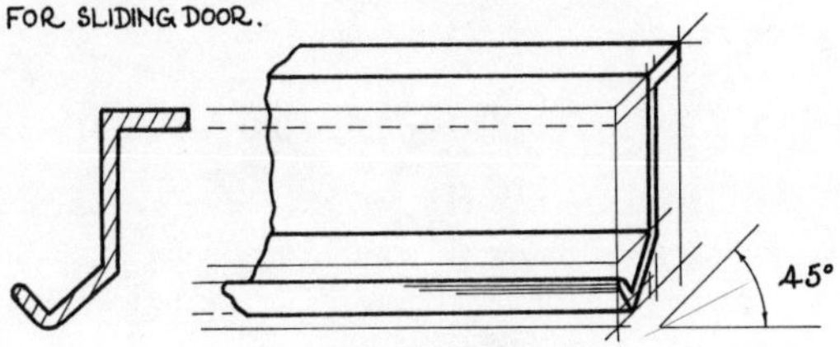
45°

CABINET OBLIQUE.

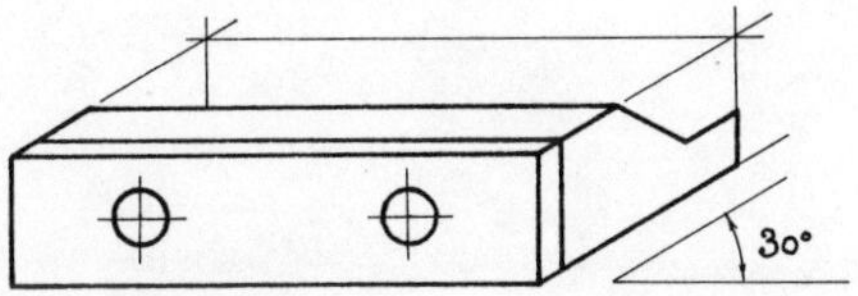
30°

FIBRE VISE JAW.
CAVALIER OBLIQUE.

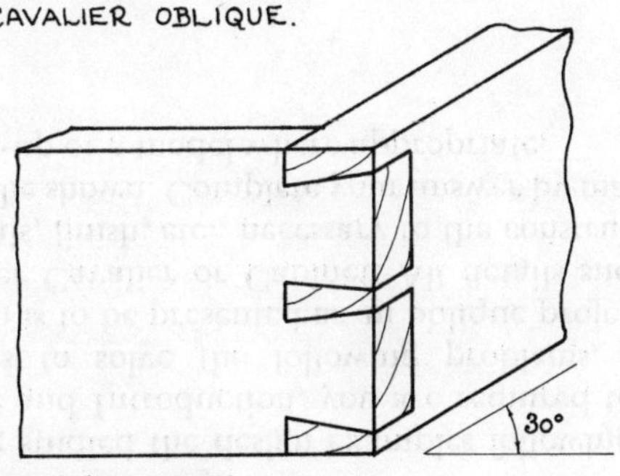
30°

DOVETAIL JOINT.
CABINET OBLIQUE.

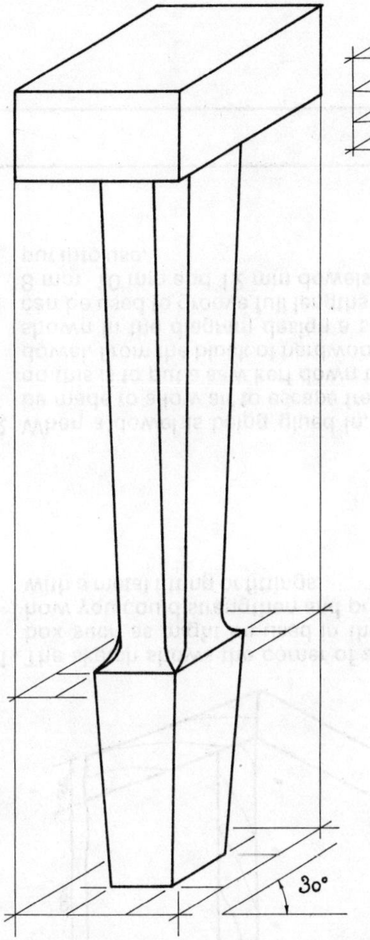
30°

SQUARE BOTTOMING STAKE.
CAVALIER OBLIQUE.

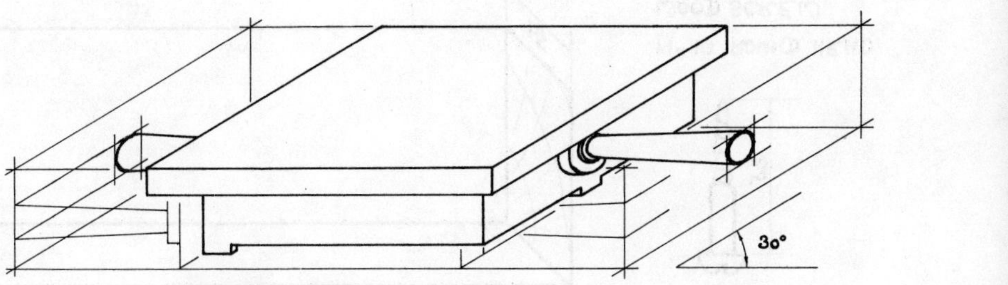
30°

SURFACE PLATE.
CAVALIER OBLIQUE.

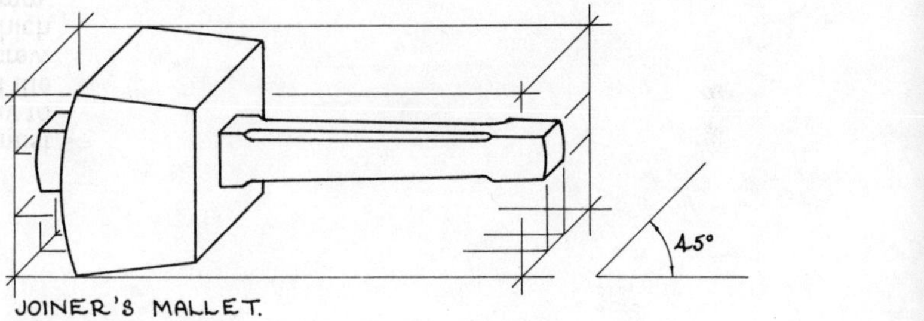
45°

JOINER'S MALLET.
CAVALIER OBLIQUE.

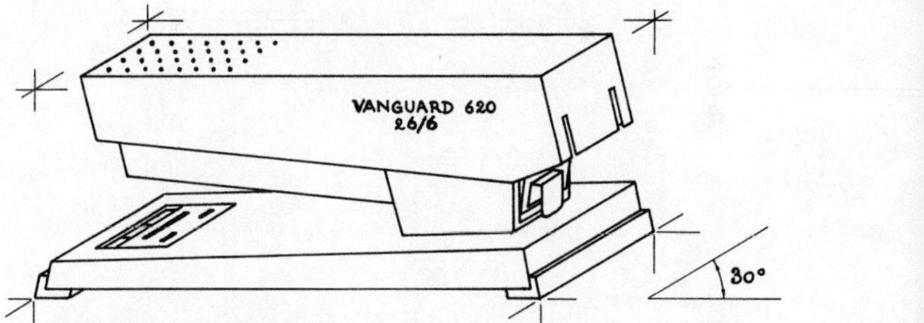
VANGUARD 620
26/6
30°

STAPLING MACHINE.
CAVALIER OBLIQUE.

ALTHOUGH CABINET OBLIQUE OFTEN GIVES A MORE ACCEPTABLE PROJECTION IT IS SOMETIMES DIFFICULT TO HALVE THE WIDTHS WITHOUT MAKING THE CONSTRUCTION VERY CONFUSED. THIS DOES NOT ARISE WITH CAVALIER PROJECTIONS WHERE FULL WIDTHS ARE USED.

Oblique design problems

Having studied the design examples following the Preface and Introduction, you are required to use sketches to solve the following problems, each solution is to be presented as an oblique projection in either Cavalier or Cabinet. All details such as materials, finish, etc., necessary to the construction should be shown. Complete your answer by making a mock-up or a model where appropriate.

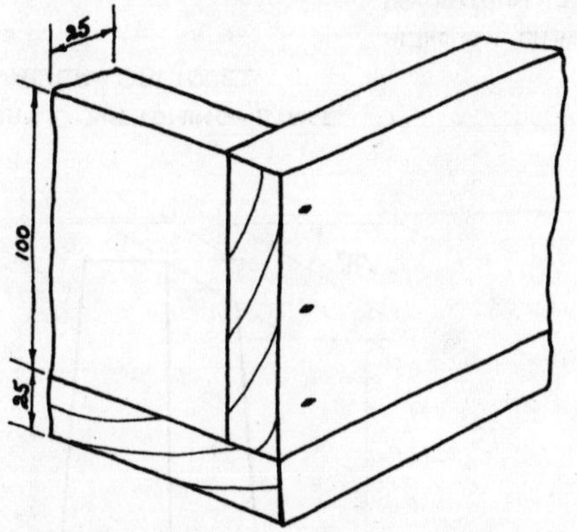

25
100
25

1 The sketch shows the corner of a rough wooden box such as might be used in the garden. Show how you could strengthen and protect this corner with a metal fitting or fittings.

2 When a dowel is being glued in, provision must be made to allow air to escape freely. One way to do this is to put a saw kerf down the length of the dowel. From the block of hardwood and the screw shown in the diagram design a small tool which can be used to groove full lengths of 5 mm, 6 mm, 8 mm, 10 mm and 12 mm dowels before they are put into use.

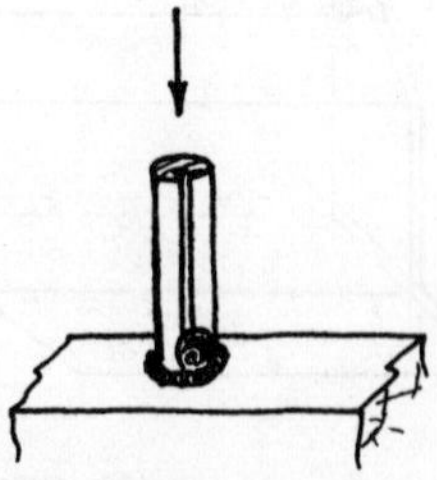

BUBBLE OF AIR BEING
FORCED OUT THROUGH
THE GLUE.

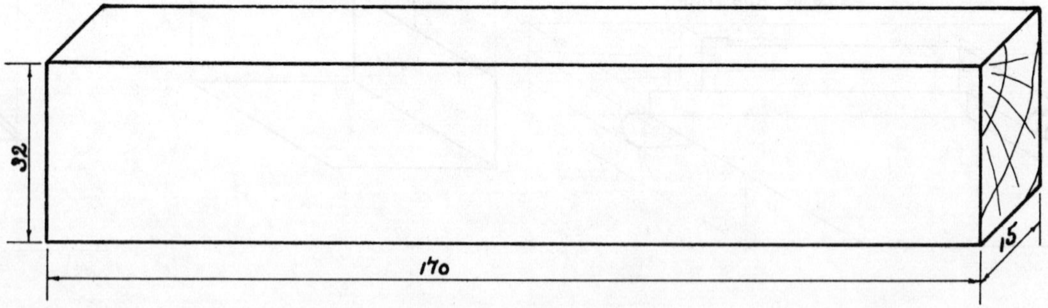

32
15
170

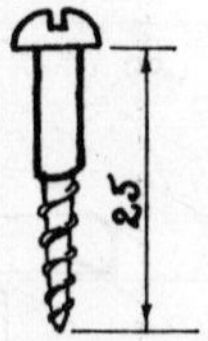

25
Nº 10 ROUND HEAD
WOOD SCREW.

3 Design a bracket to hold the car reversing lamp shown in the drawing, to the rear bumper.

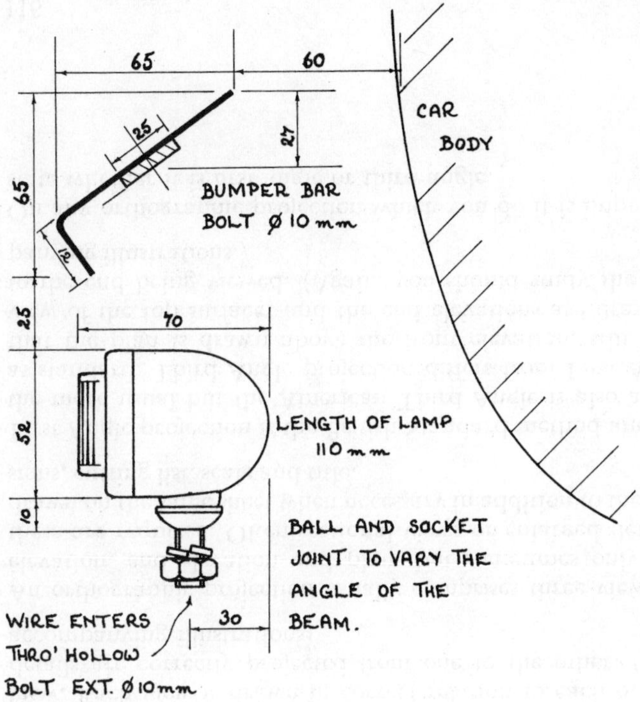
65
60
25
27
CAR
BODY
65
BUMPER BAR
BOLT Ø 10 mm
25
70
52
LENGTH OF LAMP
110 mm
10
BALL AND SOCKET
JOINT TO VARY THE
ANGLE OF THE
BEAM.
WIRE ENTERS
THRO' HOLLOW
BOLT EXT. Ø10mm
30

4 The angle of slope for dovetails used in woodwork is usually accepted as 1 in 8. Design a template to be made in wood or from sheet metal which will mark out this shape on the pins.

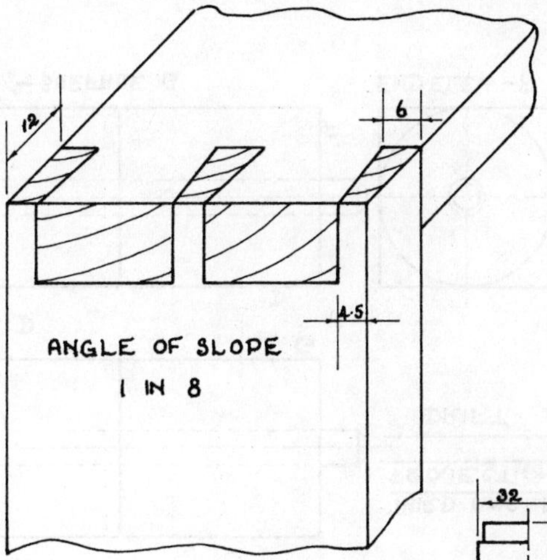
12
6
4.5
ANGLE OF SLOPE
1 IN 8

5 You are provided with two lengths of Bright Drawn Mild Steel each 10 mm x 10 mm x 130 mm and two standard socket cap screws M5 x 25. Show how you would construct a simple tap wrench from these materials.

6 Show how by suitably cutting and folding a piece of sheet metal 1.2 mm thick or by building up a laminated shape from industrial veneers or 1.5 mm plywood suitably glued together over a former, you would produce a fruit tray. It should hold a selection of the fruits common to most households.

7 To avoid bringing dirt from your garden into the house you wish to make a shoe scraper of *black mild steel* to be fixed with 'Rawlbolts' to the house wall. The scraper blade should be at right angles to the wall, and horizontal when in use; when not required it should be folded upwards to the wall for safety.

8 Design a pair of stilts for a younger member of your family. Find out how long the upright should be, how to make them comfortable to hold and how to make a secure footrest which can be adjusted for height from the ground. Provide oblique projections of the handles and footrests.

9 You wish to keep a tropical shrub in the entrance to your home which can be lifted indoors during severe weather. Design a suitable square sectioned tub, paying particular attention to drainage.

10 Design a modern wine rack to be made of plywood and finished with acrylic paints to hold twelve bottles similar in shape to the one illustrated.

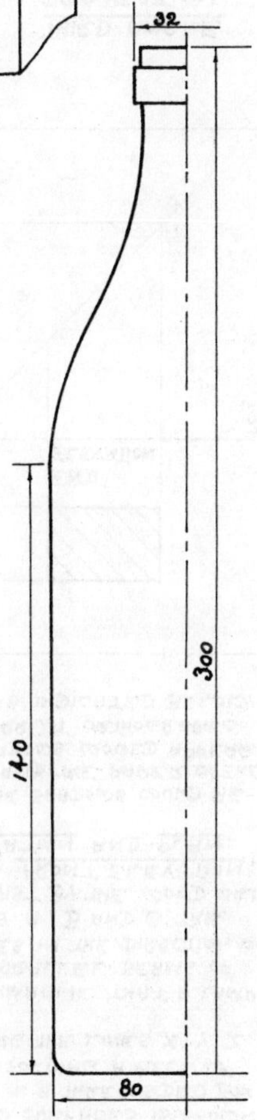
32
300
140
80

Orthographic or Orthogonal Projection

Once you have studied the examples of designing in the preceding part of this book you will realise that very often it is difficult to show all the details [on a sketch] which are necessary to make a piece of work. If the shape is to be fully understood and the correct position of parts in relation to each other made clear you may find that you have to draw a number of 2-dimensional or 3-dimensional views in different positions which would be both very laborious and tedious.

Orthographic projection is the universal method adopted to overcome this difficulty and is a system based on lines and planes at right angles, the name being derived from the Greek, orthos-right and gonia-angle.

The principal dimensions of any 3-dimensional object are length, width and height. Each view in an orthographic projection shows only two of these, e.g. length and height; height and width; length and width plus the relevant details for that particular view. Each view is drawn in correct relation to each other and details are correctly projected from one to the other. (See the accompanying illustrations)

An orthographic projection usually comprises three views, front elevation, end elevation and plan, but sometimes only two of these are required. Often sectional views or enlarged details are drawn on the same sheet when necessary in addition to the dimensions, cutting list, scale and title.

First Angle projection is the British Standard method and is still the more usual but the American Third Angle is also accepted as standard. Third Angle projection differs from First Angle in that the plan is drawn above the front elevation, still being a view of the top surface; and the end elevations are drawn near to the end being viewed. (Again, you should study the accompanying illustrations.)

On any orthographic projection which you do it is important to state whether it is first angle or third angle.

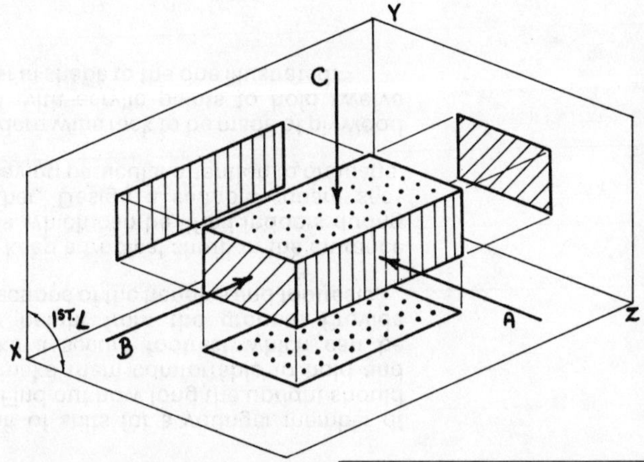
Y
C
1ST. L
X
B
A
Z

A BLOCK OF WOOD WITH MARKED OR PAINTED SURFACES IS SHOWN SUSPENDED IN A THREE SIDED BOX FORMED BY FOLDING A PIECE OF PAPER ALONG THE LINES X : Y : Z.

IF YOU NOW IMAGINE THAT A LAMP THROWING PARALLEL BEAMS OF LIGHT SHINES IN THE DIRECTION OF THE ARROWS A, B AND C THE SHADOWS CAST BY THE WOOD WILL BE OF THE FRONT ELEVATION, END ELEVATION AND PLAN.

NOW, IF THESE SHADOWS COULD BE RETAINED AND THE PAPER OPENED OUT, THE SHADOWS WOULD APPEAR IN THEIR CORRECT ORTHOGRAPHIC POSITIONS AS INDICATED BELOW.

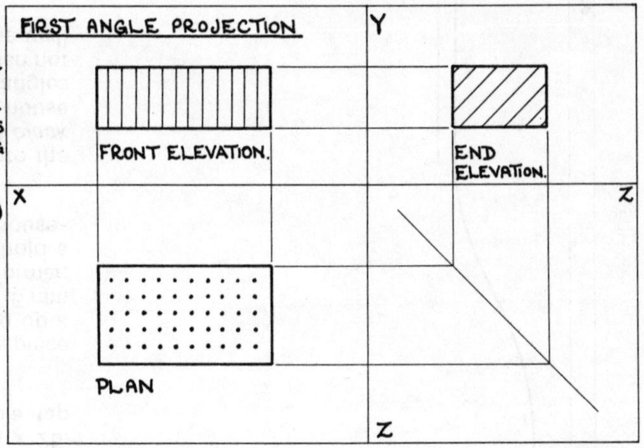
FIRST ANGLE PROJECTION
Y
FRONT ELEVATION.
END ELEVATION.
X
Z
PLAN
Z

THE SKETCH SHOWS A TURNING AND DRILLING JIG DESIGNED TO PRODUCE A NUMBER OF IDENTICAL BARREL NUTS OF THE TYPE USED IN THE ASSEMBLY OF THE TROLLEY. (PAGE 77) THE GRUB SCREW HOLDS THE BLANK IN THE JIG WHEN TURNING TO LENGTH AND WHEN DRILLING THE TAPPING SIZE HOLE.

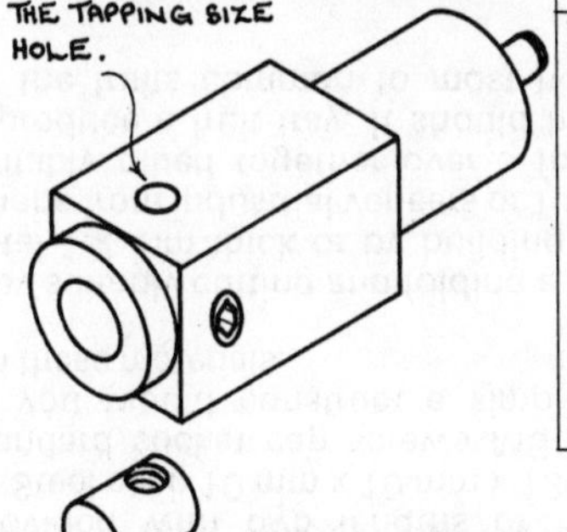

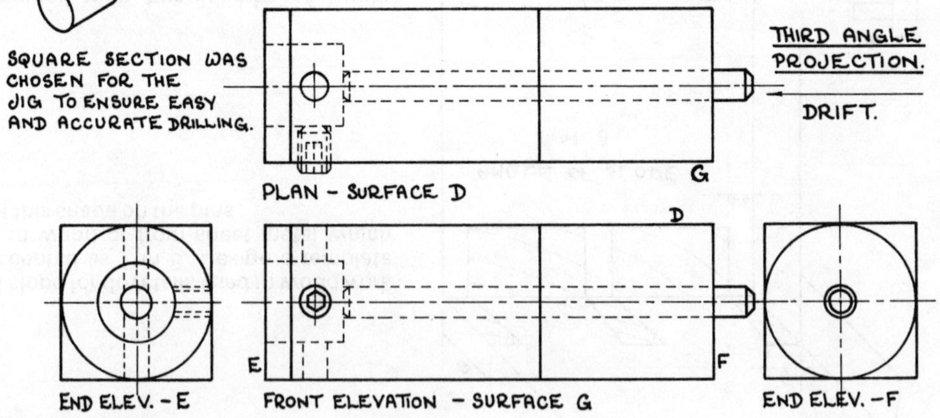
SQUARE SECTION WAS CHOSEN FOR THE JIG TO ENSURE EASY AND ACCURATE DRILLING.
THIRD ANGLE PROJECTION.
DRIFT.
G
PLAN - SURFACE D
D
E
F
END ELEV. - E
FRONT ELEVATION - SURFACE G
END ELEV. - F

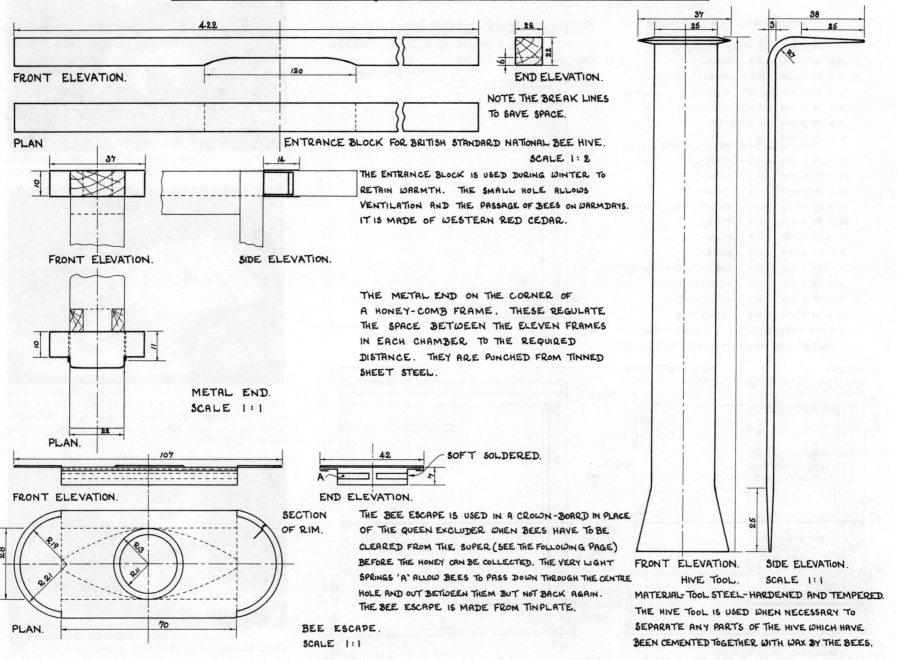

EXAMPLES OF ORTHOGRAPHIC (ORTHOGONAL) PROJECTION – FIRST ANGLE PROJECTION.

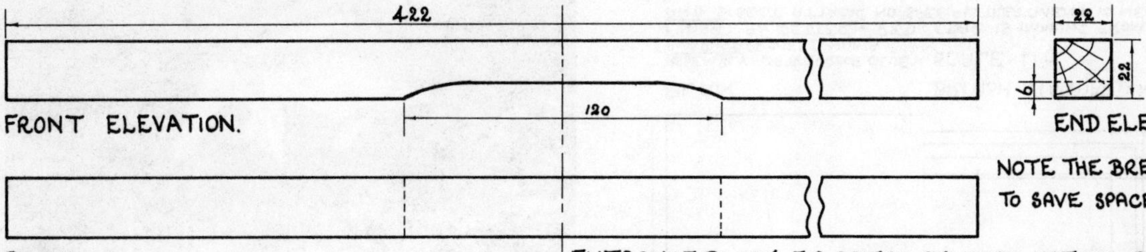
422
120
FRONT ELEVATION.
PLAN
22
22
6
END ELEVATION.

NOTE THE BREAK LINES TO SAVE SPACE.

ENTRANCE BLOCK FOR BRITISH STANDARD NATIONAL BEE HIVE.

SCALE 1 : 2

THE ENTRANCE BLOCK IS USED DURING WINTER TO RETAIN WARMTH. THE SMALL HOLE ALLOWS VENTILATION AND THE PASSAGE OF BEES ON WARMDAYS. IT IS MADE OF WESTERN RED CEDAR.

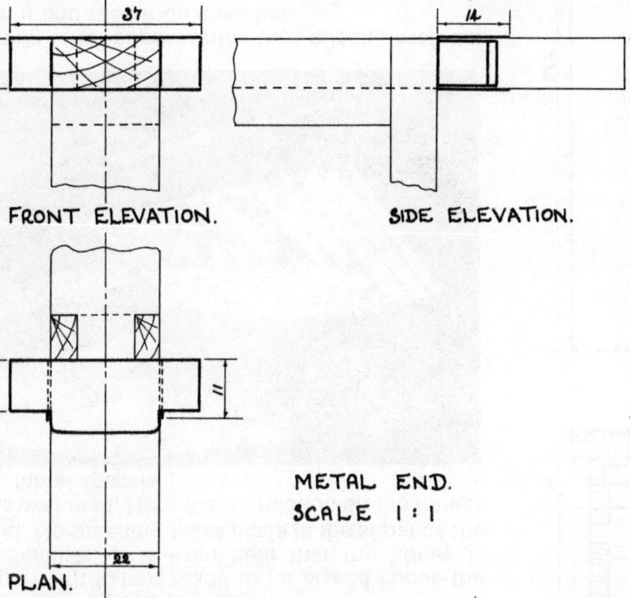
37
14
10
FRONT ELEVATION.
SIDE ELEVATION.
10
11
22
PLAN.

METAL END.
SCALE 1 : 1

THE METAL END ON THE CORNER OF A HONEY-COMB FRAME. THESE REGULATE THE SPACE BETWEEN THE ELEVEN FRAMES IN EACH CHAMBER TO THE REQUIRED DISTANCE. THEY ARE PUNCHED FROM TINNED SHEET STEEL.

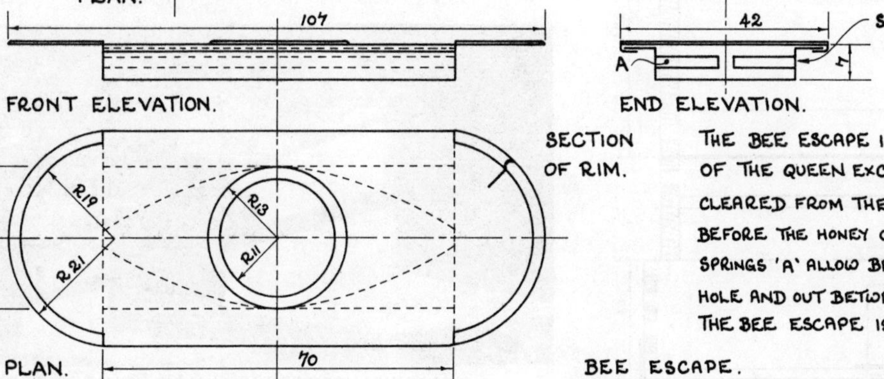
107
FRONT ELEVATION.
42
SOFT SOLDERED.
A
4
END ELEVATION.
SECTION OF RIM.
28
R19
R21
R3
R11
70
PLAN.

BEE ESCAPE.
SCALE 1 : 1

THE BEE ESCAPE IS USED IN A CROWN-BOARD IN PLACE OF THE QUEEN EXCLUDER WHEN BEES HAVE TO BE CLEARED FROM THE SUPER (SEE THE FOLLOWING PAGE) BEFORE THE HONEY CAN BE COLLECTED. THE VERY LIGHT SPRINGS 'A' ALLOW BEES TO PASS DOWN THROUGH THE CENTRE HOLE AND OUT BETWEEN THEM BUT NOT BACK AGAIN. THE BEE ESCAPE IS MADE FROM TINPLATE.

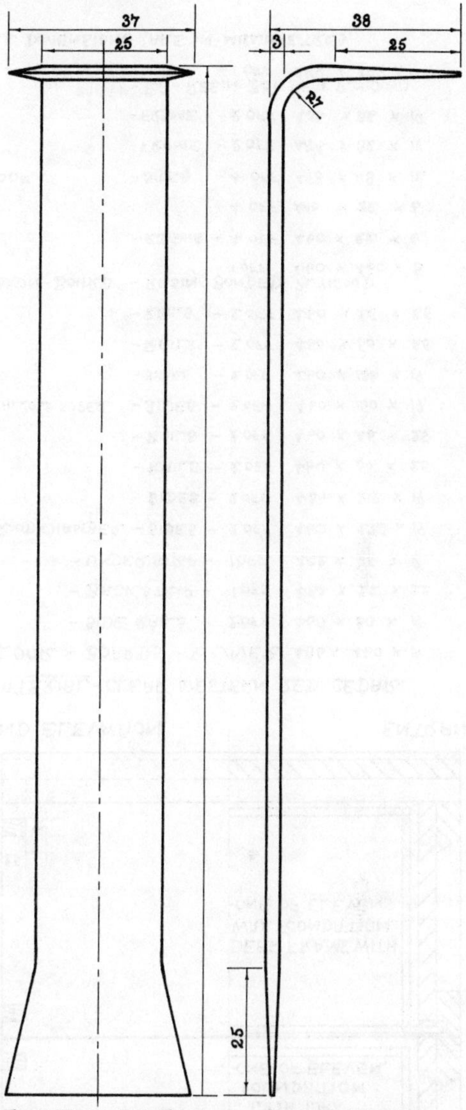
37
25
38
3
25
R7
25

FRONT ELEVATION. SIDE ELEVATION.
HIVE TOOL. SCALE 1 : 1

MATERIAL – TOOL STEEL – HARDENED AND TEMPERED.

THE HIVE TOOL IS USED WHEN NECESSARY TO SEPARATE ANY PARTS OF THE HIVE WHICH HAVE BEEN CEMENTED TOGETHER WITH WAX BY THE BEES.

EXAMPLE OF ORTHOGRAPHIC (ORTHOGONAL) PROJECTION - FIRST ANGLE PROJECTION.

The brood chamber as in winter. The entrance block (see following drawings) has been removed.

The super with frames ready to be placed above the brood chamber. It is from here that the honey is collected. No breeding takes place in the super as the queen is excluded. Note the foundation on the frames and the metal spacers.

Positioning the super with the queen excluder between it and the brood chamber.

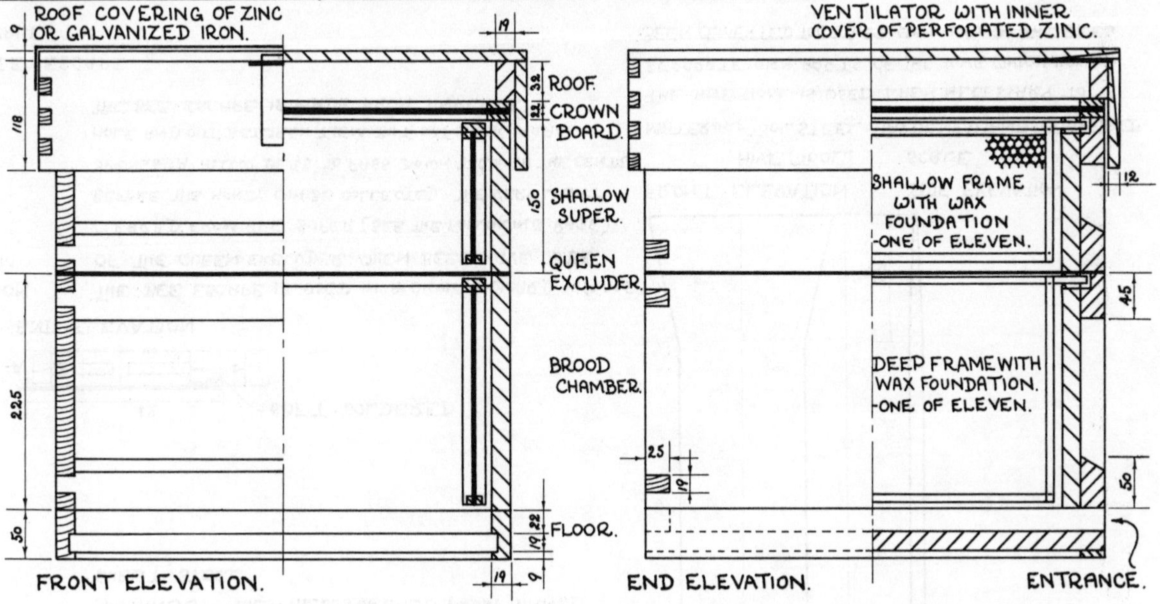

ROOF COVERING OF ZINC OR GALVANIZED IRON.
ROOF
CROWN BOARD.
SHALLOW SUPER.
QUEEN EXCLUDER.
BROOD CHAMBER.
FLOOR.
FRONT ELEVATION.
VENTILATOR WITH INNER COVER OF PERFORATED ZINC.
SHALLOW FRAME WITH WAX FOUNDATION -ONE OF ELEVEN.
DEEP FRAME WITH WAX FOUNDATION. -ONE OF ELEVEN.
END ELEVATION.
ENTRANCE.
9
19
118
38
22
150
225
50
22
19
9
12
45
50
25
19

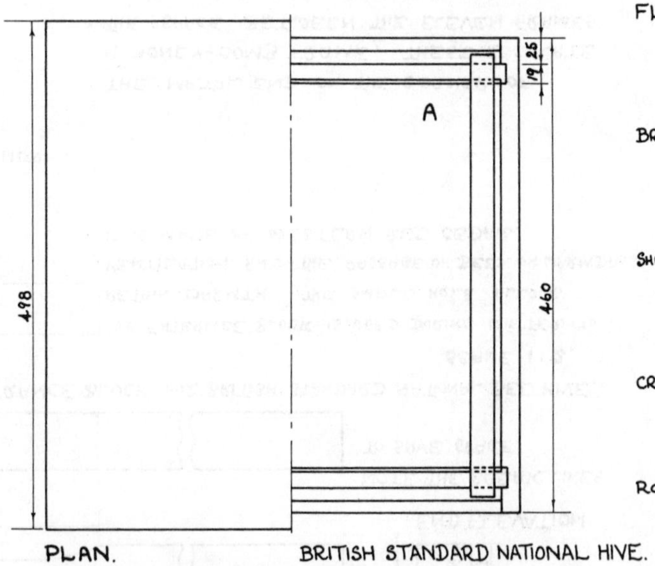

A
498
460
25
19

PLAN.

BRITISH STANDARD NATIONAL HIVE.

SCALE 1:5

ASSEMBLY - WATERPROOF GLUE AND RUST-PROOFED NAILS.

FINISH: AS WESTERN RED CEDAR IS IMMUNE FROM DECAY AND INSECT ATTACK NO SPECIAL TREATMENT IS NECESSARY.

MATERIAL - CLEAR WESTERN RED CEDAR.

FLOOR	- BOARDS - TO COVER		486 x 460 x 19
	- SIDE RAILS	2 OFF	460 x 50 x 19
	- BACK STRIP	1 OFF	422 x 22 x 22
	- UNDER STRIP	1 OFF	422 x 25 x 9
BROOD CHAMBER	- SIDES	2 OFF	460 x 225 x 19
	- SIDES	2 OFF	434 x 212 x 19
	- RAILS	2 OFF	460 x 50 x 25
	- RAILS	2 OFF	460 x 45 x 25
SHALLOW SUPER	- SIDES	2 OFF	460 x 150 x 19
	- SIDES	2 OFF	460 x 136 x 19
	- RAILS	2 OFF	460 x 50 x 25
	- RAILS	2 OFF	460 x 45 x 25
CROWN-BOARD	- RESIN BONDED PLYWOOD	1 OFF	460 x 460 x 5
	- EDGING	4 OFF	460 x 22 x 6
	-	4 OFF	416 x 22 x 6
ROOF	- SIDES	4 OFF	498 x 118 x 12
	- FRAME	2 OFF	474 x 32 x 19
	- FRAME	2 OFF	436 x 32 x 19
	- TOP - RESIN BONDED PLYWOOD	1 OFF	498 x 498 x 9

ALL DIMENSIONS ARE IN MILLIMETRES.

FURTHER EXAMPLES OF ORTHOGRAPHIC - FIRST ANGLE PROJECTION.

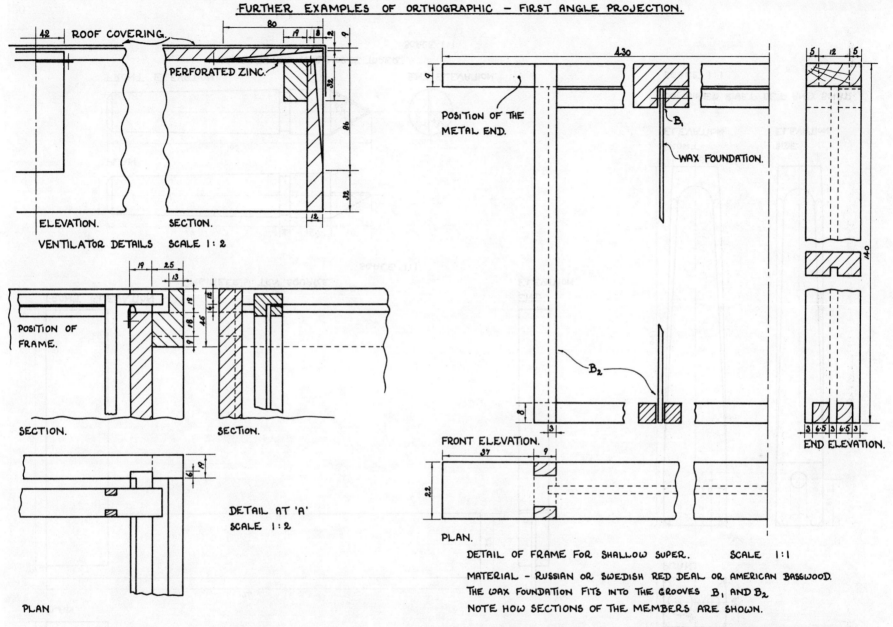

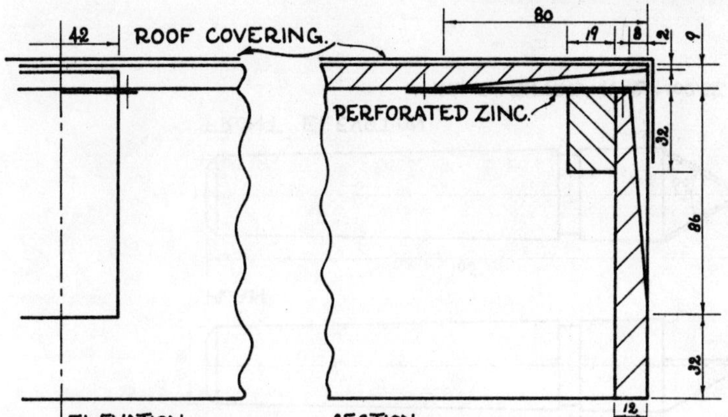
42
ROOF COVERING.
80
19
8
2
9
PERFORATED ZINC.
32
86
32
12
ELEVATION.
SECTION.

VENTILATOR DETAILS SCALE 1 : 2

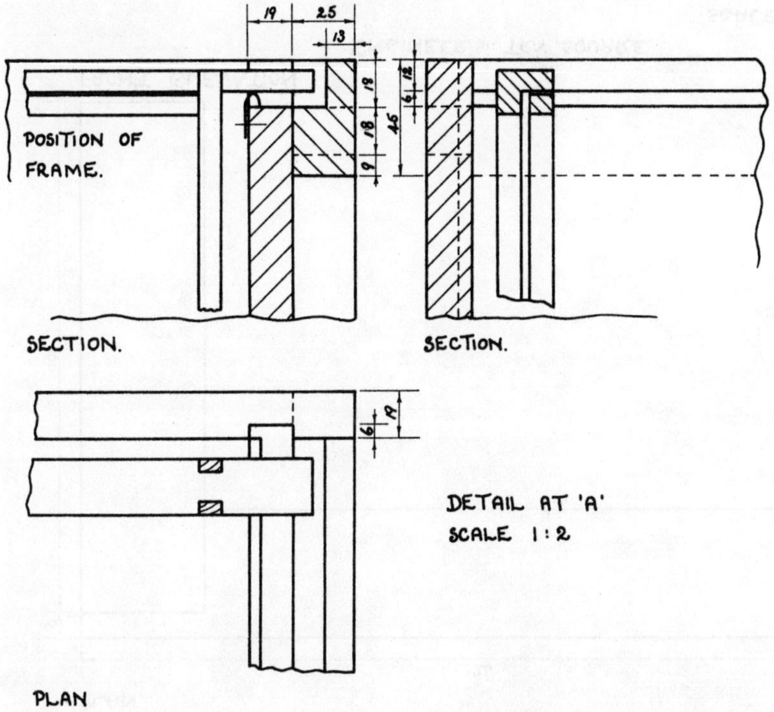
19
25
13
12
6
19
18
45
9
POSITION OF FRAME.
SECTION.
SECTION.
6
19
PLAN

DETAIL AT 'A'
SCALE 1 : 2

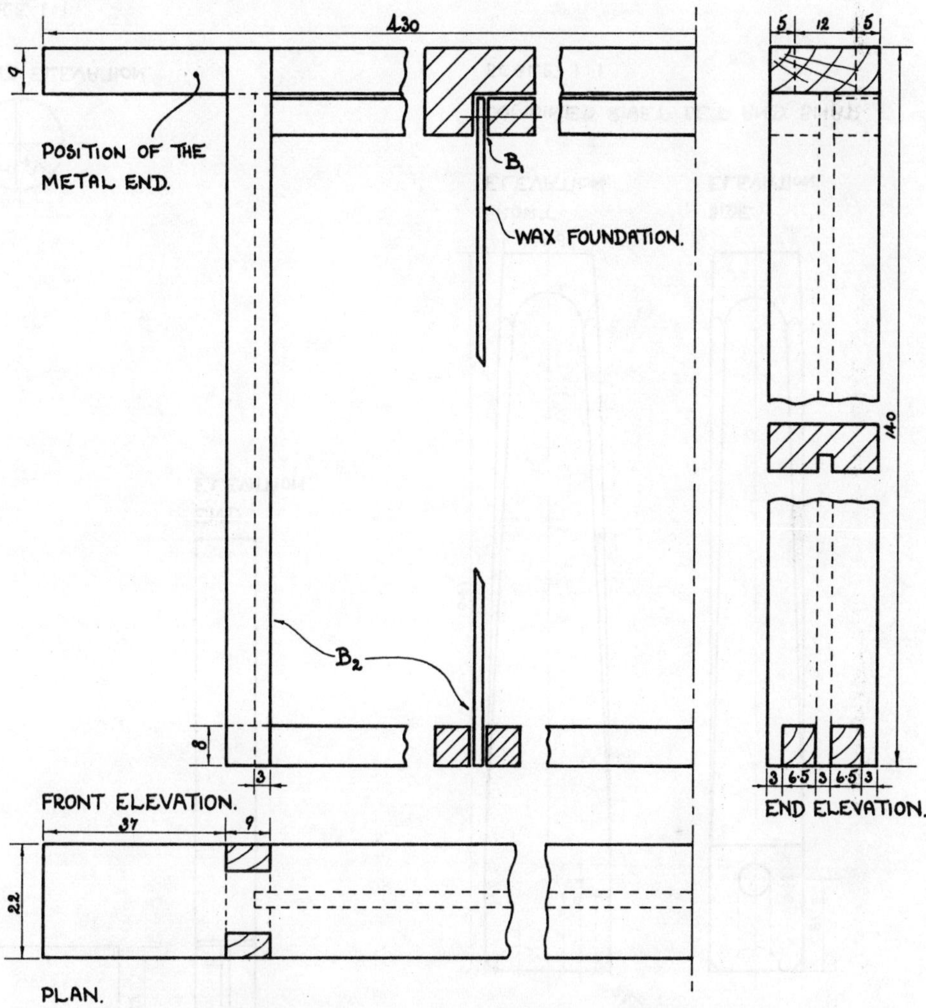
430
9
POSITION OF THE METAL END.
B1
WAX FOUNDATION.
B2
8
3
FRONT ELEVATION.
5
12
5
140
3
6·5
3
6·5
3
END ELEVATION.
37
9
22
PLAN.

DETAIL OF FRAME FOR SHALLOW SUPER. SCALE 1 : 1

MATERIAL - RUSSIAN OR SWEDISH RED DEAL OR AMERICAN BASSWOOD.

THE WAX FOUNDATION FITS INTO THE GROOVES B_1 AND B_2

NOTE HOW SECTIONS OF THE MEMBERS ARE SHOWN.

ALL DIMENSIONS ARE IN MILLIMETRES.

IT IS A COMMON PRACTICE TO DRAW DETAILS TO A LARGER SCALE TO MAKE THEM EASILY UNDERSTOOD.

EXAMPLES OF ORTHOGRAPHIC PROJECTION – THIRD ANGLE.

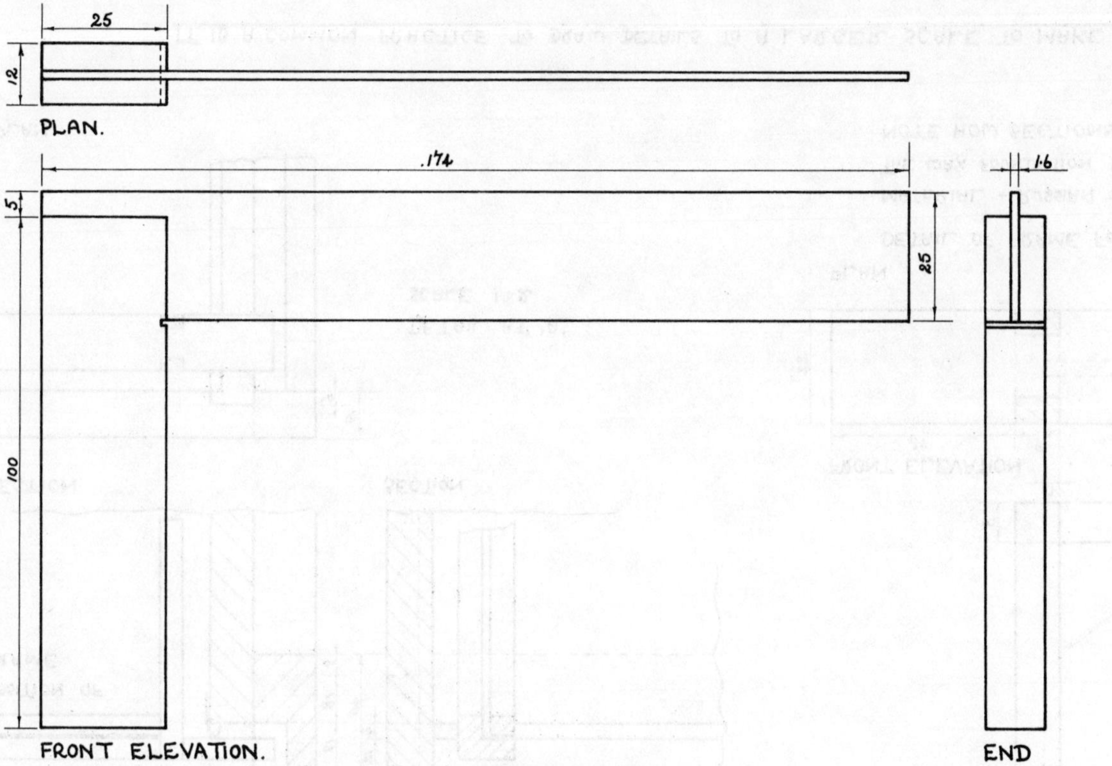
25
12
PLAN.
174
1·6
5
25
100
FRONT ELEVATION.
END
ELEVATION.

ENGINEER'S TRY SQUARE.

SCALE 1:1

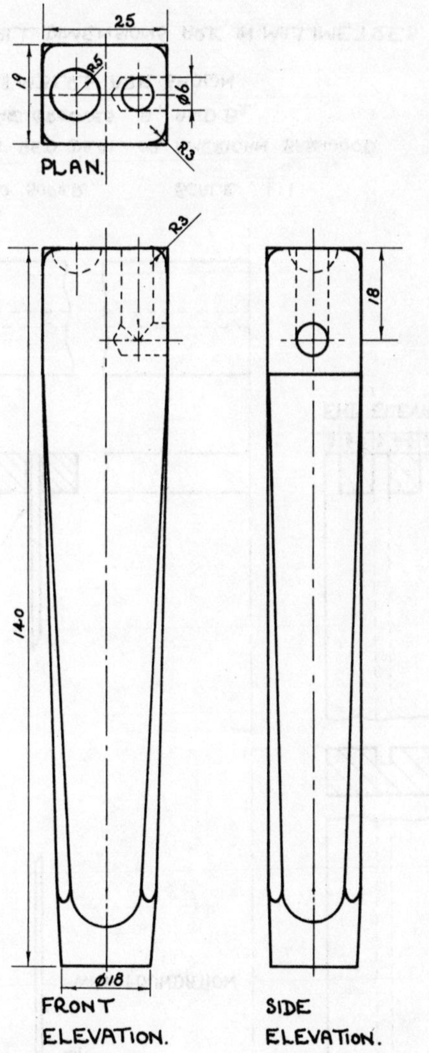
25
19
R5
ø6
R3
PLAN.
R3
18
140
ø18
FRONT
ELEVATION.
SIDE
ELEVATION.

COMBINED RIVET SET AND SNAP.

SCALE 1:1

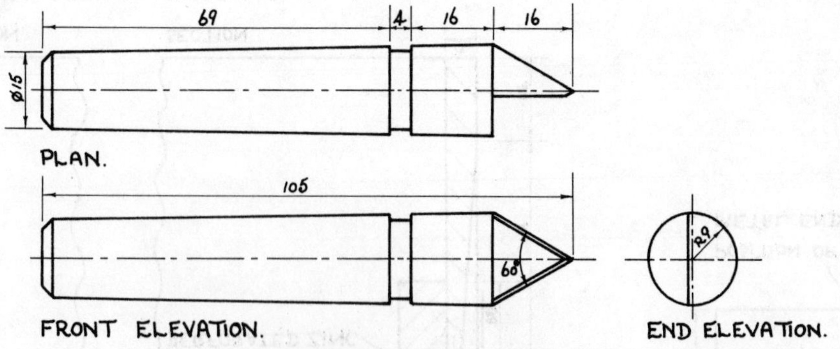
69
4
16
16
ø15
PLAN.
105
60°
R9
FRONT ELEVATION.
END ELEVATION.

HALF CENTRE : Nº2 MORSE TAPER.

SCALE 1:1

ORTHOGRAPHIC PROJECTION – THIRD ANGLE.

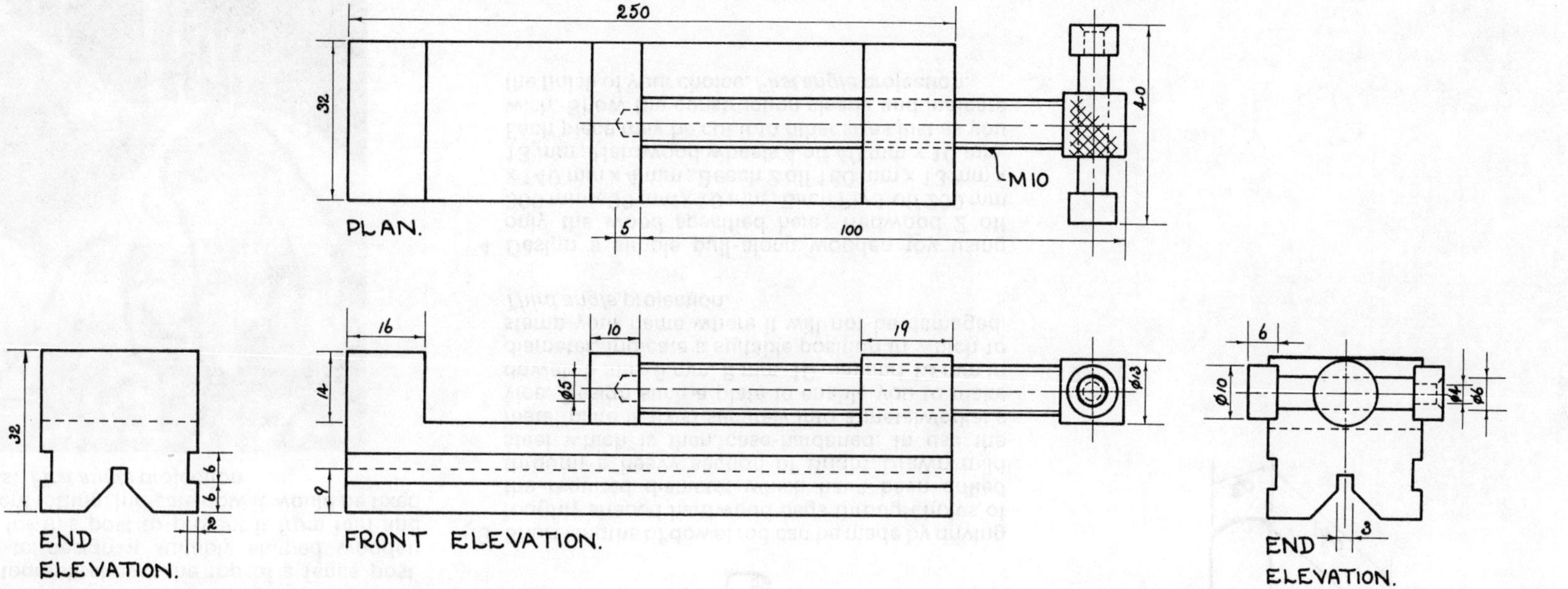
250
32
PLAN.
5
100
M10
40
16
10
19
14
ø5
ø13
32
6
6
2
9
END ELEVATION.
FRONT ELEVATION.
6
ø10
ø4
ø6
3
END ELEVATION.

MATERIAL – BRIGHT DRAWN MILD STEEL.

VICE BODY	1 OFF – 250	× 32	× 32
MOVING JAW	1 OFF – 32	× 14	× 10
SCREW	1 OFF – 105	× ø13	
TOMMY BAR	1 OFF – 40	× ø6	
ENDS	2 OFF – 6	× ø10	

FINISH – ALL WORKING FACES CASE-HARDENED : BRIGHT POLISH.

ALL DIMENSIONS ARE IN MILLIMETRES.

DRILL VICE AND VEE BLOCK.	SCALE 1:1	DESIGNED BY	FORM	DATE	SCHOOL

Design problems

For each of the following design questions you should study the details of the orthographic projections illustrated in this chapter and also refer to the examples of designing which follow the Preface and Introduction, then select a technique to use and work out a solution to each problem. From your freehand sketches you are then to prepare an orthographic projection of the work to be made; include a cutting list where appropriate and state the finish to be used. Use first or third angle projection as indicated in each question and make a mock-up or a model as may be necessary.

1 Design a hardwood wedge which can be used to hold a door open, making some provision for it to be hung up when not in use. *First angle* projection.

2 The photograph shows the top of a fence post. You are to design a suitably shaped wooden capping for this post to protect it from rain and subsequent rotting. Indicate how it would be fixed to the post. *First angle* projection.

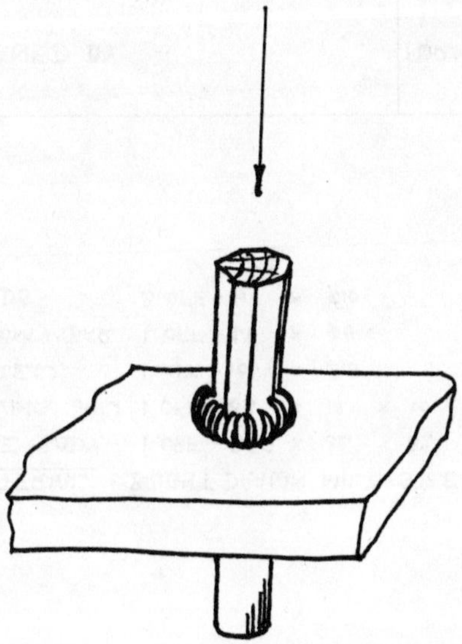

3 Short lengths of dowel rod can be made by driving roughly shaped hardwood pegs through holes of the required diameter which have been drilled through a heavy section of Bright Drawn mild steel which is then case-hardened. In use the metal plate is fixed securely into a metalworker's vice. Design such a plate to enable you to make dowels 5 mm, 6 mm, 8 mm, 10 mm and 13 mm in diameter. Indicate a suitable position in which to stamp your name where it will not be damaged. *Third angle* projection.

4 Design a simple pull-along wooden toy using only the wood specified here: Redwood 2 off 300 mm x 30 mm x 10 mm; Birch Ply 1 off 200 mm x 140 mm x 4 mm; Beech 2 off 160 mm x 13 mm x 13 mm; Hardwood wheels 4 off 40 mm x 10 mm. Each piece may be cut into other sizes just as you wish. Show the construction clearly and indicate the finish of your choice. *First angle* projection.

5 Design, either from wood or metal, or a combination of both, a pair of modern book supports to hold a row of books in place on a desk top. There are twelve books similar to the one illustrated. *Third angle* projection.

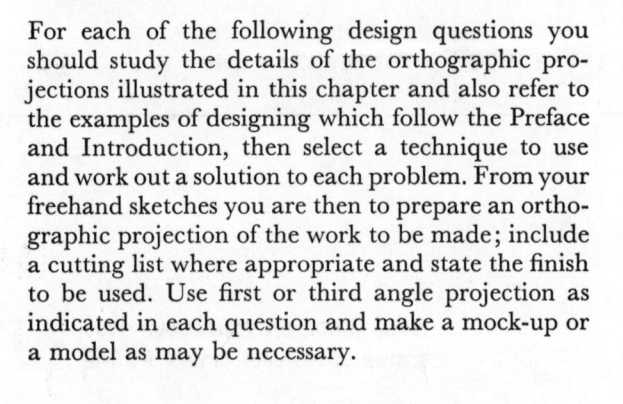

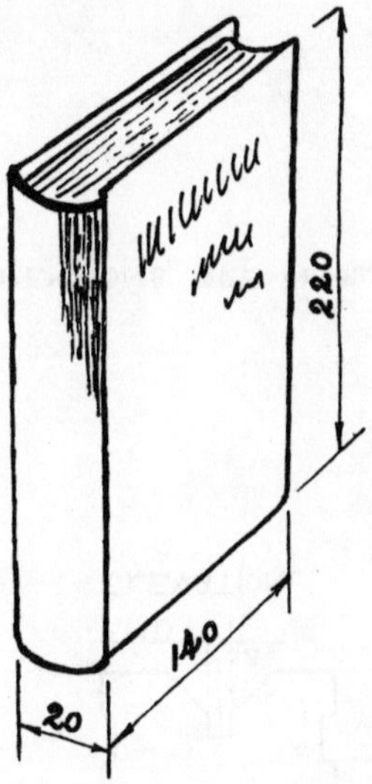
220
140
20

6 Your mother requires an expanding clothes prop for which you obtain two pieces of hardwood, each 1·524 m long x 40 mm x 22 mm. Design the metal fittings necessary to join these pieces of wood together so that you can close the prop down to 1·524 m in length or expand it to 2·590 m. How will you hold the two at this length? How could you make the prop adjustable to give a variety of lengths? Be sure to give all dimensions, indicate material to be used and finish to be employed.

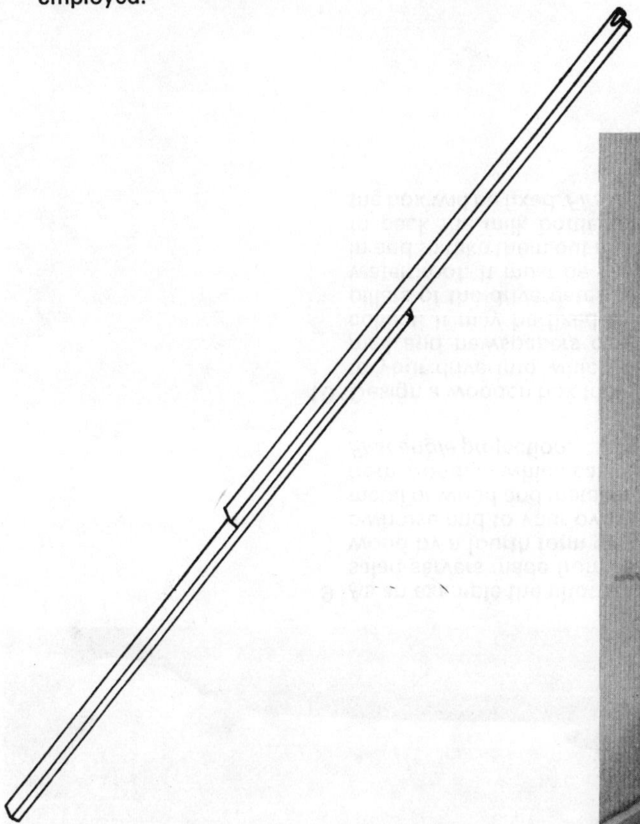

7 The screw-on cap through which the piston rod of the footpump passes has cracked off at the bearing. Design a suitable piece to be turned on the lathe which can be fitted to the cap to make a permanent repair.

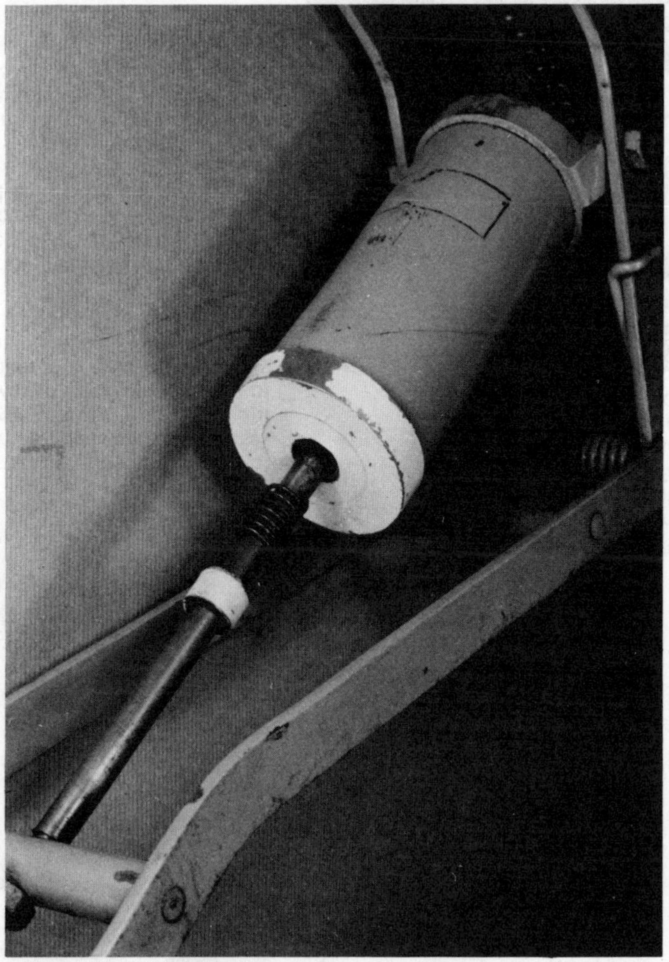

8 The sketches show the shape of scratch-stock blade and the shape of the bead produced by it. The cutter has been home-made from an old hacksaw blade. Many different shapes and variations are possible because the cutters can be quickly made to meet individual requirements. You are to design a wooden holder into which the cutter can be clamped so that it can be drawn along the wood scratching out the shape. *Third angle* projection.

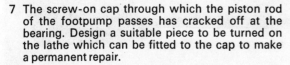

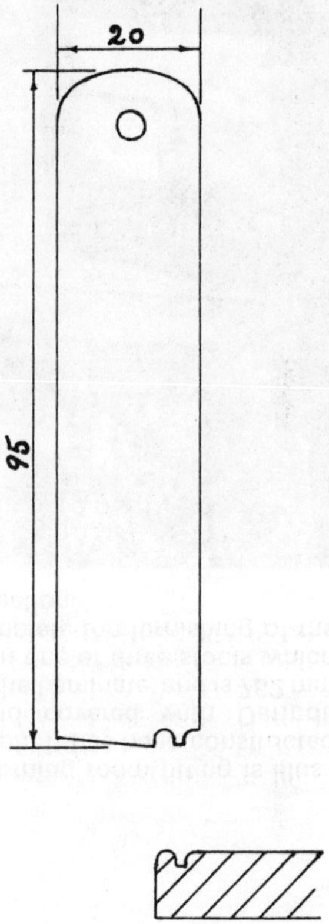
20
95

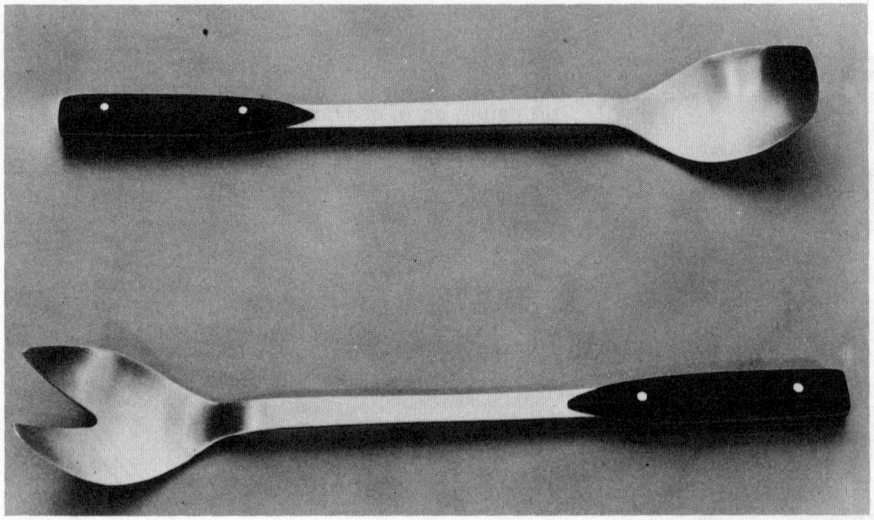

9 As an example the photograph illustrates a pair of salad servers made from stainless steel and rosewood by a fourth form girl. Design a pair for your own use and to your own shape. They may be of metal or wood and metal or may be carved entirely from wood, in which case teak would be suitable. *First angle* projection.

10 Design a wooden box to be placed at the entrance to your drive into which daily deliveries of milk, mail and newspapers can be placed for you to collect. It may be fixed to a post or to the brick pillars of the drive gates and must be thoroughly waterproof. It must be easy to put the deliveries in and to take them out and birds must not be able to peck the milk bottle tops. Show clearly how the box will be fixed. *First angle* projection.

11 The table unit of a morning room fitting is illustrated in the photograph. It has been constructed of Japanese Elm and covered with Daffodil Furniture Finish, Arborite Laminate, and is 762 mm high. You are to design one of three stools which are to be made to complete the furnishing of the room. *Third angle* projection.

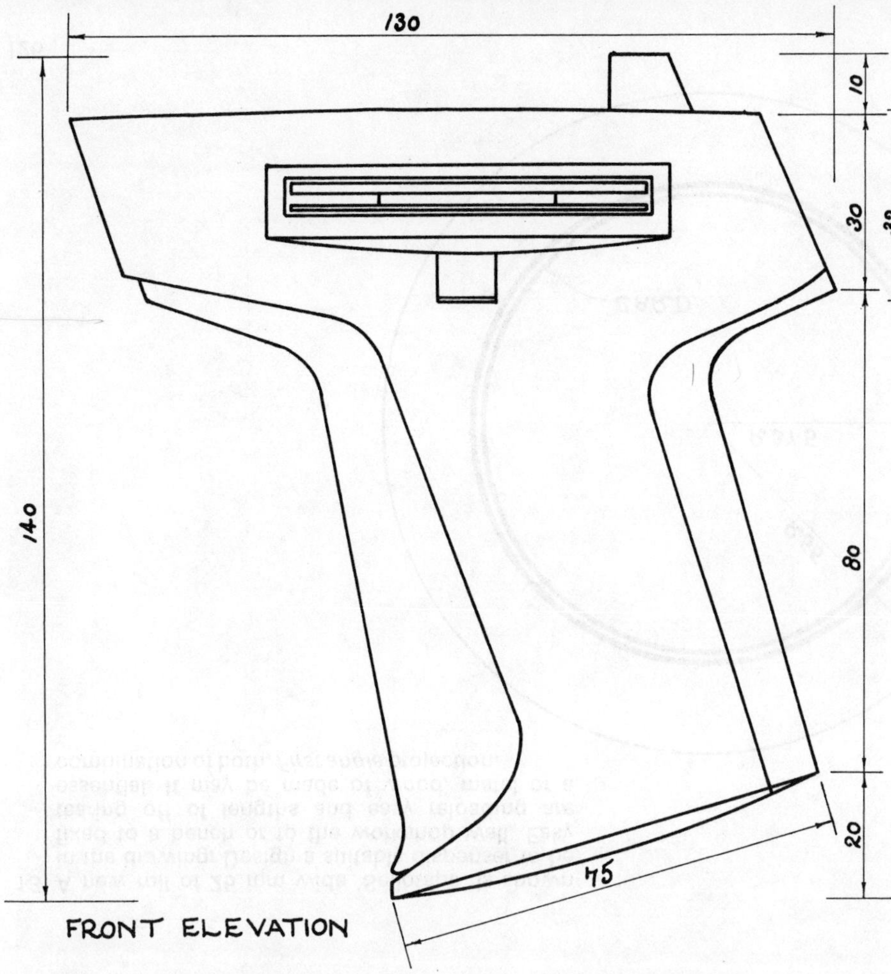
130
10
30
140
80
20
45

FRONT ELEVATION

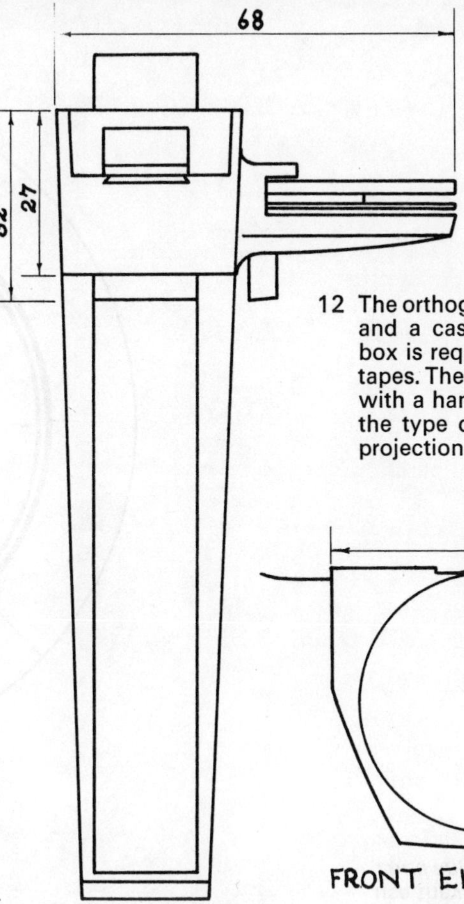
68
32
27

END ELEVATION

12 The orthographic projection shows a Dymo printer and a cassette. A soundly constructed wooden box is required to hold the printer and two spare tapes. The box should close firmly and be provided with a handle for carrying. Prepare the design for the type of box you would suggest. *First angle* projection.

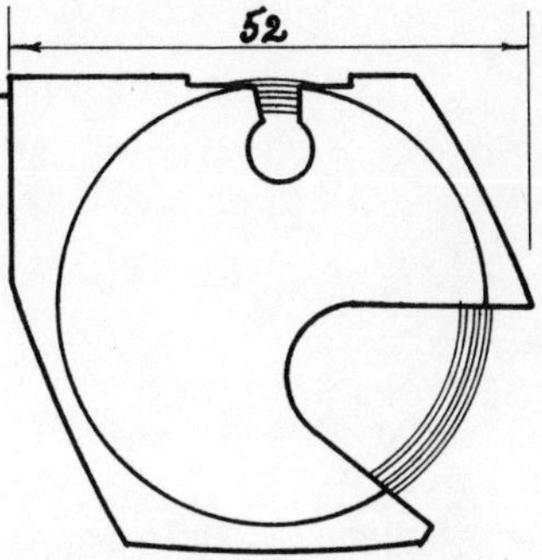
52

FRONT ELEVATION

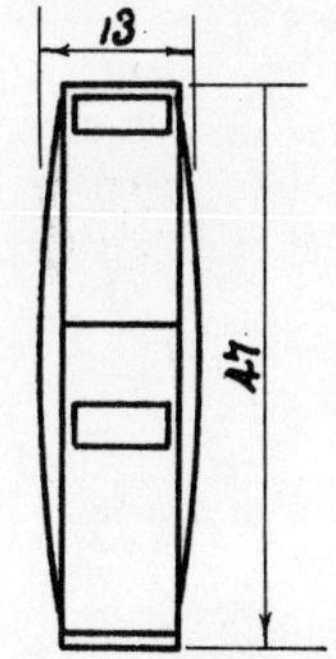
13
47

END ELEVATION

CASSETTE FOR DYMO TAPES.

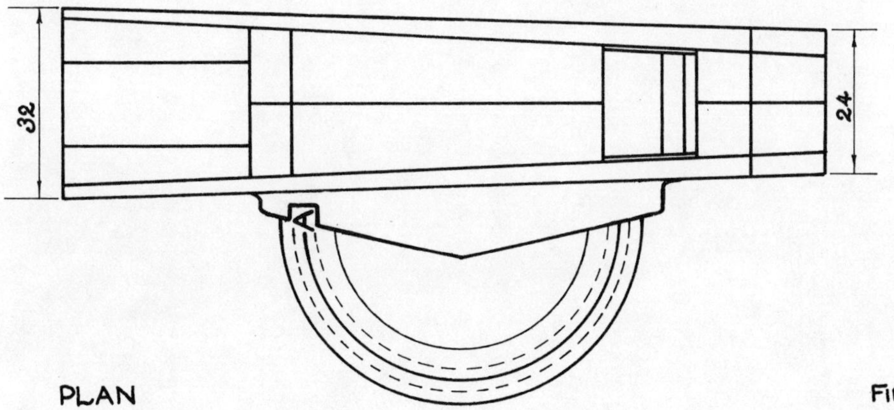
32
24
A

PLAN

DYMO - MODEL 1710.

FIRST ANGLE PROJECTION.

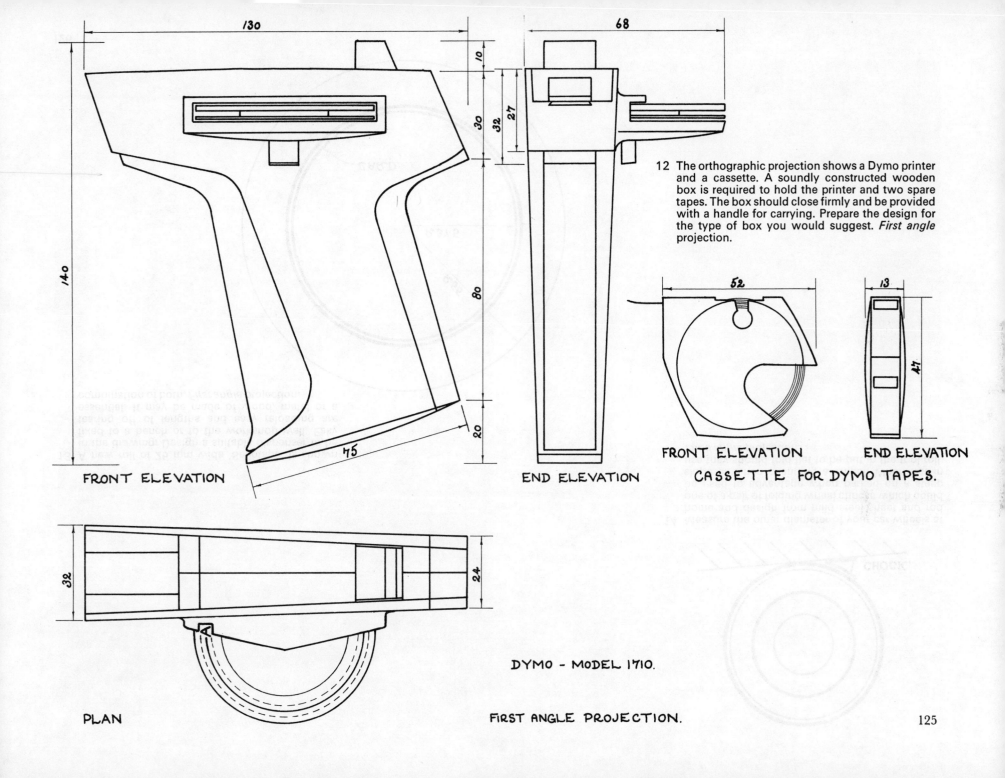

13 A new roll of 25 mm wide 'Sellotape' is shown in the drawing. Design a suitable dispenser to be fixed to a bench or to the workshop wall. Easy tearing off of lengths and easy reloading are essential. It may be made of wood, metal or a combination of both. *First angle* projection.

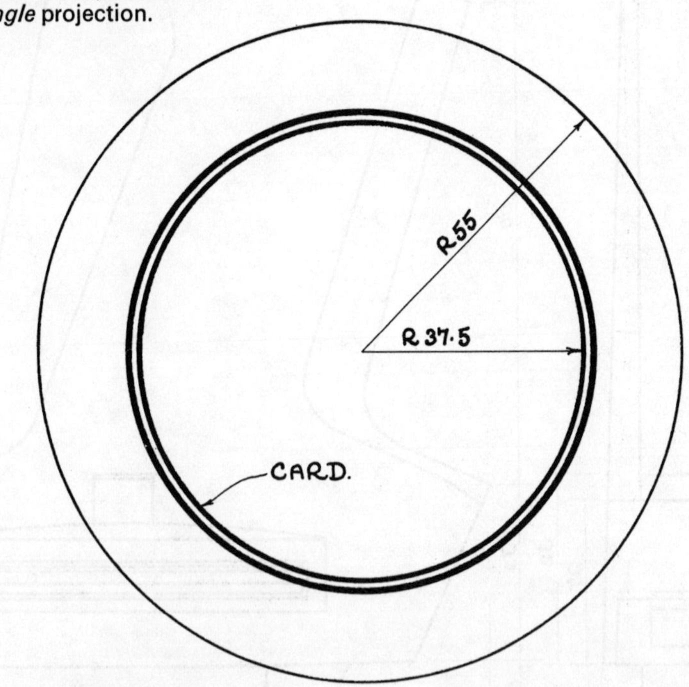
R 55
R 37.5
CARD.

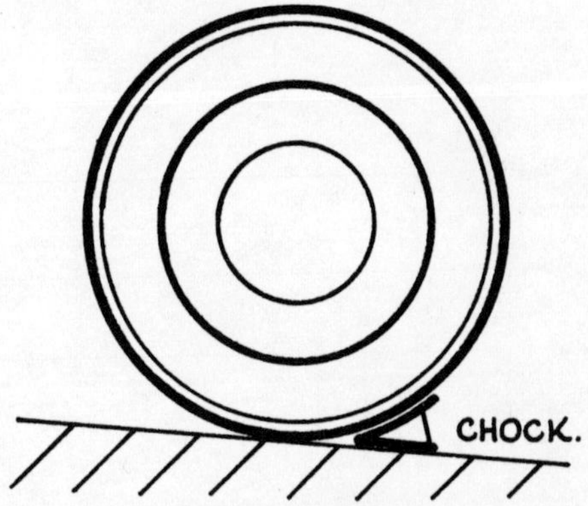
CHOCK.

14 Measure the outer diameter of your car wheels at home and design from mild steel sheet and rod one of a pair of folding wheel chocks which could be used to advantage when parked on a steep slope or when changing a wheel. When not in use they should fold flat to be put in the tool roll. *Third angle* projection.

15 The corner of a fitted wardrobe with top cupboards is shown in the photograph. It is of matt finished beechfaced plywood. You are to design a matching L-shaped ladies' vanity fitment for the corner of the bedroom shown in the sketch. Pay particular attention to the sitting position, arrangement of drawers for storing cosmetics, etc., and the fitting of a mirror and the lighting you would provide. *First angle* projection.

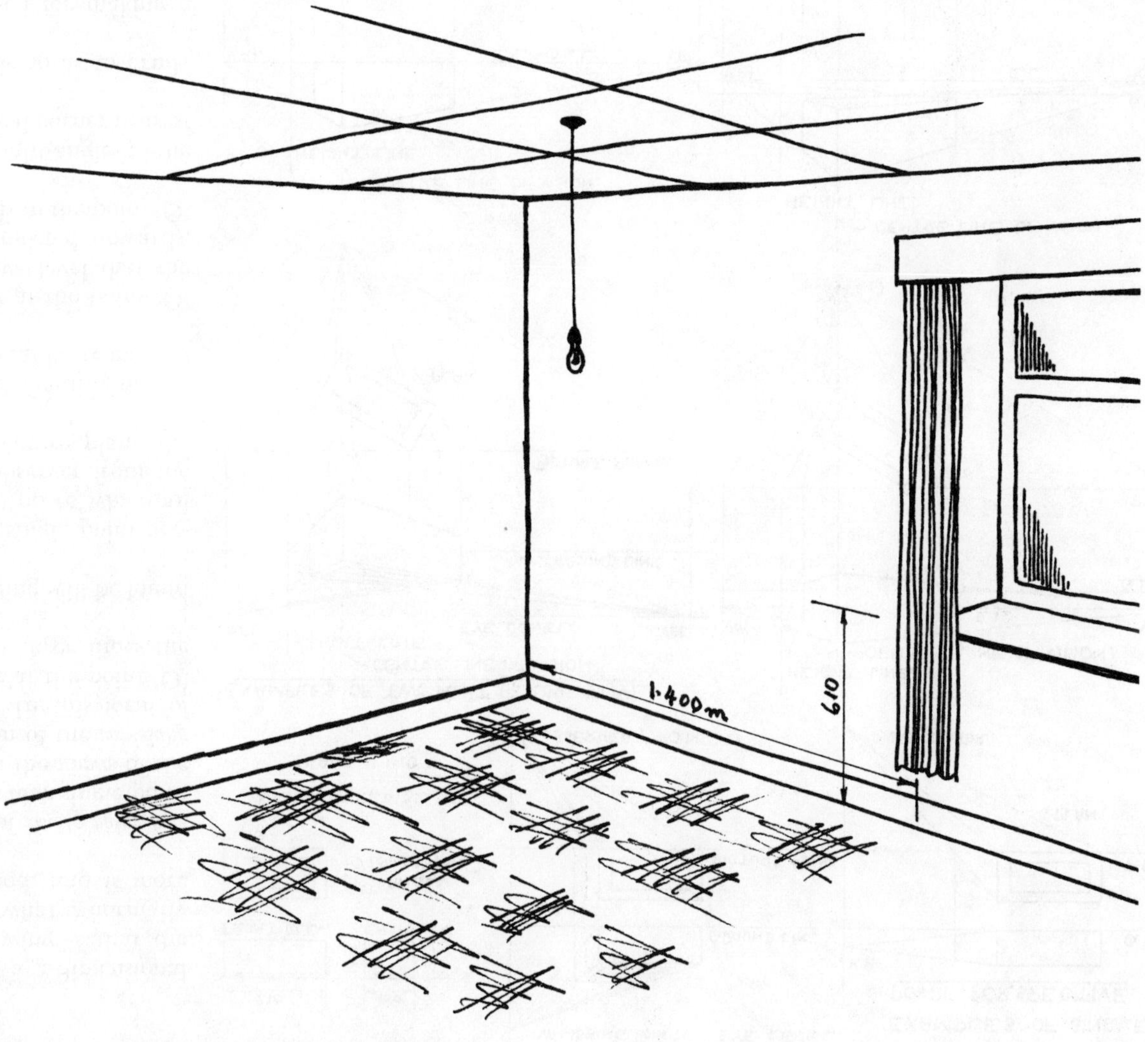
1·400m
610

Perspective Drawing

Perspective drawing is a third method of producing a 3-dimensional view of an object. The importance of perspective drawing is that the resulting view conveys an impression closely resembling what is normally seen by the eye and is therefore more easily understood, and is more acceptable than a 2-dimensional drawing.

Illustrated on the accompanying pages are examples of *single point perspective* and *two point perspective*. For simple work in particular single point perspective gives satisfactory results as can be seen from the views of the builder's brick although, as you see, varying the position of the *vanishing point* can result in a view showing only two surfaces. In this form of perspective drawing the eye of the observer or spectator at the point 'O' is vertically in line with the vanishing point and about three times the height of the object away from the front edge of the plan.

A brief explanation of the terms used in perspective drawing will be found useful at this stage.

Picture Plane – a vertical plane standing in front of (for single point perspective) or behind the plan (for two point perspective) on to which all details of the object are projected by the eye of the observer from the point 'O'. Once these points are established on the picture plane the final perspective view is projected from them.

Ground line – a horizontal line which can be positioned depending on the wishes of the draughtsman and above which the various heights are marked on the *height line*.

Eye level – the assumed height of the eye of the observer at the point 'O' and is measured from the ground line. It is on the eye level that the vanishing point or points are marked having been projected upwards, from the picture plane and are obtained by lines drawn from the point 'O' parallel to the end and side of the plan.

Centre Line of Vision – a line drawn from the observer at right angles to the picture plane and projected forward to become the vertical corner nearest to the observer on the completed perspective drawing.

A careful study of the examples shown should be made so as to firmly relate these definitions to actual drawing situations.

Two Point Perspective – the method most frequently used for making a perspective drawing and when completed with care and accuracy is most acceptable to the eye. You should note from the four simple examples of two point perspective how differing aspects of the object can be emphasised by changing the position of the eye level.

Within the limits of the paper the further the vanishing points are apart, and this depends on how far the observer can be in front of the plan, the perspective angles are less obtrusive and the final view becomes even more acceptable. This is even more obvious in free-perspective drawing where the vanishing points can be set up a considerable distance away.

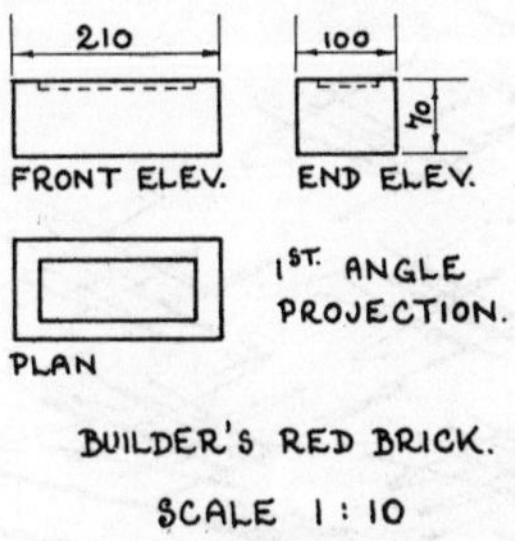
210
100
FRONT ELEV.
END ELEV.
70
PLAN
1ST. ANGLE
PROJECTION.
BUILDER'S RED BRICK.
SCALE 1 : 10

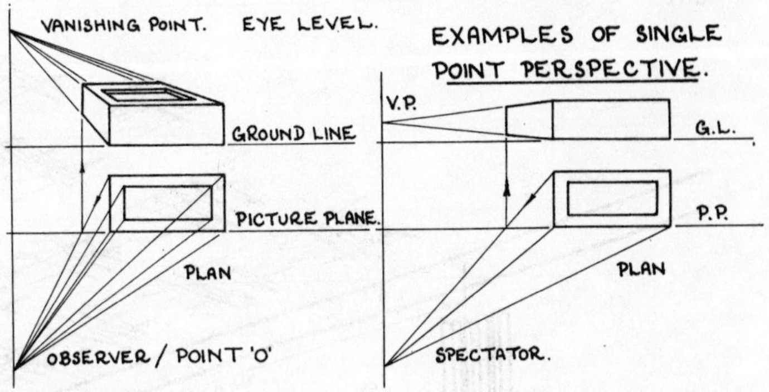
VANISHING POINT.
EYE LEVEL.
EXAMPLES OF SINGLE POINT PERSPECTIVE.
GROUND LINE
PICTURE PLANE.
PLAN
OBSERVER / POINT 'O'
V.P.
G.L.
P.P.
PLAN
SPECTATOR.

EXAMPLES OF TWO POINT PERSPECTIVE.

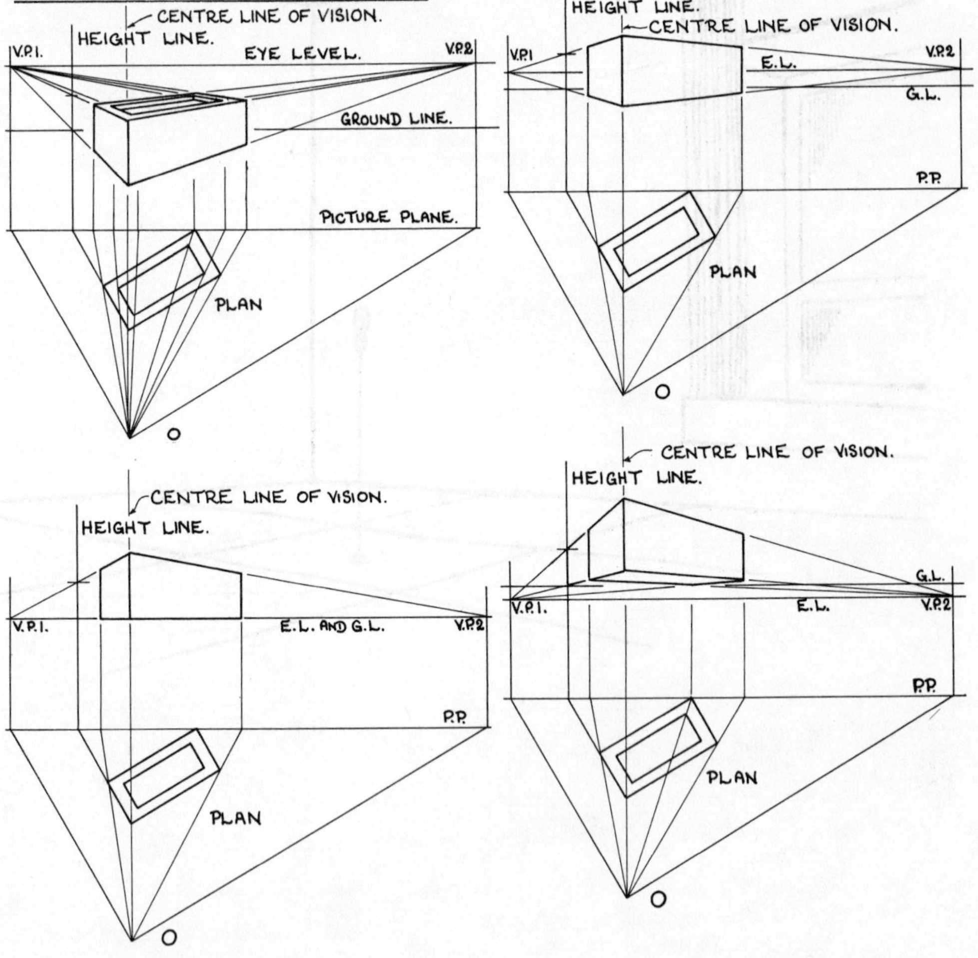
CENTRE LINE OF VISION.
HEIGHT LINE.
V.P.1.
EYE LEVEL.
V.P.2
GROUND LINE.
PICTURE PLANE.
PLAN
O
HEIGHT LINE.
CENTRE LINE OF VISION.
V.P.1
E.L.
V.P.2
G.L.
P.P.
PLAN
O
CENTRE LINE OF VISION.
HEIGHT LINE.
V.P.1.
E.L. AND G.L.
V.P.2
P.P.
PLAN
O
CENTRE LINE OF VISION.
HEIGHT LINE.
G.L.
V.P.1.
E.L.
V.P.2
P.P.
PLAN
O

EXAMPLES OF PERSPECTIVE DRAWING.

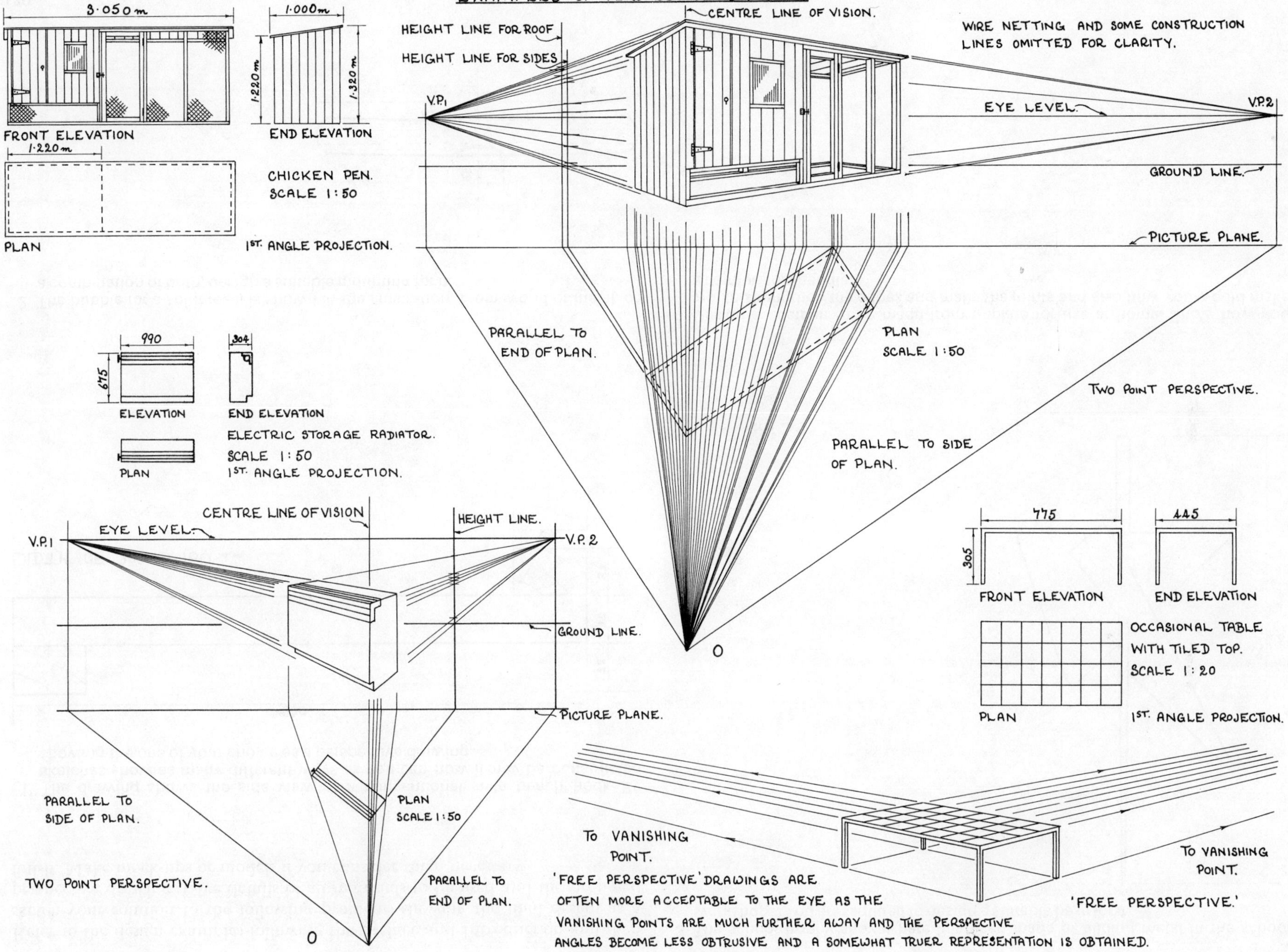
3.050 m
1.000 m
1.220 m
1.320 m
FRONT ELEVATION
END ELEVATION
1.220 m
PLAN
CHICKEN PEN.
SCALE 1:50
1ST. ANGLE PROJECTION.
CENTRE LINE OF VISION.
HEIGHT LINE FOR ROOF
HEIGHT LINE FOR SIDES
WIRE NETTING AND SOME CONSTRUCTION LINES OMITTED FOR CLARITY.
V.P.1
V.P.2
EYE LEVEL.
GROUND LINE.
PICTURE PLANE.
PARALLEL TO END OF PLAN.
PLAN
SCALE 1:50
TWO POINT PERSPECTIVE.
PARALLEL TO SIDE OF PLAN.
O
990
304
675
ELEVATION
END ELEVATION
ELECTRIC STORAGE RADIATOR.
SCALE 1:50
PLAN
1ST. ANGLE PROJECTION.
CENTRE LINE OF VISION
HEIGHT LINE.
V.P.1
EYE LEVEL.
V.P.2
GROUND LINE.
PICTURE PLANE.
PARALLEL TO SIDE OF PLAN.
PLAN
SCALE 1:50
TWO POINT PERSPECTIVE.
PARALLEL TO END OF PLAN.
O
775
445
305
FRONT ELEVATION
END ELEVATION
OCCASIONAL TABLE
WITH TILED TOP.
SCALE 1:20
PLAN
1ST. ANGLE PROJECTION.
TO VANISHING POINT.
TO VANISHING POINT.
'FREE PERSPECTIVE' DRAWINGS ARE OFTEN MORE ACCEPTABLE TO THE EYE AS THE VANISHING POINTS ARE MUCH FURTHER AWAY AND THE PERSPECTIVE ANGLES BECOME LESS OBTRUSIVE AND A SOMEWHAT TRUER REPRESENTATION IS OBTAINED.
'FREE PERSPECTIVE.'

Perspective drawing problems

Refer to the design examples following the Preface and Introduction and then sketch your solution to the following problems showing the final design as a perspective drawing. Give details of all materials to be used and the proposed finish. Make mock-ups or models if you consider them necessary.

1 The drawing shows the side view of a conventional style bench hook. By sketches show as many different ways as you can how it may be constructed showing the one of your choice as a perspective drawing.

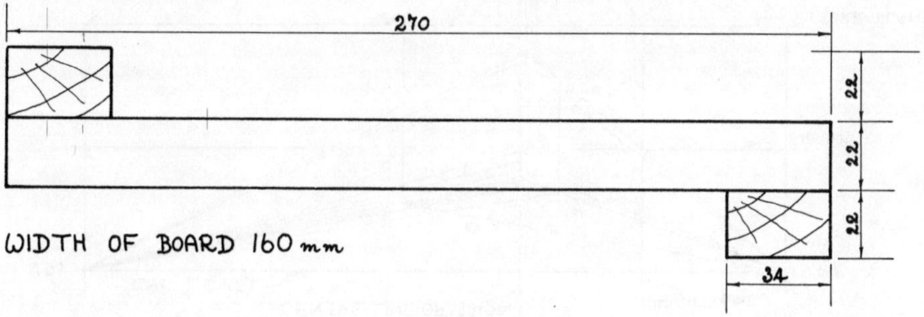

270
22
22
22
34
WIDTH OF BOARD 160 mm

2 The bubble for a spirit level is shown in the illustration. From wood or metal, or a combination of both, design a suitable mounting for it.

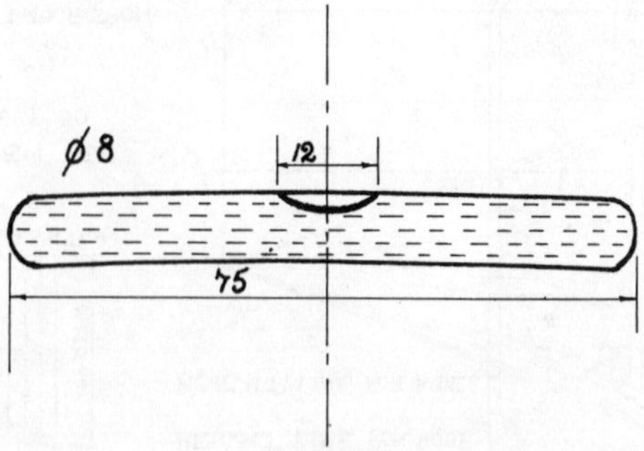

ø8
12
75

3 The school trophy shown here has been made of gilding metal in the school workshops. You are required to design a suitable base for it.

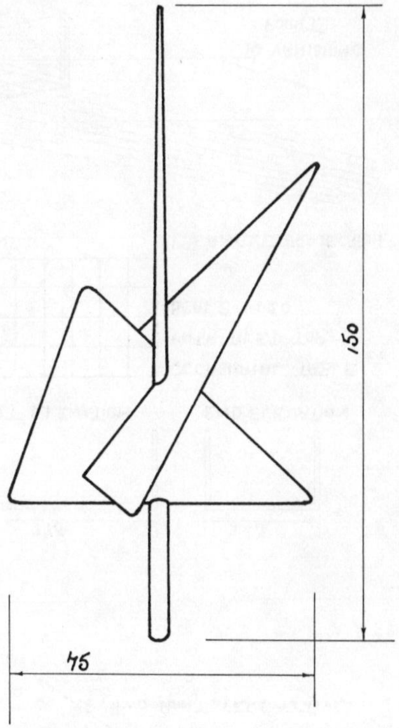

150
45

4 Design a dustpan to be made from tinplate for use at home. Show how you would strengthen the edges and make the joints and also how you would make a comfortable handle.

5 The binder which holds six copies of the *National Geographical Magazine* measures 275 mm high x 195 mm wide x 66 mm thick. Design an open fronted unit to hold forty of these which have been collected. The unit should stand on the floor against a wall and be so designed that similar units can be stood on it as further copies of the magazine are collected.

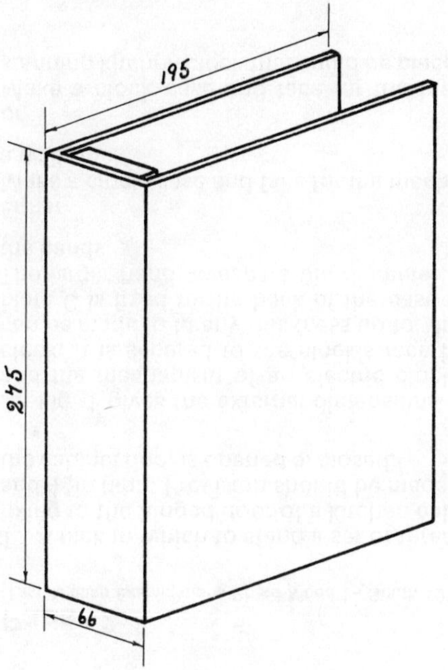

195
275
66

6 You are to design a record cabinet on which to stand a record player and which will hold at least one hundred records in four compartments each holding twenty-five. It should be of modern construction using manufactured boards.

7 Make an enquiry at home or at school into the type and quantity of crockery etc. which is in frequent use in a breakfast room. Using this information, design a wall cupboard which will contain the necessary items. For convenience in use it is suggested that sliding doors are employed.

8 Design an occasional table to match the trolley (pages 76 and 77). Pay particular attention to the styling of the top, its surface and how it is to be fixed.

9 It is suggested that you design a desk. It may be for a child or an adult; it could be for yourself for your own use at home, if so it may have to fit into an existing scheme of furnishing. Think carefully of the work to be done at the desk and what it has to hold. You should also study the ergonometry involved so that the correct proportions are applied to enable you to sit and work comfortably at the desk.

10 You are to prepare the design of a garage-cum-workshop in which there will be room to house your cycle, or motor cycle and the family car. There should be provision for a bench at which to do any maintenance you wish to carry out, with adequate storage for tools and materials. You may also want to include an area for use as a home workshop for woodwork. Pay careful attention to the provision of heating, lighting and ventilation. The garage may be constructed of any conventional fireproof building materials.

Design Questions from Examination Papers

The following design questions have been taken from papers set by some of the various CSE and GCE examination boards. They are included here to give further practice in solving design problems using the methods illustrated in the previous chapters.

Paper 1

(East Anglian Examinations Board Mode 1—South 1971, Metalwork CSE)

1. Design a portable holder for the electrician's soldering iron shown below. The holder must have provision for holding a reel of solder, also shown, so that it can be used from holder. The holder must ensure that the hot bit will not be able to touch the holder, lead of iron or reel of solder.

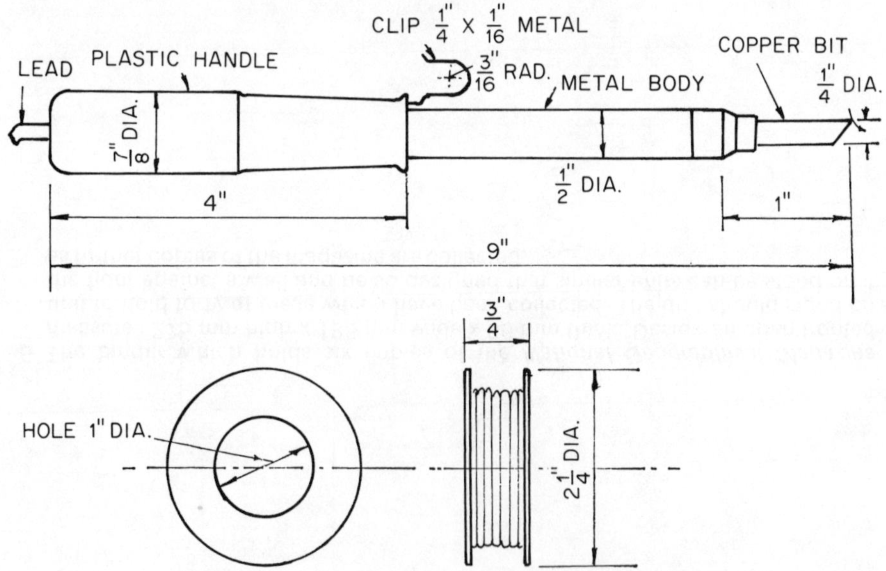

CLIP 1/4" X 1/16" METAL
COPPER BIT
LEAD
PLASTIC HANDLE
3/16" RAD.
METAL BODY
1/4" DIA.
7/8" DIA.
1/2" DIA.
4"
1"
9"
3/4"
HOLE 1" DIA.
2 1/4" DIA.

2. Design a small box with lid suitable to hold collar studs and cuff links, preferably made in a non-ferrous metal. The box may be any shape or size as long as it will fit into a cardboard presentation box 3in x 3in x 2in high. Include in your design some simple form of decoration on the lid.

3. Design a clamp that will hold sheet metal down to a drilling machine table (shown in section below) so that the metal can be drilled safely. The clamp must be able to be fixed to the table temporarily (no holes are to be drilled in the table) and then be operated with one hand.

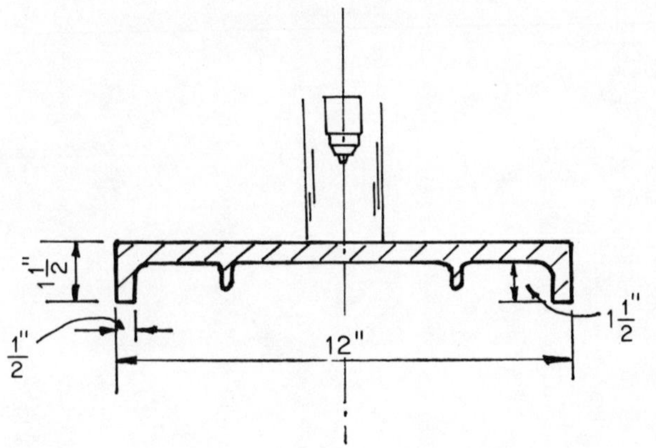

1 1/2"
1/2"
12"
1 1/2"

Paper 2

(East Anglian Examinations Board Mode 1—South 1971, Woodwork CSE)

1. A rack in which to stand a set of three identical spice jars. It must be suitable for fixing to the hinged door of a kitchen cabinet. The cylindrical jars are 2¼in diameter and 4½in high. Provision should be made to ensure that the jars do not fall out when the cabinet door is opened or closed.

2. Fig. 1 gives the external dimensions of the outer case that encloses the battery and the mechanism of an electric clock movement that is suitable for a kitchen clock. It is secured to the clock's face by a knurled nut A and a locknut B. They can be made to fit any thickness up to ½in by adjusting the locknut. A brass hanging plate C is fixed to the back of the case but it can be removed if it is not required. The larger hand sweeps a 6in diameter circle. You are not required to make or fit the hands.

Either
Make a clock-case and face for the mechanism so that it can be used in a kitchen as a wall clock.

or
Make a clock-case and face for the mechanism so that it can be used as a free standing kitchen clock that could be placed on a working surface.

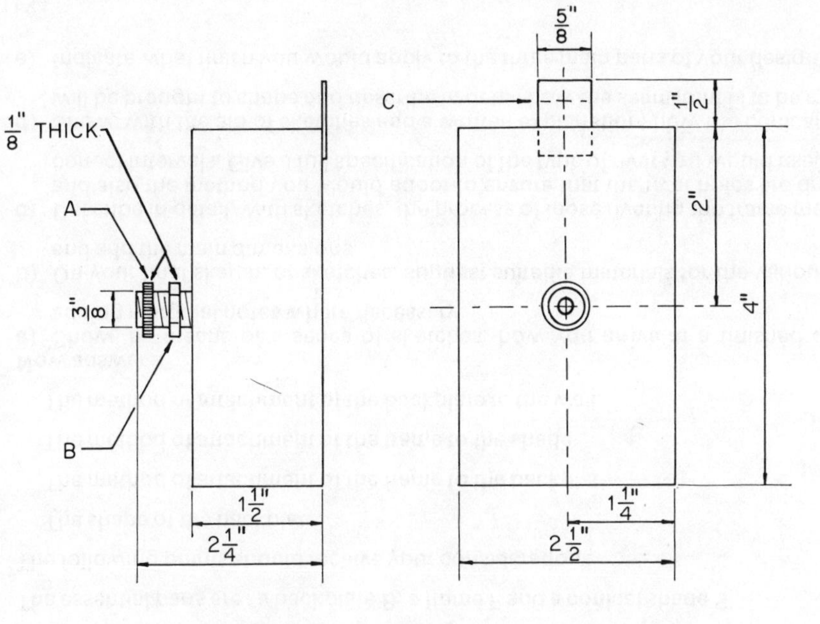
5"/8
C
1/2"
1/8" THICK
A
3/8"
2"
4"
B
1 1/2"
1 1/4"
2 1/4"
2 1/2"
ALL DIMENSIONS IN INCHES
NOT TO SCALE

Fig. 1

3. A mahogany needlework box has a hinged lid that is 1in deep. The internal dimensions of the lower part of the box are 16in by 10in by 8in deep. Two $\frac{1}{2}$in square runners have been made so that they can be screwed inside the box along the 16in sides to support a loose tray which can either be removed from the box or slid from side to side to give access to the bottom of the box.

4. You are required to make a jointed tray with the bottom let into a groove or a rebate that will fit inside the box and rest on the runners. It should be made to house:

1 pair 6in ladies' scissors.
1 needle wallet 3in by 2in by $\frac{1}{2}$in.
1 pin cushion 3in by 2in by $\frac{3}{4}$in.
6 cotton reels 1 $\frac{3}{8}$in diameter by 1 $\frac{3}{8}$in high.
1 coiled 60in draper's tape measure.

Paper 3

(South-East Regional Examination Board 1968, Metalwork CSE)

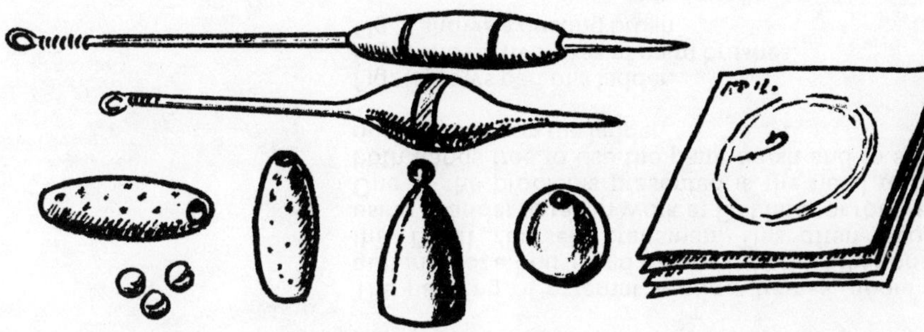

1. A small box is required by a fisherman to hold certain pieces of fishing tackle:

Four floats, maximum size 5in long by $\frac{1}{2}$in diameter.
Spare hooks and lines in packets, 2in by 2in.
Ledgers or small lead weights, 1in long by $\frac{1}{2}$in diameter and about six in number.
Odd corks, 1in long by $\frac{3}{8}$in diameter and about six in all.
A small quantity of split lead shot.

The box is to be made in sheet metal and requires a lid and the whole design should be capable of being made in the school workshop.

a) Make a sketch, or sketches, of such a container giving the main dimensions and details of all the joints employed.

b) State the material, or materials, from which your box is to be made and then make a list of all the parts required, giving their sizes.

c) Sketch the shape of the development of the body of your box, indicating the fold lines.

d) With the aid of notes and sketches, describe the stages, in making the box from a flat sheet.

e) Describe, using notes and sketches, how you would produce one of the corner joints of the box, naming the tools and materials required.

f) Make an enlarged sketch showing clearly the method you would employ to fasten the lid to the box.

2. A small tea-towel airer with two or three horizontal swinging arms, pivoted at one end to a backplate, is required for a kitchen. The arms are to be about 10in in length and made from $\frac{3}{16}$in diameter mild steel and finally covered with thin-walled plastic tubing, which is readily available.

In being asked to design the completed towel airer you should, firstly, consider:

The method you would employ to fasten the rods to the backplate so they can freely swing through 180°.

The shape of the backplate and its method of fastening to the wall.

Suitable materials from which the completed design could be made, assuming a well-equipped school workshop is available complete with a foundry bay.

Now answer:

a) Make sketches of your completed design, clearly showing the pivoting mechanism and giving the main dimensions. Number or name the separate parts.

b) Where metal is joined, label the appropriate places on your sketch with the name, or type, of joint employed. Where metal is shaped, label with the process used.

c) Make a list, in table form, of all the parts of your design, including the swinging arms, under the following headings:

PART NUMBER, OR NAME	NUMBER REQUIRED	SIZES	MATERIAL	FINISH

d) Explain in detail, using sketches as well if you wish, how you would make one of the joints connected with the pivoting mechanism. Name all the tools and materials used.

e) Say how you would clean up the completed job and what finish you would apply to the parts, other than the arms.

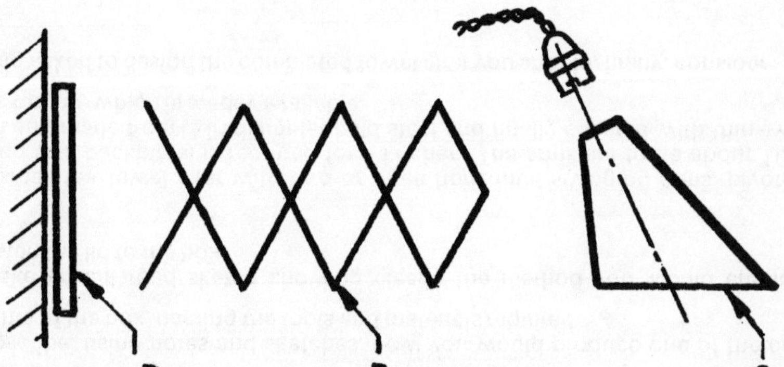
B
F
S

4. You have been asked to make in the school workshops an extending lamp, on the lines suggested by the sketch above.

The essential parts are: a backplate B, a frame F and a conical shade S.

The following points should receive your consideration:

The shape of the backplate.

The method of attachment of the frame to the backplate.

The method of attachment of the frame to the shade.

The method of attachment of the backplate to the wall.

Now answer:

a) Show, by means of a series of sketches, how you arrive at a finished design, adding marginal notes where necessary.

b) On your final sketch, or sketches, suggest suitable materials for the various parts and add the main dimensions.

c) Describe in detail, with sketches, the process of loose riveting the frame members and also the method you would adopt to ensure that the rivet holes are drilled at correct intervals. Give a full specification of the type of rivet you would use.

d) Show, with the aid of sketches and a written explanation, how the conical shade will be brought to shape and describe in detail how the seam joint is to be made.

e) Indicate what finish you would apply to the three main parts of your design.

Sketches in this section, although not necessarily to scale, should be large, in good proportion and can be either freehand pictorial or freehand orthographic but if orthographic projection is used then two views must be given.
Preliminary sketches must not be erased as marks will be awarded for the logical development of an idea.
Your completed design should be capable of being made at school using the normal tools and equipment of a well equipped workshop.

Paper 4

(Associated Examining Board 1972, Craftwork—Metal 'O' Level)

The painting of external window frames, doors and guttering of a house and garage is frequently done by the 'Do It Yourself' craftsman. This often involves using a ladder to reach work at first floor or roof level. One of the problems presented is the need to have both hands free to use the paint brush and to steady oneself safely on the ladder.

Fig. 1 shows part of a ladder.
Fig. 2 shows two sizes of paint brushes.
Fig. 3 shows a dusting brush.

Design a ladder tray or platform to accommodate a paint tin of 115 mm maximum diameter, 135 mm high and weighing 2 kg, together with one brush of each size illustrated in Figs. 2 and 3.

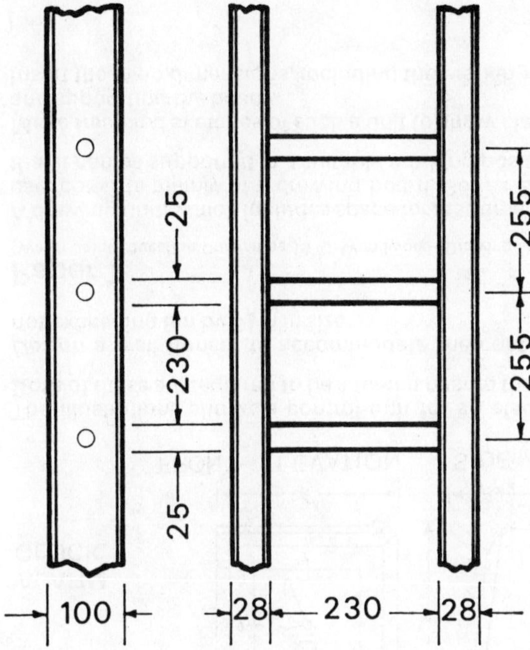
25
230
25
255
255
100
28
230
28

Fig. 1

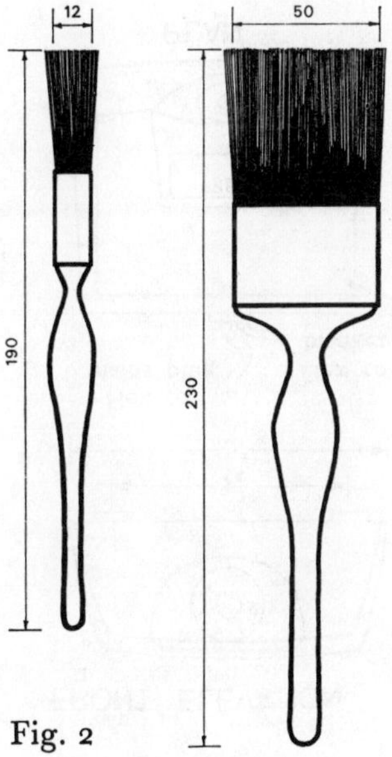
12
50
190
230

Fig. 2

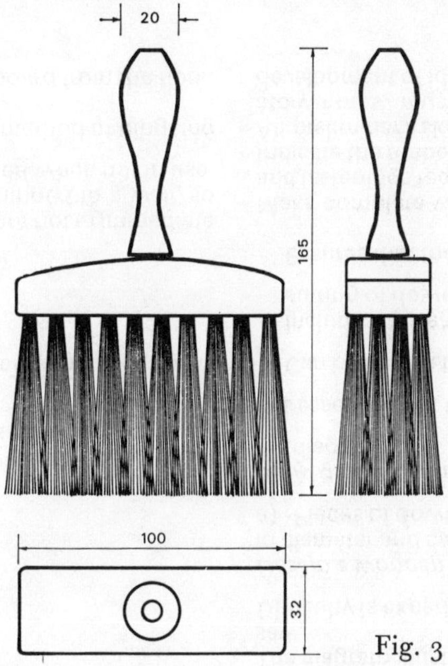
20
165
100
32

Fig. 3

It is essential that the ladder tray/platform:

(a) Fits firmly to *any* rung of the ladder and can be quickly attached and adjusted to a level position.

(b) When in the working position, does not impede the painter.

(c) Ensures that the paint tin and brushes cannot fall.

(d) When not in use, is easily stored away taking up as little space as possible.

Make complete working drawings and a list of materials required. Indicate the 'finish' of your choice. All preliminary sketches leading up to your final design, together with any explanatory notes, must be attached to your drawing. Marks will be awarded for the development of ideas in sketch form.
Candidates are expected to show by their solutions to this problem an appreciation of the materials, processes and constructions of the craft.

Paper 5

(Oxford and Cambridge Schools Examination Board 1970; Drawing, Design and Theory—Metalwork 'O' Level)

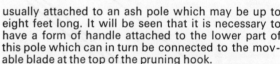

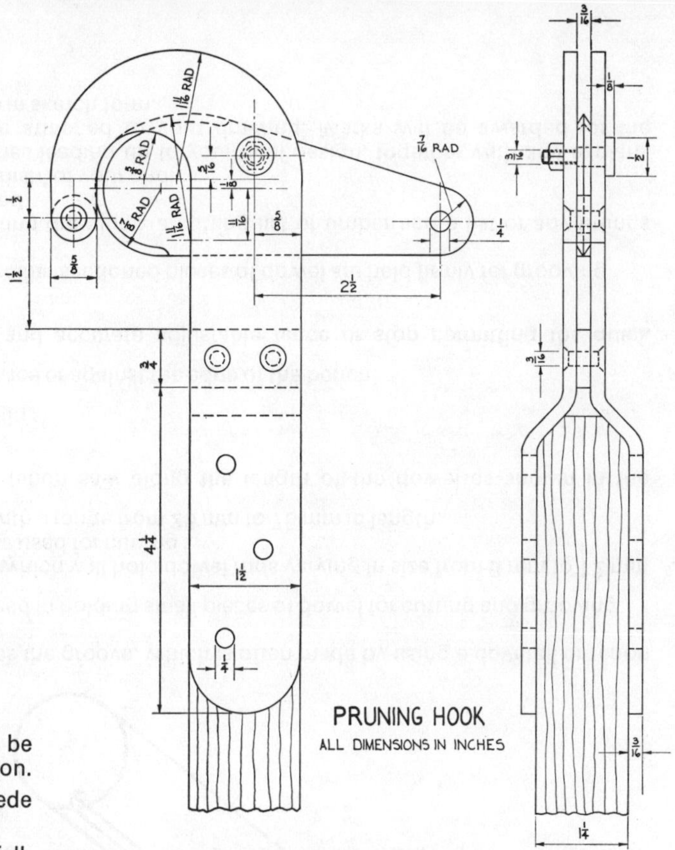
PRUNING HOOK
ALL DIMENSIONS IN INCHES
RAD
2½
4¼
1½

1. The drawing shows incomplete views of a pruning hook used for cutting small branches from trees when pruning. The part of the hook used in the drawing is usually attached to an ash pole which may be up to eight feet long. It will be seen that it is necessary to have a form of handle attached to the lower part of this pole which can in turn be connected to the movable blade at the top of the pruning hook.

On the squared paper provided you are required to design a handle and linkage which would be suitable for operating the pruning hook. The freehand drawings which you make for this handle should be clearly annotated where necessary and sizes indicated.

Then fix your 15in x 11in drawing paper with the *short* edge at the top of your drawing board. Do *not* draw a border round your paper.

Use your discretion to supply dimensions or other details not given on the drawing. Make clear pencil lines and do *not* erase any construction lines.

In the bottom right-hand corner of your paper you are required to draw a plain scale, $\frac{3}{4}$in to 1in, to measure up to 8in, dividing the first section to read $\frac{1}{16}$in.

Paper 6

(Associated Examining Board 1970, Craftwork—Wood 'O' Level)

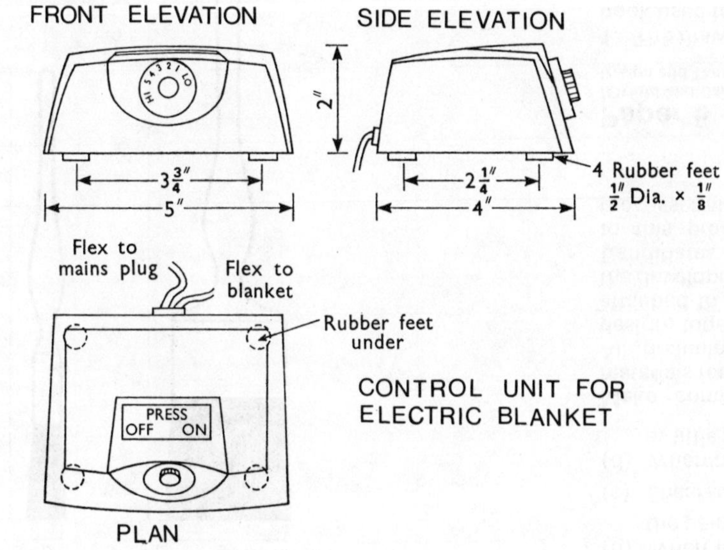
FRONT ELEVATION
SIDE ELEVATION
2″
3¾″
5″
2¼″
4″
4 Rubber feet
½″ Dia. × ⅛″
Flex to mains plug
Flex to blanket
Rubber feet under
PRESS
OFF ON
PLAN

CONTROL UNIT FOR ELECTRIC BLANKET

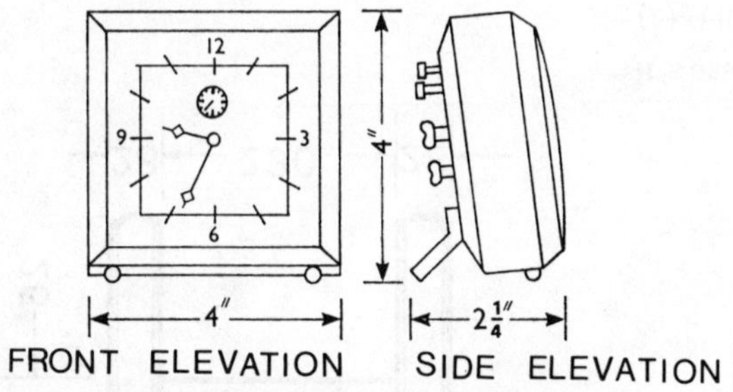
12
9
3
6
4″
4″
2¼″
FRONT ELEVATION
SIDE ELEVATION

ALARM CLOCK

The illustrations show: a control unit for an electric blanket; and an alarm clock. Both of these are required to be situated near to the head of a bed.

Design a wall fitment to accommodate the control unit, the clock and two books not exceeding 8in by $5\frac{1}{2}$in in size.

Paper 7

(Welsh Joint Education Committee 1970, Woodwork—Drawing and Theory 'O' Level)

A drawing unit, which includes space for instruments etc. which are not in immediate use, consists mainly of a drawing board, 36in x 24in, which is hinged to a wall, so that it can be supported in a suitable working position, and lowered when not in use.

Make freehand sketches of such a unit to show clearly a suitable method of hingeing and supporting the board.
Insert the main dimensions, including the working height of the board from the floor.

Paper 8

(Associated Examining Board 1972, Craftwork—Wood 'O' Level)

One method of jointing pieces of wood together is by the use of dowels. In frame construction such as stools, this entails the cutting of several pieces of dowel of the same diameter and *short* length. When using dowel for joints it is necessary to cut them accurately to length and to groove the small pieces of wood so that the surplus glue is not trapped in the joint.

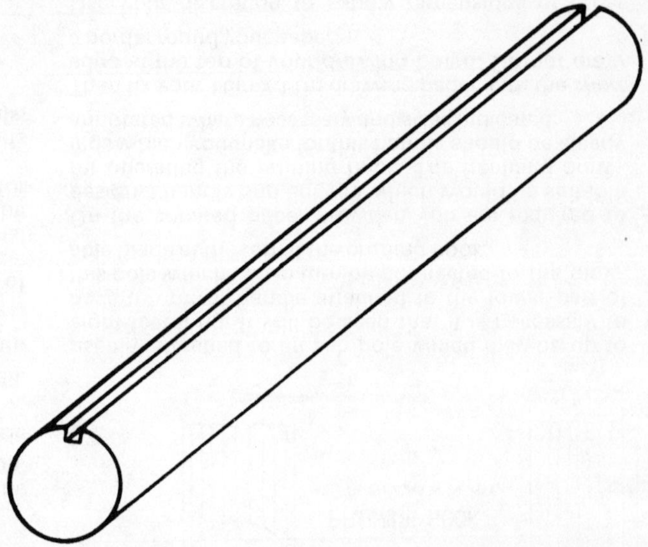

The diagram illustrates the groove, which is often made by using a dovetail or tenon saw.
Difficulty is experienced in holding small pieces of dowel for cutting and grooving.

Design a wooden jig which will hold dowel rods varying in size from 6 mm to 12 mm in diameter and can be used for cutting:

a) Pieces of dowel with a range from 25 mm to 75 mm in length.

b) A groove with a tenon saw along the length of the dowel as shown in the diagram.

It is essential that the jig:

Can be held in the vice or against the edge of the bench.

Includes an easy and accurate adjustable fence or stop permitting the quick cutting of dowels.

Ensures that the circular sectioned pieces of dowel are held firmly for grooving.

Make complete working drawings, a cutting list of timber and a list of any fittings and fastenings required.
Indicate the timber 'finish' of your choice.
All preliminary sketches leading up to your final design, together with any explanatory notes, must be attached to your drawing. Marks will be awarded for the development of ideas in sketch form.

Paper 9

(Associated Examining Board 1969, Craftwork—Metal 'A' Level)

2 Kings
2 Queens
4 Knights
(Heads carved)
4 Bishops
4 Castles
16 Pawns

The illustration shows in elevation the pieces of a set of chessmen which were turned and carved in red and white marble about seventy years ago. Designs and choice of materials have changed since then.
You are required to:

1. *Design,* in a modern style, any one piece of a set of chessmen. It is to be made mainly on the lathe from a suitable piece of aluminium bar. Specify the treatment you would use to distinguish 'black' from 'white' chessmen.

2. *Draw* full-size the template which will be required for the repetition work involved in the making of a number of these chessmen.

3. *Design* a holder for this template. Provision must be made for the template to be pulled down to check the work as it progresses, and to spring clear when released. The base of the holder is to be secured to the bed of the lathe by a clamp in a position clear of the saddle.

Paper 10

(Associated Examining Board 1971, Craftwork—Metal 'A' Level)

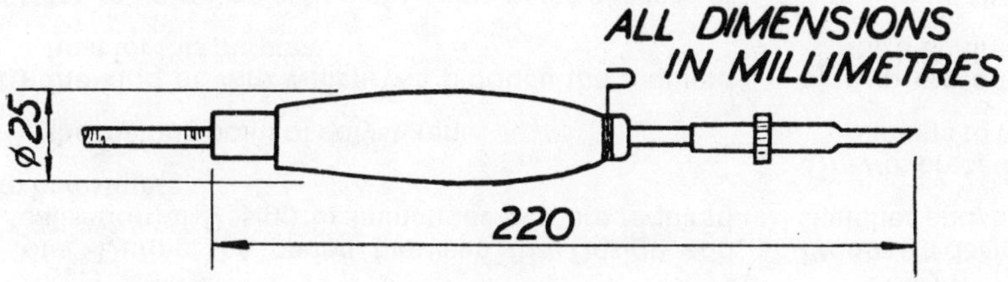
ALL DIMENSIONS
IN MILLIMETRES
ø25
220

The assembly of electronic components necessitates the soldering of small components to a board faced with copper.

Design a device that will hold such a board which is up to 240 mm long, 150 mm wide and 2 mm thick.

When held in the device the board should be so mounted that both sides are accessible to the operator in as flexible a range of positions as possible. The device may be mounted on a base, in which case it must have working stability, or clamped to the edge of a table or bench top which may be from 25 mm to 50 mm in thickness. It should also incorporate a support for an instrument soldering iron of the size given in the accompanying sketch.

Make complete working drawings and a list of materials required.
Indicate the 'finish' you intend to use.
All preliminary sketches leading up to your final designs, together with any explanatory notes, must be attached to your drawings. Marks will be awarded for the development of ideas in sketch form.

Paper 11

(Southern Universities' Joint Board 1971, Metalwork—Drawing and Design—'A' Level)

a) Make freehand sketches to show six different designs for brooches. You should indicate on your sketches the type of metal, constructional details and type of finish you would use.

b) By means of freehand sketches and notes show two types of clasps which could be used on the brooches.

Make sketches to show a suitable design for a trinket box which is to contain small items of jewellery. The lid should be hinged but, apart from this, there are no restrictions or limitations on your designs. Full constructional details should be given on your drawings.

Paper 12

(Associated Examining Board 1972, Craftwork—Wood 'A' Level)

Serving meals to people confined to bed is frequently a problem as there is clearly a requirement for a flat and firm surface to ensure both safety and comfort.

Design a small fitment which will assist the invalid who has to take meals in bed and which will also serve as a base for playing cards and writing letters. The same fitment should also include a folding rest or stand which can be used to support at a convenient angle, a book, a magazine or a folded newspaper. This may be either separate to stand on the flat surface or may be an integral part of the whole piece. The bed has a maximum width of 900 mm.

It is necessary that:

a) It may be used comfortably by a semi-reclining patient so that slight movement will not upset anything.

b) Items on the flat surface cannot slide off.

c) It is compact and the overall size for storage is not greater than 600 mm by 380 mm by 100 mm.

Make complete working drawings, a cutting list of timber and a list of any fittings and fastenings.
Indicate the timber and 'finish' you intend to use.
All preliminary sketches leading up to your final design, together with any explanatory notes, must be attached to your drawing. Marks will be awarded for the development of ideas in sketch form.

Paper 13

(Associated Examining Board 1972, Craftwork—Design 'O' Level)

1. Fig. 1 shows a sectional view of the construction of the window cills in a school corridor.

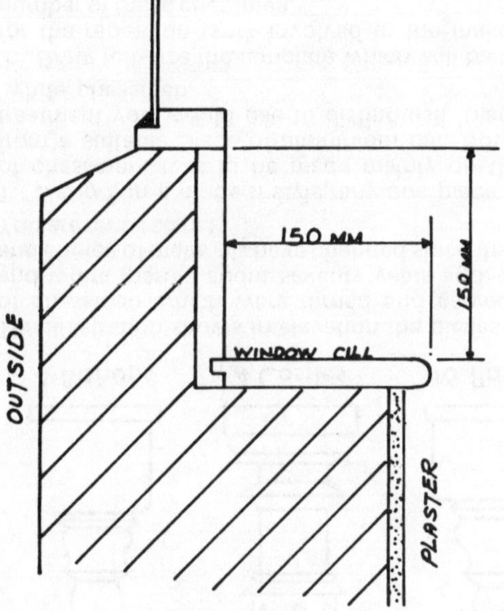
150 MM
150 MM
OUTSIDE
WINDOW CILL
PLASTER
CONCRETE

Fig. 1

Design a container for plant pots to be used on the window cills which would satisfy the following conditions.

a) Hold three pots each 120 mm diameter by 120 mm high.

b) Permit the watering of the plants without the water draining onto the cill.

c) Not protrude into the corridor.

2. Polystyrene sheet is cut by using an electrically heated wire which is fixed at right angles to a baseboard made from 18 mm blockboard as shown in Fig. 2.

The Art Department in a school wishes to cut a quantity of discs, without a centre hole, ranging from 75 mm to 150 mm diameter from square blanks of expanded polystyrene varying from 6 mm to 25 mm in thickness.

Design a jig which can be attached firmly to this baseboard and which can be adjusted so that the required sizes of disc may be cut. Your design should include some method of locating the blanks on the jig.

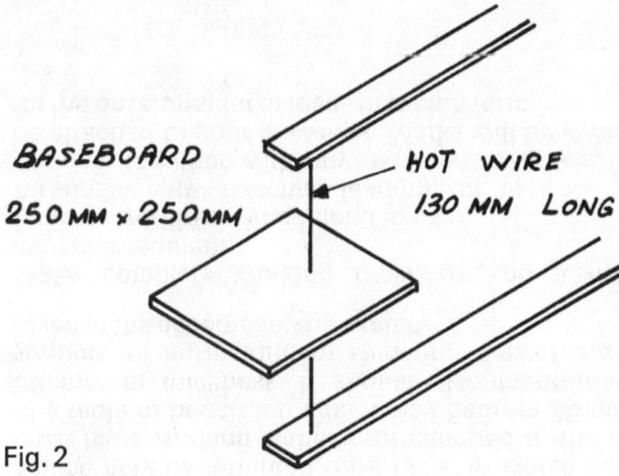
BASEBOARD
250MM x 250MM
HOT WIRE
130 MM LONG

Fig. 2

3. *Design* a piece of apparatus suitable for cutting the expanded polystyrene as in Question 2. This apparatus is to operate in a 6-volt supply and candidates examination pieces will be treated at 6-volts but the power source which you use will not be required.

Note: During the period between the Design and Realisation of Design Examinations you are required to investigate

a) the melting point of polystyrene

b) the kind of wire which will produce the required heat for this purpose.

Attach to your Realisation of Design piece a record of your investigations.

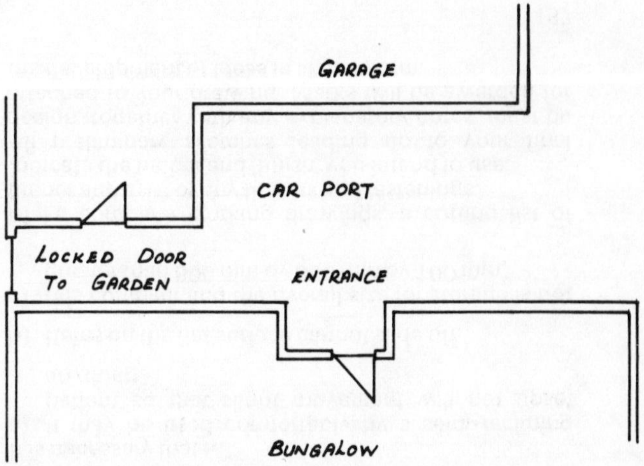
GARAGE
CAR PORT
LOCKED DOOR
TO GARDEN
ENTRANCE
BUNGALOW

4. The main entrance to a bungalow leads off a covered car-port as shown above.

Design a device to give audible warning inside the bungalow of anyone entering the car-port.

Make complete working drawings and a material list.

Include preliminary sketches leading up to your final design, together with any explanatory notes.

Marks will be awarded for the development of ideas in sketch form.

Candidates are expected to show by their solutions to this problem an appreciation of materials, processes and construction.

Paper 14

(Associated Examining Board 1972, Craftwork—Communication and Application 1972)

1. A pedestal drill and a lathe are positioned near to each other in a workshop. Certain safety precautions are common to both machines.

Produce a design for a wall poster, which by means of sketches and/or statements warns users of

a) two precautions which must be taken to avoid damage to themselves

b) two precautions to be taken to avoid damage to the machines.

Write down the precautions at the top of your design sheet.

2. A friend has asked for your advice in designing and making a circular table for use in the garden and which will remain outside during the summer months. List all the factors you would advise him to take into account.

3. An advertisement states that garden seats are available 1500 mm in length and it describes them as being made of solid wood with slats running the whole length of the seat. Two views are shown as in Fig. 1.

Make a pictorial impression of the garden seat which will allow the features to be more fully appreciated.

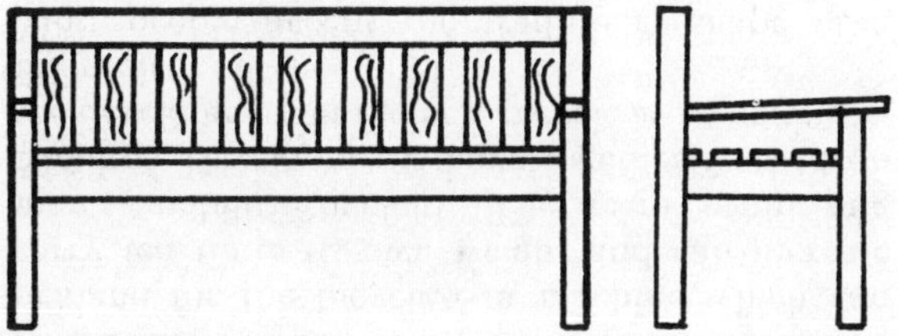

Fig. 1

Part 2

1. The Model Boat Club wishes to produce a number of identical model boat hulls in glass reinforced plastic. These would be fitted out individually by members of the club. Show graphically, in detail, preferably in the form of a flow chart, the order of procedure for making the hulls. Start with the making of the mould and finish with the removal of the hull from the mould.

2. Fig. 2 shows the plan of a garage/workshop. It is intended that the garage area should be separated from the workshop area by means of a divider such that the garage can be left open but the contents of the workshop left secure. The divider should be capable of being moved into the position shown by dotted lines so that the car can be moved into the workshop area when working on the engine.

Design a divider comprising two parts which move as shown by the dotted lines.

Each part of the divider is to be held securely in both positions.

Suggest ways in which the larger part of the divider can be used for storage purposes on the workshop side.

Fig. 2

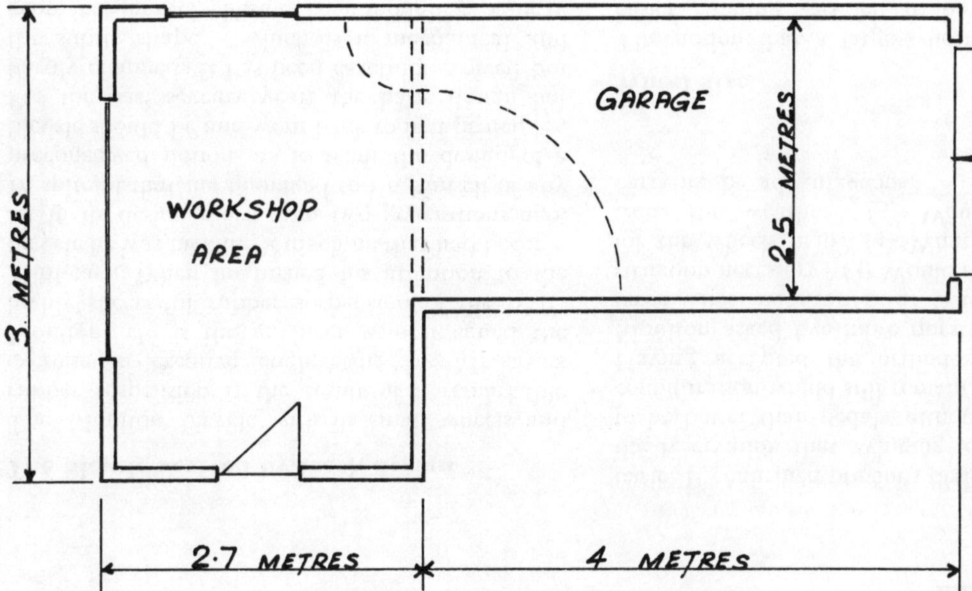
GARAGE
2·5 METRES
WORKSHOP
AREA
3 METRES
2·7 METRES
4 METRES

3. Design a jig to be used for making skids for children's sledges.

Each skid is to be of 25 mm square section with curved fronts as shown below and laminated from strips of ash.

Indicate how your jig would be used.

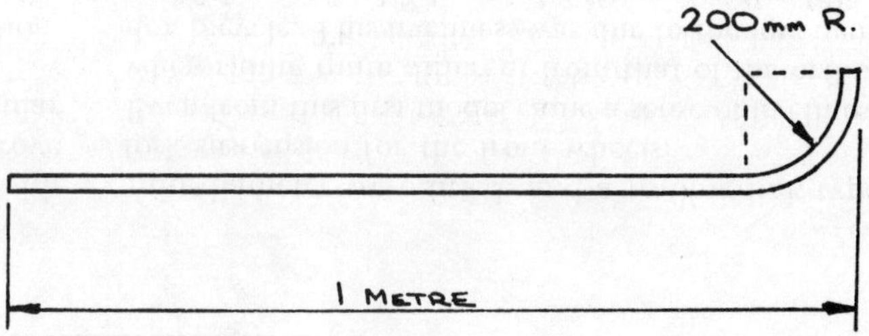
200mm R.
1 METRE

Design in Industry and Architecture

Examples of the use of freehand sketching and graphics, technical drawing and model making by professional designers.

The bicycle revived by fresh design

The Moulton bicycle with its small wheels and rubber suspension is the result of a remarkable exercise in creative engineering by Mr. Alex Moulton. He is the engineer who designed the highly successful rubber suspension of the BMC Mini-cars. When he turned his attention to the bicycle he was tackling a machine that had become set in its design more than two generations ago. In spite of that, he managed to rid himself of any preconceived notions as to what the design of a bicycle should be and went back to first principles. For the past seventy years the basic design has hardly changed. It has been carefully evolved but the subtle shape – which is a mechanical and geometric marvel – has not been thought capable of further development; it was considered to have reached its ultimate. In recent years, all the wrong emphasis has been on improving production methods rather than improving the design.

Alex Moulton believes there will be an everlasting demand for the bicycle – a machine which can carry ten times its own weight and can increase man's mobility fivefold. The team comprising Moulton Developments have together worked on the development of the new bicycle as an engineering project.

Most people accept the traditional shape of a bicycle, but Moulton asked several basic questions. First: is the existing ergonomic position of the rider in relation to the machine the best? He reconsidered the prone position, but early experiments confirmed that it was not practical. Although high thrust was possible and wind resistance was low, the fatigue of holding the thighs in the horizontal position was considerable.

He soon accepted, therefore, that the classic position was the best. The triangle, formed of saddle, handlebars, and pedals fixed relatively, is absolutely basic. It confirmed previous design thought – with the reservation that swinging levers might prove to be better than pedals, although the triangular configuration would still remain.

Having accepted the orthodox riding position, Moulton asked five more questions: (1) Was the large wheel necessary? (2) Was small tube construction necessary? (3) Would resilient suspension for the wheels help? (4) What about protection from the weather? (5) Would safe luggage-carrying be advantageous?

Wheel size

The notion that a large wheel was essential for easier running was felt to be wrong. Moulton believed that rolling resistance of a small wheel could equal that of a large one provided sufficiently high pressures were used, rolling resistance being primarily a function of inflation pressure. Moulton had Dunlop's confirm these theories and they carried out rolling resistance tests with tyres down to 14in diameter, similar in design to the normal 27in Dunlop Sprite sports tyre. The new bicycle actually has 16in diameter tyres inflated to 60 lb per sq.in, but racing versions will be inflated up to nearly 200 lb per sq.in.

It was also felt that a longer wheelbase – approximately 3in more than standard – would give greater directional stability and better braking, with less tendency for the back wheel to lose adhesion.

Fig. 1 shows the development range where Moulton was searching for form rather than function. In this search for form and the desire to be original in thought the early experimental models were constructed on aerodynamic lines – but always with small wheels.

The first machine, built in 1959, employed monocoque construction, using 22 g Duralumin. Wheels 14in diameter were fitted, and a trailing-link-type fork suspension for the front wheels.

Even from this first model came a sense of liveliness when riding quite different from that of the orthodox bicycle. This liveliness was due to the low inertia of the small wheels and the responsive flexibility of the front suspension which ironed out the bumps.

The monocoque construction, however, produced an unacceptable 'road noise' as in some unitary construction cars.

It was also evident that a sub-frame was necessary to secure accurate alignment of the heavily loaded components. The torque in a bicycle crank axle can be similar to the maximum torque of a car engine. So in addition to not looking right or particularly attractive, monocoque construction was disappointing in its efficiency.

Later in 1959 a model with a large diameter tubular backbone frame was produced. It took the form of an 'F' frame, the tubes being 20 g by 2in diameter mild steel and all parallel. Glassfibre mouldings were used for weather protection at front and rear.

The front suspension was modified to use rubber in compression instead of tension – rear suspension was not yet fitted – and front and rear load carrying capacity was introduced. The ability to carry loads such as shopping, for instance, was considered a necessary feature if the full potential of the machine was to be realized. The wheels were increased to 16in diameter.

This model showed up two basic faults: (1) the round frame tube was not stiff enough in bending which resulted in annoying vibration; (2) the good isolation of the front suspension showed up the lack of any at the rear. The answer to (2) it was felt, did not lie in fitting deep saddle springs – as a rigid base is necessary for efficient pedalling – so the decision was taken to add rear suspension.

Another model was immediately produced – still

using round tube but of heavier gauge. It had front suspension of the leading link type and rear suspension was introduced.

A complete break

Moulton then decided to make a complete break and use flat-sided oval and tapered tubes. These are used in the production model and are supplied by Tube Products Limited of Oldbury. They collaborated in evolving manipulating techniques for the special sectioned and tapered tubes to allow lug-less construction. At present mild steel ERW is used.

A wholly new type of single telescopic front fork was finally evolved (Fig. 2), while the rear suspension is of the trailing-link-type using rubber in compression and shear plus a small friction damper (Fig. 3).

The majority of the parts are standard components, e.g. brakes, saddle, chainwheel, crank and pedals. One universal model is equally suitable for men and women.

One version, called the 'Stowaway' has a frame which divides across the main beam and fits together with a quick positive locking device. It can be put into the boot of a car. Altogether five versions are available; standard, stowaway, de luxe, safari and speed. The de luxe weighs $32\frac{1}{2}$ lb with carrier and the speed version $26\frac{1}{2}$ lb.

Lest the Moulton bicycle be considered as purely utilitarian, many speed trials have been carried out which, it is claimed, have proved its performance is at least equal to that of the best orthodox racing machine.

Certainly creative thought, the ability to question the accepted vogue and ingenious development has led to a revolutionary design (Fig. 3).

Fig. 1 The range of monocoque models produced when Moulton was searching for form rather than function. They were constructed on aerodynamic lines but always with small wheels.

Fig. 3 Rear suspension on the production model showing the trailing link pivot point, friction damper and rubber suspension block.

Moulton deluxe

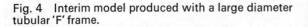

Fig. 4 Interim model produced with a large diameter tubular 'F' frame.

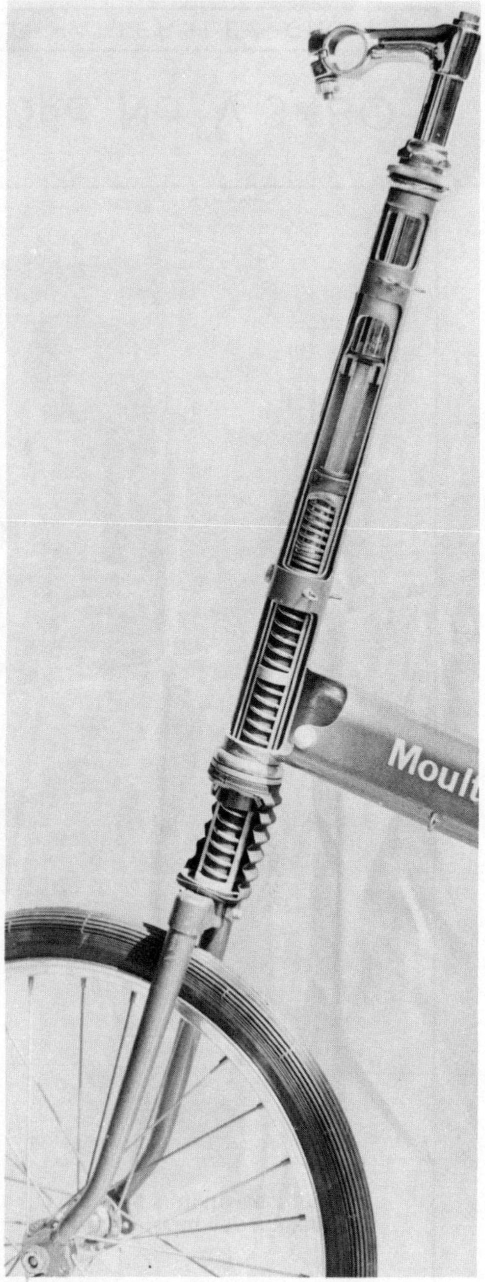

Fig. 2 Front fork and steering column assembly on the production model.

ALL SIZES IN MILLIMETRES

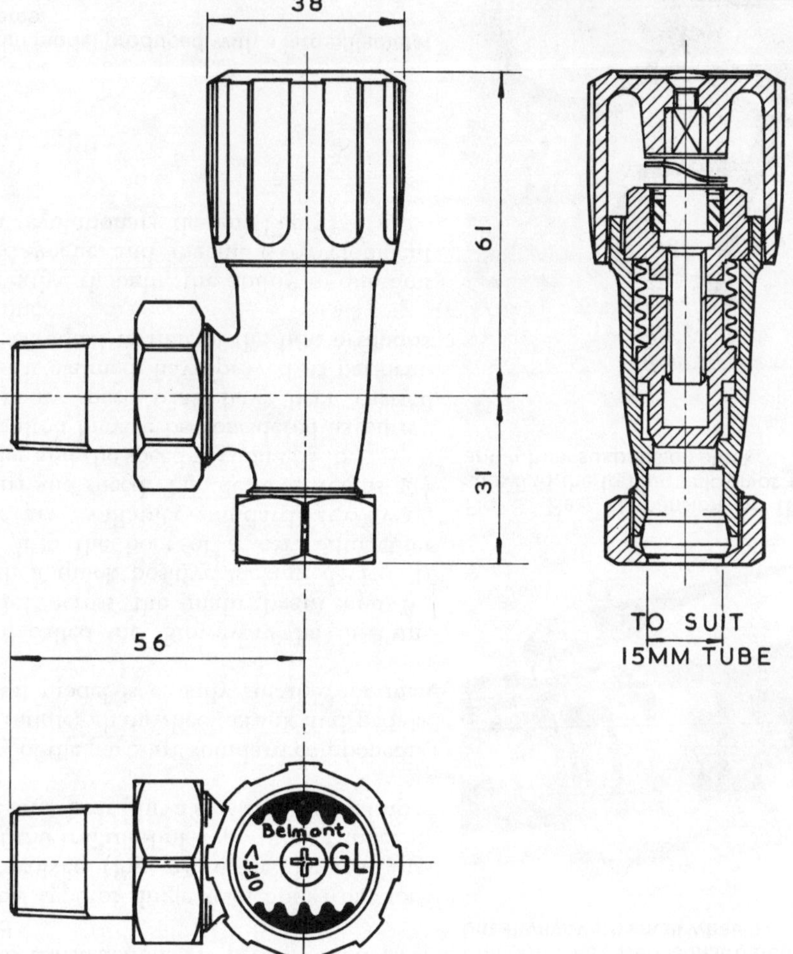
38
61
31
1/2 B.S.P.
BS 21
56
TO SUIT
15MM TUBE
Belmont
OFF
GL

An example of a typical industrial production drawing. It is useful to compare the drawing with the sectioned photograph

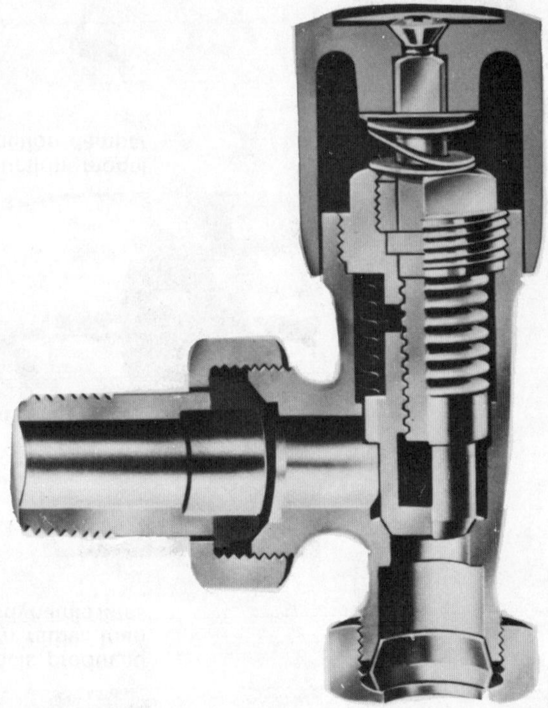

TITLE ASSEMBLY DETAILS OF 1/2" M12OGL GLANDLESS RAD. VALVE	DRAWN [signature] CHECKED [signature] DATE 3-5-72	DRG. NO. V 3480

PEGLERS LIMITED DONCASTER — NON·FERROUS DIVISION OF THE PEGLER·HATTERSLEY GROUP

Six graphic designs by Anthony Beams for the Myriad Range of decorative plastic laminates produced by Arborite Ltd. These laminates consist of multi-layers of specially processed papers impregnated with phenolic and melamine resins fused together by heat and pressure into a homogeneous solid panel. They are widely used on modern furniture where heat and stain resisting surfaces are required.

This circular style greenhouse has twelve sides and was designed by Maurice Juggins.
The original idea was to create a controlled environment of minimal size but maximum accessibility and control.
Simply by turning on the spot, the user can reach all the plants. This makes it particularly suitable for disabled people.

Other features:

Configuration The circular shape is ideal for maximum light transmission, and is pleasing and easy to site in the garden.

Ventilation There is a vent at the bottom of each panel and they all open together by pulling on a cord. The top dome can be operated manually or automatically as the temperature rises. This circumferential air flow is ideal for plant growth.

Construction The main frame is made from aluminium extrusions and the top dome is perspex vacuum formed.

This model was made from balsawood and plastic sheet and was one of a series leading up to the final design.

A production greenhouse in use, complete with circular staging.

6 mm New Generation Sapphire Drill, Model 3495 by Wolf Electric Tools, Ltd. This is a single speed, 420-watt double-insulated drill approved by the British Standards Institution. It features a 'palm-grip' for maximum working effectiveness and has capacities of 6 mm in steel, 16 mm in hardboard and 10 mm in masonry.

The three-dimensional cut-away line drawing shows much more detail than the simple line drawing and is a method much favoured by manufacturers to advertise their products.

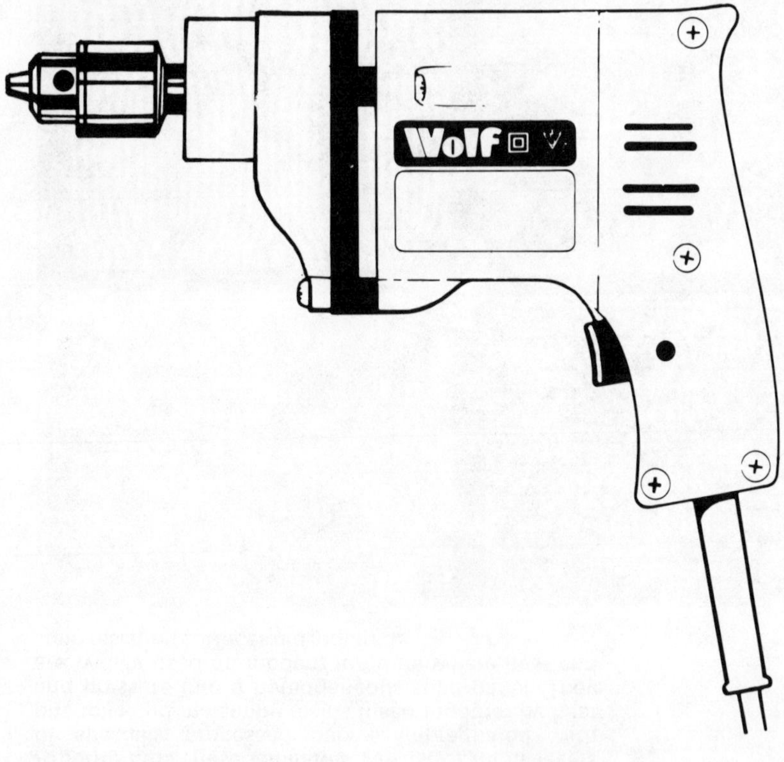
Wolf

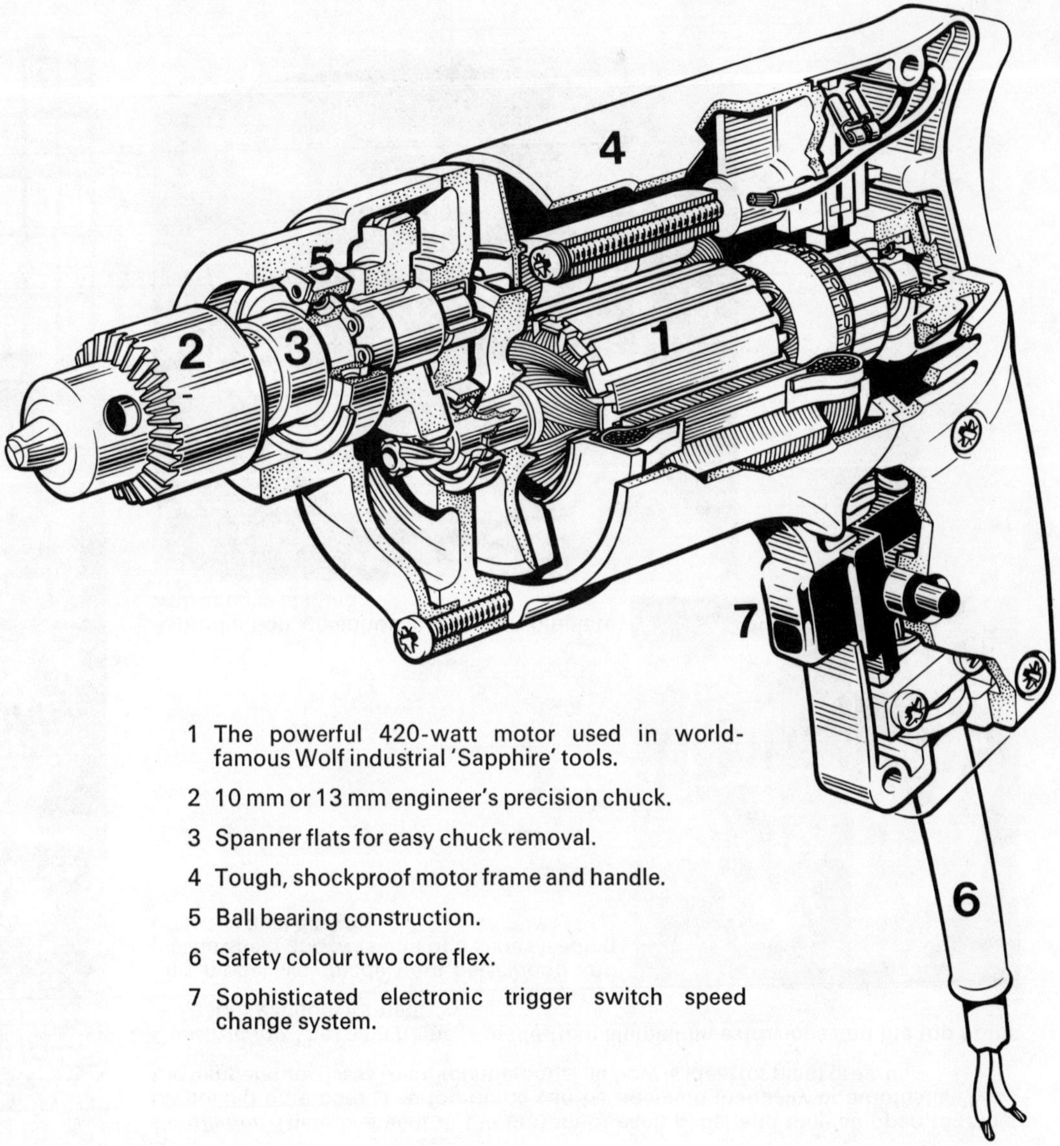
1
2
3
4
5
6
7

1 The powerful 420-watt motor used in world-famous Wolf industrial 'Sapphire' tools.

2 10 mm or 13 mm engineer's precision chuck.

3 Spanner flats for easy chuck removal.

4 Tough, shockproof motor frame and handle.

5 Ball bearing construction.

6 Safety colour two core flex.

7 Sophisticated electronic trigger switch speed change system.

The British Leyland (Austin-Morris) Marina.

This is a further example of a three-dimensional cut-away drawing.

An artist's impression in colour of the engine, again as a three-dimensional cut-away. (Tones of red, yellow and blue were used to distinguish the various parts of the engine.)

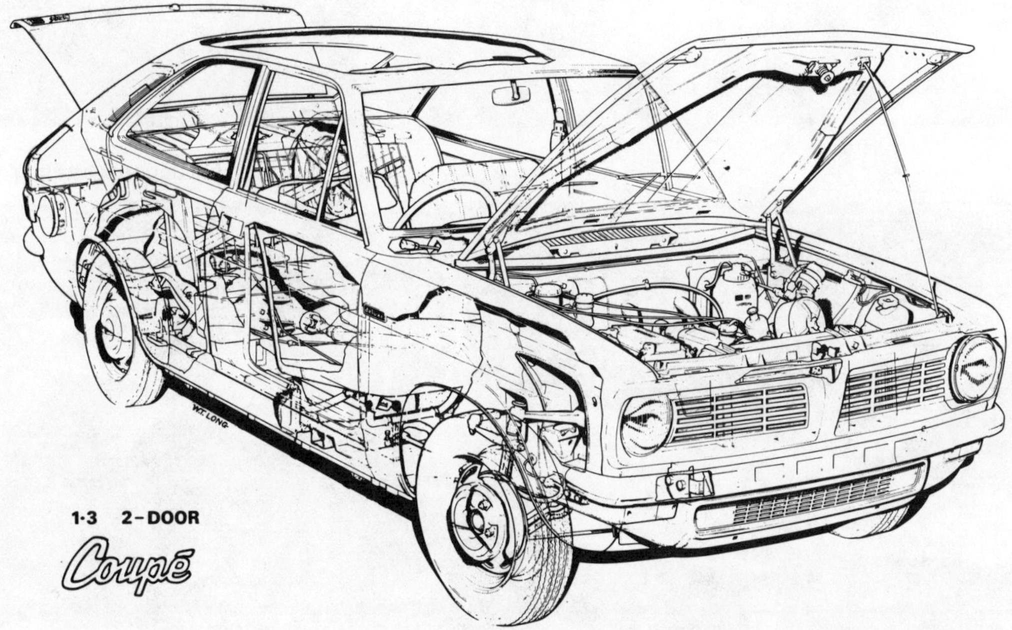
1·3 2–DOOR
Coupé

The technical artist at work.

Mock-ups and models in the production of Concorde

Concorde

Full size wooden mock-up of Concorde.

A wooden mock-up, electrically driven, to illustrate the three positions of Concorde's variable geometry nose section.

Concorde
SUPERSONIC FLIGHT

Concorde
SUBSONIC FLIGHT

Concorde

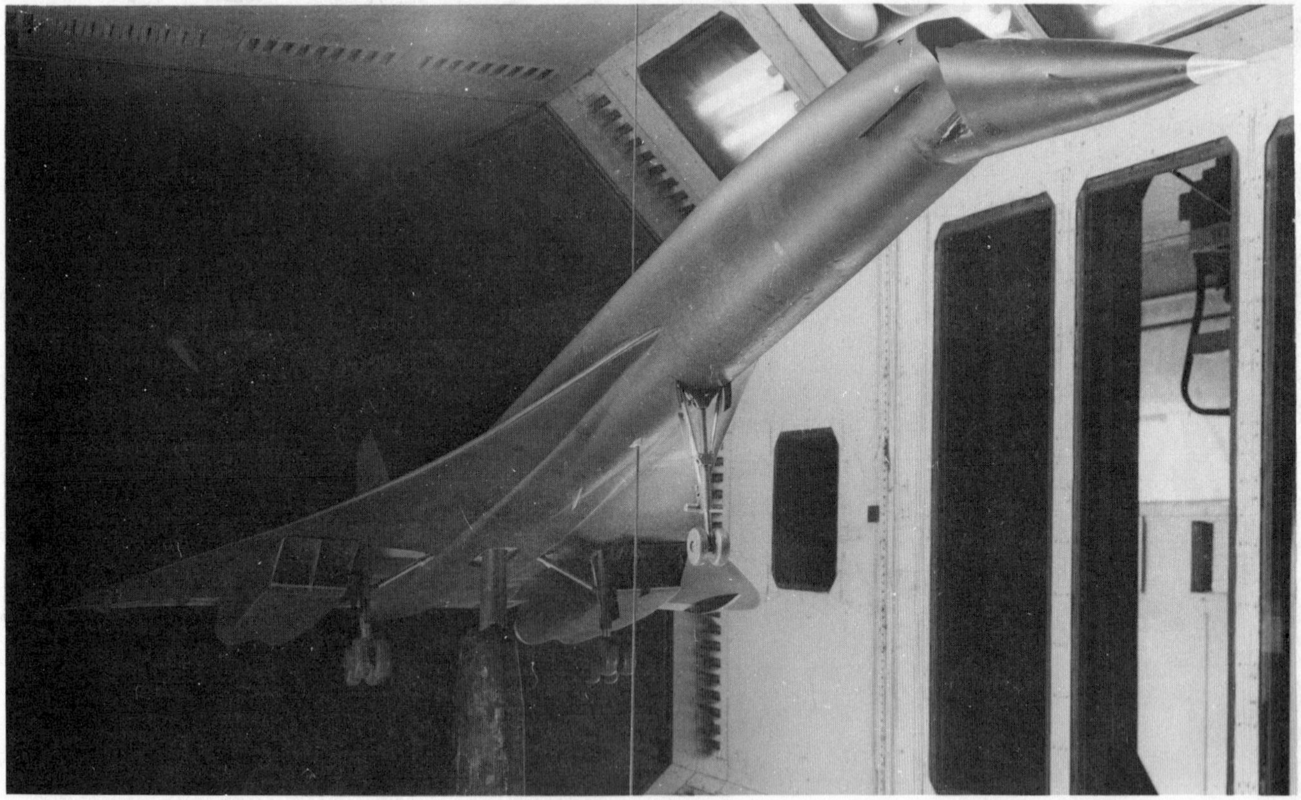

1/18th scale Concorde model of complete aircraft in condition for approach to the 3.5 m x 3 m working section of a low speed tunnel at Bristol.

This model is suspended from an overhead balance on a steel strut, which is shielded from the airstream over most of its length by a fibreglass fairing of aerofoil section. A pivot at the model attachment permits incidence to be varied during a test run by means of a cable attached to the forward fuselage. The wing is machined from aluminium and the fuselage and nacelles are constructed of fibreglass and wood.

The model shown is intended for subsonic testing only. It is used to measure the overall aerodynamic forces and moments, in order to assess aircraft loadings and flying characteristics.

1/15th scale model of Concorde engine intakes on port wing.

In this picture, a panel has been removed from the nacelle cowl showing the radial assembly of tubes which measure pitot pressures at the position of the compressor entry face. This is shown detached from the model inset.

This model intake is mounted on a part model wing, representing only the portion of the aircraft which may effect the nature of the intake flow.
Machined from steel and aluminium the model is used for transonic and supersonic studies. It has been tested in the RAE 2.4 m supersonic tunnel at Bedford, the ARA 2.4 m x 2.7 m transonic tunnel also at Bedford, and in the ONERA S2 supersonic tunnel at Modane, France.
The intake is fitted with representative ramps which can be remotely actuated. The flow through the intake is controlled by remotely operated valves at the downstream end of the nacelle.
The model provides information on the nature of the flow arriving at the engine, the operating limits of which could be affected by poor quality. The sharp leading edges of the intake splitter and sidewalls which are a feature of the Concorde intake, are shown here protected by plastic strips during model assembly work.

Three-dimensional cut-away drawing in colour of the latest version of the Olympus engine. (Tones of brown, green and blue were used to distinguish the various parts of the engine.)

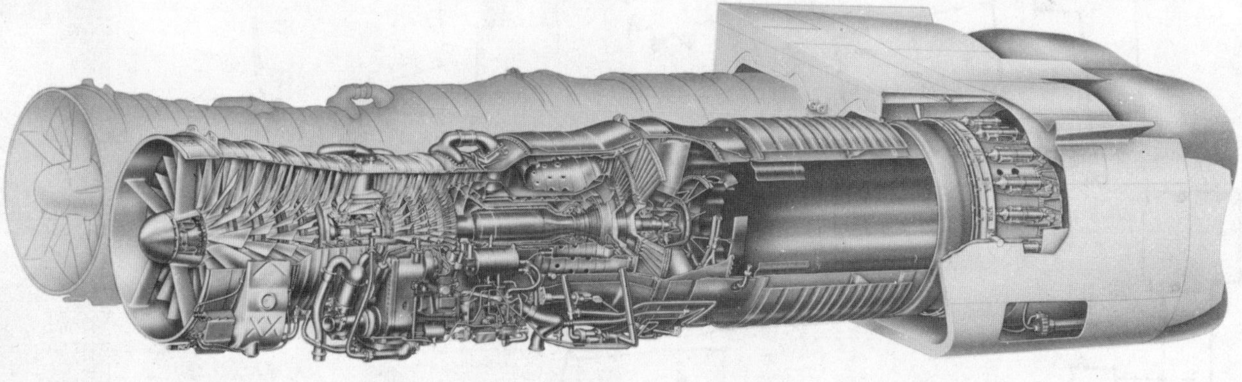

Views of Coventry Cathedral from Priory Road.
Architect Sir Basil Spence, A.R.S.A.

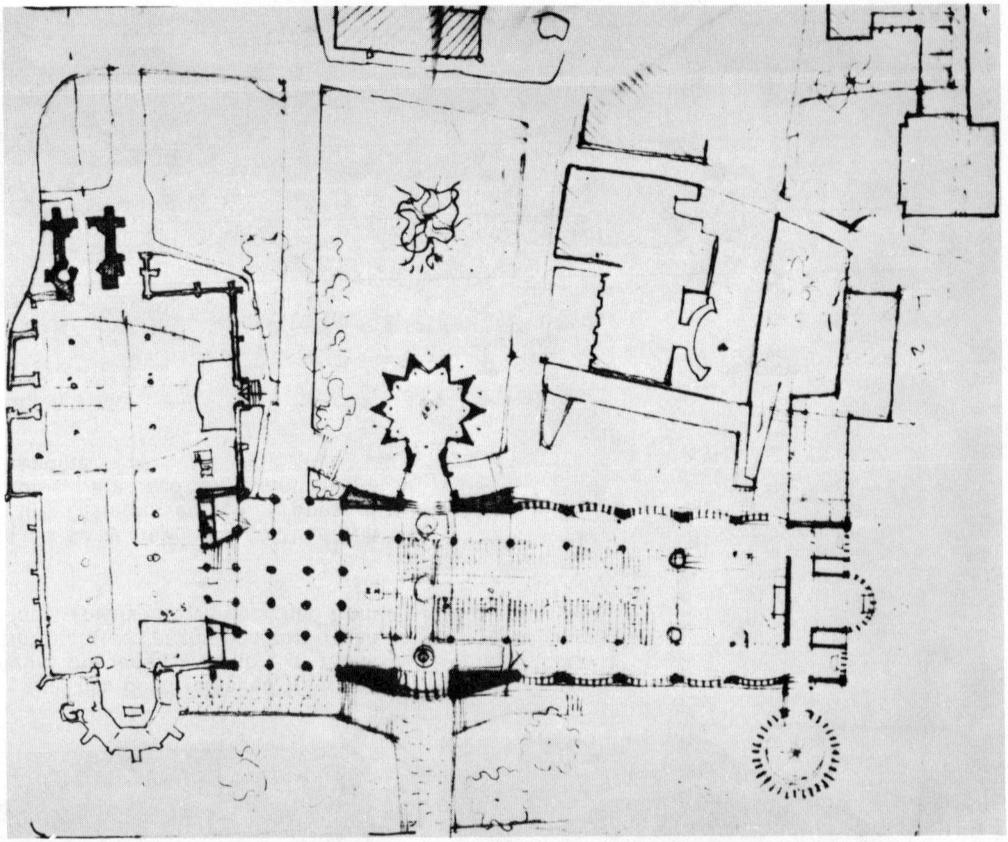

Reproduction of Sir Basil Spence's very first sketch for his design for Coventry Cathedral.

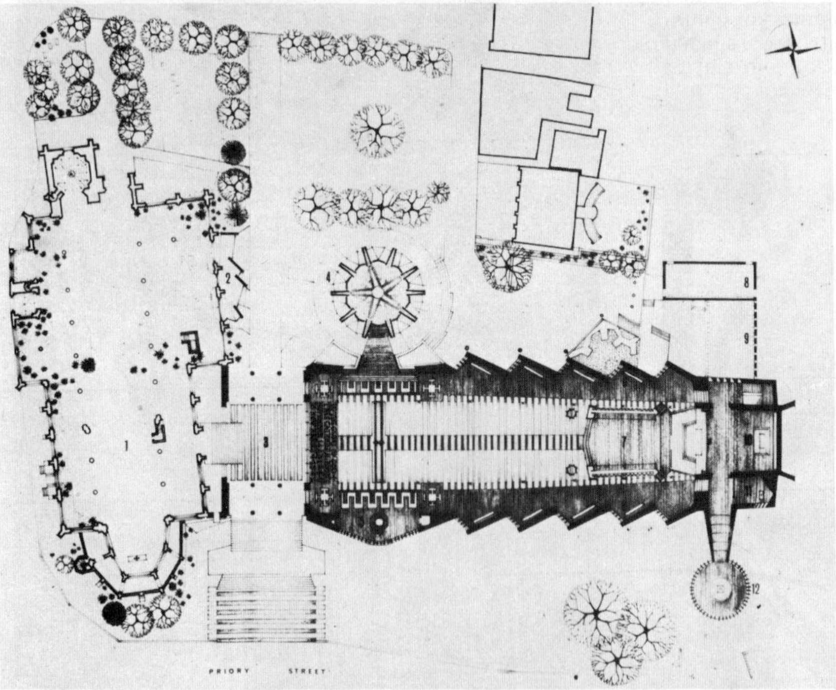
PRIORY STREET

The Cathedral Church of St Michael, Coventry.

The scale drawing produced from the sketch.

CO OPERATIVE

Perspective sketch of Merseyway Shopping Centre, Stockport.

Model of Merseyway Shopping Centre, Stockport.

Design and the Community

An awareness of design should not be restricted to the immediate confines of the workshop. Design in some form or other, both good and bad surrounds us and in its own way its quality affects our standard of living. In this chapter we are concerned with the design of items which are not of a purely personal nature and work made at school for the benefit of the school community or the community at large which can give great personal satisfaction.

The previous chapter gave an indication of how important sketching, drawing and model making are to professional designers. Some design situations are suggested to you here and further examples of the work of professional designers are illustrated, you are to consider carefully the designs, paying particular attention to shape and appearance. Many of the items illustrated are essential to our modern way of living and in accepting this fact you are to consider how well or otherwise these products affect our environment. You are then invited to design similiar work to meet particular requirements. These designs can be in the form of sketches, workshop drawings or scale models and can form part of a general design project.

AIREVILLE
SECONDARY SCHOOL
SKIPTON

Ceramic tiles at the entrance to the metalwork, woodwork and pottery workshops at a Danish school. You are to suggest designs for similar plaques for use at your own school. Metal, wood, plastics or any other suitable material may be used.

The original stone sculpture from the niche in the chimney was so badly affected by the weather that it became unsafe and had to be removed. Suggest designs for an abstract form to be made in mild steel of welded construction which can be galvanised to prevent rusting. The niche is approximately 2 m high. Alternatively, design a similar piece of work to stand in a corridor or in the grounds of your school.

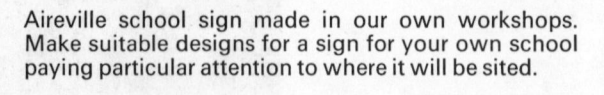

Aireville school sign made in our own workshops. Make suitable designs for a sign for your own school paying particular attention to where it will be sited.

Design brief

You are required to design a wrought iron railing to fit into the area bounded by the letters ABC. The railing should be designed to fit either over the stone sphere or it may fit round it, but the general line should be on the line DE. The finished railing may be of modern or traditional design.
You should indicate on your design sheet all methods of construction and how the railing is to be secured.

A group of boys working on this problem as part of Aireville School's contribution to the Schools Council Curriculum Development Project in Design and Craft Education. The work is being done as Community Service at the West Riding County Council's Countryside Park, Studley Royal with Fountains Abbey estate near Ripon. (Now within the county of North Yorkshire.)

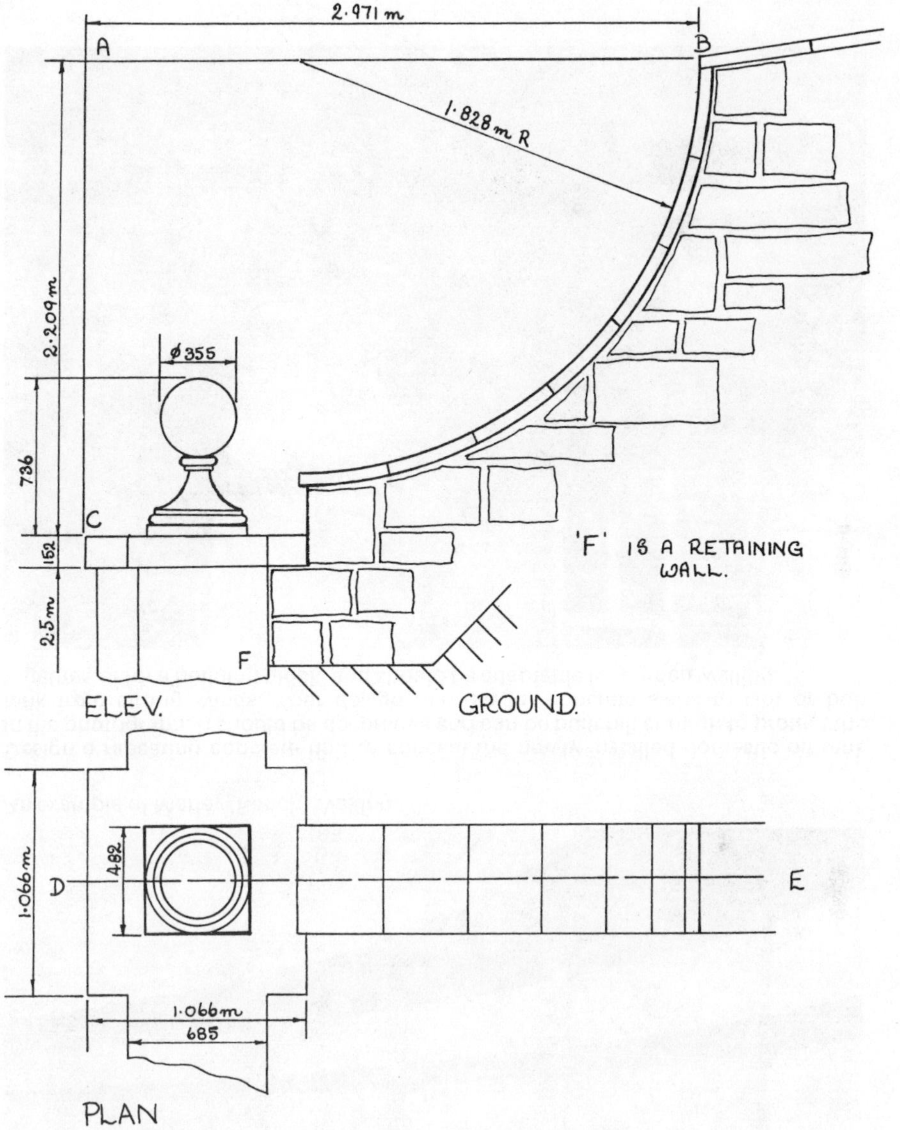
2·971 m
A
B
1·828 m R
2·209 m
ø355
736
C
152
2·5 m
F
'F' IS A RETAINING WALL.
ELEV.
GROUND.
1·066m
482
D
E
1·066m
685
PLAN

PlayCubes came about as a result of thorough research with educationists, child psychologists, community leaders, government officials and children. They are a clustered grouping of glass fibre units, interlocked and tunnelled for safe, creative play.

Each PlayCube unit is moulded of high-stress glass fibre. They are available in vivid colours with joining fixtures, and can be assembled to fit any size or shape of space.

They are safe, durable, and require virtually no maintenance. Each unit is light, easy to assemble, and when connected form a practically indestructible play unit.

Play Cubes

Make sketches and models in card, of your own suggestions for a children's adventure playground. The units may be constructed in concrete or timber and must be durable and weather resisting. The safety of the child when playing should be a prime consideration.

An example of Marley 'Ranch' Walling.

Design a repeating concrete unit to conceal the newly installed domestic oil tank in the photograph. It should be decorative and can be built tall enough to protect the tank from strong winds. Your design may be for concrete slabs to slot or bolt together, or for a building block, and should be adaptable for garden walling.

Study the examples of street lighting, then design a suitable lamp to light the road leading to the village in the photograph. Care should be taken to ensure that your design blends with the rural atmosphere.

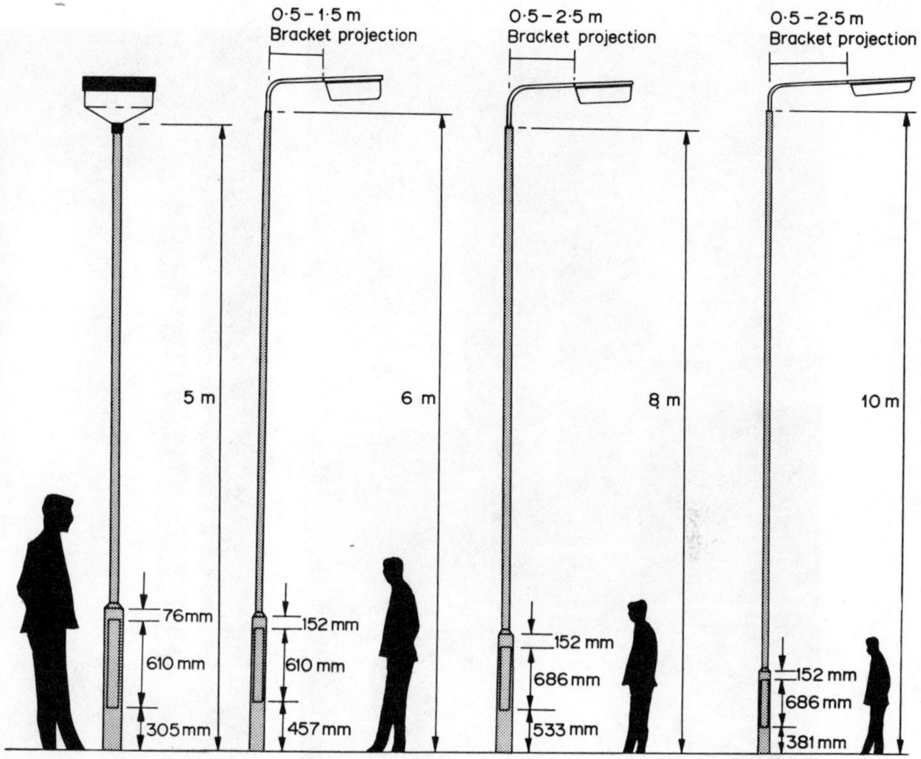
0·5–1·5 m
Bracket projection
0·5–2·5 m
Bracket projection
0·5–2·5 m
Bracket projection
5 m
6 m
8 m
10 m
76mm
610 mm
305mm
152 mm
610 mm
457mm
152 mm
686mm
533 mm
152 mm
686mm
381mm

You are shown examples of outdoor seating, lighting bollards for pedestrian ways and litter bins. Study these and then design a matching seat, bollard and litter bin for the paved area illustrated. There is no restriction on the type of materials you may suggest or the final finish to be applied. Make a scale model in wood, card or other suitable materials of your final design.

This elevation shows the clean and exceptionally attractive outline of the Butterley footbridge. It can be seen how well the curve of the spiral ramp blends with the bridge design.

In plan view the symmetrical outline and elegance of the design are apparent.

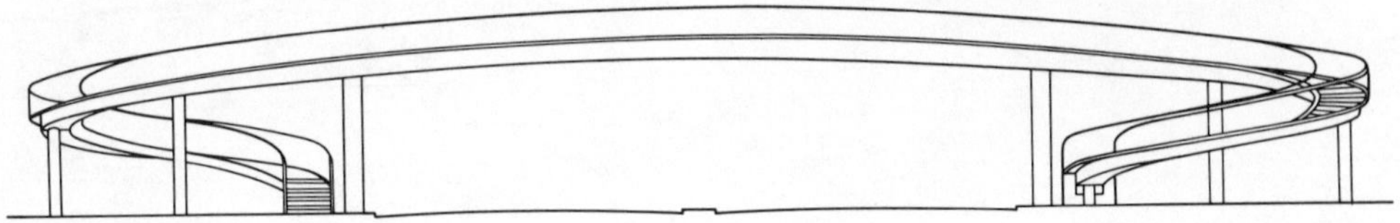

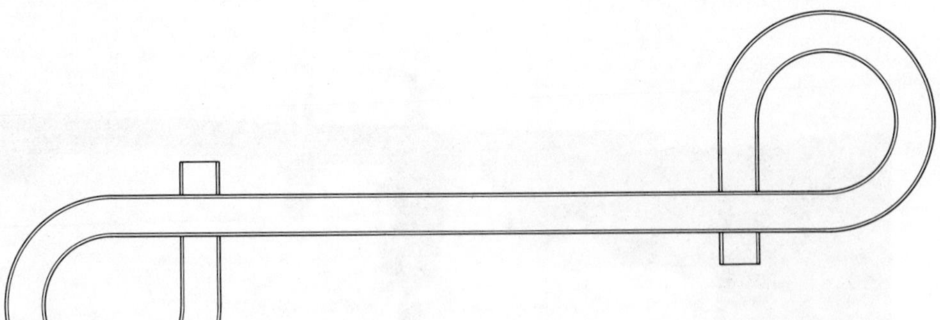

Wentbridge Viaduct

Designed by the West Riding County Council, acting as agents for the Department of the Environment, under the supervision of the County Engineer and Surveyor, J. A. Gaffney B.Sc., FICE.

Scammonden Bridge

Designed by the West Riding County Council, acting as agents for the Ministry of Transport under the supervision of the County Engineer and Surveyor, Col. S. M. Lovell C.B.E., E.R.D., T.D., FICE.

Study the model and photographs of the Butterley footbridge and the form of the heavier duty bridges over the M62. Then suggest designs for a hikers' footbridge to cross the motorway at the point indicated by the arrow. Make a simple wooden model.

Suggestions for further design problems of a similar nature.

Pre-school playgroup equipment.

Outdoor flower tubs for public places.

Road signs.

Petrol pump.

Repeating module for a wall feature in concrete, wood or polystyrene depending on the situation.

Vending machine for hot and cold drinks.

Wireless set.

Bed-sitter for a student.

Telephone.

Refrigerator – exterior/interior.

Television set and stand.

Trailer caravan – exterior/interior.

Kitchen – modern fittings.

Study/bedroom for a teenager.

Book List

Craft Education–Metalwork Design	T Pettit	(E Arnold)
Design in Metalwork	Bridge and Crossland	(Batsford)
Designs in Wood	Bridge and Crossland	(Batsford)
An Approach to Design in Metal	V Austin	(Macmillan)
Metalwork Design	R N Wheeler	(Cassell)
A Designer's Approach to Woodwork	D W Egglestaff	(Pergamon)
Design your own Craftwork	W E Brooke and K Barkley	(Murray)
Sketching for Woodwork and Metalwork	G T James and P W Millard	(Bell)
Freehand Technical Sketching	Hubert Cook	(Methuen)
Attitudes in Design Education	K Baynes	(Lund Humphries)
Design in Metalwork – 3 sets of 8 design sheets	R L Andrews and G S Dobbs	(Blond Educational)
Looking and Seeing Books 1/2/3/4	Kurt Rowland	(Ginn)
Learning to See Books 1/2/3/4/5	Kurt Rowland	(Ginn)
Educating the Senses	Kurt Rowland	(Ginn)
Creative Form in Woodwork Books 1/2	E W Bond and J T Fisher	(McGraw-Hill)
Modern Workshop – Practical Constructions and Assignments	Donald Fisher and Arthur Moore	(Holmes McDougall)
Education through the use of Materials	Schools Council Working Paper 26	(Evans/Methuen)
Metric Data for Craft Teachers	A W Lewis	(Methuen)
Measure for measure – a guide to metrication for workshop crafts and technical studies	Schools Council	(Evans/Methuen)
Metric Standards for Engineering	B and S Handbook No. 18	(British Standards Institution)
Engineering Drawing Practice	BS 308 PARTS 1 : 2 : 3 : 1972	(British Standards Institution)
Creative Design Metalwork	R Sandham, F R Willmore, K Smith	(E Arnold)

Acknowledgments

To past and present students of Aireville Secondary School, Skipton, for the original and edited design sheets.

The author also wishes to thank the following for their active assistance in compiling the text and giving permission for the reproduction of photographs and other copyright material (page numbers in brackets):

Abacus Municipal Ltd. (154 *top left*, 155); Arborite Ltd. (143); Berol: Eagle Pencil Company Ltd. (87, 88 *top and bottom left*, 92); British Aircraft Corporation (146, 147); British Leyland 'Austin-Morris' Ltd. (145); British Pens Ltd. also UK agents for A. W. Faber-Castell (84, 91 *bottom right*, 92 *bottom left and middle, and top right*); British Standards Institution (98, 99, 101); British Thornton Ltd. (85, 86, 89); Butterley Engineering Ltd. (156); Churchouse Ltd. (154 *top right*); Concrete Utilities Ltd. (153 *left and top right*, 154 *bottom right*); the Craven Herald (23 *bottom*); Darque Bros. Ltd. (160); the Department of the Environment (157 *top right*); Donaldson and Sons (149); Eleco Ltd. (153 *middle*); Entec S A, Geneva (152 *left*); Harbutts Ltd. (92 *top left*, 94 *bottom*); Hartley Reece and Co. (90, 91); Humex Ltd. (143 *left*); Letraset Ltd. (96); Marley Buildings Ltd. (155 *top right*); Mono Concrete Ltd. (154 *bottom left*); Moulton Consultants Ltd. (140, 141); the Provost and Chapter of Coventry Cathedral (148); Solarbo Ltd. (94 *top*, 95); The Science Museum, London (25); Unique Slide Rule Co. Ltd. (86 *bottom right*, 87 *bottom right*, 88 *top and bottom right*); Tim Widdowson (143 *right*); Geliot Whitman Ltd. (95 *top right*); Windsor and Newton (84 *bottom and middle*, 93); Wolf Electric Tools Ltd. (144). Other photographs by R. W. Holmes, Worth Photofinishers, Keighley, Yorks; Allan Hargreaves and the author.

Items of woodwork illustrated in the text, other than industrial products, are of timber supplied by Porter (Selby) Ltd.

INCHES	FRACTIONS	FEET	1	2	3	4	5	6	7	8	9	10	11
		METRIC											
0		0	304.8	609.6	914.4	1219.2	1524.0	1828.8	2133.6	2438.4	2743.1	3047.9	3352.7
	1/8	3.2	308.0	612.8	917.6	1222.4	1527.2	1832.0	2136.8	2441.6	2746.3	3051.1	3355.9
	1/4	6.4	311.1	615.9	920.7	1225.5	1530.3	1835.1	2139.9	2444.7	2749.4	3054.2	3359.0
	3/8	9.5	314.3	619.1	923.9	1228.7	1533.5	1838.3	2143.1	2447.9	2752.6	3057.4	3362.2
	1/2	12.7	317.5	622.3	927.1	1231.9	1536.7	1841.5	2146.3	2451.1	2755.8	3060.6	3365.4
	5/8	15.9	320.7	625.5	930.3	1235.1	1539.9	1844.7	2149.5	2454.3	2759.0	3063.8	3368.6
	3/4	19.0	323.8	628.6	933.4	1238.2	1543.0	1847.8	2152.6	2457.4	2762.1	3066.9	3371.7
	7/8	22.2	327.0	631.8	936.6	1241.4	1546.2	1851.0	2155.8	2460.6	2765.3	3070.1	3374.9
1		25.4	330.2	635.0	939.8	1244.6	1549.4	1854.2	2159.0	2463.8	2768.5	3073.3	3378.1
	1/8	28.6	333.4	638.2	943.0	1247.8	1552.6	1857.4	2162.2	2467.0	2771.7	3076.5	3381.3
	1/4	31.7	336.5	641.3	946.1	1250.9	1555.7	1860.5	2165.3	2470.1	2774.8	3079.6	3384.4
	3/8	34.9	339.7	644.5	949.3	1254.1	1558.9	1863.7	2168.5	2473.3	2778.0	3082.8	3387.6
	1/2	38.1	342.9	647.7	952.5	1257.3	1562.1	1866.9	2171.7	2476.5	2781.2	3086.0	3390.8
	5/8	41.3	346.1	650.9	955.7	1260.5	1565.3	1870.1	2174.9	2479.7	2784.4	3089.2	3394.0
	3/4	44.4	349.2	654.0	958.8	1263.6	1568.4	1873.2	2178.0	2482.8	2787.5	3092.3	3397.1
	7/8	47.6	352.4	657.2	962.0	1266.8	1571.6	1876.4	2181.2	2486.0	2790.7	3095.5	3400.3
2		50.8	355.6	660.4	965.2	1270.0	1574.8	1879.6	2184.4	2489.2	2793.9	3098.7	3403.5
	1/8	54.0	358.8	663.6	968.4	1273.2	1578.0	1882.8	2187.6	2492.4	2797.1	3101.9	3406.7
	1/4	57.1	361.9	666.7	971.5	1276.3	1581.1	1885.9	2190.7	2495.5	2800.2	3105.0	3409.8
	3/8	60.3	365.1	669.9	974.7	1279.5	1584.3	1889.1	2193.9	2498.7	2803.4	3108.2	3413.0
	1/2	63.5	368.3	673.1	977.9	1282.7	1587.5	1892.3	2197.1	2501.9	2806.6	3111.4	3416.2
	5/8	66.7	371.5	676.3	981.1	1285.9	1590.7	1895.5	2200.3	2505.1	2809.8	3114.6	3419.4
	3/4	69.8	374.6	679.4	984.2	1289.0	1593.8	1898.6	2203.4	2508.2	2812.9	3117.7	3422.5
	7/8	73.0	377.8	682.6	987.4	1292.2	1597.0	1901.8	2206.6	2511.4	2816.1	3120.9	3425.7
3		76.2	381.0	685.8	990.6	1295.4	1600.2	1905.0	2209.8	2514.6	2819.3	3124.1	3428.9
	1/8	79.4	384.2	689.0	993.8	1298.6	1603.4	1908.2	2213.0	2517.8	2822.5	3127.3	3432.1
	1/4	82.5	387.3	692.1	996.9	1301.7	1606.5	1911.3	2216.1	2520.9	2825.6	3130.4	3435.2
	3/8	85.7	390.5	695.3	1000.1	1304.9	1609.7	1914.5	2219.3	2524.1	2828.8	3133.6	3438.4
	1/2	88.9	393.7	698.5	1003.3	1308.1	1612.9	1917.7	2222.5	2527.3	2832.0	3136.8	3441.6
	5/8	92.1	396.9	701.7	1006.5	1311.3	1616.1	1920.9	2225.7	2530.5	2835.2	3140.0	3444.8
	3/4	95.2	400.0	704.8	1009.6	1314.4	1619.2	1924.0	2228.8	2533.6	2838.3	3143.1	3447.9
	7/8	98.4	403.2	708.0	1012.8	1317.6	1622.4	1927.2	2232.0	2536.8	2841.5	3146.3	3451.1
4		101.6	406.4	711.2	1016.0	1320.8	1625.6	1930.4	2235.2	2540.0	2844.7	3149.5	3454.3
	1/8	104.8	409.6	714.4	1019.2	1324.0	1628.8	1933.6	2238.4	2543.2	2847.9	3152.7	3457.5
	1/4	108.0	412.7	717.5	1022.3	1327.1	1631.9	1936.7	2241.5	2546.3	2851.0	3155.8	3460.6
	3/8	111.1	415.9	720.7	1025.5	1330.3	1635.1	1939.9	2244.7	2549.5	2854.2	3159.0	3463.8
	1/2	114.3	419.1	723.9	1028.7	1333.5	1638.3	1943.1	2247.9	2552.7	2857.4	3162.2	3467.0
	5/8	117.5	422.3	727.1	1031.8	1336.7	1641.5	1946.3	2251.1	2555.9	2860.6	3165.4	3470.2
	3/4	120.7	425.4	730.2	1035.0	1339.8	1644.6	1949.4	2254.2	2559.0	2863.7	3168.5	3473.3
	7/8	123.8	428.6	733.4	1038.2	1343.0	1647.8	1952.6	2257.4	2562.2	2866.9	3171.7	3476.5
5		127.0	431.8	736.6	1041.4	1346.2	1651.0	1955.8	2260.6	2565.4	2870.1	3174.9	3479.7
	1/8	130.2	435.0	739.8	1044.6	1349.4	1654.2	1959.0	2263.8	2568.6	2873.3	3178.1	3482.9
	1/4	133.4	438.1	742.9	1047.7	1352.5	1657.3	1962.1	2266.9	2571.7	2876.4	3181.2	3486.0
	3/8	136.5	441.3	746.1	1050.9	1355.7	1660.5	1965.3	2270.1	2574.9	2879.6	3184.4	3489.2
	1/2	139.7	444.5	749.3	1054.1	1358.9	1663.7	1968.5	2273.3	2578.1	2882.8	3187.6	3492.4
	5/8	142.9	447.7	752.5	1057.3	1362.1	1666.9	1971.7	2276.5	2581.3	2886.0	3190.8	3495.6
	3/4	146.1	450.8	755.6	1060.4	1365.2	1670.0	1974.8	2279.6	2584.4	2889.1	3193.0	3498.7
	7/8	149.2	454.0	758.8	1063.6	1368.4	1673.2	1978.0	2282.8	2587.6	2892.3	3197.1	3501.9
6		152.4	457.2	762.0	1066.8	1371.6	1676.4	1981.2	2286.0	2590.8	2895.5	3200.4	3505.1
	1/8	155.6	460.4	765.2	1070.0	1374.8	1679.6	1984.4	2289.2	2594.0	2898.7	3203.5	3508.3
	1/4	158.8	463.5	768.3	1073.1	1377.9	1682.7	1987.5	2292.3	2597.1	2901.8	3206.6	3511.4
	3/8	161.9	466.7	771.5	1076.3	1381.1	1685.9	1990.7	2295.5	2600.3	2905.0	3209.8	3514.6
	1/2	165.1	469.9	774.7	1079.5	1384.3	1689.1	1993.9	2298.7	2603.5	2908.2	3213.0	3517.8
	5/8	168.3	473.1	777.9	1082.7	1387.5	1692.3	1997.1	2301.9	2606.7	2911.4	3216.2	3521.0
	3/4	171.5	476.2	781.0	1085.8	1390.6	1695.4	2000.2	2305.0	2609.8	2914.5	3219.3	3524.1
	7/8	174.6	479.4	784.2	1089.0	1393.8	1698.5	2003.4	2308.2	2613.0	2917.7	3222.5	3527.3
7		177.8	482.6	787.4	1092.2	1397.0	1701.8	2006.6	2311.4	2616.2	2920.9	3225.7	3530.5
	1/8	181.0	485.8	790.6	1095.4	1400.2	1705.0	2009.8	2314.6	2619.4	2924.1	3228.9	3533.7
	1/4	184.2	488.9	793.7	1098.5	1403.3	1708.1	2012.9	2317.7	2622.5	2927.2	3232.0	3536.8
	3/8	187.3	492.1	796.9	1101.7	1406.5	1711.3	2016.1	2320.9	2625.7	2930.4	3235.2	3540.0
	1/2	190.5	495.3	800.1	1104.9	1409.7	1714.5	2019.3	2324.1	2628.9	2933.6	3238.4	3543.2
	5/8	193.7	498.5	803.3	1108.1	1412.9	1717.7	2022.5	2327.3	2632.1	2936.8	3241.6	3546.4
	3/4	196.9	501.6	806.4	1111.2	1416.0	1720.8	2025.6	2330.4	2635.2	2939.9	3244.7	3549.5
	7/8	200.0	504.8	809.6	1114.4	1419.2	1724.0	2028.8	2333.6	2638.4	2943.1	3247.9	3552.7
8		203.2	508.0	812.8	1117.6	1422.4	1727.2	2032.0	2336.8	2641.6	2946.3	3251.1	3555.9
	1/8	206.4	511.2	816.0	1120.8	1425.6	1730.4	2035.2	2340.0	2644.8	2949.5	3254.3	3559.1
	1/4	209.6	514.3	819.1	1123.9	1428.7	1733.5	2038.3	2343.1	2647.9	2952.6	3257.4	3562.3
	3/8	212.7	517.5	822.3	1127.1	1431.9	1736.7	2041.5	2346.3	2651.1	2955.8	3260.6	3565.4
	1/2	215.9	520.7	825.5	1130.3	1435.1	1739.9	2044.7	2349.5	2654.3	2959.0	3263.8	3568.6
	5/8	219.1	523.9	828.7	1133.5	1438.3	1743.1	2047.9	2352.7	2657.5	2962.2	3267.0	3571.8
	3/4	222.3	527.0	831.8	1136.6	1441.4	1746.2	2051.0	2355.8	2660.6	2965.3	3270.1	3574.9
	7/8	225.4	530.2	835.0	1139.8	1444.6	1749.4	2054.2	2359.0	2663.8	2968.5	3273.3	3578.1
9		228.6	533.4	838.2	1143.0	1447.8	1752.6	2057.4	2362.2	2667.0	2971.7	3276.5	3581.3
	1/8	231.8	536.6	841.4	1146.2	1451.0	1755.8	2060.6	2365.4	2670.2	2974.9	3279.7	3584.5
	1/4	235.0	539.7	844.5	1149.3	1454.1	1758.9	2063.7	2368.5	2673.3	2978.0	3282.8	3587.6
	3/8	238.1	542.9	847.7	1152.5	1457.3	1762.1	2066.9	2371.7	2676.5	2981.2	3286.0	3590.8
	1/2	241.3	546.1	850.9	1155.7	1460.5	1765.3	2070.1	2374.9	2679.7	2984.4	3289.2	3594.0
	5/8	244.5	549.3	854.1	1158.9	1463.7	1768.5	2073.3	2378.1	2682.9	2987.6	3292.4	3597.2
	3/4	247.7	552.4	857.2	1162.0	1466.8	1771.6	2076.4	2381.2	2686.0	2990.7	3295.5	3600.3
	7/8	250.8	555.6	860.4	1165.2	1470.0	1774.8	2079.6	2384.4	2689.2	2993.9	3298.7	3603.5
10		254.0	558.8	863.6	1168.4	1473.2	1778.0	2082.8	2387.6	2692.4	2997.1	3301.9	3606.7
	1/8	257.2	562.0	866.8	1171.6	1476.4	1781.2	2086.0	2390.8	2695.6	3000.3	3305.1	3609.9
	1/4	260.4	565.1	869.9	1174.7	1479.5	1784.3	2089.1	2393.9	2698.7	3003.4	3308.2	3613.0
	3/8	263.5	568.3	873.1	1177.9	1482.7	1787.5	2092.3	2397.1	2701.9	3006.6	3311.4	3616.2
	1/2	266.7	571.5	876.3	1181.1	1485.9	1790.7	2095.5	2400.3	2705.1	3009.8	3314.6	3619.4
	5/8	269.9	574.7	879.5	1184.3	1489.1	1793.9	2098.7	2403.5	2708.3	3013.0	3317.8	3622.6
	3/4	273.1	577.8	882.6	1187.4	1492.2	1797.0	2101.8	2406.6	2711.4	3016.1	3320.9	3625.7
	7/8	276.2	581.0	885.8	1190.6	1495.4	1800.2	2105.0	2409.8	2714.6	3019.3	3324.1	3628.9
11		279.4	584.2	889.0	1193.8	1498.6	1803.4	2108.2	2413.0	2717.8	3022.5	3327.3	3632.1
	1/8	282.6	587.4	892.2	1197.0	1501.8	1806.5	2111.4	2416.2	2721.0	3025.7	3330.5	3635.3
	1/4	285.7	590.5	895.3	1200.1	1504.9	1809.7	2114.5	2419.3	2724.1	3028.8	3333.6	3638.4
	3/8	288.9	593.7	898.5	1203.3	1508.1	1812.9	2117.7	2422.5	2727.3	3032.0	3336.8	3641.6
	1/2	292.1	596.9	901.7	1206.5	1511.3	1816.1	2120.9	2425.7	2730.5	3035.2	3340.0	3644.8
	5/8	295.3	600.1	904.9	1209.7	1514.5	1819.3	2124.1	2428.8	2733.7	3038.4	3343.2	3648.0
	3/4	298.4	603.2	908.0	1212.8	1517.6	1822.4	2127.2	2432.0	2736.8	3041.5	3346.3	3651.1
	7/8	301.6	606.4	911.2	1216.0	1520.8	1825.6	2130.4	2435.2	2740.0	3044.7	3349.5	3654.3